# Chinese Women and Rural Development

## Sixty Years of Change in Lu Village, Yunnan

Laurel Bossen

ROWMAN & LITTLEFIELD PUBLISHERS, INC.
Lanham • Boulder • New York • Oxford

ROWMAN & LITTLEFIELD PUBLISHERS, INC.

Published in the United States of America
by Rowman & Littlefield Publishers, Inc.
An Imprint of the Rowman & Littlefield Publishing Group
4720 Boston Way, Lanham, Maryland 20706
www.rowmanlittlefield.com

12 Hid's Copse Road, Cumnor Hill, Oxford OX2 9JJ, England

British Library Cataloguing in Publication Information Available

**Library of Congress Cataloging-in-Publication Data**

Bossen, Laurel, 1945–
    Chinese women and rural development : sixty years of change in Lu Village, Yunnan /
Laurel Bossen.
        p. cm.
    Includes bibliographical references and index.
    ISBN 0-7425-1107-3 (cloth : alk. paper) — ISBN 0-7425-1108-1 (pbk. : alk. paper)
    1. Women in rural development—China—Lucun (Yunnan Sheng) 2.
Women—China—Lucun (Yunnan Sheng)—Social conditions. 3. Sex role—China—Lucun
(Yunnan Sheng) 4. Footbinding—China—Lucun (Yunnan Sheng) 5. Lucun (Yunnan
Sheng, China)—Social conditions. I. Title.

HQ1240.5.C6 B67 2002
305.42'0951'35—dc21                                                        2001044378

Printed in the United States of America

∞™ The paper used in this publication meets the minimum requirements of American
National Standard for Information Sciences—Permanence of Paper for Printed Library
Materials, ANSI/NISO Z39.48-1992.

To

Nathan

Ingrid and Stephan

Annika

# Contents

# Maps, Figures, and Tables

## MAPS

## FIGURES

## TABLES

# Weights and Measures

| | |
|---|---|
| 1 *gong [kung]* | 0.4 mu (local unit used in Lufeng region, originally one day's work), 0.027 hectare |
| 1 *gongjin* | 1 kilogram |
| 1 *jin* | ½ kilogram, 1.1 pounds |
| 1 *hectare* | 2.47 acres |
| 1 *li* | ½ kilometer, or 1/3 mile |
| 1 *mu* | 1/6 acre = 0.067 hectare |
| 1 *yuan* | U.S.$0.20 in 1990 |

## CONVERSIONS, VOLUME TO WEIGHT

1 liter of husked rice = 0.85 kgs
1 liter of unhusked rice = 0.54 kgs

# Preface: Discovering a Matriline

I first came to Lu Village in Yunnan Province in 1989, just a month after the cataclysmic events of June 4 at Tiananmen Square in Beijing—a tense moment in China's history. The timing of my receiving an opportunity to visit the village was a surprise. On my field trip to China in 1988, Lu Village was in one of the many regions of far away Yunnan that was still off limits to foreigners. In June 1989 I had been in China for six months, conducting research on rural women in villages in central China. Immediately after the suppression of dissent in Beijing and across China, relations between China and the West grew very strained. Most foreigners left China on the advice of their governments, fearing that instability and violence might continue. I remained, however, and traveled from Henan Province to Yunnan in July, as I had planned. At this time of sharp Western condemnation of China, I was suddenly invited by officials of the Yunnan Academy of Social Sciences (YASS) to make my first visit to Lu Village. This unexpected opportunity seemed like a clear message that China wanted to keep its doors open.

Accompanied by a small, semiformal delegation of outside officials, all men, from YASS, the county, and the local township, I arrived aboard the township jeep, which stopped at the stone marker at the entrance to the village. My appearance as the "first" North American to visit their village—at least in current memory—prompted the villagers to interrupt their routine activities and come out of their doorways to stare. Indeed, villagers told me I was the first foreigner ever to visit their village and some even said I was the first *waiguoren* (foreigner) they had ever seen in person.[1] As crowds gathered, officials protectively shepherded me to the second-story sanctuary of the Lu Village headquarters, where they served tea in a large meeting room lined with chairs and tea tables. They then conducted a public meeting with more than two dozen village leaders and observers, myself, and my official entourage from the provincial and township organizations. There, my escorts formally introduced me to the local officials, who in turn introduced their village, reciting the basic economic conditions, following the protocols that village leaders employ whenever any distinguished outside guests or authorities arrive. (As a university professor with a doctorate, I qualified as a distinguished guest.)

I explained my interest in women and rural development, specifically women's social and economic life, and that I wanted to study the changes since China's most renowned anthropologist, Fei Xiaotong, conducted research there in the 1930s. The party secretary pointed out two women leaders, the women's affairs director and the family planning officer. He invited me to ask them questions about the role of women in the village, so I did. These women, smiling and straightforward, briefly outlined the kinds of work women did in the community. They were not unnerved by the fact that most members of the audience were men. They spoke confidently in a room where the majority were fellow villagers. The portrait they sketched of women's work was very positive and factual, yet superficial. Their frank attitude seemed to say, "Now we have told you about women and their work. What else is there to know?" When I asked about women's nonfarm opportunities, leaders arranged to take me on a village walking tour to "inspect" the local homes where women made bean curd for sale.

This kind of public performance, structured to transmit information from local authorities to superior, outside authorities, always made me uncomfortable, particularly as I observed the not-so-subtle status differences enacted among powerful township authorities, the prestigious scholars from the city, the "exalted foreign guest," and the obliging villager leaders. Nonetheless, when the meeting broke up I finally managed to slip away (as was my habit) from the formal script and entourage to have a casual chat with several women, including the women leaders. Once "off stage" we were soon laughing together about the formalities, and I knew we could get along. Middle aged, smiling, sturdy, and physically strong, they seemed confident and pragmatic as representatives of village women, and comfortable among the political leadership. They also understood my interest in studying women in the context of development and my emphasis on speaking to women directly.

After the meeting we filed down the narrow main street of the village on our walking tour. At the end of town, we stopped in front of a new two-story building and admired the modern construction. It was the home of the branch party secretary, the most important village leader, and he cordially invited us inside for more tea. I dreaded stilted occasions when everyone sat and exchanged pleasantries, but once I was inside the family courtyard, the atmosphere became less formal and, while sipping tea, with small children running about, we visitors began to relax.

To fend off the feeling of being constantly engulfed by male officials and formal protocols, I chatted with the women of the household, inquiring about the relationships among them—there seemed to be so many women! The party secretary had five grown children, four of them daughters. In the household that day, I first met his wife, an erect, self-assured middle-aged woman who greeted the officials with dignity and confidence. I then met a tall, elderly woman, lean and wiry, with bright eyes shining from her well-lined face, dressed neatly in traditional blue pants and jacket, whom the party secretary called "Mother." Next, I was introduced to some of the younger women, his married daughters, then the husband of one daughter.

I began to write down names, looking forward to a time when I might be able to return for more than a visit. Then, I discovered somewhat awkwardly that the party secretary was living in an uxorilocal household—a household in which a man becomes a member of his wife's family rather than the reverse. The surnames of his mother and his daughter did not match his own, as one would expect in a patrilineal system. The woman he addressed as "Mother" was his wife's mother, and the family names of his daughters were his wife's family name. Indeed, one of his daughters was even uxorilocally married, having "brought in" a husband rather than marrying out. No one offered any sign that there was anything unusual about these marriage arrangements. Once I realized that all these women bustling about the courtyard were mothers and daughters, it came as no surprise to discover that the smallest girl, a toddler who expected the party secretary to carry her about everywhere (which he often did), was a fourth generation, and the youngest member of a coresidential matriline consisting of great grandmother, grandmother (the party secretary's wife), mother, and daughter.

This was certainly different from the rigidly patrilineal families of the villages in Henan Province where I had lived over the preceding months without encountering *any* cases of uxorilocal marriage in my interviews. Not only was this household unusual in its deviation from the patrilocal standard, but it also differed in the status of the husband. The literature on Chinese families stresses that men in uxorilocal marriages were generally looked down on, yet this was clearly not true of the party secretary. He was the long-serving leader of a village district comprising fifteen different village divisions, and held the highest-ranking position of some two dozen local cadres. Such was my introduction to Lu Village and, of course, it piqued my interest and desire to return. After relatively short-term comparative research in four other villages (two in Yunnan and two in Henan), I realized that Lu Village, with its previous study by Fei Xiaotong, represented a unique opportunity to examine the changes women experienced with development from the prerevolutionary period to the present.

## NEGOTIATING ARRANGEMENTS

I returned to Lu Village in 1990 to conduct research for a longer period, of several months, accompanied by only one assistant, a young woman, as I requested from YASS. Township officials greeted us warmly. Since conventional fieldwork involving long-term residence in the village was then little understood by officials, and since they could not easily imagine the content or repercussions of such research (which might bring them political disapproval), they insisted that I live in the township guest house in the market center. Both to sustain politically correct images and to protect the health and safety of a foreign woman, assumed to be politically unreliable, weak, and unaccustomed to physical hardship, the authorities were determined not to budge on my frequent requests to live in the village.

While the official concerns often seem arbitrary and senseless to foreign researchers, ineffectual as political pretense and yet a nuisance to serious research, I tried to put myself in the position of the officials. They were the ones who would be held responsible should I become seriously ill, the victim of a crime, or "embarrass China" by publicly denouncing some shortcoming of utopian images of socialism (in the early days of China's reopening after the Cultural Revolution, people had vivid memories of hapless officials suffering unpleasant consequences for political misjudgment). Officials also believed, with a common urban prejudice, that villages were more dangerous than the town center, where officials commanded the police force. I suspected that another motivation might have been to have guests fill up money-losing government guest houses. Thus, I had little choice but to live in their official guest house, where I stayed in the same room that was allocated to Fei Xiaotong when he made a two-day revisit in 1990.

I made arrangements with several villagers for help. I hired a young woman, newly graduated from polytechnical school, as a research assistant, to help locate households and conduct interviews in eighty sample households. Other officials and neighbors helped in a great many ways throughout the project. In particular, the women's director and the family planning official—bright, capable women—and their families cheerfully offered explanations, contacts, and exposure to local conditions and family life. We made arrangements for regular meals at one home and were frequently invited to eat, rest, and visit at others.

Over the years since then, I have returned a number of times to Lu Village for short and longer field trips and visits, sometimes with a woman assistant from YASS, and sometimes alone or with a family member. Following Margery Wolf's advice (Wolf 1985) relating to officials treating women researchers as lower priorities in the presence of their husbands, I avoided bringing my husband until I was well established, even though he is not an academic. Indeed, on his first visit, local officials rushed off and, before I knew it, had decapitated a lovely turkey for a banquet in his honor!

As China has become more open and more accustomed to visitors, the formality of the arrangements has decreased, but villagers' hospitality has always been remarkable. In 1991 and 1993, I collected life histories from a number of women and, in 1995 and 1996, I returned again, conducting more interviews, attending weddings, and generally gaining further insights into various aspects of village life and change. A more recent trip in 1999 coincided with the rice harvest, giving me an opportunity to observe and participate in some of the work and to catch up on other changes. It also allowed me to meet a doctoral student from Iceland, Sigrun Hardardottir, who had also come to conduct anthropological research in Lu Village.

## PLAN AND SERENDIPITY

In addressing the subject of Chinese women and rural development, my goal was to obtain both quantitative and qualitative information through fieldwork. For quantitative data, I requested information from village and township officials, often copying it out by hand from handwritten forms. This kind of data presents the official view of the village and is important for understanding the overall economic and social characteristics of Lu Village. It is useful for identifying variations within Lu Village and for comparing averages from Lu Village to those of other areas in the township, the province, or to the nation as a whole.

I used the official household registry books of the administrative office of Lu Village in order to select a random sample of households for interviews. From this I selected two interview samples. The first set of interviews, with over eighty households, was conducted in 1990 and the second, with fifty households, was completed in 1997 by an assistant. These interviews covered topics such as household membership, employment, the agricultural division of labor, incomes and expenses, wedding and housing costs, reproduction and birth control, travel, political experience, and modern possessions. Older women became the focus for another set of fifty questionnaires administered in 1996 to gain a clearer idea of the conditions women experienced in the period of Fei's study. These questionnaires asked about marriage, about women's work for their own and their husband's families, and about footbinding practices in their families. In addition, I selected a number of individuals for longer interviews and life histories.[2] These individuals were mostly chosen on the basis of congeniality or interest from among those I had already interviewed in my random sample. Thus, the people whose lives are presented in greater detail probably are those who are more accustomed to speaking to strangers. Their stories may, therefore, draw less attention to those who are less skilled or interested in communication with the outside. Government officials, also known as cadres (*ganbu*), are among those who are most comfortable in speaking to strangers. But while they may have fairly standardized ways of presenting village affairs, their own lives tend to be full of colorful experiences that are far from formulaic.

In most of my field trips, I was accompanied by someone from YASS who came as a *peitong*, or companion. At first, like most foreign researchers, I felt that this was required in order to keep an eye on me (and it probably was) and resented it. Indeed, I was also required to pay for their expenses and time, as well as various administrative costs. But I realized that if I negotiated for my *peitongs* to be women, and enlisted them as research assistants, they could be invaluable aids to my research. In the chapters that follow I refer at times to assistants who accompany me without providing a name. I do this in order to avoid confusion, since I worked with three different young women assistants in Lu Village: Yu Wenlan, Wang Fen, and Zhu Xia. Yu Wenlan and Wang Fen helped me in 1990 and Yu Wenlan came with me again in 1991. In various visits between 1993 and 1997, I hired Zhu Xia as my very capable assistant. In each case, I felt very fortunate to work with these young women, each of whom was intelligent and very hardworking. Zhu Xia, in particular, who helped me administer my questionnaires in 1996 and 1997, made an important contribution. In the end, however, I am responsible for the research and interpretation of the data collected.

It is worth mentioning that the relationship between foreign researcher, research assistants, and local residents is always complex. I found that in my earliest visits, when my assistants were young, single women, certain topics concerning women were taboo. Discussions of sex, birth control, and childbirth initially caused discomfort to them and to the village women we interviewed when they were aware that my assistant was unmarried. Yet they were quite willing to discuss such subjects with *me* because they knew I was married and had a daughter. Wang Fen at first used to leave the room when I asked about birth control, even though my pronunciation was hard for local women to understand and Wang's assistance would have been useful. As the years passed, each of these young women married and bore children, and then it became much more acceptable to discuss a wider range of topics in their presence. Village women carefully guard these subjects from the uninitiated, even though information about birth control is widely and publicly disseminated.

The qualitative aspects of my fieldwork involved simply passing as much time as I could in the village, visiting and observing different activities. I ate meals in the village nearly every day and was invited to meals at many homes. I visited the gardens, the pig sties, and the latrines. (I learned to appreciate the efficiency of the waste recycling system but never got used to the aromas.) I was also invited to attend weddings and other celebrations, and I generally socialized and watched daily life. Some of my favorite memories are of playing basketball in the schoolyard, watching children play with fighting crickets, climbing the mountains to look for wild mushrooms, sitting with groups of friends chatting at the side of the street or in village courtyards. I also have vivid memories of the feverish heat and fatigue of the rice harvest. Attending village meetings was less strenuous, but they were long and slow. I visited local sites, attended the markets in the market town, and visited villagers' relatives who have town jobs or town apartments. I also had meetings and feasts with town officials, copied records in township offices, shopped, rode around on my bicycle, visited the local temple and the dinosaur museum, and rode horse carts and buses. In the town, I was called upon to translate into English the signs for the government guest house and explanations for the town's dinosaur museum (the region is known for its dinosaur fossils). Town officials also invited me to attend and photograph the local cultural performances in which performers from Lu Village competed for awards with other villages in the township. By participating in town life, I did not feel that I was being drawn away from village life, since I often encountered villagers in town and realized how often they came there to shop, visit, or do other business.

The results of my research have been both planned and serendipitous. I planned to get basic population and economic data, but I did not know that I would learn about female suicide or footbinding. I did not expect to be able to attend a land division meeting and I certainly did not expect to attend many rehearsals of village cultural performances that would culminate in a big variety show held in the town. There is always a sense in which fieldwork is opportunistic, and I certainly felt my opportunities were limited by the heavy constraints imposed by the government: the requirement that I go through a complicated set of processes to get permission to do research, the authorities' refusal to permit me to sleep in the village, and the requirement that most of my early visits be short and that I be accompanied by a government employee. At the same time, the fact that I was able to spend a great deal of the time with villagers and township officials, who can be extremely hospitable and helpful, meant that any feelings of exasperation that I might have felt toward faceless, anonymous bureaucrats in the provincial Foreign Affairs Office were dissipated by all the people who offered me friendly assistance. After a decade of field trips, my visits to many old friends in the village were warm and informal, whereas my ties with officials (who had changed in the interim) were more distant.

## NOTES

1. People may have seen U.S. soldiers in the vicinity during World War II, but many would have been too young to remember.

2. Throughout this work, to protect the privacy of individuals interviewed, I have used pseudonyms for Lu Villagers.

# Acknowledgments

Many people helped and encouraged me in this project over the past decade. My research has been generously funded by individual and team grants from the Canadian Social Science and Humanities Research Council (SSHRC) and the Québec Fonds pour la Formation de Chercheurs et l'Aide à la Recherche (FCAR), as well as by the McGill University Graduate Faculty and Department of Anthropology. At McGill, I also received institutional support from the Centre for Society, Technology and Development (STANDD), the McGill Centre for Research and Teaching on Women (MCRTW), and the Center for East Asian Studies. Among institutions in China, I thank the Yunnan Academy of Social Sciences for providing my primary affiliation and opportunities to meet helpful colleagues, while Yunnan University frequently served as a home base, meeting place, and information center when I was in Kunming. Other helpful institutions include Yunnan Provincial Women's Federation, Lufeng County government, Lufeng County Women's Federation, and the Jinshan Township and Lu Village governments. In Hong Kong, the library at the University Services Center at the Chinese University of Hong Kong was enormously useful. The center itself is an oasis, full of information and lively intellectual exchange.

Colleagues at McGill University have been unfailingly supportive. Among them, I particularly thank Don Attwood, John Galaty, Fumiko Ikawa-Smith, Philip Salzman, Deborah Sick, Bruce Trigger, and the late Richard Salisbury. Tony Masi and Tom LeGrande provided helpful comments on chapter 8, while Nathan Bossen, Norma Diamond, Paula Friedman, Hill Gates, Sigrun Hardardottir, Judith Mitchell, and Margaret Swain commented on the full manuscript. I thank Catherine Brown, Chen Chun, Hu Xiaowen, Hu Xiaocong, Ethan Michelson, Scott Simon, Brian Thom, and Tianying Zhao for research and map assistance, and I thank Rose Marie Stano, Diane Mann, and Cynthia Romanyk for departmental help.

Many others shared information, ideas, and encouragement at different moments. Among them are Susan Blum, Myron Cohen, Eugene Cooper, Stevan Harrell, Maria Jaschok, Ellen Judd, William Lavely, Heather Peters, Gloria Rudolf, Alan Smart, Josephine Smart, Margaret Swain, Toby Shih, Sydney White, and Margery Wolf. Special thanks to Hill Gates for her help in studying footbinding and for sending me copies of her questionnaires to try out in Yunnan, and to Sigrun Hardardottir for making my field trip in 1999 so delightful.

In China, I received assistance from many more friends and colleagues than I can name. These include He Yaohua, He Zhixiong, He Zhonghua, Li Ceng, Qiu Baolin, Yu Wenlan, Zhao Junchen, Zhou Yonghua, and Zhu Xia as well as the late Guo Zhengbing and Yuan Dezheng of Yunnan Academy of Social Sciences, Li Xiaojiang of Zhengzhou University, and Chen Chun of Fudan University. Pan Zhengfu, He Jiaming, and Qian Chengrun of Lufeng County generously provided books about the county. Gu Xiangran, Wang Qingsheng, Lei Hong, and Guo Ping are among those of Jinshan government who provided data. Those who helped with my fieldwork include Yu Wenlan, Zhou Yonghua, Wang Fen, Wang Xiying, Huan Ruzhen, and many others who cannot be listed by name. Zhu Xia was particularly helpful in conducting interviews and administering questionnaires. Hu Fu and Yang Yang helped prepare me for Yunnan. I thank the eminent anthropologists Fei Xiaotong and Tian Zukang, who offered counsel and encouragement. The late Patrick Xiang Jingyun and his wife Pearl Liu Dewei provided great support, friendship, and hospitality whenever I was in Kunming and taught me a great deal about China. In Hong Kong, Jean Hung (Xiong Jingming) offered great friendship, encouragement, and hospitality as associate director of the Chinese University of Hong Kong's Universities Service Center. Former Canadian Ambassador to China Fred Bild and Eva Bild hosted me in Beijing and presented me with an opportunity to meet Fei Xiaotong.

I wish to thank executive editor Susan McEachern at Rowman & Littlefield as well as production editor Jehanne Schweitzer, and copyeditor Dave Compton for helping me prepare this book. I also thank Stanford University Press for permission to use the poem, "Complaint of the Weaving Wife," in chapter 3.

We can look at the past century and be thankful for some of the momentous technological changes that have occurred. These changes permitted vast numbers of women to give up weaving cloth on looms and turn to writing words on computers. I acknowledge the help of Nathan by recalling how he parodied the "Complaint of the Woman Weaver," performing her endless work at home, with her husband standing by, giving her moral support.

Complaint of the Woman Writer

Hungry, she still writes.
Numbed with cold, she still writes.
Page after page after page.
The days are short,
The weather chill (in Montreal),
Each chapter hard to finish. . . .
Her husband wants to urge her on,
But he has not heart to do so.
He says nothing,
But stands beside the computer.

My deepest thanks go to my family, to Nathan, who first brought me to China and encouraged me, sharing good times and bad, and to Ingrid, who has had to put up with an anthropological mother, and who has survived the experience with good humor and wit. She finally visited China with me in 1999 and was warmly welcomed. It's too late to thank my parents again, although their support has sustained me long after they departed.

# Note on Orthography

Throughout the text, I have used the contemporary *pinyin* system of orthography developed in the People's Republic of China. Older spellings are preserved only when English speakers are likely to be more familiar with them, as in the case of Chiang Kai Shek. Older publications using different spelling systems are introduced the first time with the original name spelling in brackets as, for example, "Fei and Zhang [Fei and Chang]." To improve consistency, names of people and places cited in Fei and Zhang [Chang] and Tian [T'ien] using different spellings have been converted to contemporary *pinyin* or English spelling, even in direct quotes. Thus Luts'un, which means "Lu Village," becomes Lu Village, Tali becomes Dali, Chang becomes Zhang, Soong becomes Song, kung becomes gong, mow becomes mu.

*Chapter One*

# Lu Village in Southwest China: Unearthing Gender

Yunnan is China's southwestern frontier province; its name, "South of the Clouds," carries with it a sense of distance. Far removed from the Center of China, it hangs on the ridge of the continent, separated from the basins of the great rivers by chains of mountain ranges. It is not very accessible from the central provinces; and, since distance breeds suspicion, only yesterday the age-old belief was still current that Yunnan was a wild region overrun with beast-like aborigines, in early times held in subjection only by the resourceful god-like hero, Chu-ke of the Three Kingdoms, and later by the fearless Mongols. (Fei and Zhang 1945:7)

If you have money, fear not to go wherever you like, even to Yunnan or Kue-ichou [Guizhou]. Couplets on a popular depiction of the wealth god, early twentieth century. (Gates 1996:148)

It is said that in former times, the ethnic Han of Yunnan were descendants from two groups: the exiled officials and the exiled convicts.
—Xiang Jingyun, exiled to Yunnan in 1959. (Xiang and Liu 1999)

Embraced by the mountains of central Yunnan, about one hundred kilometers west of Kunming, the provincial capital, Lu Village is one among many compact villages and hamlets dotting a large valley of irrigated rice fields. From the exterior, in 1989, this small, closed, earth-tone village looked much as it did when China's most famous anthropologist, Fei Xiaotong, photographed the village and dubbed this community "earthbound" after his research in 1938–1939. The surrounding fields, abutting and surrounding the walls of the oval-shaped village, shimmered with their bright green expanse of rice paddies, extending smoothly over the flat land, up to a nearby hill, denuded of tall trees, and surrounded by a background of taller, darker mountains. In summer, scattered figures worked in the fields, weeding or spraying.

1

*Lu Village with windowless earthen walls as seen from the rice fields (1989).*

From the hilltop, the large town of Lufeng was visible in the distance, toward the center of the valley, across a small river. Unlike earthen Lu Village, Lufeng's predominant color was the urban gray of cement streets and cement buildings, with darker, massive structures and smells at the far end where its industry stood.

The asphalt road from town approached the walls of Lu Village and then veered around it, heading on up the green valley. People walked or biked to town, and occasionally a noisy tractor chugged along, and even more rarely a car or truck. Once inside Lu Village, you caught few glimpses of vegetation. Unless you climbed to a rooftop, you could not see the fields. The main street was straight and narrow, slightly muddy although recently paved, with open drainage channels running along the sides. The surrounding houses and courtyard walls on both sides of the street were a light tan, the color of dried leaves and dried mud, which blended with the narrow dirt footpaths branching off between the walls of other houses crowded together. Along the main artery of Lu Village (there was no central square), street life was animated by geese splashing in roadside ditches, children chasing about, old men dressed in dusty blue cotton sitting on doorsteps or squatting by the roadside playing chess. Women clustered along another section of the roadside and chatted while they sat on small straw stools, cleaning and sorting vegetables, some of them sewing cotton shoes. Carts drawn by water buffalo or horses occasionally ambled by. It was easy to imagine that Lu Village was just the way it was in prerevolutionary days, largely "untouched"—to use the ethnographic cliché—by modern urban and industrial development, with its slow-paced agricultural lifestyle proceeding much as it always had. Indeed, there was much about the place that seemed "timeless"—the colors and smells, the mud paths, the farm animals and drainage ditches on the main street, the separate groups of old men and women, wearing blue or gray cotton clothing and black cotton shoes. But no one should succumb to such imaginings for long.

Buildings with mud walls, rather than kiln-baked bricks, look old to a Westerner even when they are new. Old buildings that once housed community and clan temples had been converted to other uses: some housed several families; others served as warehouses for agricultural equipment and threshing machines. Looking carefully, one could make out traces of former temple paintings, with scrawls of revolutionary slogans fading away on the high walls. A former landlord's large house and walled garden now embraced the school and school yard. With a basketball court at one end, this space had an old shade tree at the other end, the only whiff of the tranquil charm of the gentry garden that once was here.

A fairly new two-story rectangular cement structure of standard "Stalinist-modern" design housed the village headquarters. And down the street at the end of town stood the party secretary's home, opening behind a metal gate to a new two-story house with yellow and white glazed ceramic tiles, a gleaming contrast to the prevalent earth tones of neighboring homes. Lu Village had not stood still. Nor was it standing still when Fei Xiaotong arrived in 1938. The village has its history and changing fortunes. The ten years during which I conducted my research, however, was a time when change visibly accelerated, as the village, like villages across China, opened up. New kinds and colors of housing, clothing, and vehicles heralded wider exchanges with the outside world as the traffic between village, town, and city grew.

## REVISITING THE FRONTIERS OF CHINESE ANTHROPOLOGY

Many anthropologists have been drawn to China's mountainous southwestern province of Yunnan. This frontier province—bordering on Tibet and Burma to the west, Laos and Vietnam to the south, the provinces of Guangxi and Guizhou to the east, and Sichuan to the north—is a patchwork of diverse cultural groups scattered throughout its rugged mountains and valleys. By comparison with the relative conformity of completely Han areas, Yunnan brims with color, contrast, and exotic mixtures of people. This made it a kind of "laboratory for community analysis" for Chinese and a magnet for foreign anthropologists throughout the twentieth century (Fei and Zhang 1945:7).[1] Contemporary anthropologists look to Yunnan for a chance to observe China's ethnic minorities, but in the 1930s, Chinese social scientists conducting research there were as likely to study the Chinese, or Han (the predominant Chinese ethnic identity), even when the "aboriginals" were close at hand. They viewed Yunnan as a reasonable place to study variations in Chinese rural communities. I, too, came to Yunnan to study Chinese villagers, but I particularly came to study the impact of development on rural women.

Over sixty years ago, in 1938, China's most famous anthropologist, Fei Xiaotong, and his colleague, Zhang Zhiyi,[2] conducted a landmark study of land tenure and rural development in Yunnan Province. They were among the many social scientists, displaced by the Japanese occupation from their homes and universities in coastal China, who moved to Free China's southwest frontier, where they set up a research station based in Kunming, the capital of the province. Fei and Zhang studied three communities in central Yunnan, as described in their classic study of Chinese landownership, *Earthbound China: A Study of Rural Economy in Yunnan* (1945). One of these three communities was Lu Village (originally transcribed as Luts'un),[3] located on

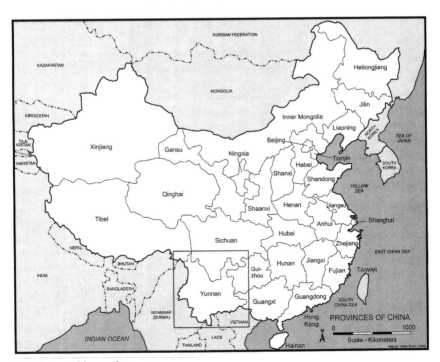

**Map 1.1.　China and Yunnan**

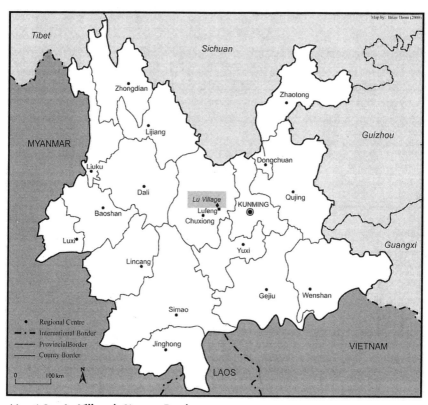

**Map 1.2.  Lu Village in Yunnan Province**

the then famous Burma Road, a supply route to Free China during World War II (see maps 1.1 and 1.2).

Fei's research had been a major factor in my original choice of Yunnan as a province where I could evaluate the changing forms of gender organization in China. His classic study in *Earthbound China* suggested that Yunnan exhibited interesting differences from the anthropological portraits of other parts of China, such as the North China Plain along the Yellow River, and the east China communities near the Yangzi Delta. However, his work focused largely on land tenure, and his descriptions of the gender system were incidental to his main purpose. My goal was to understand how gender systems related to agricultural systems, both of which have always varied within China, and to see how the revolutionary changes of the late twentieth century affected women in their relations to men and farms.

In 1938, Lu Village was a small community with only 122 households and a population of 694. Its name, a pseudonym chosen by Fei and Zhang, emphasizes the link between the village and the better-known county and market town of Lufeng. The village studied by Fei Xiaotong and Zhang Zhiyi is no longer a discrete entity. After the revolution, villagers were reorganized into new units and Lu Village was enlarged. In 1990, I could identify houses and families that Fei Xiaotong had visited in the central, congregated part of the village. Today, however, Lu Village encompasses a total of fifteen "small organizations" (*cunmin xiaozu*), formerly called "production teams" (*shengchan dui*). These small units are still often called "teams" in common parlance—the term I continue to use for the sake of convenience.[4] In 1988, the population governed by Lu Village had reached 2,943, in 693 households, more than four times the size of the population Fei and his colleague studied fifty years earlier.

*Greater* Lu Village refers to the administrative village structure as a whole, which encompasses all fifteen teams. When I examine the differences between those who live in the central area and those who reside in more peripheral hamlets, I distinguish Lu Village *Center* and Lu Village *Hamlets*, respectively. The eight teams of Lu Village Center form a single, fairly compact settlement beside the paved road to Lufeng County town. They account for 57 percent (or 1,680 people) of the total population of Lu Village. Lu Village Hamlets include the seven outlying, dispersed teams. Lu Village Center and Lu Village Hamlets are not formally recognized administrative divisions and only serve to contrast those who reside in the dense cluster bordered by the paved road with those who live farther off road, in areas that are harder to reach.

In Lu Village Center, teams are neither discrete territorial units nor discrete kinship units. Neighbors living in the center often belong to different teams and teams include various lineages or surname groups. The focus of unity for all fifteen teams is their jurisdiction over certain parcels of farmland; those who receive land from a given team are under its jurisdiction. This was an arrangement established at the time of land reform in the 1950s.

Upon learning that Fei and Zhang had studied only an area that is now in Lu Village Center, I recognized a problem of (mis)representation that has plagued most anthropological and development studies, including my own: "road bias."[5] In the literature on rural China, a large proportion of the villages studied are close to major cities and transportation arteries because these are more conveniently reached by outside researchers.[6] Lufeng was located near the Burma Road, and the center of Lu Village was not far from the town center. If I focused only on the central part, I would reproduce the road bias inherent in the original study, a bias toward the richer communities that government officials had already tried to steer me toward. I would learn only about the living conditions of those who were most likely to be better off, because they were more centrally located.

Even though *Earthbound China* portrayed Lu Village as a relatively isolated rural village with no industry, the central village has advantages that are lacking in its surrounding hamlets. Today, the center has the schools, the road, and administrative resources that the hamlets lack. Lu Village Center had a prestigious lineage that traced its ancestry back to an official of the Ming dynasty. This lineage produced university-educated sons in the early twentieth century, and its descendants were still living there in Fei's time and the present. I reasoned that I might get a better glimpse of China's less-privileged rural life if I also tried to gather information about the more remote hamlets of Greater Lu Village. Using household registry books, I selected a random sample for interviewing, drawing from the entire population of fifteen teams, not just from Lu Village Center. While certain teams had reasonably good transportation connections to town, others were located off dirt roads or even narrow dirt paths, which were sometimes impassable to horse carts due to mud. Unlike those in Lu Village Center, some of the other teams lacked running water and relied on wells for drinking water and small roadside channels or irrigation ditches for washing clothes. The walk to the market town for the farthest teams could take up to two hours, in contrast to the half-hour walk from Lu Village Center.

## LUFENG TOWN: COUNTY SEAT AND MARKET CENTER

As the next higher administrative level and nearest major market, Lufeng is definitely within the ambit of weekly (if not daily) life for the villagers. Fei described this town in 1938 as "the center of almost all the marketing activities of the villagers," noting that "nearly every household sends a representative there every market day to sell produce and buy needed commodities" (Fei and Zhang 1945:47–48).

As can be seen in figure 1.1, Lufeng County belongs to Chuxiong Yi Autonomous Prefecture, indicating that the territory under Chuxiong's jurisdiction has a large population ethnically identified as Yi, one of the many aboriginal populations that predated Han settlement of Yunnan. In the 1930s, Fei described the minorities as living outside of Lu Village, mainly in the surrounding mountains, but attending the Lufeng town market. Today, the Yi and other minorities are much less evident in Lufeng's markets. One occasionally spots a few minority individuals there, but if they attend in significant numbers, they must be much less distinctive in dress than in the past.

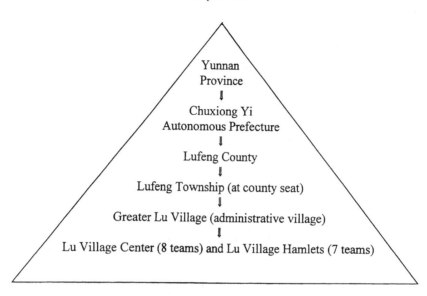

Yunnan
Province
⇩
Chuxiong Yi
Autonomous Prefecture
⇩
Lufeng County
⇩
Lufeng Township (at county seat)
⇩
Greater Lu Village (administrative village)
⇩
Lu Village Center (8 teams) and Lu Village Hamlets (7 teams)

**Figure 1.1.    Political Structure**

## GENDER IN CHINA

My attraction to Lu Village stems from my general interest in gender relations in rural China. Until gender burst into the North American university
curriculum in the 1970s, research on *women* and land was out of bounds. But
in recent decades interest has grown. In this study I examine factors that contribute to different kinds of gender relations. I describe in detail the gender
system found among the Han Chinese in Lu Village, Yunnan province, and
illustrate the ways that economic development has affected this village since
the time that Fei Xiaotong first wrote about it.

Like many North Americans, I first became aware of gender inequality and
women's historical struggles to gain equal rights and respect in my own society and then began to examine other societies from a desire to understand
these inequalities more generally. From a North American perspective, the
degree of gender inequality in China has always seemed particularly serious
and troubling. Reports of women confined to the home, of footbinding, female infanticide, the sale of daughters, and female suicide readily capture the
attention of any feminist reader of Chinese history. Intense curiosity about
China's past, present, and future gender relations has motivated my research.
A desire to know how a society could have developed such extreme practices,
who benefited from them, and what made them change sparked my interest.
My curiosity is not just directed at China's history, however. In contemporary

China, census data showing highly unbalanced sex ratios suggest that even after more than four decades of a revolution promoting gender equality, girls are still less desired. In a country of 1.2 billion people, a "small" shift upward of 1 percent in the ratio of males to females affects millions of lives. Reports of female infanticide, abandonment of infant Chinese girls (and adoption of them by westerners), and trafficking in Chinese women are once again found in the press.[7]

"Whence come these evils?" Were and are they simply a part of a "patriarchal Chinese culture"? If so, this tells us little about their origin or reasons for persisting. Can they be viewed as strategies chosen by people under certain kinds of social, economic, or political conditions? If so, what are these conditions? Can they be specified? How widespread were these practices that have so captured the attention of past observers of Chinese society? Contemporary news reports tell us that some of them, such as female infanticide, female abduction, wife selling, and high rates of female suicide, continue, particularly in rural areas. Do these practices have their roots in agrarian society? If so, how does behavior that seems so indisputably harmful to girls and women fit into the larger social context where rural Chinese men and women are creating families and struggling to survive and prosper? How serious are the gender inequalities found in contemporary China?

Related to these questions are the effects of the cold war divergence between the East and West, between Chinese communism and the Western democracies. How much was China's Communist system of planned development able to improve women's lives? Did it succeed in areas where other systems had failed? Does market-driven development offer a better or worse future for Chinese women? These are obviously big questions that cannot be answered by the study of one village. Lu Village is, however, a rich example of what happened in a particular setting and reflects the ways different conditions and relationships—historical, local, global, economic, political, and cultural—lead to particular outcomes.

Research in a single village, privileged with an excellent earlier study by Fei, lets us examine how these larger concepts and abstractions—Chinese culture, Communist planning, and market-driven development—impinge upon gender in daily life. It allows us to see how people who live within these larger constructs treat each other in a local context, taking into account a variety of other factors, more local and personal, that also influence the quality of life. Thanks to Fei's research, we have in Lu Village a rural community where China's development can be viewed over time, where regional diversity can be discovered and appreciated, and where we can gain at least some sense of how women lived beside men. The historical and regional setting creates an exceptional opportunity to consider the variables that shape gender relations in China, giving women greater power and value in some cases, and less in others. It allows us to ask how and why the gender system of Lu Village differs from that of Han Chinese villages on the North China Plain, in inner Mongolia, in the Yangzi Delta, or the Pearl River Delta. While no village can be taken as typical of rural China, we can better understand and locate the origins of China's more troubling gender relations through the analysis and comparison of detailed local studies.

## CHANGE AND DIVERSITY IN CHINESE VILLAGES

Since China began its gradual and controlled opening to Western scholars following Mao's death, political restrictions on information and access have made it difficult to conduct independent field research there, particularly in rural areas. As a result, anthropologists have conducted relatively few village studies in relation to China's vast rural population, and research on gender has been even more limited (Judd 1994; Pasternak and Salaff 1993; Potter and Potter 1990). During the revolutionary years under Mao, Chinese anthropology was suspended, while the younger generations, still restrained by politics and by limited training and funds, have only recently begun to publish their research. Foreign anthropologists have encountered a slew of political obstacles to fieldwork and have often been prevented from staying a long time in a single rural setting (Wolf 1985; Cooper 2000). Due to the difficulties of conducting research in rural China, other valuable local sources have been biographies, written by and about village men (or urban women who were sent to the countryside during the Cultural Revolution) from diverse parts of the country.[8]

Many of the first long-term village studies in the reform period focused on China's wealthy southern Guangdong Province with its many overseas connections (Potter and Potter 1990; Chan et al. 1992; Siu 1989). Only recently have villages in China's other provinces received more attention (Pasternak and Salaff 1993; Jing 1996; Yan 1996; Gao 1999; Ruf 1998). These village studies explore the diverse, local consequences of revolutionary political and economic change and the current challenges of China's development. Yet few studies based on fieldwork have systematically examined gender as part of the development process. The main exception is Ellen Judd's comparison of three villages of Shandong Province in northeast China (1994), illustrating local differences in women's employment. Judd shows that in Shandong women have limited power, and that the empowerment of women officially promoted during the revolutionary years was in many ways limited and eroded by local resistance as well as state power, findings supported by other studies of gender in rural reform China.

Although gender among the Han population is often contrasted to that of China's ethnic minorities, the Han gender system is not monolithic. Beneath the general rubric of patriarchy, Han gender relations are complex and variable. Increased recognition of different local and regional gender patterns in rural China helps locate and identify the conditions and relationships that nurture or block women's development. Comparable ethnographic studies of gender from different regions are needed to identify the local factors which favor gender equality or discrimination.

Burton Pasternak and Janet Salaff give an important example of China's regional dynamics affecting Han Chinese settlers on China's northern frontier (1993). Examining the interaction of ecology, technology, culture, and gender during the time when Han settlers introduced their intensive farming systems into Mongolia, Pasternak and Salaff outline the long history and expansive tradition of the "Chinese Way" of life in a culture that "absorbs and reshapes the cultures of those with whom it has come in contact."

> The Chinese Way is associated with an economy based on dense settlement and intensive farming. China is an "involuted" society (Geertz 1970).[9] Peasants transfer increasing population pressure to the land. They apply ever more labor and attention to squeeze marginal increments out of limited space. Long ago the Chinese found an adaptation that worked most of the time. To get the workers needed for this labor-intensive regime, farmers favor the patrilineal-patrilocal extended family, and strongly prefer sons. This adaptation allowed the Chinese to fill all areas of China possible, and her long history testifies to that success.
>
> But there are also limits, places where the Chinese Way might intrude but not really vanquish. These were areas hostile because of their harsh environments." (Pasternak and Salaff 1993:4)

In comparing "ecoareas" (ecological areas) of farmers and pastoralists on China's northern borderland, Pasternak and Salaff note that in the farming area, Mongols

> adopted the north Chinese mode of farming and the Han manner of life, . . . they live interspersed with the Han and have become culturally indistinguishable from them. In architecture, clothing and activity, we find few indications of a major departure from the Chinese Way. They make their livings much the same way and enjoy much the same income. They often intermarry. Like the Han they favor early patrilocal marriage, two to three children, and stem families. (1993:265)

By contrast, in the ecoarea where farming could not succeed, Han pastoralists came to "resemble pastoral Mongols more than farming Han. . . . As Han moved into Inner Mongolia and adapted to the grassland ecology, they abandoned farming and many of the ethnic traditions of the Chinese Way" (266).

Pasternak and Salaff concentrate on environments that favor farming or pastoralism, but a similar approach can be used to distinguish between dry farming and irrigated-farming systems. This is usually associated with north-south differences.

Hill Gates (1996) criticizes an ecological approach that views agriculture in terms of a climatic gradient from north to south, with shifts in crops grown. She simultaneously argues against ecology, ethnicity, and Confucian education theories:

> A north-to-south continuum in all kinds of phenomena is a cliché of Chinese stud-
> ies. This gradient represents both different regional costs and regional differences in
> spending patterns: the poor north and the richer south, as well as the subsistence
> economy of the north and the more commoditized south. It is useful, then, to turn
> to some other regions in which north-southness—interpreted as climate/ecology, as
> mixes of migrants and indigenes, or with Jack Goody, as exposure to Confucian let-
> ters (1990:109–110)—can hardly be argued to have had much relevance. (Gates
> 1996:282–83)

In rejecting the north-south continuum as a cliché, Gates does not reject ecological factors per se, as much as a simplistic model of them that assumes the north and the south each contain a single, uniform pattern of economic adaptation. Most ecological models of China take into account a variety of climatic and geographic features of China as well. Location in the mountains or plains, and proximity to rivers, obviously affect the distribution of rice farming even in the south. In this study, I maintain that it is important to examine the rice farming adaptation as a factor in China's gendered household economy. Only through a detailed knowledge of how local household economies and farming systems operate can we determine whether particular patterns of agricultural production, or particular combinations of gendered responsibilities, hold women back. The study of Lu Village and its evolving traditions of rice farming holds out the possibility of better understanding the dynamics of Han Chinese gender hierarchies.

## GENDER AND DEVELOPMENT

The strong emphasis on gender in the United Nations' *Human Development Report* (UNDP 1995) reflects growing recognition of this important issue in development. For years, feminist scholars have criticized the exclusion of women from development planning and the treatment of women as passive recipients (Boserup 1970; Bossen 1975; Sen and Grown 1987; Davison 1997; Nussbaum 1999). They have called for increased efforts to document the variety and multiplicity of women's economic roles, social adaptations, and family strategies, demanding that women be counted and considered as agents. Economist Amartya Sen has argued that recently there has been a shift from concentration on women's *well-being* to a broader emphasis on women's *agency* (1999:189). In anthropology, this is reflected in a shift from recording women's work and economic conditions to recording women's "voices." Clearly, it is important to spend time listening to women and not only recording data about them. But Sen reminds us that "the changing focus of women's movements is, thus, a crucial *addition* to previous concerns; it is not a rejection of those concerns" (1999:190).

What is "development"? It is unrealistic to assert that a general goal of development refers to but a single state of being or has a commonly accepted meaning. Rather, it is a mixed bundle of goods and dreams, varying with cultural settings but sharing some recognizable commonalities. What I mean by development is a diverse cluster of ongoing improvements in living standards, wealth, health, education, communication, technology, consumer goods, comfort, and choice—not merely conformity with the goals of development planners, or ever-escalating "growth." Sen has argued that development can also be seen as "a process of expanding the real freedoms that people enjoy" (1999:3).

Elsewhere, I have argued that women's integration into development is uneven and too complex for a simple formulaic solution (Bossen 1984, 1999). Inequalities and asymmetries do not inevitably increase or shrink with development. Rather, development leads to diverse, disruptive changes and a shifting mix of gains and setbacks in specific domains that differently affect specific age, gender, class, and ethnic groups. In recent years, analyses of gender and development in Asia have increasingly examined the subjects of women's property rights and population sex ratios along with more conventional measures of economic and social well-being (Agarwal 1994; Caldwell et al. 1988; Jeffery and Jeffery 1997; Miller 1981). Gender is slowly but steadily being integrated into studies of Chinese economic development, with its labor-intensive production, its social strata, and its population problems (Croll 1994; Gates 1996; Greenhalgh 1990; Huang 1990; Lavely 1991; Lee 1998; So 1986). By examining the gender dynamics in Lu Village across sixty years, I seek to contribute to larger perspectives on Chinese women and patterns of Asian rural development as technological change accelerates.

## Research on Chinese Women

> There is no differentiating feature in Chinese life that is more profound, continuing and asymmetrical than gender. (Judd 1994:257)

The subject of women's status in China before and after the revolution and during the current reforms generates widespread interest but all too often yields to stereotypes. Numerous scholars have discussed, analyzed, praised, and criticized China's efforts, as a socialist country, to bring women into the public economy and to establish sexual equality (Diamond 1975; Croll 1981; Johnson 1983; Wolf and Witke 1975; Wolf 1985; Rosen 1987–1988; Stacey 1983). More recent studies examine a wider range of feminist issues in contemporary China. Some take a general approach, drawing on surveys, interviews, anecdotes, and news reports from all over China in order to create a national mosaic or composite view of women in the world's most populous nation (Croll 1994, 1995; Hall 1997; Jacka 1997; Honig and Hershatter 1988), while others examine representations of women, sexuality, and gender in shifting, largely urban settings as part of China's quest for modernity (Jankowiak 1993; Rofel 1999; Schein 2000).

Despite this broad interest, the quantity of on-site, in-depth anthropological field research on *rural* women in contemporary China remains minuscule. This is particularly unfortunate given the size and cultural diversity of the rural population as well as the important social and economic issues involved. Relatively few anthropologists and sociologists address this void. By contrast, research on Chinese women in earlier historical periods (Ebrey 1991, 1993; Gates 1989; Ko 1994; Mann 1997), and particularly in south China's Canton Delta and Hong Kong (Jaschok 1988; Stockard 1989; Topley 1975; Watson 1991a; 1994) is flourishing. This deficiency is linked to the ongoing difficulties of gaining permission to do long-term, comprehensive research in rural China. Despite China's well-publicized opening for business and tourism, researchers who want to study rural China (particularly noncoastal and less wealthy areas) face many obstacles and frustrating delays.

Research on *rural* China, gender issues aside, is also characterized by disproportionate coverage of the eastern coastal provinces (Chan et al. 1992; Friedman et al. 1991; Huang 1990; Huang 1989; Siu 1989; So 1986; Vogel 1989) and relatively little from the interior provinces (Endicott 1989; Gao 1999; Jing 1996; Ruf 1998). While some recent village and regional studies include explicit discussions of women, the literature as a whole is not yet sufficiently rich and detailed to address theoretical issues with great confidence. This study of Lu Village is intended to expand our knowledge of China's rural women and to contribute to the systematic examination and theoretical treatment of gender in the context of China's regional and local cultural and economic variations.

## HISTORY AND MEMORY

Lu Village should not be seen as a place divorced from history or "relatively unchanged" by the outside world. History is vital for understanding rural Chinese communities and their gender systems. Ignoring history, earlier generations of anthropologists often assumed falsely that communities they studied had fairly stable traditions, reaching a kind of equilibrium and maintaining themselves as distinct, isolated units. The modest community of Lu Village, however, was for centuries a stage, or overnight stop, on one of Yunnan's many crisscrossing caravan routes. Some sons of Lu Village went out to become statesmen, soldiers, or scholars; their deeds are recorded in clan and family histories. (It is harder to find out about the daughters, who usually married out, or the wives who married in.) Lu Village has sent merchants, miners, and migrant workers to far away places and has accepted migrants as well. "Far away" to eastern Chinese, beyond the clouds in central Yunnan, Lu Village is one of many settlements located at the edge of a populous valley. For centuries these villagers have engaged in trade and tribute relations beyond the valley borders, connecting them with larger empires. Lu Village has been poor, but not isolated. Time and again, China's historical dramas have come to Yunnan, and played in Lu Village.

Building on Fei's earlier study, I reconstruct the roles women played in the community in the past. Present-day research in Lu Village reveals strong continuities in some domains, as well as significant and accelerating changes in others. Continuities are visible, for example, in farming practices and in family organization, while conspicuous changes include the disappearance of footbinding and the spread of modern transport, education, and television.

Revisiting the past with Lu Village elders provides insights into Fei's portraits of women. Elderly women confirm, expand, and sometimes correct his interpretations. Their memories of their lives and activities in Lu Village in the 1930s illuminate, for example, Fei's puzzling statements about the prevalence of female footbinding and its interference with work in the fields (see chapter 3). They illustrate how footbinding, now a memory, was once embedded in a way of life. Set within a larger historical context of economic change, a radical new view of rural women and footbinding emerges.

Viewing Lu Village from a historical perspective makes it possible to reexamine gender in the course of development. Have Lu Villagers on China's periphery transplanted or subverted the Han system of strongly patriarchal household economies, the "Chinese Way," formulated and elaborated in central China (Pasternak and Salaff 1993)? Have patriarchal institutions eroded through local contact with indigenous inhabitants or foreign trade, allowing women greater opportunity and autonomy than in China's heartland? Has gender in Lu Village been shaped by the ecological setting, which favors rice cultivation over wheat? As the last surviving elders born in the 1920s die off at the century's end, this precious opportunity to deepen our knowledge of an extremely dynamic period of village life vanishes. Knowledge of the early-twentieth-century gender system in Lu Village, drawn from the elderly and from Fei's pioneering work, provides a valuable baseline for comparing developments under revolutionary and reform policies.

This historical perspective illuminates the ways sixty years of economic, social, and political change have transformed the gender system of Lu Village at the beginning of the twenty-first century. Did the Communist state's revolutionary political agenda and rhetoric of gender equality produce a significant, enduring change in Lu Village? Did the agricultural system and women's role in it change? Did China's changing family planning policies liberate or oppress women? Revisiting Fei's early report revises current perceptions of change. Combining historical insights with systematic examination of the economic, social, and cultural dimensions of gender in Lu Village in the 1990s yields a profound appreciation of the changes rural women have experienced.

## Tradition and Reform

As China's first generations of educated rural women reach maturity with greater awareness of the outside world, and encumbered by fewer children than their foremothers, they play different roles and seek new goals under China's reforms. How have economic development and reform affected them? Does the rice-farming tradition of Lu Village foster gender equality, preparing women for new market opportunities better than do traditions in other parts of China (Bossen 1992)? Do flexible local gender traditions regarding family, work, and property persist, or does market integration promote standardization? Do national policies still foster gender equality in the reform period?

The reform period has hastened urbanization. As those born in the late 1970s, with fewer siblings, reach adulthood and marriage age, their experiences show how education, family planning, and market reforms influence economic and family choices for rural women. Does a better-educated, more open generation of rural young adults reject farming and choose urban types of occupation, family, and residential arrangements?

China's family planning policy is also revealing some of its longer-term effects on gender in rural areas. How does family planning affect son preference and land distribution? What happens to rural families that, under strict family planning, have no sons? Do couples without sons subvert the policy by migrating and having babies illegally outside the village? Do they divorce or try to adopt children (sons)? Do they abandon daughters or raise them and encourage them to "bring in" a son-in-law? All of these practices occur in rural China. Which are most common in rural communities like Lu Village?

What does economic reform mean for rural women's property rights? Do village rules regarding inherited membership rights shift toward a more open residential system? Regional variations in Chinese patrilineal inheritance and property management (Cohen 1993, 1999) need to be identified. While pressures for reform of the village property system come from many different sources, including national laws (Ocko 1991), local village customs influence the respect for women's property rights and, in turn, have a bearing on post-marital residence, son preference, resistance to family planning, and investment in female education. Examining narratives of divorce, widowhood, remarriage, endowments, and inheritance in Lu Village from women's perspective illuminates the scope of women's rights to land and other forms of property.

## RURAL CHINA AND LU VILLAGE

Lu Village, off the path of tourists seeking ethnic contrast, is a dynamic Chinese community. The story of its farming households and their quest for development is an ongoing challenge shared in many ways by villages across China. As an ethnographic study of change and continuity in Lu Village over a sixty-year period, my approach focuses on women in relation to men, and on the role of gender in villagers' experiences. Beyond these intrinsic interests, however, studying Lu Village engages issues of great interest to both anthropologists and sinologists and is intended for comparison with other studies of China's development and regional gender variations. Three major issues are the relationship of gender to agricultural environment and practices, to changing political agendas, and to the growth of markets.

### Gender and Agriculture

The exploration of gender in relation to specific agricultural systems and changing divisions of labor reveals historical and regional variations in patriarchal practices. The variable relationship between gender and agriculture has significant implications for contemporary development and demographic change, as traditional gender patterns influence emerging rural and urban economic institutions.

> Although many scholars *assume* connections between women's work on the one hand and such factors as household organization, marriage payments, post-marital residence, marriage forms, infanticide, and footbinding on the other, these connections have yet to be examined in any detail. (Watson 1994:25, italics added)

> No one has yet systematically measured the effect of work outside the home on women's status or autonomy in China. Nor have we. The clues are ambiguous, even contradictory. (Pasternak and Salaff 1993:263)

Through ethnographic study of Lu Village, I look for connections and analyze clues linking gender in rice farming and other work with women's property rights and family planning. I also look for links between forms of
women's work and the regional expression of Chinese culture in the mountainous southwest, the cultural borderland. This research explores the dynamics of gender variation among Han Chinese and the significance of the
"Chinese Way" among farmers in one of China's regional farming systems, a
rice farming ecoarea. Examining Lu Village in light of accepted views and
findings from other parts of China tests and refines theories about work, gender, and inequality.

Ecological theorists, such as Jared Diamond (1997) and Burton Pasternak
and Janet Salaff (1993), emphasize that certain macro and micro regions can
sustain specific kinds of crops and animals, and that others cannot. This gives
rise to different sorts of crop-animal combinations for farmers and different
kinds of household divisions of labor. But environment alone does not dic-
tate how farming will be carried out. Successful cultural traditions and know-
how also spread, transform environments, and configure the way work is ap-
portioned among family farmers. Lu Village illustrates how regional
environments affect the starting points and pathways of gender in relation to
development. In Lu Village, irrigated rice farming combined with beans and
raising pigs and water buffalo yields different family patterns and strategies
compared to other crop and animal combinations found in north and east
China. This is not, however, a simplistic north-south contrast, where latitude
is a deciding factor. Indeed, even within Yunnan there are microenviron-
ments where farmers do not grow irrigated rice. Rather, this approach invites
further microlevel scrutiny into the way that growing tobacco, cotton,
opium, silk, or tea in combination with varied food grains entails modifica-
tions of the "patriarchal blueprint" that has been so long associated with
Chinese culture.

## National Political Agendas

Over the past sixty years, China has experienced a variety of political
regimes and policies affecting small farmers and gender. Much ink has been
spilled debating which of these regimes offered better programs and
prospects to women. In many ways, women have been held up as a symbol,
or an index, of how well a nation has been able to develop. What is surprising is that, as China proceeded through republican, revolutionary, and reform governments, each phase has witnessed change and development, and
in each phase women have obtained some benefits and made some gains in
the direction that we might call "development." These benefits have been

different in each period, but they have been important in each case in constituting the current, vastly improved conditions of women in rural China. This position differs from the polarized views that credit one type of government or another with improving women's lives. Clearly, during the revolutionary period the state was most vocal in promoting gender equality, trumpeting the achievements of women under socialism. Neither the republican nor reform governments have made grandiose claims or investments specifically on behalf of women. Yet from the long-term perspective of Lu Village, the process seems more continuous or incremental. Many of the traditional institutions that disadvantage women persist, but gradual improvements are also undeniable.

China's quest for development has not followed a smooth, linear course; it has been punctuated by setbacks. It was particularly hindered by the prolonged war against the Japanese (1937–1945), a ferocious civil war (1945–1949), and by the misguided policies of the Great Leap Forward (1959–1961) and the Cultural Revolution (1966–1976). Despite these low points, both rural and urban China have been developing, in different ways, in the sense defined above. What's more, during each of the major political periods—republican, revolutionary, and reform—China has shown some progress in integrating women into large economic, political, and cultural changes that have taken them beyond the household and village. This suggests that there has been a larger process at work, a process that transcends particular political regimes. The trouble with this position is that it pleases neither the advocates of progressive, redistributive state planning nor those with faith in liberalism and free markets. My hope is that this account of Lu Village will advance our understanding of the complex problem of balancing state intervention on behalf of women against the importance of allowing women to negotiate their own solutions.

Integrating women into the social, economic, and political life of nations has been on the global agenda throughout the twentieth century. One cannot say that the process in rural China, or anywhere else, is complete, that women are fully integrated, or that they have come significantly closer to equality with men within the enlarged public space. But in many ways, their lives are better—their social and intellectual scope has been enlarged and their life expectancy has increased. Women have not been left at a standstill while men progressed. The study of Lu Village examines different benefits of twentieth-century development for women: the end of footbinding, greater recognition of women's economic contributions, improved female health and education, lower infant mortality, a wider variety of employment options and family choices, more labor-saving technology and modes of communication, and a greater public voice.

None of these gains is "conclusive" or comprehensive in the sense of cul-
minating in ideal, stable standards of gender equality; none are secure in the
sense that there is no erosion of benefits and no backsliding into more restrictive patterns of life. Patriarchal relations in rural China are not dead. But
they have been weakened and quite likely will continue to weaken, particularly if China's greater economic openness evolves toward more democratic
political institutions. If forced to identify the underlying cause of this long-
term trend, I might point to the eroding or destabilizing force of more open
markets and growing individualism that have been weakening patriarchal institutions in many nations throughout the past century. This destabilization
does not come without costs or without some borne more heavily by women.
Also, the evolution of more open markets depends greatly on the diplomacy
of nations and their ability to avoid war.

## Opening Markets

The opening of labor markets has the potential to erode patriarchal powers
by allowing subordinate family members to seek their own livelihoods, but
states can also play a significant role in hastening (or retarding) the integration of women into society and markets as full citizens. Conservative religious states have often opposed granting and upholding rights for women
that would allow them to appear in public, to attend school, to marry or divorce by choice, to work outside the home, to own property, or to vote in
their own names. Socialist states like China, however, promoted gender
equality, public education, and public labor for women as a basis for development by overriding the authoritarian power of family heads. Ironically,
both kinds of state have often restricted the development of freer markets in
order to achieve social goals.

In 1949, when the Chinese Communists took power, patriarchal authority
was only beginning to be eroded by global trade and growing labor markets,
mainly in the cities. Revolutionary policies required women to participate in
public labor at a time when rural women were not yet clamoring for such
privileges. In the 1980s and 1990s, the reformist agenda similarly imposed
state family planning, with the well-known one-child policy for urban residents and the lesser-known two-child policy in most rural areas. The Chinese
state thus achieved fertility reduction before increased prosperity, and a more
open market economy voluntarily gave rise to a demographic transition to
smaller families, a transition that Amartya Sen suggests could have been
more effectively achieved through empowerment of young women
(1999:217–18). The point here is that the Chinese state, eager for development, outpaced the market by imposing public labor and family planning (as

well as education) well before liberalizing market forces undermined the patriarchal power of the family and established them by more democratic processes. Viewed from a distance, some of these state-supported changes appear beneficial for women. But only with a closer look at local conditions, such as those of Lu Village, and at the changes rural women have actually experienced, do we begin to understand which benefits were genuinely achieved and what kinds of costs they entailed. During these sixty years in Lu Village, women have experienced ups and downs, and twists and turns, in a many-stranded development process.

## RURAL WOMEN IN CHINA'S DEVELOPMENT

What are some of the specific ways that rural women, such as those of Lu Village, experienced the ambitious project of development? In the republican period, the painful practice of footbinding declined dramatically and was nearly wiped out in most of China, although it lingered on in parts of rural Yunnan. As we shall see, this decline was not just the product of changing fashion, missionary persuasion, or government decree and enforcement. Changes in the household economy, driven by the industrial and transport revolutions, as well as trade and more open markets, made the bound foot an impediment to economic success—which it had not been before. The opening of China's markets and the abandonment of footbinding opened the door to other gains for women, such as through the spread of formal public schooling for girls.

In the revolutionary period, official socialist discourse (inspired by Western industrial capitalism and its critics) prescribed equality of the sexes, insisting that women work outside the home to achieve equality. The state established new laws granting rights to women (and men) to make personal decisions about marriage and divorce. It also established universal education and health care for both sexes, thereby laying the foundation for future gains. The Chinese state's vision of development and equality for women was not a direct response to market demand or to a vigorous rural women's movement. The revolutionary state primarily sought to bring China to a level of national development that would enable it to compete with other nations. Women's labor, health, education, and mobility outside the family were deemed essential for national progress and were part of what Amartya Sen and Jean Drèze have called a "support-led" process (Sen 1999:46; Drèze and Sen 1996).

In the reform period, the emphasis on market revival and reform of the state sector has meant a loss of pro-equality propaganda, of state-mandated

*The road from Lufeng to Lu Village (1999) shows that new-style homes of brick and glazed tile with two and three stories have become common.*

employment of women, and of women's political visibility (if not real power—which they did not achieve) in the chambers of power. Yet this period has arguably brought women greater control of their own income through market employment, greater exposure to society at large, and better (if not too much) access to contraceptives. The state has compelled families to have fewer children (limiting women's choice in the matter), thereby reducing one of the heaviest and most heartbreaking burdens women faced in the past: that of bearing and rearing more children than they could feed and watching them die.

During the reform period, the revival of markets and market incentives have brought greater food security to the countryside. Infant mortality, which soared under the antimarket policies and famine of the Great Leap Forward, has dropped and remained low through the 1980s and 1990s. Women in the reform period rarely lose their babies because of poverty or disease. Nonetheless, son preference is still a factor that, under the current policy, results in a high proportion of missing female infants. In addition to economic and demographic changes, women have been exposed to new worlds through new consumer goods such as televisions. Although this process certainly introduces many new "wants" and "needs" to the rural population, it also provides information that was previously lacking. Women can now "see" alternative lifestyles, as they watch national and international news and a myriad of new products enter their purview through television and advertising. This has eroded one of the larger barriers to women's participation in town and urban life: fear of the unknown. They can now see how to dress, how to act, how to speak, how to buy. Only by doing fieldwork, and experiencing the intricate questioning about prices and products year after year, did I realize how much the lack of this sort of information was experienced as a handicap by homebound and villagebound women and men. The city used to be a more terrifying place. And women, with less experience of migrant labor, were more intimidated by it.

This change struck me most vividly on a trip to Lu Village in 1999, when I was taking an afternoon bus from the big city of Kunming to the town of

*The main street of Lu Village Center covered with drying rice as children walk home from school.*

Lufeng. Seated behind me was a group of four happily shouting and laughing young rural women, returning home after a day at the market. What was the source of their exuberance? They had left Lufeng early that morning with mushrooms to sell and had rapidly sold them in Kunming for good prices, and then they had gone shopping. They were delighted with their sale and with their purchases (including a handbag and a rice cooker). Their infectious joy kept them laughing and joking for most of the ride home. All this in one day! Ten years earlier, the same trip would have taken more than four miserable bladder-holding bus hours each way, making it necessary to stay overnight in the city, and hence expensive for villagers. These young women did not have to worry about the poor latrines (or the lack of them) en route, or the cost of spending a night in the city: they were home before dark.

This chapter introduced Lu Village and its significance for the study of rural China and for pressing questions about agricultural work, national development and demographic policy, and expanding markets in relation to women's rights, gender equality, and human dignity. In the following chapters, I describe the challenges of local development and economic, social, political, and cultural change experienced by women of Lu Village. Drawing on surveys, interviews, and personal narratives, I show how these experiences, often unexpectedly rich and diverse, reflect the changing course of development.

Chapter 2 outlines the sixty-year perspective on change provided by Fei Xiaotong's pathbreaking study of Lu Village in 1938. Although anthropological research has changed in many ways, most emphatically in its recognition of gender, significant continuities link our interests in rural development over time. Throughout this book, I frequently refer to and reinterpret Fei's work in order to assess changes over the past sixty years. Drawing on my own ten-year perspective on Lu Village from repeated visits between 1989 and 1999, I sketch the remarkable changes over that decade.

Chapters 3 through 6 consider economic themes, beginning at the ground level, by looking at female footbinding. This notorious custom, now extinct, formerly shaped gender, literally and figuratively, in much of China. Chapter 3 weaves together the oral accounts of elderly village women with local and regional history. This interpretation of the economics of the gender system found in Lu Village in the early twentieth century shows how it was changing even before the revolution. Chapter 4 traces changes in the gender division of labor in village farming and nonfarm occupations from the 1930s to the present, including conflicts with child care. Lu Village refutes the common view that Chinese women did little work in farming until the revolution. Chapter 5 highlights other aspects of economic change through the story of a most unusual woman shaman, once labeled the richest woman in the village. An account of her long life over China's decades of turmoil illustrates overlooked economic and gender themes of the past and present, as well as the conflicting views of different villagers. Chapter 6 examines the distribution of wealth and poverty in Lu Village, and the stories of women and families at different ends of the spectrum.

The next three chapters present social and cultural aspects of gender and development in Lu Village. Chapter 7 depicts marriage and family dynamics among different generations, including unusual patterns of marital residence, such as uxorilocal and long-distance marriage. It shows how marriage payments, wedding arrangements, family rituals, divorce, family division, inheritance, sworn sisterhood, and care of the elderly contribute to complex textures of family life, and how such institutions exert a strong influence on women's experience of development. Chapter 8 grapples with thorny issues of demographic change, and especially China's controversial family planning policy and census reports of growing sexual imbalance implying the return of female infanticide. It examines and compares the evidence from Lu Village to the township, Yunnan Province, and China as a whole. Chapter 9 looks at gender in the local political system and political culture, highlighting the positions women occupy and their political experiences in leadership, official meetings, and political performances. Finally, chapter 10 considers the overall process of development and many changes that have occurred in the lives of Lu Village women.

External forces propelling China toward development have combined with local history, environment, and culture to give Lu Village its unique configuration and flavor in gender relations. While no other village will have taken exactly the same path, many have been moving in the same directions. Knowing how these rural women have experienced and responded to the dramatic changes of the latter half of the twentieth century helps to answer complex questions about Chinese women and development, questions that still must be addressed as we enter the twenty-first century.

## NOTES

1. Early ethnographies of Yunnan include Hsu (1952, 1967), Fitzgerald (1941), Osgood (1963), and Tian (1944).

2. Zhang Zhiyi was originally transcribed both as Chang Chih-I and Tse-yi Chang in *Earthbound China*. Fei was the principal investigator and author of part I, on Lu Village, and will henceforth be referred to as the author of the Lu Village study. The period of Fei's research in Lu Village, according to Arkush, was November 15–December 23, 1938, and August 3–October 15, 1939. Arkush notes that "the dates in *Earthbound*:12 are off by a year," and that the study was finished in January 1940 and published under the title *Lu-cun nongtian* (Paddy fields of Lu-cun; Arkush 1981: 80).

3. Fei gave the community a pseudonym, Luts'un, now written Lucun in *pinyin* (the official transcription system of the People's Republic of China), meaning Lu Village. The name recalls its link to the nearest county town of Lufeng.

4. Carter et al., describing China's reform as a whole, explain: "the *cunmin xiaozu* is the equivalent of the former production team, and consists of about twenty to thirty households" (1996:10, 99).

5. See Chambers (1983) for the concept of "road bias." Caldwell et al. (1988) found significant difference between towns and dispersed villages in south India.

6. Long Bow, made famous by Hinton (1966), is a suburb of Changchun City. Kaixiangong, Jiangsu, studied by Fei (1939), is close to Suzhou, while P. Huang's work (1990) is on the Yangzi Delta. Zengbu, the village described by Potter and Potter (1990), is in the Pearl River Delta, close to Guangdong and on a railway. Woon (1990) and Johnson (1993) also conducted research in the Pearl River Delta. Chance studied a Beijing suburb. In Sichuan, Endicott's village is on a railway (1989) and Ruf's (1998) is nine kilometers from a railway (and ninety from Chengdu City). Similarly, Greenhalgh's three villages in Shaanxi (1993) and Judd's three villages in Shandong (1994) are near major urban centers.

7. See, for example, "Kidnapping in China," a report in *The Economist* (5 January 2001: 53–54) claiming that it is "impossible to know how much kidnapping is going on in China, but the 'authorities' crackdown on kidnapping this year is said to have found 110,000 women."

8. See Huang (1989) and Seybolt (1996) for biographies of men as village heads in Xiamen and Henan, respectively. Jung Chang's best-selling three-generation biography, *Wild Swans* (1991), written by the daughter of urban cadres, is not village based. An autobiography by an educated villager (of the Bai minority) offers valuable insights on rural gender through his close ties to several women in Yunnan (He 1993).

9. Historian Philip Huang also elaborates the concept of involution in Chinese history (1990).

*Chapter Two*

# Perspectives in Time

If the course of economic development can be read from human geography, Yunnan should serve as one of the best fields for study. (Fei and Zhang 1945:9)

## FOLLOWING THE STEPS OF AN ANTHROPOLOGICAL FOUNDING FATHER, FEI XIAOTONG

Because Fei Xiaotong's study of Lu Village in *Earthbound China* provided a reference point for my research on development in Yunnan Province, it is important to outline his work and some of the differences in our approach. The most obvious difference is that Fei focused on the economics of land tenure, while I focus on gender relations. Despite our different priorities, there is actually considerable continuity between Fei's concerns in the pre-Mao era (before 1949) and mine in the post-Mao era (after 1976).

An enduring figure in Chinese anthropology, with a career and influence that spans most of the century, from the 1930s to the 1990s, Fei was a student of Bronislaw Malinowski at the London School of Economics and of Robert Parks at the University of Chicago. Fei's writings have been widely cited in works on rural China, and several biographies of him have even been written (Arkush 1981; McGough 1979). He has been a key figure, not only in the development and revival of China's social sciences, but also in national politics, as leader of the Democratic League (Minmeng). He has been both praised and punished, as China's political priorities changed course. Among his many anthropological accomplishments in analyzing Chinese social structure, his descriptions of rural Chinese women have received limited recognition.[1]

By today's standards, Fei provided a limited account of village women. Reflecting many of the gendered assumptions of his times, he gives far more

27

time to rural men than women.[2] Yet considering the context in which he lived and wrote, he stands out as one of the few Chinese anthropologists who included women in his descriptions and commented on their hardships.[3] To be sure, his data about women are often meager, and claims sometimes rest on dubious evidence, but one has only to compare the chapters written by Fei and Zhang in *Earthbound China* to realize the difference. For the two communities where Zhang was primary investigator (Yu Village and Yi Village, originally written as Yuts'un and Yits'un),[4] there is notably less information about women, apart from a discussion of the decline of women's weaving in Yu Village. To take a minor point, we never learn whether women in Yu Village and Yi Village were footbound. In contrast, part I on Lu Village, written by Fei, includes a comparatively detailed description and analysis of women's roles in the agricultural division of labor, in marriage, and in other aspects of community life.

## CHANGING RESEARCH AGENDAS: FROM CLASS AND LAND TENURE TO GENDER RELATIONS

Fei Xiaotong selected Lu Village to fulfill a specific role in his research strategy of comparing four communities.

> We started our study with this village because we found here a simple form of economy in which neither commerce nor industry plays an important part. The main occupation of the people is the management and cultivation of farms, and the villagers are either petty landowners or landless laborers. Landlords with large holdings are lacking, and absentee owners are few and insignificant. It seems to us that this village represents a basic type of farming community in interior China. The life of the peasants is characterized by the use of traditional farming techniques on rather fertile land and under a strong pressure of population. In these fundamental ways Luts'un represents, in miniature, traditional China. (Fei and Zhang 1945:19)

He believed that villages should be studied with theoretical questions and analytical relevance in mind, "not mainly for convenience and by chance" (18). Yet Fei's choices of village sites were indeed influenced by convenience and personal contacts (as, of course, were my own), kinswomen and classmates, as well as theoretical considerations. Most obviously, the Japanese occupation influenced the choice of Yunnan as a site for a makeshift research station composed of displaced social scientists.

Fei and Zhang were interested in the relationship between degrees of land concentration and absentee ownership. Their criteria for village selection emphasized this. The first three villages listed in figure 2.1 were those in Yunnan, studied by Fei and Zhang. The fourth was the village Fei originally studied in Jiangsu and reported on at length in *Peasant Life in China* (1939) and in an abridged version in *China Village: Close-up* (1983).

The Chinese villages studied by Fei and Zhang cannot be seen as "typical" or average in a statistical sense. They were neither typical for China as a whole nor for Yunnan Province, but they did present significant contrasts in terms of conditions deemed important for successful economic development. Chinese social scientists like Fei and Zhang were concerned with the path of rural development. They sought for China to avoid the impoverishment, bankruptcy, dispossession, and abrupt displacement of small holders that accompanied rapid development in many parts of the world. They feared that absentee landlords who accumulated land from impoverished peasants neglected agricultural investment and productivity. They hoped that their comparative studies of Chinese patterns of land tenure, and of combinations of agriculture with cottage industry, would help to reveal the appropriate path to rural development and prosperity.

Through the turn of the century, the search for an appropriate path to rural development and prosperity remains a vital concern in large agrarian nations such as China. Having experienced a Communist program of social change for over fifty years, the uncertainties of landownership remain. Moreover, the rights of women to own or manage land are also shaky, and it is questionable whether they are better defined today than they were in Fei's youth.

Today it is widely understood that development involves shifts in a wide range of social and economic institutions, and that the study of change must explicitly consider women as well as men. Increasingly, indicators of the health and well-being of the entire population are used to measure success in "human development."[5] Aggregate national wealth is no longer a sufficient measure of development success. Distribution of wealth in ways that enable each individual to attain good education, good health, and long life is now considered an important dimension of development. These aspects of development can be quantified. Yet successful development, if it is to describe a quality of life that populations desire, is not simply wealth, health, and education. It involves opportunities to make choices about the quality of one's

| Village, Province | Smallholders |
|---|---|
| 1  Lu Village (Luts'un), Yunnan | Smallholders, owner-occupants, few tenants |
| 2  Yi Village (Yits'un), Yunnan | A few large landowners with land in other villages, smallholder owner-occupants, and no tenants. |
| | *Absentee owners and tenants* |
| 3  Yu Village (Yuts'un), Yunnan | Many tenants, some big owners live in nearby town. |
| 4  Kaixiangong, Jiangsu | Mostly tenants, absentee landlords in big towns. |

**Figure 2.1.  The Four Villages Studied by Fei and Zhang**

life and to find satisfying ways of achieving personal goals without denying these options to others. This means looking more intimately at the quality of life, and the presence or absence of physical coercion, of occupational and marriage choices, and of mobility. This study proposes to examine these dimensions of development and to make more explicit the gender differences in the way Chinese rural development is experienced.

## The Accuracy of Fei's Study

Because Fei Xiaotong holds a prominent position in Chinese social science and because he produced some of the most outstanding Chinese anthropological studies of the prewar period, his work has already been subject to extraordinary scrutiny. Many scholars have drawn heavily on his work and continue to do so to this day (Goody 1990; Jacka 1997). In general, they attempt to take into account the limitations of his methods and of the times in which he conducted his research. While his work is not flawless, it is generally considered to be of high quality. He often provided descriptions of how he obtained his data, of whom he interviewed and where he lived, and he combined insightful anecdotes with attempts to gather more comprehensive and systematic data on the economic questions that interested him most.

During the Cultural Revolution, his work was harshly criticized in China for class bias, for as he himself indicated, he drew more heavily on information provided by the wealthier and better-educated segments of the rural population. These political criticisms were, of course, extremely unfair. Fei's work provides a wide range of qualitative and quantitative information on the life of both poor and wealthy villagers. His intentions certainly were to seek solutions to rural poverty rather than to perpetuate it. Nonetheless, his professional life was suspended and he was ostracized until China's antiintellectual policies were reversed in the reform period.

Fei's work has also been criticized in the West for inaccuracies. Arkush has pointed out that Fei's studies were "hastily done. . . . Not much of his important analyses of the agricultural year and its seasonal labor requirements could have been based on firsthand observation. In neither village did he take a census of the population, but made calculations on the basis of local government figures he knew to be inaccurate." After detailed analysis of quantitative problems in Fei's work, Arkush concluded "Fei's quantitative data should be handled with caution" (1981:85, 87).

This assessment is certainly correct and consistent with my own efforts to analyze Fei's quantitative data. But it is balanced by the qualitative data he provided. He included numerous rich descriptions of various aspects of village life. These descriptions, anecdotes, and portraits of life in Lu Village in the prewar period are largely consonant with what older people today recall about the past and also reveal clear continuities with the present. They provide an excellent point of departure from which to trace the course of tradition and change in village conditions and, in particular, the shifting understandings of gender and development.

In addition to the benefits of looking at Lu Village from a sixty-year perspective, my own visits to Lu Village have now spanned more than ten years and bear witness to some remarkable changes in the town center and in the village.

## Current Approaches to Anthropological Research

At the 1998 International Congress of Anthropological and Ethnological Sciences, anthropologist Jerry Eades contrasted Eastern and Western approaches in recent research on rural China. He observed that Chinese scholars trained in Japan took a more holistic, or classic ethnographic, approach, giving considerable detail on varied aspects of village life as they related to each other. Chinese scholars trained in the West, he found, focused on a single theoretical problem, analyzing it in great detail, but providing little information about other aspects of village life.[6] By these standards, this study is closer to the classical approach and to that of Fei Xiaotong. I do not seek to resolve a single narrow problem as much as to examine a wider set of interrelated aspects of gender and development. In part, I chose this more classic approach because Fei's work begged for contemporary comparison with respect to the many topics he covered. But examination of an expanded range of factors is also consistent with the more comprehensive definition of development employed by contemporary development economists such as Amartya Sen (1999). Highly focused studies often leave too many unanswered questions about the importance of other aspects of village life. Yet it would be unrealistic to claim that I tried to treat all topics equally. Some of my choices were guided by personal preference, and some by the political climate and the interests of villagers themselves.

My first priority was to understand how the periods of revolution and economic reform had transformed the village economy and the gender system. Fei's study was firmly rooted in the domain of economic anthropology and a concern with the problems of development in rural areas. My own study follows upon his interests in farming, development, family, and population— topics I explore in detail. However, I have very little information on religion. Villagers did not show interest in religion and brushed aside my questions. When I attended the local temple on days that a few older women of the village suggested would be busy, there was little activity. When I inquired about the presence of Christianity in the village prior to the revolution, people denied that there ever were many Christians and both older and younger people claimed ignorance of religion or a lack of religious affiliation. There is probably more going on in ritual and religious life than I encountered,[7] but with limited information in Fei's account, and a lack of enthusiasm toward my inquiries, I did not pursue the matter as much as other researchers might have. During my 1999 visit, however, family rituals toward ancestors were widely practiced on designated days, with a lively commerce in ritual paper goods in the town market.

## A DECADE OF CONSTRUCTION: BRIGHT LIGHTS IN LUFENG TOWN

A noble stone bridge of seven arches—the most substantial and artistic I have seen in Western China—spans a stream which flows southwards to the west of the district city of Lu-feng, on its way to swell the Song-koi. The city itself is badly ruined, but the place in which it lies contrasts very favourably in an agricultural point of view with the valley occupied by the next city to the east—Anning. (Hosie 1890:143)

In 1990, Lufeng was considered a dull town by my Kunming colleagues. The main point of fame was still the "noble stone bridge" described above by Hosie, although the river it crossed had greatly shrunk, probably due to diversion of water for irrigation. Lufeng's stores were few and drab, stocked with little of interest to a city dweller. The main item visitors could hope to bring back from Lufeng was wild mushrooms, collected in the hills around villages like Lu Village. I myself was impressed by the lack of urban consumer goods. For instance, in 1990, one could not find a store that sold toilet paper or aspirin. As a researcher I hunted in vain for photocopy machines, bright light bulbs, good quality pens and paper, good batteries. The supply of packaged foods or drinks was extremely limited, and no one sold Yunnan's famous cheese. The fresh fruit, sold at curbside, was in poor condition, looking like it was rejected by larger cities. By contrast, the daily fresh produce market was fairly well stocked, and on market days one could find a rich variety of agricultural products, wild mushrooms, grains, seeds, vegetables, handmade baskets, tools, and plain clothing. Market days, held twice a week, were the most lively times, when villagers from all directions would come, shop, and meet friends and relatives on the street. There were a handful of small Muslim restaurants in the town, and another handful of small Han restaurants. One would occasionally see a few minority women, usually Miao, who came down from mountain villages wearing distinctive clothing, bamboo baskets on their backs. There was not much car traffic in the town, and in the evenings people went out and strolled up and down the street, snacking, gossiping, and relaxing.

When I traveled to Lufeng by bus, the bus would stop at a point on the highway (the Burma Road) about two kilometers outside of Lufeng, where a small settlement had grown to service highway traffic. There was always a string of horse-drawn taxicabs (in the original sense) to take passengers into town for one yuan. On the way into town, there was a broad, empty boulevard, a large paved street yet without any buildings. Then one reached a "traffic circle" without any traffic on it, in the center of which was erected a large, fanciful, and modernistic sculpture of a dinosaur, to celebrate the fact that Lufeng County was the center of a region rich in dinosaur fossils. A new museum had just been completed to house dinosaur fossils. Behind the dinosaur landmark, the several main streets of the town became narrower and the traffic thicker, for here were the old buildings and commercial business of the town. There was one brand new tall building in the town, a structure of about ten stories (meaning it had the only elevator in town) that was to be a hotel, probably in anticipation of throngs of tourists who would come to visit the dinosaur museum (the throngs have yet to arrive, but some foreign delegations pass through).

Lufeng had county and township government building compounds, a hospital, a high school, a movie theater, some banks, three or four large stores, the dinosaur museum, a bus station, an area where horse cabs and bicycle carts could be hired, and various small shops, food shops, bicycle repair shops, and the produce market. There were also a few industries on the outskirts, one producing steel products with a fair amount of pollution. Just outside the town were a Buddhist temple and a cemetery for revolutionary heroes. Perhaps the saddest shop in this quiet town was the bookstore on the main street. It had hardly any stock, and the books were mainly sets of dusty, moldering government-printed volumes of Marx, Lenin, or Mao's thoughts, along with various agricultural how-to booklets. There were no maps of the region, for these were still treated like state secrets which could help anyone planning an invasion; only government officials could have them.

Since then, each year that I have returned, major changes have taken me by surprise. The number of stores and restaurants has multiplied; entrepreneurs have rebuilt their storefronts to make display windows and have installed glass display cases. Many have installed florescent lights so the products can be seen in bright light. The scale of available products has mushroomed. I stopped having to bring my own toilet paper, batteries, pens, and paper. I stopped having to beg from suspicious government officials to let me photocopy my data on the one machine in town, or return to Kunming if I wanted to copy questionnaires. In 1996, there were several shops with photocopy machines and computer services available. In 1999, a few shops had internet connections, although they were slow and unreliable. Beauty salons and beauty products proliferated. Suddenly, many brands of all imaginable toiletries were stacked in the stores, and hardware and furniture stores appeared. The department stores began to stock more modern bicycles, then motorcycles, stereos, color TVs and videos, electric fans, washing machines, refrigerators—ever more appliances. Music stores and discos opened. The state-run bookstore remodeled itself and carried a wider, more colorful selection. Commerce has become ever livelier. Mushroom sellers no longer sell only fresh mushrooms on the street; they now dry and export them wholesale—one of Yunnan's specialties in the provincial trade fair. Bamboo basket sellers have disappeared from the main street, losing business to sellers of plastic bags and brightly colored plastic buckets and tubs.

There is no way that I could have predicted in 1990, after my first research trip, that change would come so fast to this region. Commerce is transforming Lufeng town, yet government expansion is evident as well. Lufeng's once empty boulevard and side streets are filling up with new six-story apartment buildings for government employees. More banks, hospital buildings, and government office and residential buildings seem to appear every year. One hospital employee in Lufeng (a daughter of a Lu Village family) showed me the new glazed-brick residence for hospital employees. She pointed to a shabbier building made of cement, remarking sarcastically that it was "old" when it was erected less than a decade earlier. Then she took me to the prior employee residence, a red brick building probably less than twenty years old that was now abandoned. The same construction mania was evident in the government guest house where I originally stayed in the new building completed in 1989. Since then two other new buildings have been completed, and the building where I stayed in 1990, brand new at the time, has been allowed to run down and will probably soon be demolished. By 1999, on the outskirts of town, newly completed high-rise buildings were selling units in private ownership.

The formerly dull market town is becoming a busy commercial center and the forces of change in the town are also propelling the residents of Lu Village. The thirst for new commodities is powerful in a population suffering from years of commercial drought, and there is no knowing when it will be slaked. Yet beneath these material acquisitions there rests a set of cultural understandings, practices, and institutions that do not change so rapidly. People are still farming, marrying, raising children, and building social networks based on familiar gender traditions.

## A DECADE OF CONSUMER "CATCH-UP": TV IN LU VILLAGE

During the 1990s, the village and villagers have also been changing rapidly, with more access to modern communication and transportation technologies. The main street in town has been paved, and another village office building has been erected, next to the old one, with a futuristic spiral staircase in the middle of the courtyard leading to the offices on the second floor. A new factory has been built on the edge of town. Most villagers have bought televisions, and televisions now show more advertising—stimulating desire and providing information about an explosive growth of available new products. Where most homes used to have but two old wooden chairs, and stools or straw cushions for seating, families are now purchasing stuffed sofas and armchairs. In prospering households, dark wooden cupboards have been moved out of sight, replaced by showy, tall, white enamel cupboards. The Western concept of a "living room" is mingling with the traditional formal symmetry of the front room. Fashionable clothing, home furnishing, and appliances are all proliferating. A consumer revolution is taking place, only a few paces behind the big cities.

Forms of transportation have also evolved. A growing number of villagers now drive motor vehicles. I used to join people who were mainly riding bicycles or walking on the road to town while a few diesel tractors puttered by, but now there are many trucks and motorcycles as well as buses. Surprisingly, horse-drawn cabs have begun to make frequent trips taking villagers between town and village—an option that was not available in the past. Horse cabs have been banned inside the town, but villagers who used to walk now have more disposable income and choose to ride. In 1991, when I hired a car from Kunming to bring me to Lufeng, I decided to take the opportunity to drive to an archeological site at Yuanmo and invited some villagers to come along. Later, one woman told me that was the first time she had ever been inside an automobile. It was a vivid memory for her then, she reminded me, but she now daily rides on the back of her husband's motorcycle into town. About twenty households in Lu Village have purchased minivans in the last few years. Private telephone lines are also making inroads. In 1991, when I arrived unexpectedly and went to the home of a village friend (hoping to avoid ceremonies), a man was dispatched to town by bicycle to inform township officials, who then drove out to greet me while villagers rushed to prepare a banquet. In 1996 the same home had a telephone. In autumn 1999, the entire village was being wired for telephones for anyone who wanted to subscribe.

The restful atmosphere of the village is changing as new houses in the 1990s no longer present dull, earth-tone mud walls. Houses popping up on the village outskirts and near the road, outside the former protective core, display shiny white and pastel glazed bricks, with large windows that open to the outside and to commerce.

In order to appreciate the significance of changes over the sixty years and over the past decade, it is worthwhile to step back to earlier points of reference. In chapter 3, I examine the subject of footbinding as it was once practiced in Lu Village. Reexamination of this important dimension of women's experience in local history provides a deeper understanding of the gendered behaviors and values that villagers have brought forward, and those which they have cast aside in pursuing China's dramatically shifting paths to development.

## NOTES

1. Feminist scholars have, however, often cited Fei's ethnographic work for information on women (see Davin 1975; Jacka 1997:24–25; Johnson 1983; Stacey 1983; Wolf 1985).

2. During the Cultural Revolution, he was accused of bias in favor of the rich, but not of gender bias (see Arkush 1981). In his controversial essays, *Xiangtu Zhongguo*, translated into English as *From the Soil*, Fei devoted a chapter to a general theory of male-female relations and the segregation of men and women in Chinese culture, citing a very traditional Confucian precept, "between men and women there are only differences" (1992: 87–93).

3. Francis L. K. Hsu (1967 [1948]) also provides considerable information on women in West Town, Yunnan.

4. These would be written Yucun and Yicun in contemporary pinyin spelling.

5. See the United Nations *Human Development Reports*, especially 1994 and 1995, which introduce the Gender-related Development Index (GDI) and the Gender Empowerment Measure (GEM).

6. Eades's examples of Chinese scholars trained in Japan are Han Min and Nie Lili; Chinese scholars trained in the West include Jing (1996), Yan (1996), and Yang (1994).

7. In 1999 I discovered that the county town had one Christian and one Muslim place of worship, located in rooms of interior residential courtyards off the main street, with little exterior sign of their existence. However, I did not find out whether either of these congregations had members from Lu Village.

*Chapter Three*

# Trade and Beauty: The Demise of Footbinding in Lu Village

A plain face is given by heaven, but poorly bound feet are a sign of laziness.
(Pruitt 1945:22; also paraphrased in Croll 1995:20)

## FOOTBINDING IN CHINA AND YUNNAN

The downtrodden status of women in imperial China has often been symbolized by the centuries-long tradition of female footbinding. Under the Qing dynasty (1644–1911), imperial edicts banning the practice were ineffective and the practice continued.[1] By the close of the nineteenth century, many Chinese and foreign reformers were calling for the eradication of footbinding, yet they encountered considerable resistance. In the early twentieth century, arguments for the liberation of Chinese women often focused on the liberation of their feet as necessary for the health of the nation. Women with feet bound, broken, and compressed to make them tiny were quite obviously oppressed by physical pain and limitations on their mobility, but the belief that binding was beneficial to women, making them beautiful and improving their marriage chances, was also deeply ingrained in the population (Ko 1994). Why did this custom prevail in so many regions of China for such a long time and how did it finally become possible to eradicate it?[2] How did it affect women in rural areas like Lu Village?

*Old woman of Luoci with bound feet.*

The history of footbinding in Lu Village illustrates the dynamics and distribution of the Han gender system in China, and particularly in the southwest. By piecing together how footbinding fit into particular known contexts, we can better comprehend its acceptance in a region so far removed in time and space from its putative origins during the Song dynasty (960–1279) in eastern China, as well as the reasons for its final rejection in the twentieth century.

Questions about footbinding are far from irrelevant for contemporary Chinese women's issues. The conditions that once permitted or produced this form of physical control by impairment of women are associated with a larger set of gendered customs and practices in China. Even in periods of rapid change and political revolution, societies typically retain assumptions about gender difference and maintain continuity in the ways they enact gender roles in families and communities. How did footbinding in Lu Village relate to other aspects of gender, particularly the nature of women's work and their economic contributions? The footbinding history of Lu Village, as part of the village's gender her-

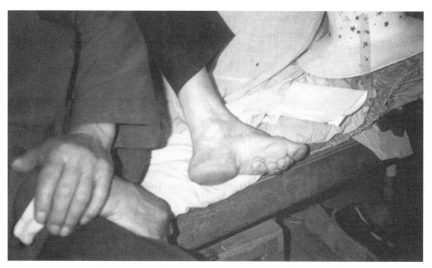

*The misshapen foot of an elderly footbound woman of rural Tonghai.*

itage and as part of the greater Chinese pattern, provides insights into the particular ways that gender has evolved and is experienced today.

## FOOTBINDING: CLASS, FARMING, AND ETHNICITY

Many observers have stressed that footbinding was related to class and implicitly to urban-rural differences. Women from poor, rural families that required their heavy labor in the fields were less likely to have their feet bound than women of elite families, who tended to live in towns and cities. Wealthy families did not need their daughters' labor and could afford the conspicuous luxury of keeping a woman with dainty feet. Small feet, wealth, and idleness, then, went together, as did large feet, poverty, and farmwork. From this perspective, the oppression of daughters by binding and compressing their feet to fit a three-inch ideal would ironically give them a better chance of escaping the oppression of poverty and heavy labor—but only if they could marry into a wealthy family, where they could live a leisured, indoor life. The price of these benefits, however, was a loss of mobility and freedom. The footbound woman was more fundamentally housebound than the footloose woman. The bride with small feet conformed more closely to the ideal of a proper woman as an "inside person."

But what about the vast rural population, neither elite nor impoverished? Footbinding was indeed not confined to an elite class of women. Until the twentieth century, it was widespread and almost universal among women in many rural regions. The regional variation has been interpreted largely in terms of farm labor practices and ethnicity. Various authors, such as Davin (1975, 1976:118) and Jacka (1997:23), interpret regional variations in Chinese women's status by referring to John L. Buck's agricultural surveys of the 1930s. Buck reported that women performed more field labor in the rice region of south China (16 percent) and less in the wheat region of the north (9 percent). The theory is that where women did a great deal of work in the fields, as in double-cropping rice areas, women's feet were less frequently bound (Jacka 1997:24). Yet these authors have noted that some regions had varied degrees of female participation in farming but similar footbinding practices.[3] Quite clearly, then, whether or not women farmed was only one possible influence on footbinding.

The farm labor theory is not very satisfying because footbinding and female exemption from farmwork do not closely correspond. Exemption from farm labor can hardly account for footbinding in regions where virtually all women, rural and urban, had their feet bound. In rural areas, it is hard to believe that such a large proportion of the population could be excused (for life!) from economically valuable labor in order to be "attractive" to men. When much of rural China was desperately poor and hardworking, it seems unlikely, if not irrational and mysterious, that many women should have their feet bound only to become beautiful and idle playthings for their laboring, small-farmer husbands.

Ethnicity has also been proposed as a factor affecting distribution. China's non-Han minority groups generally did not bind women's feet.[4] To the Han, *not* binding was interpreted as a sign of these people's lack of civilization and their wildness (*yexing*); the splayed toes of the unbound foot were seen as unruly or untamed. Han footbinding may have been reinforced by the desire to maintain visible ethnic boundaries and signs of "civilization" in regions where there were many minorities. Similarly, bound feet may also have been a sign of assimilation of subordinate ethnic groups toward dominant Han culture. To my knowledge, however, no one has directly argued that Han Chinese families across China bound women's feet *primarily* to indicate that they were Han.

While class, ethnicity, and farm labor requirements influenced footbinding, they do little to explain it.[5] The most common cultural explanation assumes that binding was primarily done to appeal to Chinese male aesthetic preferences, which inexplicably drifted toward this ideal. These culturally constructed preferences valued the helpless, modest, housebound female, presumably because she could not flee or challenge male potency. Her weakness became erotic. The study by Howard Levy (1991 [1966]), which Hill Gates (1995) describes as "resolutely masculinist," takes this approach, using literary sources to demonstrate the "sado-masochistic appeal" of the bound foot to elite men.

Anthropologist Elizabeth Croll (1995) and others suggest that footbinding did not just evolve independently in response to male erotic fantasies, but that it was a bodily extension of sexual segregation and female seclusion, confining nubile daughters and sisters to chaperoned spaces while sons and brothers ran free. The constant sexual supervision and control of the well-bred, footbound daughter destined for marriage is contrasted with that of the slave or servant who had no such protection from male advances. Describing a woman with unbound feet in the early twentieth century, one woman asked, "How will the servants be able to tell whether it's the bride or a newly bought slave girl?" (Chao in Croll 1995:23). Of course, despite the "sexual" attraction theory of bound feet, big-footed servant and slave girls were unlikely to remain free of their masters' attentions.

Classical writings and traditional sayings often explain that feet must be bound to prevent girls from running around or running away, or going out on the street (Croll 1995:24). Why is this confinement so desirable? Is it only to ensure sexual propriety, or more directly, to control sexual property? An exclusive concern with sex, propriety, and paternity suggests women mattered only as reproducers, sex symbols, and status symbols. Although this luxury might apply to families of fabulous wealth, how could it hold for the vast numbers of rural women across China? Was their labor of so little consequence? We need to consider more explicitly the kinds of labor that women and girls were socialized to perform, under such firm control, within the family.

## BOUND FEET AND PROPER TRAINING

In my encounters with old women who still have tightly bound feet in other parts of Yunnan, many still conform to the aesthetics of their day, which called for a controlled demeanor from proper women. These women maintain a very upright, stiff-backed, almost Victorian posture; they comb and pull back their long hair tightly and neatly into a bun, and wear a very tailored traditional style of cotton or silk jacket and pants tightly bound by white cloth at their ankles, just over their tiny shoes. Even today, these outfits speak indefinably of good breeding and self-control. This self-control associated with bound feet and careful movements seems to have signaled moral virtue in women, much the way upright bearing, impeccable clothing, and precision marching symbolize rigid military discipline among soldiers.

Hanna Papanek (1990:176) notes that "painful practices mark the passage to adulthood for both males and females in many societies." She speaks of

"the foot-binding paradigm" as a form of female socialization to accept inequality and pain, and as a form of mutilation "linked to erotic appeal." She
writes that this extinct practice is important, not only as an example of extreme inequality, but also "because it was decisively stopped in conjunction
with major political, social, and economic changes in the society. It is evidence of the possibility of changing even the most grievous inequality
through appropriate actions" (1990:176–77). Aside from speculating about
its psychological importance in socializing some women (but again, why not
all women?), Papanek does not suggest which "appropriate actions" finally
brought about its extinction.

There were, of course, variations in the degrees of binding. Some feet were
bound so tightly that after the small toes were bent back under the foot, the
arch was folded and broken so that the front of the foot was pushed back toward the heel; others were less deformed and merely rendered small and slen-
der by bending and binding the small toes under the foot without breaking
the arch. But the economic mystery about the assumed waste of female labor
potential remains unsolved.

## FOOTBINDING, TEXTILES, AND HOUSEHOLD ECONOMICS

Recently, anthropologist Hill Gates (1995, 1997) has pioneered the task of
showing how a closer look at household economic conditions and local work
activities of women provides greater insights into the significance of this
evocative custom. She maintains that women with bound feet were not exempt from work, but were required to do forms of work that could be classified as "light labor." Light labor here does not mean that the economic value
of the labor was necessarily light, or less than heavy labor (one does not assume a "light" computer programmer produces less than a "heavy" brick-
layer). Nor does it mean such labor was less onerous (e.g., "blind" stitching
in lace making, or rug knotting). Rather, it has connotations referring to the
bodily demands placed upon the worker. Her hypothesis is simple: "footbinding was likely to be common where light labor for women was general"
(1995:7).

What qualifies as light labor is not always obvious, although the concept
of "light work" as female work is well established in China.[6] Gates includes
all forms of textile work but is less definitive about forms of work such as oys-
ter shucking and tea picking, both practiced in Fujian in areas where women
used to have bound feet. Gates excludes porterage, fuel and fodder collecting
in the mountains, and work in wet paddy fields from the category of light labor.[7] Thus, in areas where women did these types of work, they would be un-

likely in her view to have bound feet. Through surveys conducted in Fujian, Sichuan, and Taiwan, she pieces together the types of work that were associated with high and low rates of footbinding, and early and late ages of footbinding.

## Quick Hands and Slow Feet

My own conception of "light" work compatible with footbinding emphasizes the place of work, its pace, and the parts of the body used to perform it successfully. This would be work that women could do indoors or within a limited physical terrain. It would be best done with deft hands and dull feet, primarily at home or in nearby fields. It would require dexterity but little pedestrian mobility. It would be, literally, "handiwork."

Many forms of women's work in nineteenth-century China required degrees of dexterity, immobility, and patience, but none so much as "manual" labor in textiles, which literally made use of the hands more than the feet. As Gates (1995) has noted, spinning and weaving cotton, twisting and weaving hemp, and reeling silk were all highly compatible with footbinding, as were making straw mats and mosquito nets.[8] I would add embroidery, sewing, making cloth shoes, and weaving straw shoes and baskets. In a complex, highly commoditized commercial system, there were many types of domestically produced commodities that women could make for sale. Specialization was common. For this work, women had to become accustomed to sitting in one place for hours at a time, working with their hands. Other types of work also required dexterity: picking tea, scraping opium pods, shucking oysters, and raising silk worms were partly compatible with footbinding, even though they often required women to move to a work site. Once there, their foot movements could be slow while their hands whirred away.

By this theory, footbinding lost much of its raison d'etre when sedentary, home-based work, such as hand spinning and weaving, was driven out of the home by modern factory-based spinning and weaving of textiles. The decline of home spinning and weaving of cotton cloth and other forms of sedentary textile work, then, should be associated with a decline in female footbinding in areas where women used to perform this work (Gates 1995, 1997).

The pathbreaking theoretical and empirical research by Gates requires that scholars examine the economic implications of this painful and debilitating custom. Reexamining the early evidence from Sidney Gamble (1954) charting the distribution and decline of footbinding and recent work by economic historians[9] documenting the textile revolution in eastern China, it is increasingly clear that the footbinding complex cannot be explained by cultural and symbolic values alone. While "small feet" may well have evoked male admiration and sexual desire among the gentry (Levy 1991 [1966]; Chang 1991; Chang 1996) and symbolized affiliation with the leisured classes, the uneven spread and rapid disappearance of this practice across rural China probably had as much to do with varying economic conditions and economic motives as with a sudden change in aesthetic and moral values. Aesthetic values favoring small feet in this "textile model" did not, as often implied, override or contradict economic interests through the refusal to use female labor. Rather, they placed a premium on the very physical constraints that tied women to useful and lucrative textile handiwork. As Gates's research has shown in Fujian and Sichuan, when female footbinding by villagers ended, those villagers were scarcely aware of any antifootbinding movements emanating from Chinese reformers or Christian missionaries. In Lu Village, however, police enforcement clearly hastened the end of footbinding, even though ideological movements evidently made little impression upon the women who experienced it.

In almost every account of a Chinese girl's childhood experience of footbinding, there follows an account of her indoor activities thereafter, which invariably include embroidery, spinning, weaving, or other work with needle or thread. Jung Chang (1991:24) described her grandmother, footbound at age two, who was taught to embroider as well as draw and play music. Hill Gates (1995:11) cites women in Fujian who spoke as if weaving cloth was synonymous with having bound feet. Croll (1995:20) quotes Hsieh Ping-ying describing footbinding, the resistance, and the aftermath—working indoors, spinning thread: "I, like a condemned prisoner . . . shouted and howled. . . . I felt as if the bones of my feet were broken and I cried and fell down on the ground. . . . From henceforth I spent most of my days sitting by the fire *spinning*" (1995:21- 22, italics added).

Unfortunately, as Gates observed, because women generally performed their work within the home, we rarely learn the details about the products of women's textile labors, and what they were worth. Were they exclusively for household use? Were they sold to contractors or in markets, or given as "priceless" tributary gifts on special occasions? How much did it cost to buy equivalents? Without this knowledge, the natural tendency is to assume their value was negligible.

The amount of money saved by having wives, mothers, and daughters make shoes for a family was undoubtedly insignificant in the budget of a wealthy household. But poor families cut corners when women made family clothes, and they could turn to women for income by selling their textiles, their skilled textile labor, or their persons. The woman who could avoid spending money on purchased textiles, and use needle and thread to embellish and restore them for the family, or embroider fine textiles for the gentry enabled poor households to get by. This skill, requiring little capital, gave women an income when men's fortunes went up in smoke (as they did all too often in China's opium dens).

Toward the end of the nineteenth century, the economic revolution bringing industrial technology, capitalism, transport, and commercial integration began to displace certain types of household craft production by women: first spinning and later weaving. If homemade cloth was no longer economically competitive, the underlying reason for footbinding disappeared. The industrial revolution in textiles pulled the rug out from under the footbound domestic textile producer. This perspective on changing household economic conditions suggests peasant men or small farming households were never as irrationally governed by their aesthetic or erotic preferences as commonly believed. Power, the labor of women, and economic interests were always at stake. In this chapter, I reconstruct the prevalence and demise of footbinding in Lu Village, but begin by summarizing information from northeast China for comparison.

## THE DEMISE OF FOOTBINDING IN NORTHEAST CHINA

From 1926 to 1933, sociologist Sidney Gamble conducted detailed, rich surveys in Ding Xian, a county in Hebei Province, northeast China (Gamble 1954). The surveys showed that the cultural hold of footbinding started to loosen among the cohort of women born from 1900 to 1904. Decisions against binding were being made when girls were around age five, in 1905–1909.[10] This was just after the Boxer Rebellion against Western influence, and just before the fall of the imperial Qing dynasty (1911) and the beginning of republican China. Girls born from 1910 to 1914, who reached footbinding age from 1915 to 1920, were the first cohort in which the majority were allowed to grow up with their feet unbound.

Gamble's data demonstrate that the timing of the change in footbinding coincided very closely with major changes in local women's textile production. In Ding Xian most village women were heavily involved in textile production. Cotton spinning was found in 453, or 98 percent, of the villages in the county, where 95 percent of the spinners were women. Cloth weaving was found in 378, or 83 percent, of the villages. Thirty percent of the population were weaving families, and weavers were just under 10 percent of the village population. Over eighty percent of the weavers were women producing salable cloth (Gamble 1954:298–301). These families abandoned footbinding at the same time that domestic weaving technology momentously switched to machine-made yarn from Tianjin and to more productive looms.

Spinning was probably already undermined by imported machine-made thread given that the average gain per person was less than a third that for other home industries, primarily weaving (Gamble 1954:16). But the increased supply of cheaper factory thread would have enhanced the weaving income of those with the best access to the new sources of supply. From 1882 to 1932, Gamble found an increase from 58 to 86 percent of families weaving cloth in a sample village (1954:16). Unfortunately, he did not examine the impact of imported factory thread on spinning households in the county. We can only speculate that spinners were switching to weaving wherever they had access to cheap, machine-made thread and could afford a loom. Where such access was impossible, due to difficult roads or inability to purchase good looms, households would have lost a domestic occupation and a dependable income.

The three different types of loom were "locally known as clumsy, pulling, and iron machines." The original "clumsy" loom was a wooden loom, with shuttle thrown by hand. The "pulling" loom was improved because the shuttle was "thrown from shuttle boxes activated by pulling a string that hung in front of the operator." The iron loom "was an automatic model driven by foot power transmitted through pedals, chains and gears. The pulling model was introduced around 1908, the iron loom around 1920" (301). Weavers rapidly switched from wooden looms, to pulling looms, and then to iron looms, which more than doubled the productivity of the weaver, who now moved the shuttle with foot-operated peddles.

Table 3.1 shows the timing of the demise of footbinding together with the transition in weaving technology used by women weavers in the home. The introduction of the new pull loom to the area around 1908 coincided with the five-year period in which the percentage of young girls getting their feet bound began to shift significantly downward. When 7 percent of the households acquired new looms in 1912, 40 percent of the young girls were not getting their feet bound. When 17 percent of the households had new looms in 1917, 80 percent of the girls were allowed to let their feet grow. What is the relationship between these two dramatic changes? Did the "spirit of the times" cause families to shift their daughters from a viable economic strategy in order to meet new standards of beauty? Or did the increasing productivity and competition of new textile technologies mean that fewer and fewer women could earn income for the household by weaving? Textile prices must have been falling as output increased, as a result of both improved domestic looms and factory production. Those who could only weave slowly using a hand shuttle were soon to be outdone by those using the iron foot-powered loom. Possibly, bound feet were a disadvantage in operating the peddles on the iron loom, but in the new factories, managers preferred hearty workers who could stand for long periods and walk back and forth between looms.

**Table 3.1.   Age of Females with Bound and Unbound Feet in Northeast China (515 families, Ding Xian, Hebei Province, 128 miles south of Beijing, 1929)**

| Birth year | Year to bind feet[a] | Total number | Percent with bound feet | Percent old looms by year |
|---|---|---|---|---|
| before 1889 | to 1894 | 492 | 99.2 | |
| 1890–1894 | 1895–1899 | 109 | 94.1 | |
| 1895–1899 | 1900–1904 | 103 | 94.1 | |
| 1900–1904 | 1905–1909 | 130 | 82.5 | |
| 1905–1909 | 1910–1914 | 129 | 56.5 | 93 (1912) |
| 1910–1914 | 1915–1919 | 149 | 19.5 | 83 (1917) |
| 1915–1919 | 1920–1924 | 161 | 5.6 | 66 (1922) |
| 1920–1924 | 1925–1929 | 169 | 0.0 | 51 (1927) |
| 1925–1929 | 1930–1934 | 294 | n.a. | 20 (1932) |
| | Total | 1736 | | |

*Source:* Footbinding data adapted from Gamble's (1954:60, table 9) survey from 1929. Loom data adapted from table 96, p. 314.

[a]Unlike Gamble, I assume binding began from age five to ten, as does Croll (1995). Gamble believed it began at age three, but this may be taking the extreme young age as the average. My interviews, admittedly from later periods and different regions, generally cite ages above five years for the beginning of binding. Year of footbinding above is assumed to be five years after the year of birth.

Gamble pointed out that as more families switched to the new, more productive looms, and particularly the iron loom, the total number of looms operated in the village decreased. From 1912 to 1932, the total number of looms decreased by 15 percent, from 280 to 239. But output during that period rose by 90 percent. That suggests that those with the new technology were driving down prices and displacing those who lacked it. Even though older women with bound feet might continue for years to operate their traditional looms, younger girls faced a different economic future. Parents must have been keenly aware that their daughters would not be able to earn much money through hand weaving, even if they acquired iron looms. Foreign- and factory-made cloth were making their work obsolete. The footbound woman was no longer an economic asset to her household.

Another striking feature from Gamble's study is that the footbound women of Ding Xian did farmwork, confounding the theory that women in north China were more oppressed than elsewhere because they did not participate in farming. "In a group of 515 families, 88 percent of the males and *80 percent of the females over 12 years of age were doing farm work.* Eighteen percent of both sexes reported primary nonfarming occupations. Twelve percent of the males and *51.5 percent of the females were doing some home industry*"(1954:7, italics added).

Combining farmwork and home industry, Ding Xian women were a flexible part of the family labor force. Yet we cannot be sure if the industrial textile revolution imposed this flexibility on female labor (and their feet) by undermining a form of domestic production that had spread and thrived for centuries, or if combinations of textile and field work were always expected of footbound women in this region.

## FOOTBINDING IN LU VILLAGE, SOUTHWEST CHINA

According to commonly held theories about women's work and rice farming in south China (discussed in chapter 1), footbinding should have been less prevalent in south China, where women did rice transplanting. According to Gates (1995:11), work in the paddy fields was not "light" work. Thus, Lu Village, as a rice-growing village where women transplanted rice, should not have had many women with bound feet, and if there were any footbound women, they should have been from elite families that did not require them to work in the fields.

Fei's observations in Lu Village in 1938, however, do not fit this theory (Fei and Zhang 1945). He remarked that footbinding did not exempt women from work in the fields. *All* women worked in the fields, regardless of the wealth of their households. He interpreted this to mean that their status was more akin to that of a labor force than to co-owners in the household. Senior and even junior males of wealthy households could enjoy the privilege of avoiding work in the fields, but not women, even those with bound feet. Fei never specified, however, how prevalent footbinding actually was at that time, nor how severe it was. He did not mention if it was disappearing as a result of economic change or of government campaigns to eradicate it. From this limited information, we might tend to dismiss Lu Village as an anomaly where ethnic considerations overran economic ones. This may have been Gates's reaction when she wrote: "But here and there, such as on Taiwan's northern Han-Aboriginal frontier, or the mixed Han/non-Han communities in northern Yunnan, footbinding became so overwhelmingly a sign of ethnic identity that correlations with labor disappear" (1995:7).

Fortunately, I obtained information on footbinding in Lu Village from the older women. Interviews with nearly all surviving older women (born before 1940) of Lu Village Center, conducted in 1996, permit me to estimate the prevalence of footbinding in the late nineteenth century and the timing of the transition to "big feet."[11] These estimates provide a closer look at the economic conditions of that period.

### How Prevalent Was Footbinding in Lu Village from 1866 to 1940?

In Lu Village and the surrounding Han villages, nearly all women had bound feet at the turn of the century. A subsample of eighteen older women (born between 1918 and 1938) interviewed at greater length provided information about their own mothers and their maternal and paternal grandmothers as well as about their husbands' mothers and maternal and paternal grandmothers whom the in-marrying wife had a chance to meet. Table 3.2 summarizes the evidence that footbinding had been predominant but not absolutely universal in this region of Han rice farmers in the late nineteenth and early twentieth centuries. It includes women who would have been born approximately between 1866 and 1913.

Four out of five of the women from the two preceding generations had their feet bound. These women include some who grew up in Lu Village itself, as well as women from surrounding communities in the same county who were part of the local marriage exchange system. Most women came from villages within fifteen kilometers of Lu Village.

Various reasons were given to explain the occasional failure to bind feet before the real transition occurred. One woman explained she was from a mountainous area where people were too poor to bind women's feet—referring to the widely recognized economic advantage of owning flat valley land as opposed to land on mountain slopes. Other factors such as early loss of parents or association with non-Han ethnic minorities also provided explanations, as we shall see below. One Han woman (with bound feet) married a man of the

**Table 3.2.   Footbinding of Lu Village Elderly Women's Forebears (estimated born 1866–1913)**

| 1st ascending generation (1891–1913) | Percent bound | 2nd ascending generation (1866–1888) | Percent bound | 2nd ascending generation (1866–1888) | Percent bound |
|---|---|---|---|---|---|
| Own mother (n = 18) | 78 | Father's mother (n = 12) | 75 | Husband's father's mother (n=8) | 88 |
| Mother-in-law (n = 13) | 85 | Mother's mother (n = 11) | 91 | Husband's mother's mother (n=8) | 88 |
| Total 1st ascending generation (n = 31) | 81 | Total 2nd ascending generation (natal kin) (n = 23) | 82 | Total 2nd ascending generation (affinal kin) (n = 16) | 87 |

*Source:* Subsample of extended interviews with eighteen older women in Lu Village, selected from larger sample based on ability to recall and describe the past clearly, 1996.

*Note:* The birth years of the subsample women interviewed were 1916–1938, a span of twenty-two years. The average age of marriage was nineteen for this generation. I estimated that the average age difference between generations is about twenty-five years, meaning that the second ascending generation is about fifty years older than the women interviewed. Subtracting twenty-five from the upper and lower age limits of the women interviewed, 1916–1938, gives 1891–1915. Subtracting fifty years gives 1866–1888. Totals are lower for the husband's side, since some of these female kin would have died before the bride joined the family, so she would not have seen their feet.

Yi minority (who generally live in the more mountainous districts), none of whose female kinswomen had bound feet.

The evidence from Lu Village shows that footbinding was rapidly declining even before the time of Fei's study. The Nationalist government, having outlawed the practice, was exerting pressure in major market towns by unbinding women's feet.[12] Antifootbinding pressures would only have increased during the Anti-Japanese War (1937–1945). There was greatly increased contact with the outside world due to the immigration of eastern Chinese fleeing the Japanese, the transfer of the Nationalist government capital to Chongqing, and the relocation of many universities and Chinese military units to Kunming. The war also brought American airmen to Kunming to help supply the forces in Free China. With the many civil servants and modern intellectuals flocking to Kunming and its environs, as did Fei, the cultural opposition to footbinding in the cities must have increased dramatically at that time. In the village, outside visitors such as Fei and his missionary aunt were rare, and certainly not remembered for preaching against footbinding.[13] But one of the most important factors consolidating the change would have been the increased demand for female labor in farming and heavy work such as porterage, given the conscription of many able bodied men from Lu Village in 1939 (Fei and Zhang 1945).

Table 3.3 shows that girls born from 1921 to 1930 witnessed the transition, with the full conversion to natural feet for girls born after 1935. Again, assuming a five-year time lag in the making of such decisions, we can date the transition in Lu Village from about 1925 to 1935. At the time of Fei's research in 1938, most young girls aged eight to twelve were no longer getting their feet bound. This must have been a topic of serious discussion among local parents deciding what was best for their daughters, but Fei did not

**Table 3.3. The Demise of Footbinding in Lu Village**

| Birth Year | Year to bind feet | Total number | Percent bound[a] |
|---|---|---|---|
| 1916–1920 | 1921–1925 | 8 | 75 |
| 1921–1925 | 1926–1930 | 12 | 50 |
| 1926–1930 | 1931–1935 | 9 | 11 |
| 1931–1935 | 1936–1940 | 17 | 12 |
| 1936–1940 | 1941–1945 | 8 | 0 |
| | Total | 54 | |

*Source:* Interviews in 1996 with all available older women of Lu Village Center, excluding women who were hard of hearing or suffering from poor memory.

[a]Most of these women had their feet bound only temporarily; their feet were loosened within a few days, months, or sometimes years and they did not experience permanent or extreme disability.

mention it. Note that the change occurred in Lu Village nearly two decades later than in Ding Xian.

Footbinding in Lu Village disappeared for most women born after 1930. Many who were born between 1915 and 1930 actually had their feet bound for only a short time before the process was terminated. Some women reported that their feet were bound for only a few days, or months, and then were released. Others in this cohort underwent up to twelve years of binding, with their feet unbound at the age of twenty, when in some cases they were still able to flatten out. The reason they gave for unbinding them was usually that the attitude of society had changed; but some women were more specific, as we shall see below. One said her father had heard at the market that government authorities were cutting the bindings of all women who entered the city. Others mentioned patrols at the city gates that were forcibly unbinding women's feet. Mrs. Gao, who appears in chapter 6, recalled that

> When my mother was young, they bound her feet but she herself feared the pain. She said it hurt, and they let them loose. So my mother's feet were not small. We also didn't have them bound. I remember the time when they burned foot bindings. It was before Liberation, when I was barely twelve years old [1938–1939]. When we went to market, on that short section of road as you entered the city you could see that at the Great West Gate Bridge there were people who burned foot bindings (*shao guo jiao*). Those people were called the "Long Arm Team" (*chang bi dui*).

The elderly women interviewed were all under twenty at the time their feet were unbound. It is unclear whether older women whose feet were permanently misshapen were also being required to remove their bindings in the 1930s. The fact that most of the surviving elderly women had their feet released before they were permanently stunted does not mean that "early release" was a practice in this area. All but one woman in my small sample had their feet released before marriage. The average age of binding was around six or seven. With only a small sample, I cannot determine whether Lu Village women born in the nineteenth century generally had feet extremely tightly bound in pursuit of the three-inch ideal, but some of them did. One woman who ceased binding (and married a Yi man) said that her feet were only bound for a short while, to make them smooth and straight. She expressed a standard somewhat less restrictive than the "three-inch golden lily," a metaphor for tiny feet.[14] Various women born in the twentieth century described this type of binding in contrast to the natural foot. They implied that binding feet was a sign of good grooming, not merely beauty.

Like Papanek, Gates agrees that footbinding played an important role in girls' socialization and that it had major symbolic significance.[15] However, Gates

emphasizes the particular kinds of work lives that young Chinese girls were being socialized to accept and perform. Without knowledge of the drastically
changing economic conditions affecting women's work, all-purpose psychological and cultural explanations are easily pasted into the blank spaces in our
knowledge, hiding our ignorance. Why the psychology of submission, sacrifice,
and pain took this particular form in some places and in some groups and not
others, and why it persisted for centuries and then suddenly ended is left unanswered. The myth of women's lack of economic value thus remains unchallenged, not just within the Chinese tradition, but also in the Western tradition
of looking at women as if marriage divorced them from the economic world.

## RECOLLECTIONS OF LU VILLAGE'S
## ELDER WOMEN ABOUT FOOTBINDING

Gates has described footbinding as a "culture-less custom" saying that, hunt as
she might, she could uncover little evidence of ritual, songs, sayings, or magic
associated with the practice in her interviews and discussions with older
women.[16] My own experience was similar. Many women simply cited the expression, "big footed servant girls do not get married" (*dajiao yatou jie bu dao*),
equating large feet with servile status. Yet the varied statements quoted below
provide insights into the experience of this transitional generation.

### Economic Aspects

Women rarely remarked on the economic implications of footbinding. Perhaps this is because the work they were raised to do has always been obvious
to all their acquaintances; they saw no need to explain particular forms of
work and how much they could earn. One woman cited a saying:

> #5. [Age seventy-six, born 1920 in Lu Village] Big feet bring in five *dou* (150 kg)
> and take out five *dou:* why marry her off?[17]

This saying implies that there was no net gain on the marriage of a daughter with large feet; the amount of grain received as bridewealth matched the
amount given in dowry. Conversely, it *may* suggest net gain for parents on the
marriage of a footbound daughter. But it also might imply that a daughter
with large feet, unlike a footbound one, could earn grain income through her
own labor. If so, there was no great incentive to marry off a working daughter early, or to marry her to someone outside the household.[18] Consistent
with this, the average age of marriage for Lu Village's older women, mostly
unbound, was about nineteen, which is not particularly young.

#49. [Age eighty, born 1916 in Lu Village, feet bound in 1923 at age seven, married 1934 at age eighteen, feet unbound in 1936 at age twenty] The households with the most difficult lives did not bind feet very small, they just bound them to be smooth feet (*shun, shun jiao*—these are also called "cucumber feet" because of their narrow, tubular shape).

This woman, unique in the accounts from Lu Village, had her feet unbound after marriage—a pattern Gates has reported elsewhere as a kind of compromise, where feet were bound primarily to secure a marriage, but undone in response to the heavier work demands on the married woman. It is unlikely this was an established pattern in Lu Village, since most women who had their feet unbound said it was due to social change, not change in marital status.

Before the footbinding transition, girls who protested received little sympathy from their mothers, who were the enforcers. The girls faced a beating if they dared to remove the bindings.

#28. [Age seventy-one, born 1925 in Heijing] When they bound my feet, they hurt and I cried. When I thought of liberating them and opened them, my mother took the shoes and beat me. Then I did not take them off.

#49. [Age eighty, born 1916 in Lu Village] It hurt to work, to climb the wall. Yet I dared not unbind them. If I unbound them my mother would beat me.

Some older women explained how their parents' early death prevented them from having someone care enough about them to bind their feet. These women placed the failure to bind their feet in the context of their unfortunate childhoods, as a sign of neglect.[19]

#7. [Age seventy-seven, born 1919 in Xiao Lu, married 1938] My adoptive mother did not help me bind my feet; she did not even give me a pair of shoes to wear. Only if I went out as a guest would they then tell me to wear shoes.

#12. [Age seventy-four, born 1922 in Nanxiong] My father died when I was two. My mother left to marry someone else. My grandmother (*nainai*) was terrible, and did not give me enough to eat or to wear. Because I had no father or mother, there was nobody to bind my feet.

## Minority Ethnicity and Free Feet

The Han woman who married a Yi explained that the Yi did not practice footbinding. Another woman, half Yi with a Yi mother, grew up in a Miao area, and emphasized not ethnicity but terrain and poverty as explanations for lack of footbinding in that zone.

#35. [Age seventy-nine, born 1917 in Lu Village] When they bound my feet, they did not bind them small, they were only bound in order to be a little finer (*xi*, also thinner)—smooth, smooth feet (*shun, shun jiao*, where "*shun*" also means "orderly"). Society still bound feet at that time. I later let my feet out. My husband was Yi, not Han. His family did not bind feet.

#40. [Age sixty-two, born 1934 in Guanzi] My mother was a Yi. She lived in the mountains where the surrounding people were Miao [a different ethnic group]. Because that was a mountainous district, it was extremely poor, so they did not bind feet. . . . When I was a girl, none of the women of my natal village had bound feet. There are only Miao around there and they did not bind feet.

These statements suggest that rugged landscape, minority cultures, poverty, and unbound feet were associated with each other in Yunnan. For the Han woman whose bound feet were not very small, marriage to a Yi man meant no danger she would be criticized for this "flaw" by her Yi neighbors.

## BINDING AND UNBINDING: THE TIMING OF CHANGE IN LU VILLAGE AND SURROUNDING AREAS

Women who married into Lu Village included some who were born in other administrative villages within the same township. Some may have begun to escape footbinding slightly earlier than those in Lu Village, around 1924–1928.

#11. [Age seventy-eight, born 1918 in Zhongcun, about ten kilometers from Lu Village] My younger sisters and I were not bound, only my older sisters were bound.

#19. [Age seventy-five, born 1921 in Caiyuan, same county] My mother and her four sisters all had bound feet. In my husband's family, my *nainai*, *waipo*, and *popo* (paternal and maternal grandmothers, and mother-in-law) all had bound feet. My *nainai*'s feet were "half slope" feet (*banpo jiao*, implying that the others were smaller).

#21. [Age seventy-three, born 1923 in Chuanjie, same county] My parents bound my feet for only a few days, and then let them go.

Footbinding was declining before 1930 in Lufeng, the market town, as well as in nearby villages (see table 3.3).

#18. [Age seventy-five, born 1921 in Lufeng town] When they had just started to bind my feet, they bound them for three days. My mother took a needle and sewed them up for me. It hurt and I wanted to die. She said, "Big footed servant girls don't get married." But then they liberated my feet and did not bind them.

#58. [Age seventy-five, born 1921 in Jiuxuecun, just outside Lufeng town] My feet were bound when I was eight years old, but not finished. They were released after about three months [1929]. There were people at the four gates of Lufeng who pulled the foot wrappings off of women with small feet. They also cut off men's braids or pigtails. They were police-like officers with big hats and insignia.[20]

## The Daughters Talked Back

In the following unusual example, the footbound mother was undecided and actually asked her daughter for her opinion about having her own feet bound. At around that time, in 1930 or so, there was strong Nationalist government pressure to stop footbinding.

#9. [Age seventy-four, born 1922 in Lu Village] My mother had "three-inch golden lilies." Whatever she wanted to do, her feet were too small; it was not convenient. The family was poor then and my mother asked me, "Should I bind your feet or not?" I said, "Don't change me by binding them. If my feet are bound small, how would I do mobile labor (*donghuo*)?" Then she did not bind them.

In some cases it was the father who raised opposition to binding the daughters' feet.

#17. [Age sixty-one, born 1935 in Luxi, forty kilometers from Lu Village, same county] My mother had the old way of thinking. One day she decided to change me by binding my feet. I cried and said, "I hurt so much I'll die! Today it's no longer good to bind feet, but you still want to bind my feet." Then I just sat there and did not do any work. When my father came home I said, "Mother is binding my feet!" My father said to her, "For this generation of young wives now, it is no good to bind feet. . . . It is not allowed." Then, she no longer bound them.

Women born in Lu Village after 1930 did not have their feet bound. The custom quickly died out, much as it had a decade and a half earlier in the northeast. In Lufeng County, the force of the law in the market town sped the process affecting surrounding villages like Lu Village. Other places in western Yunnan like Wuding, Nanxiong, and Luxi (above) also abandoned footbinding about the same time or a little later.

#50. [Age sixty-four, born 1932 in Wuding] My mother's home was Luoci. All Luoci women bound their feet very small. But when I was a girl, small girls already stopped binding their feet.

#53. [Age sixty-five, born 1931 in Nanxiong]. My feet were bound at age six [1937], for about half a year, and then they released them.

Nearly all fifteen of the surviving Lu Village women who had their feet bound, if only temporarily, were unhappy about it, but only two claimed they actually opposed it. All reported the main reason for binding feet was the fear they would be unable to marry, but about half also said it was considered good looking, and one said it was done so she could not run away. Most women interviewed had their feet unbound within a short time, before they were permanently deformed. The reasons they gave for the unbinding emphasized that "society opposed it" in almost all (thirteen out of fifteen) cases. This means their parents did not buck the tide once opinion shifted and enforcement became rigorous; parents responded to a larger societal change. Four women also cited the pain, while three noted the family needed their labor.

The women who experienced the shift to unbound feet were children at the time. They did not have profound insight into why the custom changed; they did not go to school or query their parents about changing social and economic conditions. Many stated that as children they simply did not question parental decisions. They merely perceived that unbinding was generated by larger social forces rather than a response to their own pain or resistance. Some felt it was related to the need for women's labor.

The timing of the liberation of female feet varied across Yunnan. While the end in Lu Village was late compared to Ding Xian in northeast China, footbinding came to an end still later in Yunnan's Luliang and Tonghai counties, both Han Chinese areas to the east and south of Kunming, the provincial capital. There, unlike Lu Village, one could still see numerous old ladies hobbling along on very small feet as late as 1996. These women were born in the late 1920s and 1930s, and yet kept their feet bound when Lu Village girls were flexing their toes. This is not because these villages and towns were more isolated than those in western Yunnan. After reviewing the question of long distance trade and its relation to the demise of footbinding, I will return to the complex nature of Lu Village women's work in the early twentieth century, again as it relates to footbinding.

## UNRAVELING THE MYSTERY OF
## LU VILLAGE'S FOOTBINDING HISTORY:
## NINETEENTH-CENTURY CHANGES IN COTTON
## TEXTILE TECHNOLOGY AND TRADE IN YUNNAN

Historical sources describing Yunnan's trade patterns in the late nineteenth century shed light on effects of changing textile technology and textile markets on women's work. With rugged mountainous terrain that makes transportation difficult, Yunnan presents an extremely diverse physical and human environment. Even among what seem to be culturally uniform Han villages, one discovers significant variations in the local economy and gender divisions of labor as consequences of different physical environments and the various distances from trade routes. Comparisons among villages reveal the links between economic change and footbinding.

The late-nineteenth-century household economy was in flux in Yunnan as in the rest of China. The century had witnessed an increase in opium cultivation as a cash crop, and in the later years interregional trade expanded. By the century's end, steamboat shipping was reducing the price of imported goods such as cotton and allowing factory-spun yarn to compete with homespun.

The reports of British, French, and German explorers, businessmen, travelers, and missionaries in Yunnan in the late nineteenth and early twentieth centuries demonstrate that Yunnan was experiencing a host of new economic and cultural influences, sparked by improving accessibility through steamboat, railway, and motor car.[21]

In the late nineteenth century, British explorer Major H. R. Davies scouted Yunnan's economic conditions to advise on the feasibility of a Burma-Yunnan railway to link India and China. He reported that almost no cotton was grown in Yunnan and that the entire Han population was completely dependent on imported raw cotton, cotton yarn, and cloth (Davies 1909). Exactly when the shift from importing raw cotton to importing yarn and cloth began is hard to determine, but I suspect this started in west-central Yunnan villages well before 1900.[22] Most indigenous ethnic groups did not develop dependence on imported cloth as rapidly as the Han. Well into the twentieth century, non-Han ethnic groups maintained traditions of hand weaving other local fibers and making distinctive clothing styles and colors that form the subject of many a coffee-table book on Yunnan's ethnic minorities.[23]

By 1900, machine-made cotton yarn imported from Bombay, India, and Manchester, England, had displaced locally spun cotton for the Han.[24] Although spinning had largely disappeared from Yunnan, hand loom weaving continued and possibly expanded in specialized weaving centers. Specialized weavers made handwoven cloth from machine-spun thread, which was then sold in dispersed local markets such as Lu Village. Davies mentioned that Xinxing Zhou [just north of Tonghai] in southern Yunnan was a "chief weaving center" and that Qujing in eastern Yunnan wove cloth from Indian yarn imported from Hong Kong and Vietnam (Davies 1909:162, 318). He asserted that regions having earliest access to new transportation routes importing cheap cotton yarn were those that specialized and expanded commercial hand weaving.

In Davies's estimation, Yunnan and Sichuan provinces were both almost "entirely dependent on cotton from outside sources" (1909:318). Describing Yunnan's imports, he wrote,

> Cotton is by far the most important. The whole population of Yunnan is clothed in cotton clothes, and yet practically no cotton is grown in the province. The whole

clothing of this part of China must therefore be imported. It is brought in as raw cotton, as cotton yarn, and as cotton cloth; but the greater part of it comes as yarn and is woven into cloth in the province. . . . The imported cotton cloth is usually too dear for the poorer classes, but is worn a great deal by those who are better off. (1909:318)

Describing the cotton trade he observed at Simao in southern Yunnan, he wrote,

The trade is certainly a large one. The principal cotton growing districts are in the Chinese Shan states . . . and the British Shan state of Kengtung [all now in Burma]. . . . As the whole population is clothed in cotton material, the trade in this commodity is one of the largest and most necessary in the province. . . . Much Manchester and Indian yarn and some cloth also comes into the province from the Yangzi, from Bhamo [a town just inside Burma], and from Mengzi, the treaty port near the Tongkin [Vietnam] frontier. But there is still a considerable trade in raw cotton from Burma via Bhamo, and from the Shan states via Simao. . . . The superior convenience of the foreign yarn is making it yearly more popular. (Davies 1909:97, spelling converted to pinyin)

The use of machine-made cotton yarn was relatively recent, following the transportation revolution that brought steamboats and railroads into the interior of Southeast Asia and China, with goods taken from the terminals by caravans to markets across the hinterland. Thus, as Davies described, cotton yarns and some cloth came from Bombay to Burma by steamboat, and overland to Yunnan by caravan. Another route was from Hong Kong by steamboat to Vietnam, and overland from there, by caravan to western Yunnan, or by the new French train to eastern Yunnan. The changing patterns of trade, particularly cheaper and faster transport by steamboat and railway, allowed bulky shipments of factory-made products to compete with homemade ones and begin to displace them in the latter part of the nineteenth century.

This change from consumption of raw, locally spun cotton to imported machine-spun cotton was the first phase of an industrial revolution in textiles and transportation. It clearly had an extraordinary effect on home textile production. It is hard to imagine that any gender system could remain static when one of the major sources of employment of one sex became obsolete. Clearly, hand spinning was not competitive with machine spinning. As a result, the value of the skills and labor of women must have dropped considerably, and households must have had to drastically rethink how to deploy the household labor at their disposal. Basic questions of economic survival and the search for prosperity must have led to a reconsideration of the ways daughters were viewed and prepared for the workforce, weakening the old cultural formula of binding a daughter's feet to make her more attractive, both aesthetically and economically—as a sign of labor discipline and sacrifice.

The decline in women's contribution to cloth and clothing manufacture and the increase in the production of opium were both significant trends in nineteenth-century Yunnan's rural economy.[25] Because changes in women's economic activity involved work that was domestic, invisible, and screened from the view of outside observers, its importance has often been underestimated. Contemporary observers could comment on women's minor contributions to income and believe it was always thus, that women just worked for supplementary "pin" money and were not "breadwinners" for their households (see Fei and Zhang 1945:244). But the displacement of commercial spinning and weaving in regions that began to depend on imported cotton yarn and imported cloth for clothing must have created considerable female unemployment and family hardship. As Fei (1939, 1983) had shown for the east coast village of Kaixiangong in Jiangsu in the 1930s, the loss of female employment in textiles (in that case the silk industry) could deprive a household of up to half of its annual income and bring on a spiral of debt.

The importance of weaving to the family economy under other circumstances was captured in a Qing dynasty poem by Tung Hung-tu, reproduced in Elvin (1972), called "Complaint of the Weaving Wife":

Hungry, she still weaves.
Numbed with cold, she still weaves.
Shuttle after shuttle after shuttle.
The days are short,
The weather chill,
Each length hard to finish.
The rich take their rent,
The clerk the land tax,
Knocking repeatedly with urgent insistence.
Her husband wants to urge her on,
But he has not heart to do so.
He says nothing,
But stands beside the loom. . . .
The more she tries to get it done,
The more her strength fails her.
She turns away, choking down tears,
And consoles herself they are still better off than their neighbors,
Wretched and destitute,
Who having sold their loom
Next had to sell their son. (Elvin 1972:160)

The demise of spinning and weaving in Lu Village is, of course, only conjectural. It is likely that this area would have previously employed its bound foot women in such activities at some earlier time, either weaving with imported homespun cotton or weaving hemp or other fibers. However, the abandonment of such handicraft activities might have come earlier in Lu Village, with the nineteenth-century boom in opium cultivation. If this occupation was lucrative enough, footbound women could have been drawn away from some spinning or weaving to work in opium fields. Both rice and opium production have ample work for women that emphasizes dexterity rather than mobility. Rice transplanting and weeding are tedious work, but are really handiwork in the fields. Similarly, opium scraping involved meticulous treatment of the opium pod. Footbound wives and daughters could transfer their labor to these activities without great disadvantage: their value was in their hands, not their feet or their backs. At the same time, sewing shoes and clothes remained as female tasks for the family, tasks which could earn some income as hired labor. Such are the patterns we see in the early-twentieth-century picture based on informants' memories.

## FOOTBINDING AND LU VILLAGE WOMEN'S WORK IN THE EARLY TWENTIETH CENTURY

Because women with bound feet could do no farm work, those in the poorest families didn't bind their daughters' feet. . . . But, I would say that about 80 percent of the women here had bound feet even though Houhua was a very poor village. (Seybolt 1996:21)

In the earlier discussion on farm labor, I emphasized the fact that even in the very wealthy houses, the women and girls work regularly in the fields. . . . [I]t may not seem fair that the weaker sex, with their bound feet, should toil in the mud while the men spend their days in idleness. (Fei and Zhang 1945: 111)

The first statement above, by a village leader in northern Henan Province, recalling the 1930s and 1940s, implicitly claims that 80 percent of the village women did no farmwork. The second, describing Lu Village in Yunnan Province, claims the opposite, even when the work involved walking in wet paddy fields. Like Gamble's report for Ding Xian, which showed high rates of both footbinding and female farmwork, the observations confirm the complex relationship between farmwork and footbinding. In times of rapid economic, social, and cultural change, this relationship was probably not very stable. Here I try to reconstruct what happened in Lu Village, and to some extent in Yunnan, by taking into account not just women's farmwork, but also their handiwork.

### Farmwork

In the villages of western Yunnan Province, footbinding did not prevent women from working in the fields, although its impact on their productivity is unknown. Fei described women as taking part in the significant types of farmwork without any intimation that footbinding impeded their productivity; they transplanted rice, planted beans, weeded rice and beans, and harvested rice and beans. They were not just "helpers" but an integral part of the family labor force.[26]

Those in my subsample of older women all came from villages that grew paddy rice. They uniformly asserted that women with bound feet could and did work in the wet rice fields, as well as hoe vegetables in the dry fields. Some described how they would bring an extra pair of cloth shoes and bindings to the flooded rice fields, so that they could change their bindings before they went home. Unlike women with unbound feet, who might go barefoot into the irrigated fields, the bound foot women needed the support of their bindings when they walked into the water and deep mud. Clearly it was not convenient, but it was manageable.

## Opium

In addition to work in the major staple crops such as rice and beans, a number of women in their youth also worked in the harvest of opium poppies, although this was generally only for a month or so each year. Growing opium was illegal at the time of Fei Xiaotong's visit, but not many years earlier it had been a major cash crop exported from Lu Village and surrounding villages. Fei noted that "Since Luts'un produced opium of an exceptionally good quality before its cultivation was made illegal, the use of the drug required no expenditure of money so there were a large number of addicts in Luts'un." Village elders remember Lu Village with many fields of colorful flowering poppies, but Fei apparently saw none during his visits. As Fei and Zhang noted, this western part of Yunnan had been a center of opium culture, and opium smuggling continued after its ban (Fei and Zhang 1945:103, 280).

## Porterage

Aside from work in the fields, most older women interviewed (nearly 80 percent) maintained that women with bound feet could and did carry heavy things.[27] All but one insisted that women with bound feet hauled water, and all agreed that they walked to market. Lu Village women, recalling that period, assert that footbinding did not prevent women from carrying out most of the important farm and household duties (although it could not have made their work any easier). Nonetheless, women's speed and distance, not to mention pain as they walked or carried heavy loads, must have been affected.[28] Footbinding undoubtedly made their gait slower and more tedious, but it did not exempt women from hauling water and getting firewood for their households in Lu Village. Most likely, gender and the dangers for women "on the road," as well as their slow pace, deterred them from working as intervillage human porters, and in the caravan trade carrying salt and textiles across Yunnan. But many of the women of Lu Village, including some with bound feet, had done occasional work as porters.[29]

In early-twentieth-century Lu Village, the concept of "housework" was broad; women's daily chores included cooking, washing, child care, making and repairing clothing and shoes for family members, fetching water and firewood, raising pigs and courtyard animals, and working in the rice, bean, and vegetable (and poppy) fields as needed. In addition, women generally performed exchange labor and sometimes hired their labor out to other farming households. They clearly performed a combination of outdoor work and indoor work. They could and did move beyond their courtyards and doorways as far as the family fields and the market town.

## Textiles

Clearly, the heavy participation of Lu Village women in farm labor in the early twentieth century was inconsistent with the usual assumptions about the meaning of bound feet. But field labor did not mean that women were completely divorced from Chinese traditions of housebound female textile labor. Like men, farm women did not specialize in just one economic activity. It took considerable effort to provide the family with clothing in those days before they could buy clothes "off the rack," as they increasingly do today. Just what was the nature of that work? How time consuming and essential was it? How much income could it bring, or save? How was the distribution of work to feed and to clothe the family changing?

The older women of Lu Village report that in their youth women engaged in significant economic activities that were indeed compatible with a "sedentary" or domestic lifestyle that minimized walking. These activities centered on clothing yet they did not involve the classic female work of spinning or weaving. Rather, most Lu Village women engaged in hand embroidery and sewing of clothing, particularly cloth shoes. Over two-thirds of the women reported doing embroidery, and nearly 80 percent sewed cloth shoes for their families.[30] Given the absence of spinning and weaving (which I discuss in the next section), how important could sewing and embroidery be? Could domestic sewing and embroidery be valuable enough to justify the constraints of footbinding, despite the expected contributions of these very same women to rice farming?

## Sewing and Embroidering Clothes and Shoes

The idea that household sewing and embroidery were important economic activities seems dubious initially. While they might be of use to the family, could they create salable commodities and earn income? Economic historians have not viewed sewing and embroidery as significant activities deserving the same attention as food production, or even spinning and weaving. To a modern mind, the very terms "sewing" and "embroidery" suggest embellishment rather than economy—pastimes for women rather than profit-making work. This derives from the assumption that the products were not commercial.

This view needs examination in local contexts. Economic anthropologists have long emphasized local food and cash crop production while neglecting the historical importance of locally produced textiles in regional and world trade as a source of income and a store of value. Warm clothing protects health; expensive clothing expresses wealth. Cloth has always been something that people value and trade, motivating cross-continental movements of goods, to wit, the fame of China's historic Silk Road between Europe and Asia. When crops failed, textile sales could provide households with an alternate source of income and keep family poverty at bay. In nineteenth-century China, production and trade of homemade textiles was still an important part of the preindustrial household economy, but industrial textiles were providing ferocious competition.

Francesca Bray reviewed historical contexts in which embroidery had different connotations. She observed that embroidered clothing became fashionable in the late Ming (1368–1644), when "elite women were seldom involved in the production of fine cloth for family use." Poor women could be hired as embroiderers, while gentry women could "earn money by their embroidery skills if necessary" (Bray 1997:267). She observes,

> for an agrarian like Zhang Luxiang writing of how to make a decent living by farming, embroidery was a frivolity that distracted women from proper work: women should weave cloth, not decorate it. For well-off families it was the symbol of the leisure they could give their women: it marked them off from rough-fingered peasant women. . . . Because there was as yet no real commercial market for fine embroidery, it was work and yet it was not work, "the hallmark of Qing [1645–1911] domesticity." (268)

Bray explores the significance of a skill that added symbolic value to utilitarian items; it was a cultural production that embellished the lives of the rich and became a means for some women to earn an income. When embroidery became a generalized status symbol, undoubtedly less-wealthy families attempted to copy it, and a range of quality and price levels reflected class differences.[31]

In Lu Village, embroidery and sewing of clothes and shoes were learned and practiced by most girls in their natal families and after marriage. A majority of women reported making cloth shoes, and some made them commercially. They also asserted that in their youth, before the revolution, a woman could support herself and even her children independently from textile work, although it was difficult and relatively rare.

Some older Lu Village women remembered the rates at which they were paid when they sewed or embroidered for sale, but given differences in products and time, these rates can give only an approximate sense of value. Some recalled being paid in cash (with prices experiencing inflation in the 1930s, the figures they give are not very useful without exchange rates), and others were paid in quantities of rice and beans. Sometimes cash or grain wages can be compared to the rate at which work in the fields was paid, but we do not know if hours were comparable, or if rates for working in the fields given were for busy season high wages or for slack season low wages. Even when we try to compare the amount of time needed to make a pair of shoes, there are puzzling differences, with some claiming two days a pair, and others two pairs in a day. These may have been due to differences in skill, quality (plain or embroidered), or materials (cotton or straw).

Interviews and life histories indicate that at least some women supported themselves and their children by making shoes and embroidering cloth. Unfortunately, elderly women did not clearly distinguish between sewing and embroidery, so it is difficult to know if there were distinct markets for these two skills. The spartan, unisex clothing styles of the revolution obliterated most traces of this prerevolutionary aesthetic in contemporary life in all but a few items: shoes, cloth baby carriers, pillow cases, and quilt covers.

The need for cloth shoes and clothing was very widespread. Wealthy families did not always sew their own shoes or clothes, but poor families had to devote considerable female labor time if they were to keep all of their members shod, given the speed with which cloth shoes wore out. Families could either have their own women make shoes, employ a servant to make them, or buy shoes from a shoemaker. Shoemakers were usually women who sewed together cotton shoes or plaited straw sandals, as shoes belonged to the female realm of textiles and needlework. In the 1990s Lu Village women still made these shoes in their spare time. Their handiwork, stitching in colorful designs to hold together layers of cotton cloth to form a sturdy sole, is concealed by the foot inside the shoe. Because women were traditionally responsible for supplying family footwear, in China's rural street markets today shoe repair women often repair all types of shoes. This runs counter to European shoe-making tradition, where shoes were made of leather and shoemaking evolved as a male specialty.

*Lu Village women on main street sew shoes and knit while watching small children.*

## SHOES

In the 1930s and up to the 1980s, Lu Village women made cloth shoes for the family; some even continued into the 1990s, even though plastic and leather shoes were flooding the market. When Fei listed the annual expenses of five households, he included shoes in the clothing budget.[32] Household A had six people and purchased one pair of shoes but made another fourteen pairs of shoes out of purchased cloth; Households B and C made all their own shoes with purchased cloth. Households D, with three members, and E, with only two members, were the poorest; they purchased only old clothing to wear, but they *purchased* their straw shoes: *seventy pairs for each household.* Handwoven straw shoes or sandals (rarely seen today) worn by the poor were relatively cheap, one cent a pair, but if the quantities were accurate, they probably lasted only ten to fifteen days (Fei and Zhang 1990:122–123). Cloth shoes remained the predominant type of footwear well past the revolution of 1949. Cotton cloth was used both for the upper part of the shoe and for the sole. Layer upon layer was sewn together, and stitched tightly. Cloth shoes did not last long, although they clearly lasted longer than straw sandals.[33] With normal use, they might last several months, but with heavy wear—such as from a porter trudging along cobbled roads or mountain paths—they wore out faster. The man who left home for seasonal work in construction or mining must have needed, not only extra clothing, but also extra shoes. A family of four or five people, then, would make plenty of work for the women in keeping them shod, dressed, and fed.

## Shoemaking and Transport Work: A Woman's Shifting Work Conditions

#43 [Age eighty, born 1916 in Heijing, site of salt mines, feet bound at age six, unbound soon after, married at age fifteen] I made shoes for sale. My father was a tailor and made clothes for hire. We had no house of our own. At home, we worked for other people making shoes on demand. We had no land, just a shop and rented house where we made clothes. I earned about thirty yuan per month. One pair of shoes sold for three yuan. The price of a liter of rice was ¥1.20. Thirty liters of rice was enough to eat for one month.

At my husband's family, I carried salt. When I carried fifty *jin* (one jin equals 1.1 lbs.) of salt on one round trip, it took two days, and I earned ¥1.50. There were risks. The government would not allow us to sell salt [the government had a salt monopoly]. If we were caught by the antismuggling squad, then they might dump out the salt, and you would lose your capital.

This woman, who grew up in Heijing and later moved to Lu Village, reported that women in Heijing carried salt and sewed clothing. Commenting on the ability of women with bound feet to work, she said, "Even with bound feet women could still carry salt."

Overworked mothers must have skimped on shoes and clothes for the children. When women servants in the first part of the twentieth century describe their hard lives, they referred not only to poor food and going hungry, but also to a lack of clothes and shoes. The women orphaned in childhood, described earlier, complained not only that they lacked a mother to bind their feet; they also lacked shoes and clothing—things a mother supplied to her children. In addition to constant work making shoes for the family, every woman had to know how to sew and repair clothing for the family. Although they purchased cotton cloth, most families could not afford to buy ready-made clothing, and only the wealthy bought silk. Rural China was a stratified society, and wealthier families acquired more and better textiles as emblems of wealth. They could hire women of other households to make shoes and embroider elegant designs upon their shoes and garments.

The woman who was skilled in embroidery or demonstrated exceptional artistry probably found her handiwork in demand, and salable either through private contract or in the market. Indeed, ten of the fifty-six older women interviewed reported they had done embroidery for sale before marriage. In addition, other women sold shoes and embroidery after marriage. Some remembered how much they earned. Sewing, making shoes, and embroidery were often mentioned as the means by which poor women, single and widowed, could earn a living in Lu Village. Although I lack details on the Lufeng shoe market, a description of the market in Mengzi (southern Yunnan) in 1939 suggests the trade in embroidered shoes could be large.

> It was market day in Mengzi. Everywhere were crowds and crowds of people. . . . There were shoe merchants carrying *trays of tiny slippers embroidered* in baby-blue and light pink, adorned with embroidered rosettes. The slippers were unbelievably small. They were scarcely longer than an index finger; the bound foot is still to be seen everywhere, among the older women, for Yunnan is an isolated province that clings to ancient practices. (Smith 1940:140, italics added)

## Absence of Spinning and Weaving

In my entire sample of fifty-six elderly women, none were taught to spin or weave cloth in their childhood, and none performed this work after marriage. The complete absence of home spinning or cloth weaving in the natal villages of these Lu Village women is striking given that it remained strong in other parts of Yunnan. Even in the early twentieth century in this allegedly backward province, the cloth used in Lu Village was acquired through the market rather than produced at home. While the non-Han women in many parts of Yunnan manufactured cloth from local fibers such as hemp, the Han wore cotton. According to Mrs. Gao (age sixty-two, born 1927 in Tanghai),

> We ourselves did not know how to weave cloth. In our family, we bought cloth in the market and returned home to sew it. Only the minorities could still weave cloth. They were up in the mountains, pasturing sheep and horses. They gathered "small fire straw" (*xiao huocao*) from the mountaintop. They shredded it and went home to spin thread and weave. They wove it into colored cloth, but usually not to sell. Han people all bought their cloth. . . . We also wore trousers. Minorities wore skirts. I do not know where our cloth came from. In our village, we wore cotton; only a few landowners could wear silk. . . . [O]nly a few of the landlords could afford it. Our former landlord, even though a landlord, was not equal to these children born after the revolution. He was an impoverished landlord. It was in the city that the big old bosses, capitalists, wore that silk. In the city at that time, there were no real factories.

In this passage, Mrs. Gao reveals how different cloth materials—"fire straw," cotton, or silk—and clothing styles signified ethnic, gender, and class identities.[34]

Along with salt, wood, and charcoal (and formerly opium) passing down out of the mountains by caravan through Lu Village toward the cities, there must have been a return trade in cotton and cotton cloth to dress these Han villagers, as suggested by Major H. R. Davies's report. Indeed, Fei and Zhang reported that "the most important commodities sold in the village market are firewood, brought in by the tribesmen, and clothing and foreign goods, mostly for the household, which are sold by peddlers from the city" (1945:47). Interestingly, many Han women of Lu Village reported carrying firewood as one of their tasks.

Women born between 1916 and 1940 in Lu Village and its intermarrying community network did not grow up learning to spin and weave the fibers that made cloth. They were not part of the "men plow and women weave" formula for traditional Han households. Their mode of life depended on the market to supply them with clothing. Lu Village may have already passed through the early stages of the textile revolution when commerce displaced handspun and locally handwoven cotton by introducing factory-spun thread and handwoven cloth from specialized weaving towns. Lu Village families bought cloth, but only the rich could afford factory-made cloth. Before 1949,

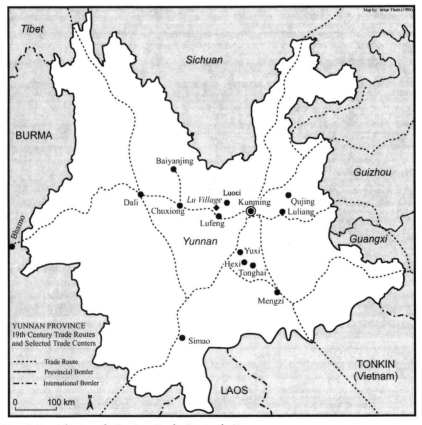

**Map 3.1.   Nineteenth-Century Trade Routes in Yunnan**

some factory cloth may have come from Shanghai. Several large textile factories were established in Kunming in the late 1930s (Tian 1944) and must
have hastened the death of home textile production in the remaining hand-
weaving centers. Not until after the Communist revolution did most people
of Yunnan begin to have access to factory-made textiles.

In Lu Village in the 1930s, the conditions of textile production reported
by Fei and elderly women are consistent with Davies's observations of
change and specialization at the turn of the century. Lu Village had no
women skilled in spinning or weaving, and the surviving women do not remember seeing these activities or seeing old disused looms tucked away in
the corners or backrooms of their natal households. Cotton cloth was purchased in the market and hand sewn at home into garments and shoes. Most
of the older women recall buying and using "rough" handmade cloth (*cubu*)
to make their own clothing. This sturdy cloth came to be less prestigious
than the finer, smoother cloth produced by machine looms, and naturally it
was less prestigious than the long, silk gowns worn by the wealthy few (Fei
and Zhang 1945).

## THE LARGER ECONOMY: YUNNAN'S MARKETS IN CLOTH

Most Lu Village women lacked precise knowledge of where the cotton cloth
that they bought in the market originated, for they had not traveled to these
places. Usually they named towns about one hundred kilometers to the south
of Kunming City: most common was Hexi,[35] followed by Yuxi and Xinxing
(see map 3.1, also Benedict 1996:33). One woman mentioned Luoci (the
woman's hometown, on the railroad north of Kunming, where women had
bound feet and were well known for weaving cloth) and one mentioned
Shanghai—obviously a distant but famous source of Chinese factory-made
textiles. The cloth women purchased was mainly handwoven, but they did
not know if the thread was machine-made or homespun. Davies's description
of the early arrival of foreign thread suggests it would have been machine-
made yarn.

If cheap and good quality factory yarn was reaching certain areas, then the
productivity of specialized weaving households may have temporarily increased (as it did in Ding Xian), for they no longer faced the production bot-
tlenecks created by hand spinning. This would have encouraged weavers in
a small number of weaving centers, located close to the yarn supply lines, to
compete for larger territories, displacing subsistence weaving in other areas.
As Davies had pointed out, the communities in southern Yunnan, near major trade centers like Simao, had an advantage in getting imported machine-
made yarn coming to Yunnan via the French railway from Vietnam.

In the 1930s, Lu Village was clearly integrated into a wider trading system by virtue of its total dependence on outside sources of cloth (and its recently lost opium cultivation). Fei's portrait of Lu Village as a largely self-sufficient farming economy (described in chapter 1), influenced by his emphasis on land and food production, underemphasized the importance of the long-distance caravan trade, and particularly its effects on clothing and the household economy.[36] Zhang's description of the third village in *Earthbound China* further clarifies the complex process of change in the economy of Yu Village (Yuts'un), near Yuxi City, as follows:

> The weaving industry is important in Yuts'un and throughout the district. Luts'un and Yits'un do not weave but buy their cloth, for the most part, from this district [Yuxi]. The work is limited to women, no men working on the loom. In Yuts'un, out of 157 households, there are 112 in which weaving is done. The clack of the wooden machines can be heard all over the village from morning to night. (Fei and Zhang 1945:239)

Yu Village can no longer be located: when Fei made a return trip to Yuxi in 1990, the area was too engulfed by urban sprawl to be identified. Yuxi is now a booming city in a county known for its tobacco industry. But in my visits to Tonghai (a market town in Yuxi County) between 1988 and 1999, I observed that a high proportion of the older women still had tightly bound feet, unlike Lu Village. This is consistent with my theory that weaving centers, located in areas having better access to imported machine-spun thread, retained footbinding longer than areas like Lu Village, which abandoned weaving at an earlier time.[37]

Zhang described the Yu Village weaving economy in 1940:

> The girls of a household learn how to weave, from their mothers or other older women, at a very early age. Each girl traditionally has a loom as part of her dowry when she marries. Although nearly all know how to weave, . . . few of the rich bother with it. . . . The total number of women in the village who work at the loom is 151 out of 201 adult women. This includes some girls as young as twelve, . . . but for the most part, the weavers are middle-aged. (Fei and Zhang 1945:240–41)

> If a woman produces more cloth than she needs for her own household, she may carry it, on the morning of a market day, to one of the dry goods stores to exchange for thread. . . . The cloth that is bought by these stores is used mainly for export, since people of the district do not ordinarily buy cloth of this sort. The cloth woven by various households is not standardized but differs somewhat in size and in quality. It cannot be sold to townsfolk but only to the peasants; and, as better machine-woven cloth is coming in, the market for home-woven materials is shrinking. (241–42)

> In one day one woman, working all day, can weave two pieces of cloth. Her actual daily wage will be, then, 70 cents, which is not sufficient to pay for her food. If

the women devoted all their time to this work, they would not earn sufficient [income] for subsistence.

The low profit from this industry is clear to the weavers. The situation at the present time is growing worse. People like to talk about the old days. Thirty years ago [around 1910], they told us, before the importation of Western manufactured thread, when the weavers of the district produced their own cotton, spun their own thread, and made their own cloth, they got much more income than they do at present. Since that time, things have been getting steadily worse. On the one hand, manufactured thread has entirely taken the place of native thread, so that the spinning is entirely wiped out. . . . On the other hand, manufactured clothes have reached the markets of the interior. They are better in quality and not much higher in price than the home woven. To compete with them the native cloth has to lower its price. . . . The weavers are squeezed on both sides. The only thing they can adjust is their own wage. (Fei and Zhang 1945:243)

According to Zhang, a woman earned less than 40 percent as much from weaving as from farmwork during the busy season.[38]

The history of textiles in Lu Village followed one of two possible paths. One possibility is that Lu Village made a transition by the late nineteenth century (or earlier) from their own homespun, handwoven cloth to purchased machine-spun, handwoven cloth, and a second transition from the late nineteenth century to 1950, from purchased machine-spun, handwoven cloth to machine-spun, machine-woven cloth. The other possibility is that Lu Village was a farming and trading community that had, since its founding, by the time of the Ming dynasty (1368–1644), imported handmade cloth from other specialized weaving centers.[39] So far, I have found no information to clarify the earlier presence or absence, say before 1850, of spinning and weaving among Han women in Lu Village to correspond with its early-twentieth-century practice of footbinding. In Lu Village, Han women's work in textiles was confined to sewing and embroidering clothes and shoes, although there were certainly many other handicrafts, such as making cloth sacks and bamboo baskets, that they could have practiced as well. From the 1950s, however, factory-made cloth fully replaced hand-loomed cloth, with distribution controlled and rationed by the state. By that time, the state controlled the two major textile factories in Kunming, which had been founded during the war.[40] Hand-loomed cloth finally lost its remaining markets in Han areas and in the last weaving holdouts, such as Luliang in eastern Yunnan, only a few women continued weaving. Ironically, the last remaining handwoven product in one of the villages I visited in 1996 was the long thin cotton binding cloth that the old ladies still use to bind their tiny feet.

From a modern point of view, footbinding—deformity of the foot—can never seem economically justifiable, but from the point of view of parents, it may have given their daughter an economic advantage. If their daughter had

small, bound feet, it would be known that she had learned patience and obedience as discussed earlier, and also that she had refined domestic (textile)
skills. Footbinding may have conveyed the message in the marriage market
that a daughter-in-law was well prepared to work in textiles: she was not
"lazy" and would not run away from this tedious handiwork. Furthermore,
when we consider the physical quality of life in some rural areas, the brutal
nature of footbinding does not seem inconsistent with other ways of teaching people to work under submission prior to the twentieth century.

Nicol Smith, for example, wrote of thin, ragged boys forced to work in
Yunnan's tin mines in 1939, their skin colored green from arsenic oxide in
the tin dust (1940:160–61).

> The number of workers in the tin mines of Kechiu [Gejiu] district varies from fifty
> thousand to one hundred thousand. . . . The miners die fast. It is necessary to replace
> them steadily by fresh recruits from other districts of Yunnan Province and Kwei-
> chow [Guizhou]. . . . Fully fifty per cent, perhaps sixty per cent, are boys *between the
> ages of eight and twelve*. . . . There is an excellent reason for the employment of boys,
> especially boys of small size. The tin mine shafts and tunnels are very narrow. No
> one but a child could squeeze through them, without stooping. . . . The death rate
> in the mines is estimated at *thirty per cent annually*! (Smith 1940:161–63)

According to Smith, deserters were shot. Harry Franck (1925) similarly
describes the miserable condition of coolies, men, boys, and even bound foot
women in Yunnan in the early 1920s.

In Lu Village, the household's needs for female labor both in the fields and
in textiles must have created ambivalence about the extreme form of footbinding, which led to an immutable "career decision" before a daughter
reached adolescence. The incompatibility of the bodily preparation of girls
for the two contrasting types of work, in textiles and in the fields, suggests
that there may have been a time when daughters did primarily one or the
other. If we abandon the assumption that there was a stable, traditional Chinese culture operating in Lu Village in the 1930s, the combination of footbinding with farmwork and portering becomes more comprehensible.

I believe that parents in late-nineteenth and early-twentieth-century western Yunnan must have observed that domestic textile production was in decline, and that prices were dropping. Yet at first they had no information with
which to predict either the revival or collapse of markets for women's handiwork. They would have been reluctant to give up binding their daughters'
feet, and would probably have responded to this unprecedented industrial
challenge in stages, first resorting to looser binding and more farmwork training for their daughters. New work in opium production may also have provided alternatives relieving the losses from growing female unemployment as
producers of cottage textiles. Caught between the choice of a hobbled daugh-

ter who could work in textiles and a sure-footed daughter who could work in the fields, Lu Village parents in the early twentieth century may have opted for the semihobbled daughters, whose feet were reshaped but not broken—the so-called "cucumber foot," which looked "tamer" than the natural foot. This may have been a transitional phase toward full acceptance of unbound feet.

## SUMMARY

Bound feet once prepared women for an anticipated life's work producing textiles or handicrafts at home. There was clearly a strong customary belief that footbound women could do no farmwork. However, under the pressure of a commercial and technological revolution, domestic textile producers could no longer compete in regional and local textile markets. Women lost their ability to produce income *inside* the household. Under severe economic pressure, women with immutably bound feet may have had to come outdoors and work in the fields, while men may have had to increase their migrations to find new sources of household income. In this interpretation, footbinding once prepared women for the classic gender system in which men plowed and women wove. But it did not prepare them for revolutionary change; it failed to protect women from the need to work in the fields or do other nondomestic work once home textile production became unprofitable. Thus we might expect a sequence of change like that charted in table 3.4 as the industrial revolution created spinning, weaving, and clothing factories to lower the costs of textile production, and the transportation revolution lowered the costs of bringing these mass-produced goods to cities, towns, and even small rural markets. The domestic textile producer would have been hit, first indirectly by the lowering of prices and loss of sales to merchants who supplied city markets, then by the direct loss of sales in local village and town markets.

In a schematic representation of the change in table 3.4, periods A through D indicate relative timing, with dates depending on the time that modern transportation reached local markets in different parts of China. Female footbinding was compatible with women's work in period A before machine-made thread reached local markets. In weaving centers, footbinding was still compatible in period B, as machine-made yarn started to reach the market but machine-made cloth was still expensive. The cheap yarn supply expanded and those on good transportation routes could then stop spinning and expand weaving for local markets, competing with other women farther from the yarn supply. In period C, women lost both spinning and weaving markets to textile factories and had limited local markets for tailoring or embroidery, which could be done at home by most women; rural women had to adapt to work requiring regular walking

**Table 3.4. Associations between Technological Change, Impact on Gendered Work, and Footbinding**

| Period | Technology | Men | Women | Market Income |
|---|---|---|---|---|
| A | Hand spinning, weaving; mule caravans, human porters, boats | Plowing, most farmwork, local construction, transport | Spinning, weaving, sewing, embroidering clothing; processing farm products<br><br>**Footbinding compatible** | Sale of grains, yarn, textiles, clothing in regional markets |
| B | Factory spinning; steamboats, train transport | Plowing, farmwork, local construction, transport | Weaving or sewing and embroidering clothing; spinners unemployed; help farming and processing farm products<br><br>**Footbinding in weaving centers, modified or stopping elsewhere** | Sale of grains, woven cloth; loss of yarn market income; some towns increase weaving with new yarn supply; some villages stop it |
| C | Factory spinning and weaving; steamboats, trains, and buses | Plowing, farmwork, construction; migrant labor—transport, construction, mining | Sewing and embroidering clothing, increasing farmwork; cash crops; local wage work; working as servants, porters<br><br>**Footbinding stopping** | Sale of grains, cash crops including opium, labor; loss of homemade cloth market; limited sewing and embroidery demand |
| D | Factory-made clothing; planes, trains, buses, private tractors, and cars | Plowing, farmwork, town jobs, or migrant labor—transport, construction, mining | Farmwork, growing cash crops; seeking factory, town jobs, domestic employment<br><br>**Footbinding ends** | Sale of grains, cash crops, labor; all cloth purchased, ready-made clothes and shoes purchased |

outside the home to the fields and to markets.[41] In period D, factory-made thread, cloth, clothing, and shoes have replaced almost all homemade textile products. Apart from farming, there is little gainful employment in the home. This set of revolutionary changes was as much a product of transportation changes as of industrial textile technology. It was only when cheap steamboat and railway transportation lowered the costs of transport that cheaper factory-made products were able to compete with local producers in remote rural areas. After 1949, government control of markets added another dimension to economic change.

For Lu Village, I estimate that period A began around 1700 (or earlier) and ended in 1800–1850, with the switch from spinning and weaving partly due to imported yarn and cloth, but possibly preceded by increasing prices for opium. Period B would have been 1850 to 1900, with Lu Village falling into the category of villages that abandoned spinning and weaving completely, while other areas specialized in weaving. Period C would be 1900–1930, when Lu Village women increased seasonal work in porterage, road construction, and rice farming, with limited sewing and embroidery, while men increased participation in porterage, mining, and road construction (when not conscripted). Period D for Lu Village is from 1930 to the present. For Han areas of rural Yunnan in general this period shifted from market access to state rationing and back to market access to factory-made cloth. In specialized communities that had persisted with hand-loom weaving up to the revolution, hand weaving finally stopped in the 1950s, when the state closed down the peasant markets, which sold home-woven cloth, and people obtained their machine-made cloth from state-run factories.

## FOOTBINDING: A "SMALL" SYMBOL IN A SEA OF CHANGE

Footbinding and its demise expressed many facets of women's changing economic, social, educational, aesthetic, and sexual conditions and illustrates both how vast and how intimate were the changes sweeping through Chinese civilization over the last century and a half (see table 3.5).

With the expansion of industrial production and changes in transportation destabilizing earlier work patterns by the late nineteenth century, Lu Village women's work increasingly required the ability to keep up with the accelerating pace of life outside the courtyard. This meant that women were worth less to almost all households, unless they could walk and move their bodies and things from one workplace to another. This change did not necessarily mean an end of "manual" work (in the narrow handiwork sense) as much as an expansion of "manual" to include backs, feet, and shoulders, as well as brains, as the changing conditions of different classes and regions required. The textile revolution nudged, and sometimes shoved, all kinds of women out of the household—spinners, weavers, sewers, and embroiderers—as, one after another, the stacks of textile products made by nimble fingers in households were dwarfed by mountains of industrial yarn, cloth, clothing, and shoes transported by cargo ships, trains, and trucks. One by one, but also in the thousands and millions, each bound foot producer found herself defeated, like America's legendary John Henry, by the machine.

Anthropologist Myron Cohen once told me that Hakka men in Taiwan boasted how easy it was to defeat and capture bound foot Han women in battle, whereas Hakka women with normal feet could run away or fight back. Likewise, a bound foot woman could not easily defend herself outdoors in a highly competitive economy. In Lu Village, women needed to be able to go out to farm, to plant, weed, and carry crops and firewood home or to market when their men were away working in mines, in construction, or long-distance trade. Women needed to carry fodder to feed their market-bound pigs, or to earn money transporting goods over mountain paths. The lines of family authority were not broken by this change, but they were loosened. The young women who began to work in textile factories in Kunming in the 1940s did begin to challenge family authority (Tian 1944).

Even today, Lu Village women's socialization still requires obedience and service to a mother-in-law, but the ways to serve increasingly require her to earn an income outside the courtyard economy. As work sites shift to factory and market town, nonfamily employers and authorities compete with the mother-in-law's control and while they, too, value young women with a tame spirit, they also want women with the stamina and flexibility to perform different kinds of jobs, not all of them sedentary.

Until the demise of domestic textile industries, the education and socialization of Lu Village women emphasized busy hands and still feet. Since the 1930s, and especially since the Communist revolution, as we shall see later, parents have prepared daughters to work in an urbanizing, literate world, even if they remain farmers. Where once tiny feet made a girl attractive to the urban elite, in the twentieth century, criteria of attractiveness have shifted many times. Sometimes they have included education, the ability to speak standard Chinese, and fashionable clothing, and other times they emphasized political fervor and revolutionary class background (He 1993; Chang 1996; Honig and Hershatter 1988; Wong 1996). In the 1990s, the criteria for female beauty increasingly converge with those of global consumer culture. Fashion designers and plastic surgeons stand ready to take up the cause of creating female beauty out of ordinary female bodies.

**Table 3.5.   Chronology of Population, Trade, and Transportation Shifts in Yunnan Province**

| | |
|---|---|
| 1723 | Japan ends copper exports to China. Qing state supports Yunnan copper mining. |
| 1729 | Road constructed from Chenggong in Yunnan to Tianyang in Guangxi, enhancing trade to Guangdong via Nanning (cuts Kunming–Nanning travel time in half) (Benedict 1996:51). |
| 1750–1800 | More than three-hundred thousand miners immigrate from Sichuan, Jiangxi, and Hunan (Benedict 1996:26, from James Lee 1982). |
| 1775 | Three million registered population. |
| 1800 | 4.5 million registered population (Benedict 1996:37; Lee 1982: 722–23). Mining declines: about one-fourth of copper mines are closed, province in recession. Growth of opium trade as "Yunnan's major cash crop" (Benedict:35). |
| 1820s | Development of domestic market for Yunnan opium. |
| 1850 | 7.4 million registered population (Benedict 1996:39). Yunnan opium widely traded in Guangxi and Guangdong (Pearl River Delta). Eastern Yunnan opium travels via Bose down You and West Rivers; opium from western Yunnan goes down Red River, then by junks to Tonkin (Benedict 1996:53). Via Bose, it takes about fifty-two days from Guangzhou to Kunming. |
| 1856–1873 | Panthay (Muslim) rebellion sparked by disputes in 1854 between Han and Muslim miners in Chuxiong prefecture (Wang Xuhuai 1968; Wei 1974; Wright 1957:113–17 in Benedict:39). |
| 1879 | Steamship service begins between Canton and Beihai (western Guangdong). |
| 1884 | 3 million population registered; population has dramatically declined due to war (Muslim rebellion), epidemics (plague), and flight (Benedict 1996:39). |
| 1889 | Foreign-operated steamships run regularly between Canton and Beihai (western Guangdong), reducing travel time between Yunnan and Guangzhou. Imported yarn (from Bombay and England via Burma, Hong Kong, and Shanghai-Yangzi routes) reaches Yunnan. Hand weaving increases in weaving centers in eastern and southern Yunnan (Xinxing, Qujing), which are first in Yunnan to gain steamship-railway access to cotton yarn imports (Davies 1909). |
| 1895–1899 | Sections of Tonkin-Kunming railway open, perhaps up to Mengzi or Simao (Davies 1909; the impression is that the railway was built by the time of his travels). |
| 1900– | No spinning or weaving in Lu Village, which is not located at early stage for overland caravans coming from the south. Bought handmade cloth from Yunnan weaving centers. Yu Village imports machine-spun thread, exports cloth, imports opium; cloth merchants numerous (Fei and Zhang 1945:285). Lu Village specializes in opium export (Fei and Zhang 1945; Bossen informants). |
| 1910 | Completion of Tonkin-Kunming railway (Barnett 1993:491). |
| 1920–1930 | Footbinding stopped in Lu Village (Bossen 1998). |
| 1930 | Dr. N. Bradley takes bus from Kunming to Anning (twenty-five miles west) on new earth road; mule caravans go west from there on old Burma Road (Bradley 1945:3). |
| 1930s | Buck's survey (1937b) includes Yiliang, Chuxiong, and Yuxi among the places representing different major zones of Yunnan: valleys in the east, south, and west. All have rice as staple, cotton as predominant material for clothing. Buck's map of cotton cultivation in Yunnan shows only a little cotton, roughly south of Yuxi or Tonghai, toward Simao. Cotton is estimated at only about 10 percent of crops, therefore there was little for market. |
| 1938 | Hand weaving continues in Yuxi (Fei and Zhang), Luliang (Bossen field notes). |
| 1950s | Footbinding stopped in Luliang, cotton weaving stopped in Luliang. Government textile factories supply cloth for Yunnan distribution; Luliang homespun is not allowed to be sold in markets (Bossen field notes). |

Across the twentieth century, the changing standards of female beauty in Lu Village and other Chinese villages also conform to changing economic conditions. Aesthetics for women have shifted from bodily signs of lifelong submission, obedience, and sacrifice to rapidly changing fashions in clothing and hairstyle. These superficial changes leave the working body more flexible in response to a rapidly changing world. Mothers-in-law and husbands have adjusted their visions of beauty to this new reality.

## NOTES

I owe great thanks to Hill Gates for inspiring me to pursue an idea that I held for a long time but had not found a way to test. By sending me blank copies of her interview forms and copies of her own work on footbinding, she showed me how I could obtain more systematic information that would help fill in more of the national puzzle about this custom.

1. The Manchus banned footbinding in 1664 but rescinded the ban in 1668 (Wang 2000:34–36; Ko 1994:149).

2. Antifootbinding societies encouraged women to stop binding their feet in order to improve their work capacity and thus improve the health of the nation. See Ebrey (1984) for writings from this movement in 1903.

3. Davin writes: "Buck, who suggested an *association between female labor participation rates and regional variations in the prevalence of foot-binding*, was troubled by this high figure of 14 percent [of female participation in farming, a comparatively high rate for the spring wheat area of the far north]. He was aware that foot-binding was still widespread in the spring wheat area, and that the bindings were so tight that women, unable to stand for any length of time, were compelled to do field work on their knees" (Davin 1975:248, italics added). The incongruity that troubled Buck may be cleared up if the declining domestic textile industry is taken into account; this change destroyed women's traditional domestic mainstay and pushed even bound foot women to seek alternate ways of contributing to the family economy, including work in the fields.

4. Historian Jonathan Spence (1990:173) notes, for instance, that during the Taiping rebellion Hakka women, "used to the life of hard farming in the mountains, . . . had never bound their feet as other Chinese females did." Also, in north China, Manchu women did not bind their feet.

5. Spence's account is an example of the lack of explanation for *why* the peculiar custom spread. Noting that Chinese resisted the Manchu decrees against footbinding, which were upheld for Manchu women, he wrote: "Despite the pain caused by this practice, the custom had spread from the elite to the peasantry, and tiny feet had become the measure of feminine beauty to the Chinese. Millions of women suffered as a result. In refusing to go along with the custom, the Manchus both asserted their cultural independence and created an effective barrier to the intermarriage of Manchus and Chinese, since Chinese men professed to find the Manchu women's normal-sized feet *sexually* unattractive" (1990:39, italics added). From this it appears that "millions of women suffered" primarily because of Chinese men's erotic culture. Blake (1994), in contrast, takes a position which is similar to Gates (1989, 1995, n.d.). Blake believes that a "sociocultural mystification"

of footbinding had occurred, ignoring women's work within an increasingly labor-intensive economy in late imperial China, and making women seem "practically worthless."

6. Jacka (1997:19, 121) sees light/heavy (as well as inside/outside and unskilled/skilled) as a conceptual dichotomy used by Chinese to describe female/male divisions of labor, but recognizes that the actual tasks so labeled are often inconsistent between regions and the subject of intense negotiation between women and men.

7. Davin also excludes porterage by women, stating, "Many women were permanently handicapped by bound feet, which precluded them from carrying heavy loads or even walking any distance" (1975: 252).

8. Blake (1994:703–4) makes similar observations. He notes that all the traditional forms of textile work preceded the advent of footbinding, but that at the end of the dynasty these were commercialized domestic occupations, sometimes contributing significantly to family cash incomes.

9. Brandt (1989), Dietrich (1972), Elvin (1972), Huang (1990), Walker (1993), and others have greatly expanded our knowledge of the role of textiles in Chinese economic history.

10. Footbinding is sometimes said to have started at age two or three, as Gamble reports. This may have been true in extreme cases or common in certain areas such as the northeast, where J. Chang (1991:24) reports her mother was bound at age two in Liaoning in 1911, but for women in my interviews it usually began around age five or six, and sometimes as late as seven or eight (see also Croll 1995; Pruitt 1945:22). Ages are sometimes given in the traditional Chinese fashion, which adds a year by counting the year in which the child is born as age one.

11. The data consist of questionnaires (adapted, with permission, from Hill Gates's surveys) conducted with fifty-six women about their own experiences, and longer questionnaires from a subset of eighteen women who were particularly capable of remembering and speaking clearly about the past in their natal villages and those they moved to just after marriage.

12. In the *Lufeng County Gazette*, the only year with a record of local antifootbinding policies is 1923. In translation: "Within the boundaries of the plains, the four counties carried out the government policy of 'Do not allow footbinding of girls twelve years and under who have not yet bound them, and immediately liberate the feet of those with bound feet.' It is strictly forbidden to bind feet" (LCG 1991:17). The *Gazette* has no record of the difficulty or success of implementation in that year or following years.

13. Fei's introduction to Lu Village was facilitated by his maternal aunt, who had spent a year there as a Christian missionary, and by a classmate at Yanjing University who was a native of Lu Village.

14. "Three-inch golden lily" refers to the most extreme form of footbinding, intended to keep the foot to three inches, by breaking the central foot bone.

15. The socialization interpretation of footbinding is also to be found in Ebrey (1990:221).

16. Ko (1994) seems to disagree. Her historical account of footbinding among elite women of the seventeenth century includes special rituals, preparations, and prayers to a goddess of footbinding. Gates has so far been unsuccessful in finding comparable practices for the late nineteenth and early twentieth centuries, but some authors describe prayers to Guan Yin and gifts of special soft dumplings to eat (to make the foot bones soft, by analogy).

17. *Jiao da, fan guo lai shi wu dou, fan guo qu shi wu dou, za ge jia?* This can also be rendered as "big feet translate/turn over into five dou (of income) and translate into five dou as dowry. Why should she marry out?" One *Lufeng dou* equals about thirty-five liters, or about thirty kilograms, of husked rice. Five *dou* is 150 kg, or about 330 lbs. At one pound of rice consumption per day, this conventional amount of grain given in marriage payment and returned as dowry is about enough to feed the bride for one year. This is similar to the kind of marriage payment traditionally given in other parts of the world (Bossen 1984, 1988).

18. Indeed, the woman who mentioned this saying was the daughter of an uxorilocal marriage. As we see in chapter 7, uxorilocal marriages are and have been fairly common in Lu Village.

19. Croll (1995:21) cites Hsien Ping-ying's biography, where a mother says, "Would not anybody who saw such a girl exclaim: 'her mother must have died when the girl was young!'"

20. It is unlikely she actually witnessed men's braid cutting. Possibly she simply made an analogy to an earlier time, based on accounts she heard. Government agents required men to abandon the hairstyle associated with Han submission to the Qing dynasty, which ended in 1911. It is unclear if this symbol was eradicated immediately in Yunnan, or slowly over a decade or so. (Army recruitment imposed rapid change on many men.) This woman had been sold at age twelve as a *tongyangxi* (adopted daughter-in-law) by her grandmother. Witty and intelligent, she was one of the rare women to give a nonformulaic reason for not binding women's feet: "If you have big feet, then in an emergency you can run."

21. Among the earliest reports are those from the French expedition of 1866–1873 (Osborne 1996). The explorers, seeking the source of the Mekong, entered China through Yunnan Province. As the expedition neared the Yunnan border with Burma, they were amazed to discover "in such a notably isolated corner of the globe, it was possible to buy English cotton goods, printed in the preferred colors of the local purchasers and bearing Buddhist emblems. Not only that, Garnier recorded with grudging admiration, the length and width of these pieces of cloth were the same as the standard product of the local weavers" (1996:118).

22. Dependence on traded cloth for some Han communities possibly began much earlier, when they immigrated, especially if they required heavy female labor in other profitable activities such as farming and road construction. This dependence did not apply to most indigenous populations in the highlands, who were less integrated into interregional commerce and retained the use of local fibers such as hemp for homespun and woven clothing.

23. Graham and his wife traveled to China as missionaries in 1911, and spent most of their lives in Sichuan, staying until 1948. Of Yunnan's minorities he wrote, "The *clothing* varies much among tribespeople of West China. . . . Lolo [Yi] men often wear thick felt cloaks which can also be used as covers when sleeping. Many Ch'iang men and women wear *undyed white hemp garments.* Ch'uan men dress like the Chinese but, the women, when they go to market and on dress-up occasions, wear embroidered dresses with short skirts" (Graham 1961:23). Describing the Yunnan Han, and probably Chinese more generally, Graham wrote:

> At the beginning of the 20th century *Chinese women wore trousers and most of them had bound feet.* The men wore long gowns that resembled dresses with long skirts. Most of these and other

clothing were made of *blue cotton cloth*. Women generally wore hats open at the top and nicely embroidered, and men wore skullcaps. Both men and women often wore blue or white cotton cloth wrapped around their heads. Laborers and farmers generally wore *straw sandals*, and both men and women sometimes wore *cotton shoes with thick soles*. During the Manchu dynasty men and women of official rank wore, on festive occasions, beautifully *embroidered* mandarin gowns . . . and elaborately ornamented hats, most of these items being discarded after the establishment of the republic. (Graham 1961:23–24, italics added)

Muegglar (1998) recently described the history of hemp production and prices in Yunnan over the nineteenth and twentieth centuries in relation to Yi villagers of Zhizuo, Yongren county, Chuxiong Yi Autonomous Prefecture. He notes that "Only during the 1890s did factory yarn begin to flow into the province from India, and some peasants begin to weave cotton cloth (Chao 1977, 181). . . . Between 1896 and 1912 [the Yi] still clearly found hemp, grown, spun and woven locally, to be competitive in price with cotton. . . . The dun-colored hempen clothing of these mountain residents signaled their poverty and backwardness, making them objects of mockery to cotton-clad lowlanders (Muegglar 1998:984–85).

24. So far, I have found no information to indicate whether imported raw cotton was sold in nonspecialized villages where it was generally spun and woven at home, or imported cotton was first spun and woven in specialized textile towns in Yunnan and thence distributed for sale to other Han communities across the province. Craig Dietrich (1972) analyzes diverse systems of cotton manufacture in Qing China, from household self sufficiency to area specialization, but his information concerns China's coastal provinces with nothing specific about Yunnan.

25. Nineteenth-century opium production in Yunnan is discussed by Benedict (1996), Frank (1925), Ruf (1998:176n46), and Bramall (1989:16).

26. It is unclear whether women with bound feet were able to transport heavy loads of charcoal and salt between stages (even if slowly) on the caravan route, one of the economic options of poor men and women during the slack season.

27. Most of the questions were answered by fifteen women who completed the longer 1996 interview form.

28. In a biography from north Henan, an elderly villager recalled the difference in speed between his own walking and that of his foot bound sisters. "It was difficult for my sisters to walk. It took my older sister over an hour to walk three *li* [one mile] to Taiping Village. . . . It is a twenty minute walk for me" (Seybolt 1996:21). Representing another view, Levy cites a traveler through Henan and Shanxi during the late Qing dynasty who "noted that even women of the lowest classes there, such as beggars and water carriers, had tiny and regular feet which pointed upwards like chestnuts" (Levy 1991 [1966]:54).

29. Although they reported women with bound feet carried loads as porters in the early twentieth century, elderly women's recollections were not sufficient to determine whether portering was common among Lu Village Han women in the same period that footbinding was prevalent in the nineteenth century. As I discuss later, Han women in poorer families may have turned to portering only when various forms of textile handiwork declined.

30. My 1996 sample of fifty-six completed interviews with elderly women about work *in their natal village* showed thirty-nine did embroidery and forty-five made cloth shoes or, in a few cases, straw sandals.

31. Countering a tendency in European tradition to view embroidery solely in cultural rather than economic terms, Rozsika Parker examines the history of embroidery in England

in terms of feminine behavior, but also shows that the nineteenth-century industrialization of textiles was continually changing the employment of working-class women in needlework.

> Initially industrialization encouraged hand embroidery. . . . Not only did the market for embroidery expand, but the mechanical production of muslin and net created new and plentiful material as a base for whitework embroidery. . . . The new techniques could be practiced without a frame, and embroiderers were thus able to work at home. Thousands of women were employed to embroider, particularly in Scotland, Ireland and in the vicinity of Nottingham, Derby and Leicester. . . . By 1857 it was estimated that 80,000 women in Scotland were homeworking muslin and some 400,000 in Ireland. . . . By the 1880s machines which embroidered had been perfected and embroidery ceased to be widely manufactured by hand. (1989:174–78)

32. Extra details on the type of shoe are found in the Chinese version (1990) of *Earthbound China*.

33. Writes Davin, "Clothes were usually made at home, and so sometimes were the cloth and the thread that went into them. Cloth shoes stitched by women took two or three days to make but lasted only five or six months" (Davin 1975:251).

34. For details on Yunnan Yi minority women's hemp weaving, see Muegglar (1998).

35. A traditional rhyme in central Yunnan praises local specialties from four places, one being the weaving center, Hexi, while Xinxing specialized in hardworking weaving girls: "Tonghai jiangyou, Lufeng cu, Xinxing guniang, Hexi bu." Translated, this means: "Tonghai soy sauce, Lufeng vinegar, Xinxing girls, Hexi cloth."

36. Fei and Zhang noted that "formerly, opium and cotton were closely linked, because, as the cotton cloth was sold to the people of the interior on the western borders, the only item the people had for exchange was opium. So opium and cotton became a balance of trade in the interdistrict commerce" (1945:288).

37. According to Zhang, Yu Village had many cotton merchants, large and small. "The most important big business in this district is the selling of cotton cloth. It has not a long history, since it started only about thirty-five years ago [around 1900]. . . . The most important business in Yuts'un is the weaving industry, which here is a traditional occupation. . . . Around 1910, with the introduction of modern, machine-produced cotton thread, the nature of the industry changed." Zhang estimated that "each household produced 200 pieces of cloth per year" (Fei and Zhang 1945:285–86).

38. Zhang calculated that the return to weaving equaled a wage of about 70 cents daily. In contrast, during the busy season, local agriculture gave women ¥0.70 to ¥1.00 per day plus food worth ¥1.00 per day, for a total value of ¥1.70 to ¥2.00. Hand weaving, earning less than 40 percent as much as field work and facing a declining market, was done only when women lacked any other work (Fei and Zhang 1945:243–44).

39. A family tree tracing one of Lu Village's old families back twenty generations, including an official who served under the Ming, attests to long Han settlement. The famous official who remained loyal to the Ming when the Qing dynasty was established was the seventh of these twenty generations. As Rubie Watson (1985) has pointed out, family trees often contain a considerable fabrication and post hoc justification, but within the area people generally agree that certain families are descended from the official.

40. See Tian (1944) and Leeming (1985:166). Both are consistent with my 1996 field notes.

41. Myron Cohen specifies that in Yangmansa, Hebei, about ninety kilometers south of Beijing, footbinding, once almost universal in the region, ended shortly before 1930,

partly in response to government action. From late 1927, "for about two years women inspectors from the county government slapped a fine on the head of any family with a child whose feet had recently been bound." In this area, women supplemented farmwork, and worked domestically in family commercial activities such as oil-pressing and clothing-weaving up to revolutionary collectivization, when clothing-weaving and oil-pressing were forbidden by the government (Cohen 1999:82–83). This suggests that Yangmansa might have been in stage C, with footbinding declining, when government intervention hastened the process even before home weaving completely stopped.

## Chapter Four

# Gender in Land Tenure, Farming, and Employment

Although it is popularly said that land belongs to the family group, this is true only in the sense that the group is entitled to enjoy its products. . . . The principal of patrilineal inheritance excludes the females from the privilege of land ownership. Women never bring land to their husbands' families, and inheritance by the sons from the father is so absolute that a widow who holds custody for a young son is prohibited from making any disposition of the property. (Fei and Zhang 1945:66)

Most of the 140 rented kung[1] are located so far from the village that the owners are not able to manage them. A few others belong to widows, as in the case of a sister-in-law of Chao, the village headman, who has no adult males in her house and rents her farm to her nephews. (Fei 1945:76)

## LAND TENURE

The description of landowning as a male preserve is an important element in Fei's theoretical analysis of Lu Village. Landowning not only differentiates between rich and poor households, but also between men and women within a household. It is part of the discourse of Chinese patriarchy. Anyone reading Chinese history is told categorically, again and again, that women could not own land. Yet anyone reading accounts of particular families finds, again and again, that alternatives existed. The categorical statements are simplifications. They may indeed describe what occurs in the majority of cases, but they conceal the many ways that people bend, evade, or manipulate the rules of landholding. As the opening quotations from Fei suggest, Lu Village was patriarchal with respect to land tenure and practiced patrilineal inheritance, but there were always alternatives, variations, and exceptions in daily life.

How does the pattern of landholding in the 1990s compare to that of 1938? I will show how the system of land tenure and the relationship between gender and land tenure has changed under the revolutionary government. In the 1930s, the issues that concerned Fei Xiaotong and many agricultural economists were inequality in landownership and absentee landlordism. In the 1990s, economists discussed the benefits of privatization and what to do with surplus labor in agriculture. Both periods share questions about what kind of institutions can reduce rural poverty and support abundant agricultural production to feed the nation. In both periods the problems and proposed solutions for agriculture have different implications for men and women, and cannot be divorced from other aspects of social, economic, and political life.

In the 1930s, years of worldwide economic depression, China's agrarian system was in crisis. Many farmers were impoverished by the drop in commodity prices and the loss of markets for textiles. Landownership seemed to be growing more unequal as poor families went under and sold their land to larger, sometimes absentee, landowners. Social scientists, reformers, and revolutionaries were all attuned to the problem of unequal land distribution, seeing landlessness as the force that drove impoverished peasants into the cities and absentee landlordism as an inefficient way to manage food production.[2]

Land reform was key to the Communist agenda. Since the Communists took power in 1949, China has gone through three land reforms. In the early 1950s, land reform redistributed land to the peasants. In the mid-1950s, collectivization began; it reached its most extreme form during the Great Leap Forward, and continued until the death of Mao in 1976. The third reform began in 1978, when China instituted the household responsibility (*baochan dao hu*) system. Since then, China has been poised between its former fully collective system of property management and a full system of private property allowing farmers to buy and sell land.[3] Advocates of privatization argue it enables farmers to increase their efficiency and release surplus labor from farmwork. Others fear privatization can bring back the hardships of the "old society" (*jiu shehui*), referring to China before the revolution. Debates about the most suitable form of land tenure for China thus span the twentieth century and are far from resolved as China's rural-to-urban migration accelerates, propelled by rapid economic development in the reform period.

## Land Tenure in the "Old Society," the 1930s

In 1938, Lu Village land tenure was based on private family and corporate ownership and patrilineal inheritance, with a limited market in land. A 1933 official land survey showed Lu Village had 594 mu (around one hundred acres, or forty hectares) under its jurisdiction. In that era, farmers were not restricted to farming land within a single village. Land within Lu Village was owned and cultivated by outsiders, just as Lu Village residents owned and rented land in other villages. Lu Village residents owned a total of 927 mu, with about 75 percent in private ownership and 25 percent held collectively by various temple, clan, and benevolent associations.[4] These associations rented land at preferential rates to members or kinsmen (Fei and Zhang 1945:77). Beyond what they owned, Lu Village farmers rented additional land, cultivating a total of 1,080 mu.[5] At least 45 percent of their cultivated land (and 35 percent of the land they owned) was located outside their village. This hints at interesting relationships with neighboring villages, and a land rental market.[6]

In the 1930s, households differed in the amount of land they owned. There were landowners managing farms with hired labor, smaller landowners combining family and hired labor, and landless households of tenant farmers and hired laborers. Fei observed that in Lu Village women could be farm laborers but not owners:

> The statement made previously that there is a tendency for landowners to avoid working on their farms might seem to be contradicted by the fact that the women of all families, even of those with large landholdings, are invariably active in agriculture. . . . This situation, however, does not invalidate the generalization that those who do not own the land are the ones who expend their labor on it, *for women are not considered as participating in ownership.* (Fei and Zhang 1945:66, italics added)

> Against the outside, the family is the owner of its common property; but if we examine the situation from the inside, we find that individual rights over property are far from being submerged. When viewed from this point of view, it is readily apparent that the land belongs to the man. (110)

Fei clearly felt that despite the appearance of common property, power differentials *within* households were similar to those *between* households of different classes. Men's rights to family property were formally recognized; women's rights were deniable. Only men could legitimately inherit land.[7] Women's rights were contingent; they could only hold land in custody for others. Yet the widow Fei mentioned in the quote opening this chapter clearly had rights to land inherited from her husband and, similar to a male landlord, she rented land out to nephews rather than farm it herself. In another example, a widow whose husband left her and her son with a farm of 11.5 mu exemplified "the traditional virtues, worked hard and had, through careful management and thrift, *enlarged her estate* to 13.8 mu by the time her son came of age" (Fei and Zhang 1945:117, units changed to mu, italics added).

Even for men, land was typically subject to nested rights with individual rights limited by the group. Men could not easily sell land outside the patriclan. Sales were possible through private channels and intermediaries, but clan members had right of first refusal. Fei wrote, "Only if the clan members are unable to buy the land or to lend him money to extricate him from his financial difficulty, may the individual sell to an outsider. In this case the buyer must secure the signatures of all the near members of the seller's clan; if the transaction takes place without permission, the contract is both customarily and legally invalid" (126). Given these restrictions, it is not surprising that only 2.5 percent of the land owned by individual households was sold in 1938. In concluding *Earthbound China*, Fei and Zhang emphasized the impediments to transacting land, claiming that "actually, throughout China there is no open market for farm land" (127, 294).

The lack of close "fit" between the amount of land within the village and the amounts villagers owned and actually cultivated shows a fluidity in farming and land transactions that defies a simple categorical model of exclusive, patrilineal social groups defending a bounded territory. There clearly was an active *rental* market in land, although it was an imperfect one in which information flowed through private channels, and kin could demand and receive special favors. Quite likely relationships to women who married into Lu Village from surrounding areas facilitated the renting, mortgaging, and transferring of land across village boundaries, while clansmen struggled to profit from kinship and maintain solidarity by preventing outright sale to outsiders. The geography of marriage relations (see chapter 7) supports this interpretation.

Fei reported that although a new law gave females the right to equal inheritance with males, it was disregarded in rural areas (Fei and Zhang 1945:112). He believed bilateral inheritance would disperse land and require households to rent out their more distant plots in other villages. He reasoned it was impractical because land was most productive when personally tilled by its owner. Ironically, by this logic, even patrilineal inheritance was not very effective in getting men to work their *own* land; Fei claimed that landowning men avoided farm labor, leaving it to the women, while nearly 35 percent of the cultivated land was rented. Despite patrilineal inheritance, Lu Village farmers evidently wanted to rent and transfer plots across village boundaries, as their rental patterns demonstrated. Consolidation of landholdings was clearly not their only concern; indeed, diversification through renting plots in different areas may have been a common household strategy.

Fei aptly described Lu Village in 1938 as a community of petty landowners, observing it was less polarized than the village he previously studied in east China. The wealthiest landowning family had about twenty-five mu, only about four acres, while 31 percent of the families were landless, renting land and working for wages (54). Both wealthy and landless households rented land, and only 15 percent of the households managed no land (76–77). Although access was not as unevenly distributed as ownership, Fei believed (like the Communist Party, which took power a decade later) that unequal landownership led to unequal wealth. In Lu Village, as in most of China, wealth was very unequally distributed (see chapter 6).

Chinese historians note that wealthy families often had more members than poor families, since fewer of their children died of hunger or disease, and because they delayed family division to keep land intact. Fei's evidence also suggests that wealthy families supported possibly twice as many members as poor ones. Although his comparison of land distribution among *households* suggested that as many as two-thirds fell into the landless and small-farm categories, an estimate considering differences in family size suggests that half the *population* may have belonged to households in the middle or wealthy categories (see table 4.1). Fei's informal descriptions of individuals and families in Lu Village suggest that, alongside class differences, age differences and stage in the life cycle also correlated with landownership. Young families in rural China often had little land but could perform manual labor, rent, or ultimately inherit or buy land from elderly kin. In contrast, the middle aged and elderly were more likely to have accumulated land but lacked capacity for heavy physical work.[8]

## Land Reform's Winners and Losers

The 1951 land reform eliminated land inequalities between households by confiscating land from the wealthier landowning households and redistributing it to the landless and land poor.[9] Throughout China, land reform work teams were trained to identify a family's class status. Landlords and rich peasants were defined as those who had received the majority of their income

Table 4.1.   Distribution of Lu Village Landownership in 1938 by Households

| Wealth Category | Farm Size (mu) | Households Percent (n = 122) | Population Percent Estimated[a] (n = 694) |
|---|---|---|---|
| Very poor | 0 | 31 | 23 |
| Poor | 1–6 | 35 | 26 |
| Middle | 7–16 | 26 | 39 |
| Wealthy | 17–26 | 8 | 12 |
| Total | | 100 | 100 |

*Source:* Adapted from Fei and Zhang (1945:54), converting gong to mu using the current ratio of 1 mu = 2.5 gong, ⅙ acres, or 0.67 hectares.

[a]This estimate is calculated assuming poor and landless households had three members and middle and wealthy landed households had six members, based on Fei and Zhang (1945:85ff) and Qian et al. (1995).

from rent, interest, or from hiring farm laborers. Those who hired farm laborers but did little or no work on the land themselves were considered exploiters, and people of the poorer classes were taught to despise them (Potter and Potter 1990:32). In Lu Village, 22 percent of the households (24 percent of the population) were classified as landlords and rich peasants. Middle peasants accounted for 36 percent of the households (50 percent of the population). The remaining households (27 percent of the population) were classified as poor peasants, laborers, and workers, who were the main beneficiaries from land redistribution (Qian et al. 1995:52).

In evaluating the land reform, many analysts have followed the official discourse and focused on class inequality. What has received less notice is that older people, and especially widows, tended to own (even if only in trust) more land than they could farm themselves, and hence to rent out their land or hire laborers to farm for them. If widows and widowers with declining strength hired labor to cultivate or plow the land, they could have been classified as landlords. The application of class labels would most likely have expropriated the widow Fei mentioned at the beginning of this chapter, and labeled her a landlord. This is evident in Potter and Potter's description of land reform in Guangdong:

> A widow . . . had owned over 10 mu of land and 1 mu of fish ponds, plus a flock of geese that she had raised to sell commercially. She had worked this property with the help of one son and a hired laborer. Her husband had died just before the reform. Although she had never oppressed anyone and was not a hated figure in the village, she fitted the criteria of a landlord and was so classified. Left to face the villagers by herself, she was ordered to deliver a large amount of grain to the peasants' association for distribution to the poor and landless peasants. She did not have enough money to buy that much grain herself, and her husband's relatives and friends refused to lend her as much as she would need. In despair . . . she committed suicide. (Potter and Potter 1990:51)

During the collective period, class labels were hereditary, so that children acquired the stigmatized or politically approved status of their parents. These labels shaped political attitudes and the assignment of privileges or penalties to households. Although class labels were officially removed in the 1970s, they still remained a powerful part of people's memories in Lu Village in the 1990s. Older people, jealous of the wealth or success of their neighbors, still whispered fiercely about the landlord backgrounds of people they resented, and those who came from poor or landless families still spoke self-righteously about their humble origins. These attitudes can be seen in the cases of wealth and poverty examined in chapter 6.

In the 1950s, the policy of land collectivization removed management from individual households (and their patriarchs in most cases) and required all villagers, men and women, to work for the collective. There, they were as-signed work cultivating various crops and earned work points as well as a share of the collective grain output. The work points, at year's end, were con-verted into cash. Collective farming continued until the economic reforms of the early 1980s permitted the revival of family-managed farming, dividing up collective land and contracting plots to individual households. Land con-tracts required that fixed quantities of output be sold to the state at fixed prices; the surplus could be sold on the free market. Land remained under the ownership and control of the production team. This system of contracting land to individual households, called the "household responsibility system," remained in force to the present.

## Land Tenure in the 1990s: Differences and Continuities

In the 1990s, village leaders distributed arable land on a per capita basis among the households of the different teams or small groups (*xiaozu*). This process excluded a small number of people in official, nonagricultural occu-pations as well as a variable number of migrant laborers. These nonregistered residents are landless in Lu Village, whatever land rights they may hold else-where. Focusing on registered residents, as official data force one to do, thus conjures away landlessness. This should be borne in mind in assessing change.

   In the 1990s, the farmland controlled by Greater Lu Village was over four times larger than that held in 1938. Greater Lu Village now had 1,565 mu of cultivated land in the center and 1,318 mu in the hamlets.[10] After the 1952 land reform, villagers' landholdings were consolidated and confined within discrete village and hamlet boundaries. Changes in territorial and adminis-trative units impede direct comparisons between the same village divisions today, but we can compare the distribution of land per capita and the degree of inequality across this period.

### Decreased Land per Capita

In 1938, the average amount of land owned was 1.3 mu per person, while that cultivated was 1.6 mu. In 1992, Greater Lu Village reported 2,883 mu of arable land for 2,983 people, an average of just under one mu per person.[11] The amount of arable land per person dropped about 40 percent over the past five decades (table 4.2). Population growth, however, has been offset by gains in productivity. For instance, only 70 percent of the land grew two crops a year in 1938, while today virtually all land in Greater Lu Village is double cropped.

**Table 4.2.   Changes in Land per Capita, 1938–1992**

|                                  | Lu Village 1938 | Greater Lu Village 1992 |
| -------------------------------- | --------------- | ----------------------- |
| Population                       | 694             | 2,983                   |
| Cultivated land / person (mu)    | 1.6             | 1.0                     |

*Source:* Fei and Zhang (1945); Lu Village records, 1992.

## Layers of Ownership: Fragmentation and Fairness

Under the household responsibility system, one "layer" of landownership rests with the village teams that distribute land, but farm management rests with the household as tenant cultivator.[12] Households can be seen as tenant cultivators because they do not have rights to buy or sell this land, and because the village itself is, in a sense, the collective owner and rent collector. Villagers are required to sell fixed quantities of specified crops at fixed prices to the state, and the price difference between state and market prices is, in effect, a form of rent or tax. In this respect, there are continuities with the ways clan land was managed in prerevolutionary Lu Village. Clan land was preferentially rented to clan members, and even private land was to some extent viewed as clan land, since clan members had first right of purchase and rights to nullify sales to outsiders.

Because land quality varies, village teams divided areas of different quality into strips, giving every household some of each type.[13] Distribution records from one hamlet in 1990 revealed an average of 9.5 separate pieces of land per household, the average size being only ½ mu.[14] As many as sixteen households (out of fifty-seven) had eleven to sixteen separate plots, an astonishing degree of fragmentation! This is not unusual for rural China (Carter et al. 1996:21).

The policy in force in the 1990s, aiming for a fair distribution of team land, did not eliminate inequality between teams. In Lu Village, per capita distributions ranged from 0.7 to 1.3 mu per capita (see table 4.3). Land belonging to different teams had different soil qualities, irrigation and road access, hilliness or flatness, and exposure to sun and wind. Within teams, however, the policy did eliminate inequalities by age, sex, and generation, three principles of hierarchy associated with the Confucian family. Each household got the same amount of land for its senior and junior members, its men and women. Land could no longer be seen as a basis for economic inequality among registered members of a team. The household registration (*hukou*) of each person as a legitimate member of a household and village team guaranteed an equal per capita share of crop land from the team's total supply. Households still had unequal amounts according to the number of members; families with more registered members received more land to farm, but no one seemed to think this unfair.

**Table 4.3.   Lu Village Farmland per Capita, 1992**

| Team | Population[a] | Mu per person |
|------|------------|---------------|
| 1  | 168 | 1.1 |
| 2  | 158 | 1.0 |
| 3  | 184 | 0.9 |
| 4  | 182 | 0.8 |
| 5  | 145 | 1.1 |
| 6  | 128 | 0.9 |
| 7  | 255 | 1.0 |
| 8  | 452 | 0.9 |
| 9  | 237 | 0.7 |
| 10 | 105 | 1.3 |
| 11 | 138 | 1.0 |
| 12 | 132 | 1.1 |
| 13 | 141 | 1.4 |
| 14 | 298 | 1.1 |
| 15 | 260 | 0.8 |

*Source:* Village Annual Reports, 1992.
[a]Includes fifty individuals with nonagricultural registration who, unlike the other household members, are not allocated land.

## Contract Duration, Uncertainty, and Land Redistribution Practices[15]

The duration of contracts in reform China has been uncertain, despite many claims to the contrary. Journalists and scholars have variously declared that, across China, the household responsibility system involves long-term contracts of fifteen, twenty, or thirty years (Wilhelm 1992) and that these extended periods reduced householders' "uncertainties about how long they would be allowed to have exclusive use of their land" (Smith 1991:83). Some cite official and unofficial announcements that contracts were valid for up to fifty years (Endicott 1989; Bernstein 1992; Putterman 1985); others declare that "currently the leases are for thirty years" (Carter et al. 1996:10). However, the gulf between official claims and local practice in China has often been wide and uncharted.

Rural interviews and village field studies give a different, fuzzier impression of contract duration. The duration and assignment of the contracts has varied widely in different regions, even within a single province, but redistributions every five years have been fairly common.[16] In Lu Village and elsewhere in Yunnan, village officials in the 1990s claimed lands were distributed for an indeterminate period. They could not say that redistribution would *not* occur, and they were not sure precisely when it would occur. They believed county authorities made this decision. Indeed, some counties in Yunnan chose *not* to redistribute land in 1990, and villagers in those areas complained that demographic changes had led to growing inequalities at the household level. In Lu Village, three re-distributions have occurred (1986, 1990, 1995) since the original distribution in 1981. Farmers, based on precedent, expected adjustments to occur every five years. Changes in the amount of land per capita were barely perceptible at the aggregate level. At the household level, however, people experienced significant shifts in their land allocation as their households gained or lost registered members.

Redistribution involved recalculation of the total population and number of persons per household for each team before it was known how much land would be allocated per capita. In Lu Village, as already noted, these calculations treated all persons equally, regardless of age and sex. However, this was not true across China. Anthropologists Judd (1994:27) and Simon (1994) reported different principles of distribution in north and east Chinese villages, where at times women have been allocated less than men.[17]

In 1990, updating household registration records for the national census provided a convenient opportunity for village leaders to reapportion the lands. I was present in Lu Village when leaders began the work of redistribution in July of that year. They called a meeting of the villagers of each team and determined which households would have their allotment reduced because members had left, or increased because they had new members. When I returned in 1991, this adjustment was complete and apparently had gone smoothly. Although redistribution involved changes, it did not entail a total reassignment, but only adding or subtracting plots according to household growth or attrition. Describing the first division of collective land when the responsibility system was instituted in 1981, members of one hamlet said families received the same lands distributed to them in the first land reform in 1951. This suggests that some villages maintained considerable continuity despite shifting policies. Nonetheless, at redistribution each household risked losing favorite plots and hoped to retain or obtain better ones.

Economic analyses of rural landholding are often "gender blind"—not in the sense of producing unbiased data, but in relying upon forms of data that make significant gender differences invisible. Censuses provide degendered units such as villages, households, or individuals. But they do not address the politically sensitive issue raised by Fei in the opening to this chapter: Does the land also belong to women, or do women simply belong to the household? What are the different dimensions of land rights women and men can acquire? When we try to take gender into account, there is rarely information available beyond restatement of abstract principles of patrilineal inheritance, revealing the ways scholars and officials interpret the system. This information does not tell us what village people actually do.

## Land Rights and Village Gender Policy

In July 1990, when land redistribution began in Lu Village, the leaders had recently decided to enforce a policy of not permitting sons-in-law to "marry in"
to the village and receive land.[18] Following patrilineal principles, families'
holdings increased when sons brought in wives and when children were born
(up to two) and decreased when members died, daughters married out, or members registered elsewhere for employment. Exceptions to the patrilineal rule
would be made only if a family had no son to inherit; then only one daughter,
not two, could marry uxorilocally and bring a husband into the village.

Who benefits from this system? Under these rules, families with married sons
end up receiving more land, while those with daughters who move out and
have no son, or only one son, end up with less land.[19] With a two-child quota,
and in an agrarian system in which land is a much more important (scarce) in-
put than additional labor, the disincentive to have daughters becomes very
strong. The leaders of Lu Village assured me that a family without a son could
bring in a son-in-law, but their policy would not allow a family with *two* daughters to bring in *two* sons-in-law, nor would it allow a family with a son and a
daughter to bring in one daughter-in-law and one son-in-law. Thus, patrilineal
bias in local interpretation (despite what national law says about equal inheritance) discriminates in favor of villagers who have two sons.

When I asked if this policy of discouraging uxorilocal marriage violated
the constitutional principle of sexual equality, officials agreed (with some
caution) that it did, but explained that because their village has a favorable
location, many daughters would prefer not to leave. With both daughters and
sons staying and bringing in spouses, they feared that their population would
grow too rapidly and villagers would get still less land per capita. When I
asked if they could simply rule that *only one child of either sex* could inherit
and thereby keep population low without sex discrimination, they acknowledged what I had said, but no more. After all, the current policy permits families to have two children. What was most curious was that several of the
cadres in the room had daughters or nieces who would benefit from staying
in the village and bringing in husbands. My proposal would have been to
their advantage. However, as leaders they must think of their constituencies
and what is perceived as legitimate. The path of least local resistance may be
to maintain a traditionally sanctioned Confucian principle of male inheritance. I concluded that the ability of local leaders to interpret policy flexibly,
which some might see as arbitrary power, does not always bode well for
women's land rights. On subsequent visits, however, I discovered another solution. When the daughter of one of the village cadres married and brought
in a son-in-law, I was told that a village membership for an in-marrying man

could be acquired for a fee. This suggested that a very limited market in land rights was informally developing.

In 1998, village leaders declared that the rules regarding "immigration" to the village had evolved further.[20] In general, when patrilocal households bring in a daughter-in-law to marry a resident son, they do not pay any fees to the authorities. Households with no son (or whose son "emigrates" by gaining urban registration) may bring in a son-in-law but must arrange for his household registration; they must pay a low fee if their son-in-law belongs to the category that "eats rural village grain." If a household with a son registered in the village also brings in a son-in-law to marry their daughter, they must pay a large sum of ¥5,000 to ¥40,000 to handle the registration. If a son's registration is urban, and he marries a woman who comes to live in the village and "eats rural village grain," the family must pay a settlement fee (louhu fei) of ¥500. Once the household registration has been established, the individual is considered a village citizen (cunmin) and enjoys the same treatment as other villagers, including the right to participate in land division.

One cadre's only son obtained urban residence registration, so the family sought to persuade their youngest daughter to bring in a son-in-law. In terms of family membership, the son-in-law would belong to the wife's family, but it is not clear whether he would therefore replace the son as heir, or if he would be a son-in-law who would not "eat village grain" and therefore pay no fee. Given that the fees for registration appear to be discretionary, a detailed study of specific arrangements over time is needed to determine whether families substituting sons-in-law for sons are paying more for the privilege.

## Team Land Records and the Informality of Household Rights

I have examined some of the record books in which team leaders record household landholdings. Given Western expectations of meticulous recording of property titles and deeds, I was much surprised by the casual ways family holdings were recorded by the team leaders, the de facto recorders of household contracted land rights. The team leaders' only records are normally handwritten and kept in small paper notebooks. For instance, the records from the land distribution of Team 3, June 30, 1985, were kept by the team accountant in a small, battered ten-by-fourteen-centimeter notebook. They were written in ink, in semilegible handwriting showing the name of the household head, the number of people in the household, the name[21] and area of the parcel of land, a productivity figure or tax rate for that parcel, and the total tax assessment. Team members lacked written documents stating which pieces of land were theirs. They had only little red plastic-covered booklets recording the amount and kind of tax they paid each year.

I remark on this procedure, not to belittle the efforts or sincerity of the team leaders involved in these communities, but to call attention to the lack of a formal, legal infrastructure to protect family land rights against loss of, tampering with, or misuse of these booklets. Households lack documents, other than the household identity card, that would legitimize land claims before higher authorities. The claims are, then, essentially claims to shares, not to any specific plots of land. Chinese economist Zhu Ling frankly observed that in China, "a cadastral system for regulating land mobility" does not exist (Zhu 1991:156). In other words, there is no official system of recording household land claims and transactions. To a large extent, a family's and individual's rights rest on the attitudes of the community and the personal authority of their team leaders. In contrast, the area of land belonging to administrative districts and teams *is* officially recorded in county offices, in multiple copies bearing official stamps. In the meantime, family farmers have little written proof of their claims to particular plots of land.

## Women's Entitlements

Collectivization gave women formal village status. Registered members of the village, men and women, were entitled to subsistence, and required to work for the collective. The economic reforms establishing the household responsibility system entitled women, as registered members of the village, to a certain amount of land allocated to the household on a per capita basis. During the 1990s, as long as a woman was registered to a community (whether by birth or marriage), she had a right to a share of the land. This does not mean that she or anyone else in the household could transact (buy or sell) land, but the policy makes it clear that women were incorporated into a village, either as daughters or wives, with rights to land for their support. In the 1930s Fei maintained that women could not own land in their own right but, as widows, held it only in trust for their sons. The present situation has elements of continuity and of change. Land today remains under the control of the village government, which distributes land to households under contract, much as clan and temple trusts did in the past. What is different today is that, in many villages where land is periodically redistributed, the presence of women, whether they be sisters, mothers, wives, or daughters, entitles a household to additional land allotments.

This simple policy probably increases women's sense of value to their household both before and after marriage; women bring an additional entitlement of land to the private household, at the expense of the larger allocating unit, and when they depart, their natal family loses an individual's share that returns to the pool. However, the lack of integration between policies of villages in different localities has some hazards for women, who are typically the ones transferring at marriage. One woman described her family's changes in land entitlement:

> When our family divided, they also divided the land given to each family. Originally the family had fifteen gong (six mu) of paddy. There are now three families of people, with twelve gong (4.8 mu) altogether. One daughter married out, so we lost three gong of paddy. Now I have two gong, for only one person, which I plant myself. My husband has given his fields to our older son to plant. At the end of the year, our son gives him grain. My daughter married out to a worker in Anning (her mother's hometown, near Kunming), but her registration was not transferred over there. So she and her son have become "black people," a "black household." [#4-1996]

The term "black" here refers to the underground economy and to people who lack formal household registration in the place they reside. In other words, her daughter does not officially share her husband's nonagricultural registration, yet she has lost her membership in her natal community, and her share of land in her natal village has gone to another household. From one point of view, this daughter has married "up." Her husband's status as a worker with residence in a larger industrial city nearer the provincial capital is considered desirable. But the move has left the daughter, as an individual, disinherited. I return to the subject of marriage and household registrations in chapter 7.

## THE GENDER DIVISION OF LABOR IN FARMING

> There is a very clear division of labor between the sexes. In general, the men do the heavier work, that which requires more strength and energy. (Fei and Zhang 1945:30)

> Men's work: men transplanting rice seedlings. . . . Transplanting rice was women's work in Japan and throughout Southeast Asia, but in China women played little part in farming. (Caption to a picture from the sixteenth century in Bray 1997:35)

> In every human society work (or nonwork) is a fundamental element in the construction of roles and of hierarchies; this is true of gender just as it is of class. Why, then, has women's work been neglected both by economic historians of the late imperial period and by feminists studying gender? (Bray 1997:177)

The first two quotations above represent two classic approaches to the gender division of labor in rural China. One holds that men did the heavy work, while women did light work. The other holds that women did very little farmwork at all. Neither pays sufficient attention to the work women did, or the "weight" they carried for the household, whether in kilograms or financially.

To evaluate changes and continuities in the gender division of labor in Lu Village, I begin with Fei's analysis, supplemented by information from elderly women of Lu Village who lived there at the time of his visit. It is indeed rare to have access to *any* detailed, substantive baseline with explicit data about rural women's work in a specific setting in prerevolutionary China. The passage of sixty years yields an appreciation of aspects of the gender system that, through decades of revolutionary change in policy and practice, have been most resilient and resistant to change. My approach differs from the usual focus on the 1949 Communist revolution. After decades of debate over what the revolution did or did not achieve for women during the turbulent Mao years, comparable data covering longer periods allows us to assess the changes from a less-politicized perspective. In Lu Village, there has been surprising continuity in rural social and economic organization since the early part of the century. Apart from public education and improved health care, the most significant changes for women may well be the result of expanding markets and technological diffusion. Such changes, reversed or slowed to a crawl during the collective period, accelerated in the 1990s. They are reverberating in women's lives and introducing different forms of labor and wealth.

## Women as Farmers in Lu Village, 1938: A Telescope on the Past

The conventional view of gender in prerevolutionary China, and an established part of Communist discourse, has been that most rural Chinese women did little or no work in the fields. This view held that women were domestic dependents, constrained by conventional values to remain underproductive within their homes and courtyards. They thus preserved their chastity and reputations as women of virtue and paid for it by becoming economically dependent on their husbands.[22] Historians and anthropologists of China, skeptical of official history and official discourse, increasingly question these axioms, seeking more complete information about the work women and men performed in different times and places. We learned in chapter 3 that, historically, women in many parts of China worked at home producing valuable textiles. Here I outline how they contributed to farmwork in Lu Village and show that they were, and still are, integral to its farm labor force.

Fei described the division of labor in farming as if household units were managed exclusively by men. This is not surprising; his research methods were shaped by the cultural and gender constraints of rural society at that time. Social norms of gender segregation did not encourage a man from outside to engage in direct conversation with village women. Fei relied on two male landowners for much of his information because they "hire others to cultivate their farms and . . . must know how much labor is required for the various phases of cultivation" (Fei and Zhang 1945:32). He later checked information about

the amount of work done in a day and the number of workers used by interviewing about one hundred households during the rice harvest. He did not say
whether these interviews included any women, but he reported no discussions
with women concerning their views of farming or farm management.

When Fei summarized his results in a detailed estimate of the amount of
male and female labor needed to farm one unit of land (double cropped, with
rice followed by beans), something surprising emerged. Out of fifty-two labor
days required per mu, twenty-nine were provided by women and twenty-
three by men (33). Multiplying by the average amount of land cultivated per
household by Lu Villagers (8.8 mu, owned and rented), women's annual work
in cultivation required approximately 255 labor days, and men's work 202
days. Under these norms, women were clearly expected to provide more farm
labor than men.

While this arrangement would provide nearly full-time work if performed
entirely by one man and one woman per household, the seasonal schedule for
agricultural work has intense peaks and troughs, so that either the family labor supply alone is too small to get the job done quickly enough or there is
not enough work for all the family members. Lu Village farmers traditionally
solved this scheduling problem by exchanging labor with their neighbors,
and hiring laborers from their own and other villages. Outside laborers,
brought in to help during rice transplanting and harvest, generally performed
tasks associated with their gender.

Fei's analysis demonstrated that in 1938 Lu Village women were primarily
farmers and a major part of the farm labor force. They generally did more
agricultural work than the men, (see table 4.4) in the two staple crops, and
also cultivated a variety of subsidiary crops and vegetables for home consumption. Yet when Fei wrote about farm managers, he meant men.

Moreover, when writing about men Fei noted differences in wealth, age,
education, and social position and gave some of them identities, while he often merged women into a single category: they all did farmwork—even in
wealthy households—and lacked the leisure of men. Once in a while, an exception slipped through—as when he wrote about accompanying "the wife of
Uncle Chang" to a neighboring village "where she was trying to make
arrangements with some Sichuan migrants for the harvest work on the farm"
(Fei and Zhang 1945:68).

Although Fei rarely described women as individual agents, his close examination of the sexual division of labor in the staple crops, rice and beans, should
have revised standard views that their contributions to farming were minor.

> During the transplantation of rice the men pull the shoots from the nursery beds and
> transport them to the main fields, where the women plant them. In the rice harvest
> the women cut the grain, tie it, and transport it to the threshing box. The men do

**Table 4.4. Lu Village Gender Division of Labor in Rice and Bean Cultivation for One Mu of Land by Task, 1939**

| Male | Days | Female | Days |
|---|---|---|---|
| Sow rice (hand) | 1.2 | Sow rice (hand) | 1.2 |
| Break soil (hoe) | 10.0 | Collect, thresh beans (sickle and beater) | 7.5 |
| Irrigate, mend dikes | 1.7 | | |
| Fertilize | 1.2 | Fertilize | 1.2 |
| Level the field | 1.7 | | |
| Plow | 0.7 | | |
| Transport (carrying pole) | 2.5 | Transplant (hand) | 2.5 |
| | | Weed 3 times (hand) | 11.0 |
| Thresh (threshing box) | 2.5 | Reap (sickle) | 2.5 |
| Dig broad bean trench (hoe) | 1.2 | Sow broad beans (hand and dibble) | 2.5 |
| Carry straw (carrying pole) | 0.7 | Carry straw (carrying pole) | 0.7 |
| Total | 23.4 | Total | 29.1 |
| Labor days × 5.7 (avg. mu *owned* per household) | | | |
| Annual male days per year | 133 | Annual female days per year | 166 |
| Labor days × 8.8 (avg. mu *cultivated* per household) | | | |
| Annual male days per year | 206 | Annual female days per year | 256 |

*Source:* Fei and Zhang (1945:22)

*Note on calculations:* My 1990 and 1996 survey data consistently show the amount of labor needed to transplant one mu of rice land is twice as high as Fei's estimate, about 5–6 days per mu rather than 2.5 days, and three times as much as the time needed for pulling up and transporting the seedlings. Since manual techniques of uprooting and transplanting seedlings do not appear to have changed, Fei probably underestimated the amount of female labor in rice production.

the threshing and carry the threshed grain to the storehouse. The work in connection with the broad bean crop is performed mainly by the women. At planting time the men dig the trenches for the placing of the seeds by the women; but the latter do all the work connected with the harvest, including the cutting, the threshing, and the beating of the vines, while the men devote themselves to the preparation of the fields for the new rice crop. (Fei and Zhang 1945:30)

Despite such evidence, most anthropologists have yielded to the impressive quantitative evidence of John L. Buck's vast surveys (1957), which portray women in southern rice-growing regions of China as contributing only small quantities of labor to farming, in contrast to northern women, who seemed to contribute almost none.[23] Fei's detailed analysis of family labor over the crop cycle suggests that Buck's surveys seriously underreport the quantity of farmwork women performed, at least in many of the southern provinces.

For the prerevolutionary period, the stereotype of the farmer as male has been so strongly entrenched that scholars have not even considered the possibility that women may have been *more* responsible for farmwork than men. But Mao Zedong, like Fei Xiaotong, having spent some time in a rural village in 1930, in his *Report from Xunwu* also took note of the heavy contributions of women to field labor in Hunan (1990:212), where the specific tasks performed by women resemble those of Lu Village. Ethnographic accounts such as Fei's and Mao's, with their qualitative and quantitative village-based observations of women, support a reassessment.[24]

## *Bucking Buck's Legacy: Reinterpreting Women's Farmwork in 1939*

Lu Village can provide footage for many replays of the past, as we review both the systematic data and colorful details Fei presented about farm households. How might a contemporary gender-sensitive economic anthropologist reinterpret Fei's early-twentieth-century account? I identify four revised views of household farming in Lu Village in 1938.

First, there would be greater attention to the possibilities of female agency. Fei envisioned Chinese farms as family units headed by a married man acting as farm manager and family head, if not always as farm owner. While Fei was certainly aware of women's farm labor, his assumption that farmers and decision makers were adult males limited his ability to assess the full range of changes occurring in Lu Village in the 1930s. He did not explore the behavior and attitudes of women facing different arrays of economic choice, constraint, or coercion from the family, the marketplace, and the wider political economy. A modern observer might not contest the portrait of greater male control but would doubt the degree to which Fei presented women as passive, manual-menial family laborers, rather than farmer-managers and agents in their own right. He wrote, for example, "the headman . . . called on his married daughter to come from her home to help in the harvest, and later he sent his wife to his daughter's household as repayment" (Fei and Zhang 1945:65). This statement, from dialogue with his male informant, ignored the possibility that mother and daughter maintained reciprocal labor exchanges through their *own* affection and initiative. Again, Fei asserted, "Having their own female workers at command, farm owners can hire less labor and consequently realize greater profit" (74). Missing from this speculative reasoning is attention to the relationships among senior and junior women of the household, as well as between husband and wife. In financial matters, as we shall see later, women do not appear to be merely taking orders.

A second reappraisal would be the importance of women as farmers. Was Lu Village in the 1930s an early example of the "feminization of farming"? This expression is now commonly used to describe the process in developing countries whereby men vacate the village for off-farm jobs, leaving women in charge of the relatively unproductive, poorly rewarded farm sector.[25] Fei's analysis easily lends support to a reinterpretation that views women as the primary farmers and farmworkers. Women performed more labor than men in the two principal crops (to say nothing of vegetable production). Fei estimated that men in one-third of the households withdrew from farmwork while women remained active, and even compensated for male absence (Fei and Zhang 1945:65, 74). In other words, the agricultural labor force of Lu Village already looked somewhat "feminized" in the 1930s. Was this only a response to the Anti-Japanese War? Was it the historical pattern of farming in this region, or the beginning of an economic transformation that became more pronounced in the latter half of the century? The limited ethnographic information available, at odds with Buck's surveys and with official discourse, suggests women were important farmworkers in rice growing districts of Yunnan. Their importance in other districts was probably underestimated as well. The cultural constraints that hindered Fei's descriptions of Lu Village women were probably even greater for the men conducting Buck's surveys in villages across China, for they were hired assistants, not trained social scientists. These surveys have long been criticized for various methodological biases, so it should not be surprising to find they consistently underestimated women's agricultural work.

A third reinterpretation would give greater emphasis to women's labor outside the household, specifically the practices of female labor exchange and hiring female farm labor. Fei wrote:

> the farmer may work on the farms of others when his own land does not demand his attention. The farmer may either hire laborers and hire himself out or may exchange services with his neighbors. A count made during the harvest in 1939 revealed that one-half of the workers in the fields were working on an exchange basis rather than for wages. Exchange of labor is possible only because the farmers stagger the dates of their planting so that the crops do not reach the same stage of development simultaneously. If this were not done, the busy periods and slack periods would coincide on all the farms. (Fei and Zhang 1945:36)

Fei was not present in Lu Village when rice was transplanted.[26] Possibly for this reason, he underestimated the time involved and paid little attention to the exchange labor system among women of different households who worked on each other's fields and hired out in groups to transplant rice in other villages. Since the demand for female labor was so high during the busy transplanting season, Lu Village farmers usually exchanged and hired laborers from neighboring villages. Sometimes hiring was done at the village gate, but prior arrangements were also made with people in other villages. Most likely such hiring was facilitated by kin ties between married women and their natal villages. This is certainly implied by Fei's anecdote above describing the headman's married daughter exchanging labor with his wife, and is supported by contemporary labor exchange patterns. Examples are common of contemporary labor exchange between related women of different villages. One married woman, age thirty-seven, whose natal village is located two-hours' walk to the north, exchanges labor with her older sister, who lives in another village only a few kilometers from Lu Village. Another woman who married within Lu Village exchanges labor with her older sister and that sister's daughter-in-law. A woman of fifty-four explained that her daughters-in-law, born in a distant village, have their sisters come to help with rice transplanting and the harvest, and her daughters-in-law return the exchange labor.

Finally, a reappraisal would pay more attention to the complexity of the Lu Village farm economy and particularly the role of garden crops and pigs. Fei devoted most of his economic analysis to staple crops: rice and beans. These are the crops that government administrators were typically most interested in, for they could be dried, stored, transported, and used to pay wages or taxes and feed armies. But understanding how a household economy allocated its labor and provided a livelihood requires recognition of the multiple, small, perishable vegetable crops that families grew and harvested that formed part of daily diets. These aspects surfaced in Fei's description of the standard of living when he mentioned the gardens and separate pigpens of the wealthier households, noting the rich families' diet included "an abundance of vegetables, raised in their own garden, and wine, which they make themselves," as well as meat "obtained from the pigs they slaughter and by purchase in the market" (Fei and Zhang 1945:91).

Tending vegetable gardens and feeding pigs were labor-intensive tasks, part of the woman farmer's daily work, requiring attention even during the seasonal rush of transplanting or harvesting. They could also be sources of cash income, as they were often sold in small quantities in the market throughout the year, making them less obvious than the bulky sacks of rice that piled up at harvest. In Fei's account, these forms of labor and income faded into the background of house and courtyard work done by women, along with cooking meals and making and washing clothes. The importance of vegetables and meat can be inferred, however, from the family budgets, in which meat and vegetables (home grown and purchased) made up 10 to 30 percent of the total for food (87).

Fei also recognized that livestock could be a subsidiary source of income—"almost every house has 2 or 3 pigs"—yet his attempt to estimate the income from pigs, based on purchased fodder, gave a cost was greater than the selling price (49–50). However, farmers rarely purchased fodder for pigs. Rather, they grew or gathered (and cooked) their own, so that costs did not exceed income, and much of the selling price was a return to labor. This aspect of farmwork was primarily carried out by women. In the 1990s, it was still primarily women's domain (Bossen 2000).

These four reinterpretations—regarding women as agents, their importance as farmers, their participation in exchange labor and hiring, and their role in vegetable and pig production—are just a few of the possible paths to a more complete understanding of the sexual division of labor in farmwork in the prerevolutionary period.

In bringing women into clearer focus during the prerevolutionary period, it should not be forgotten that Lu Village was marked by significant social and economic inequality between households. Fei focused on landholding as a major cause of that inequality and illustrated the differences in standard of living between rich and poor households. One old woman (born in 1918) recalled the days before Liberation as follows:

> Before Liberation, life was bitter. There was a landlord in the city who rented land to us to plant. Each year after we paid the rent, there was not much left over. We could only eat squash soup; we couldn't raise pigs. We almost never ate meat, and didn't have clothes. After childbirth, you couldn't rest for the month afterward [as custom requires] but had to go right back out to work in the fields. Before and after I was married, I always worked in the fields. We were under our parents' authority. My mother-in-law was terrible. She would not let me go outside to visit anyone. My husband worked outside, driving a horse cart to transport salt. From youth, he always worked very hard. Even though we had never seen each other before we were married, he was good to me. We never fought. Before Liberation, the Nationalists took a lot of men as soldiers. My husband was a soldier for three years, before he came home. (#27-1990)

How much and what kind of farmwork women did, whether or not they could afford to raise pigs and vegetables, whether or not they could afford postpartum rest, were profoundly affected by family wealth and by the presence or absence of men due to military conscription or outside labor.

## Changes in the Division of Farm Labor and Technology

Since 1938, techniques of farming rice and beans have changed. These changes include use of new seed varieties with shorter growing seasons, chemical fertilizers (alternated with organic ones), electric water pumps for irrigation, tractors (where plot size and location permit), plastic sheets to keep rice seedlings warm and shorten their growing period, herbicidal and pesticidal sprays to reduce weeding and insect infestation, and opportunistic use of traffic on the paved road (for those who live next to it) to thresh certain grains by leaving them to be driven over.

I asked several experienced women farmers to outline the current agricultural schedule in terms of the main types of farmwork and the division of labor. The results are summarized in table 4.5. We can compare this to table 4.4 for 1939, which outlines the main tasks in rice and bean cultivation by sex. Together, these tables reveal a relatively slow pace of change in the division of labor in farmwork in Lu Village over the past sixty-odd years. Despite roughly twenty-five years (1957–1982) of collective farming when work was assigned according to Communist principles, men and women have not drastically altered the ways they divide farmwork.

The farm activities that remain in the male domain include plowing fields for rice (often done by hired men with a tractor, or with an animal-drawn plow if the plot is small), hoeing fields for broad beans, and threshing rice with a threshing machine. For women, continuity is found in transplanting rice by hand and reaping rice with a sickle, and in planting, reaping, and threshing broad beans with hand tools. Given the numerous small plots allocated to each family and the unmechanized nature of most of the work, farming continues to absorb considerable labor but has become easier and more reliable with new technologies. The main reduction in time is in laborious weeding for rice, previously done by women. This has been replaced by faster, but noxious, spraying from backpack canisters. This job can be done by either sex. My observations suggest it is more often done by women, but in my survey, people reported about equal amounts of time spraying for men and women. Tasks such as adding fertilizer and hauling rice straw remain mixed.

## Women and the Plow Question

As seen earlier, Fei explained the division of labor in terms of the heaviness of men's work. Many observers have noted that, worldwide, plowing is normally done by men (Boserup 1970), and some have explained this by claiming that plowing is too heavy for women (Maclachlan 1983). The male monopoly on farming and farm ownership is thus justified by their allegedly unique ability to manipulate the plow. In Lu Village, it is clear that men had no monopoly on farmwork (as opposed to farm management). Did they have a monopoly on plowing?

Fei observed gender differences in tool use: "the most important for the men is the hoe; for the women the sickle and the beater [the flail used for beans] are the most characteristic" (Fei and Zhang 30–31). Surprisingly, he did not mention plowing, although his description of the division of labor clearly assigned this to men. This may have been because Fei was not actually present during the plowing season and therefore had no particular im-

**Table 4.5. Lu Village Farm Calendar and Basic Tasks, 1938 and 1996 (M = male, F = female)**

| Dates | Task | 1938 | 1996 |
|---|---|---|---|
| Feb 20–Mar 10 | Harvest: | | |
| | rapeseeds | | M or F |
| | broad beans | F | M or F |
| | wheat | | M or F |
| | barley for pig feed | | M or F |
| | Haul, thresh beans, grain | F | F |
| Mar 1–Apr 15 | Plow land (hired labor, double plowing, double leveling by tractor or water buffalo) | M | M |
| | Hoe (turn over) and sun dry land | M or F | M or F |
| | Broadcast rice seeds (1996, usually 6 people together): | M or F | M or F |
| |     1 spreads pesticide | | |
| |     1 broadcasts seed | | |
| |     1 covers with earth | | |
| |     1 covers with rapeseed kernels as mulch | | |
| |     2 cover with plastic sheet | | |
| | Irrigate land (team leaders, 2–3 people) for everyone at once | | M (team) |
| | Repair dykes (team coordinates or hires) | | M? |
| | Pull up, transport seedlings | M | M & F |
| | Transplant rice (exchange, hired, 5 per mu) | F | F |
| Apr 20 | Fertilize (chemical in 1996) | M or F | M or F |
| | Weed (1938) or apply pesticide (1996) | F | M or F |
| May–June | Slack season, water fields as needed | | |
| | Weed (1938) or apply pesticide (1996) | F | M or F |
| July 15–Aug 15 | Harvest rice (women reap with sickle), men haul and thresh; about 12 (hired or exchange) laborers finish in 1–3 days | M & F | M & F |
| | Rake, clean, sun dry, and mill unhusked rice (2–3 days, family groups)[a] | M & F | M & F |
| Aug 15–Sep 15 | Plant rapeseed | | M or F |
| | Hoe land for beans | M | M or F |
| | Plant broad beans | F | F |
| Aug 20 or later | Stack rice straw | M or F | M or F |
| Sep 15–Sep 30 | Plant wheat | | M or F |
| Sep 30–Feb 20 | Slack season | | |

*Sources:* For 1996, two senior women farmers of Lu Village; for 1938, Fei and Zhang (1945:22, table 1), and table 4.4, above.

*Note:* gender norms for labor are flexible in most tasks. Plowing by men and transplanting rice, planting broad beans, and threshing beans (and other grains by car traffic) by women are the main activities where sex is specified. Informants and survey data are consistent.

[a]Participant observation in 1999 revealed a laborious, previously unnoted task made harder by rain, requiring repeated raking up and covering of the rice, and by the scarcity of threshing ground space for drying grain.

pression of its importance as a male activity. Or, it may have been because plowing was not a generalized activity associated with *all* men, as an emblem of masculinity. Plowing was, indeed, the work of men, but only men who owned draft animals. Only 16 percent of the households owned water buffaloes, so most farmers hired a man with animals to plow for them (72). Without hiring draft animals and plows, villagers were still able to prepare fields for rice, but had to do so with the hoe, a more laborious process, limiting the amount of land they could prepare in time for planting.

As to the assumed inability of women to plow due to their physical weakness, I have always doubted this explanation because of recorded examples of frontier women plowing in North American history. In a different Yunnan village, I was once given a chance to try my hand at plowing with an ox, and found the challenge was not so much one of strength (the animal supplied that) as of skill in keeping the furrow to an even depth and getting the animal to perform properly—the same difficulty an inexperienced rider has in controlling a horse. Both skills seemed a matter of practice. I was not surprised, then, while recording the life history of an elderly Lu Village woman, to discover that she had plowed the fields in her youth, prior to the revolution. She learned as a girl by practicing while men took their lunch. Later, she was called upon to plow as an adult during the Great Leap Forward, when many men were taken from the village to work on large construction projects. Another woman spoke about her plowing and farming experience in the context of her service as a village leader, or cadre, during the collective period.

> Woman: I also went into the field to plow (in 1971 when I served as team leader). Then, plowing the fields was worth twenty points a day, transplanting worth eighteen.
>
> LB: If you yourself were allowed to choose to plow land or transplant rice, which would you prefer to do?
>
> Woman: I would still prefer to transplant rice. There was an old saying that: "If women touch (*mo*) the plow, the crops (*zhuangjia*) and the ox are no good." During the time of collective production teams, there were four women in the village who used to plow. Women and men did the same work. Each day in the morning at 7 A.M., they had to go to the fields and labor. When they got home, women still had to cook, feed the pigs, and take care of the children. Men normally could just rest, and smoke.

In the context of all the unmechanized domestic work women had to do during the collective period, as in traditional times, I was not surprised to find that even strong women were not eager to add plowing as a permanent responsibility. In this light, old sayings warning of ruined crops if women touched the plow might have been used by women to prevent greater work demands, as well as by men to claim men were superior and therefore deserved higher pay.

Today, the traditional gender division of technology is still evident; a small number of men are hired to do the plowing for the majority, more often with tractors than water buffaloes. Despite images of tractors with female drivers that graced China's paper money for years, tractor driving became a male specialty in Lu Village as elsewhere. Tractors are used, not only for plowing, but also for transport, and driving them is surely "lighter" work than carrying loads from the fields on one's back or with shoulder poles as women and men still do. Tractors are simple to operate and require only a modicum of training—but until recently they were scarce and relatively expensive tools. In addition to traditional divisions of labor, customary rights of access to and ownership of productive capital may be equally important in understanding women's access to certain types of technology.

When it comes to the humble hoe, a much less productive instrument, I found nothing resembling the masculine gender association that Fei observed. Women of Lu Village, and Yunnan in general, are often seen working in the fields with hoes alongside men; they break clods of earth, level mud, raise embankments for rice transplanting, prepare fields for beans, and hoe vegetable gardens. It is possible Lu Village women worked with hoes in 1938 as well, for Fei sometimes relied on the general statements of his key male informants rather than observation. During the peak of the busy rice-planting season, one sees both male groups and families of men and women preparing the land with hoes. Often when land preparation is done by men, the women are very busy with other urgent tasks. Women literally have their hands full harvesting and threshing beans and transplanting rice into different fields when the men are preparing the land. The division of labor, then, does not appear to be based on "natural" abilities as much as on social conventions for dividing labor and acquiring skills in the complex choreography of urgent tasks during the busy season. Although families often have both sexes working together, social conventions generally require that larger work groups are gender segregated.

Table 4.6 shows the land dedicated to the main crops in different years. My 1990 survey of eighty-six farming households found the average amount of farmwork per household for rice seedlings, paddy, beans, wheat, and rapeseed (grown by over 80 percent of the households) totaled about seventy days per year for women and fifty-seven days for men. This is considerably lower than the 1938 estimate of farmwork per household (see table 4.4), resulting from both technological change and decreased land per capita. The average amount of rice land cultivated by households in 1990 was 4.5 mu, much less than the average of 8.8 mu in 1938. Even so, female farmwork was still 55 percent of the total.

**Table 4.6.   Greater Lu Village Crops, 1986 and 1992**

| | *1986* | | *1992* | |
|---|---|---|---|---|
| *Crop* | *Area (mu)* | *Output/mu (kgs)* | *Area (mu)* | *Output/mu (kgs)* |
| Rice | 2514 | 466 | 2522 | 569 |
| Yams | 105 | 45 | | |
| Corn | 6 | 74 | | |
| Wheat | 719 | 324 | 764 | 341 |
| Broad beans | 1211 | 76 | 1118 | 147 |
| Barley | 147 | 86 | 62 | 198 |
| Canola | 272 | 91 | 385 | 155 |
| Vegetables | 133 | na | 135 | na |
| Tobacco | 21 | 125 | | |
| Sugar | 10 | 495 | | |

*Source:* Village annual reports. Rice is harvested in autumn, wheat, beans, barley, and canola in spring.

Lu Village, along with the rest of China, experienced radical changes in social organization between 1938 and the 1990s. Yet the traces of any long-term impact of this period upon the gender division of labor are hard to find. There are few records for the period of collective farming, roughly 1957 to 1982. Across China, this period involved massive efforts to revolutionize rural society by taking control of production away from the family and eliminating class and gender inequalities by assigning work and rewards on the basis of egalitarian principles. In theory, these movements of radical egalitarianism should have overturned old patriarchal prejudices against women and eliminated gender differences in patterns of work. Yet the gender patterns in farmwork today show more continuity than radical change.

Reconstructing exactly what was done at the local level to change gender relations is no easy task. Village officials say they have no records for this period, and that during the Cultural Revolution little record keeping was done. Possibly, earlier records were destroyed then as well, or village leaders had only informal records. Village officials are still generally wary of people talking with outsiders. I decided that attempts to discuss this period directly, after the political suppression of 1989, would put everyone on guard and make it difficult to conduct research. Cadres could always give official accounts of which movement followed which, but in my previous experience, these accounts were standardized and followed the official line. Village leaders were uncomfortable if asked to discuss in detail those periods such as the Great Leap Forward and the Cultural Revolution, when people across China experienced serious hardship. I believe this was because no one likes being forced to lie. Also, memories of painful events are hard to revive without opening old wounds. In later chapters, I present some villagers' personal experiences of life under the collectives. But even in the late 1990s, when alluding to famine during the Great Leap Forward, an old woman with a very clear memory of the past muttered a private remark to my Chinese assistant saying she thought they were not supposed to talk about it (even though we assured her that it was internationally known that millions starved during that period and it was no longer a "state secret").

During the collective period, villagers were paid with work points in lieu of money. By asking individual team leaders if they personally had kept any records of work points from the collective period, I came up with one example of how points were distributed before the collectives were dismantled in the early 1980s. This example consisted of a small, handwritten notebook with names and work points recorded for a team in Lu Village Center in 1980–1981. It showed that women supplied most of the farm labor that year, maintaining the prerevolutionary pattern (see table 4.7).

In 1938, Fei's informants told him that Lu Village women as a rule were paid half as much cash as men for a day of farm labor (Fei and Zhang 1945). Although Fei treated this rule as inflexible, life histories revealed more variation, but women *were* generally paid less than men. In 1980, women were still paid less than men, not because they worked fewer days or hours, but because typically women were assigned to do work that was assigned lower work point values. Sometimes, daily wage rates were superceded when piece rates were used (as in rice transplanting), and women and men earned according to performance rather than pay level.

In this team, women collectively earned 53 percent of the work points and provided the bulk of the agricultural labor force. However, men earned 629 more work points per person than women for the year. On average, women earned only 83 percent as much as men, directly reflecting the discriminatory

**Table 4.7. Production Team Work Points Earned in Team Labor, by Sex (34 households, 1980–1981, total points)**

| | Number of people | Average work points/ person | Work point pay rate | Work points earned | Work points (percent) |
|---|---|---|---|---|---|
| Male | 37 | 3,735 | 12/day | 138,206 | 47 |
| Female | 51 | 3,106 | 10/day | 158,384 | 53 |
| Total | 88 | 3,370 | | 296,590 | 100 |
| Fertilizer points[a] | | | | 13,385 | |

*Source:* Team records kept by the former team leader. Work point rates come from informant statements, and are consistent with 320 work days per year.

[a]Fertilizer points were given to households for supplying fertilizer to the collective. This fertilizer came from family pigsties and was, in a sense, a byproduct of pig raising. Women usually managed courtyard pig raising and thus earned work points for the household.

pay scales: women generally earned only ten points per day, while men
earned twelve points.

This record of unequal work points recalls similar inequalities reported for
other villages across China.[27] The principles for awarding work points
changed at various times during the collective period, but equal pay was the
exception. At times, the rates were decided by national politics so that those
considered good Communists got higher wage rates and "bad elements" got
lower ones. Generally, pay rate principles were molded by traditional political views so that men were classed as high-quality labor and assigned higher
rates than women, or men were assigned the jobs that were labeled more difficult and received higher rates. On occasion, for particular kinds of tasks,
work points were paid according to output, that is, by piece rate. Under this
system, women sometimes earned more than men. One woman (a party
member) described the beginning of the Great Leap Forward as follows:

> In 1958, the villagers elected me to be treasurer (*kuaiji*).[28] I had to look after the
> team's money, work points, and distribution. At that time, work points were decided
> according to correct political thinking, and labor capacity. It did not matter if it was
> a man or a woman, everyone could earn the highest work points, twelve points per
> day. Transplanting rice was twenty points per gong. You could earn five points for
> pulling up one hundred rice bunches. When I was young, I could pull up eight hun-
> dred rice plants each day, earning forty work points.

## Women's Farmwork in the 1990s

After sixty years, changes in the gender division of labor in Lu Village farming had not been revolutionary. My economic survey[29] showed that women
were *still* more concentrated in farming than men, with a division of labor and
labor schedule for growing rice and beans that seemed like it could have been
recopied from Fei (table 4.6). It is not that farming was unchanged. Technological improvements had indeed reduced labor and increased productivity, as
I discuss shortly. But the basic responsibilities for particular farm tasks had
shifted little since Fei's time. Women performed large amounts of agricultural
labor both before and after the revolution transformed political organization.
The revolution disseminated the view that work would bring women liberation and equality. As a result, official rhetoric about women's work changed,
but the content of the work changed far less. In particular, rice and beans still
require a great deal of manual labor for transplanting and harvesting.

The intensive use of female labor groups, composed of family, exchange,
and hired labor, continues in rice transplanting today as in the past. Most
women have clear memories of how much work they have given and received;
indeed, one woman showed me a notebook going back five years in which she
had carefully kept track of these exchanges. Young women are particularly active in rice transplanting as exchange or hired labor, while older women more

often pull up and bind seedlings for transplanting, or remain at home to supervise and cook meals for the work crews. Farmers provide cooked meals to laborers as part of the remuneration, in addition to the daily wage. Large groups are able to finish transplanting a field in a single day, so that all the rice shoots begin growing and mature at the same time. By inviting exchange laborers, each household can finish its fields quickly, but the women and men who have received help must then go out to work in the fields of their exchange partners. The peak period for rice transplanting lasts about two weeks. The rice harvest also requires groups to finish the work quickly. As in the past, these groups contain roughly equal numbers of women who reap with the sickle and men who thresh the grain in the village.

## Farming Vegetables and Pigs

Raising vegetables and pigs provides a vital addition to family nutrition and cash income. Unlike with grains, which have dramatic peaks and troughs in labor demand, labor devoted to vegetables and pigs forms a daily routine for most households. This work can be somewhat integrated with food preparation, and therefore seems to "blend in" with housework. But clearly this is

*Lu Village woman reaps rice with a sickle.*

*Rice harvest in Lu Village. Men thresh in the fields with
a threshing machine.*

more than an "extension" of housework. It is also an integral part of family
farm production, providing subsistence and cash.

To illustrate the nature of this work, I present an excerpt from my field
notes for one June morning that I spent with Mrs. Wu, a farmer in her early
forties. These notes only cover a few hours. While offering some other observations, they give some sense of the activities that keep most women busy.

A morning's work in Lu Village[30]

9:20   I arrived at Mrs. Wu's house. The door was locked, but Mrs. Wu came
       from the back lane leading from the fields just when I got there,
       greeted me and unlocked the doors for me to sit down. She was just
       about to go off to the vegetable garden to water the plants. She had
       the buckets of night soil from the latrine. I asked if I could accompany
       her and see her garden. She laughed and agreed. Mrs. Wu said the wa-
       tering would only take about half an hour.

9:40   Mrs. Wu lifted two buckets of night soil on her carrying pole and set out
       from the house to the fields. The two buckets weighed about 30 kgs.

*Lu Village woman carries boiled water to laborers harvesting her rice field.*

each, so she was carrying about 120 pounds of liquid shit on her shoulder. She walked rapidly down the lane to the main street, northward to the edge of town and beyond, and then down a dirt path to her vegetable field. The buckets she carried are old sturdy wooden ones, and they have chains that are hooked to the pole. I briefly attempted to carry them and discovered it takes great skill, as well as strength, to walk smoothly without spilling the contents (which I definitely did not want to do).

*A mechanized rice harvester. Hired for the first time in 1999 by one household, the large vehicle could not maneuver around the corners of the small field without crushing rice. To avoid loss, the owner had to cut the edges by hand.*

The patch of land Mrs. Wu was watering was an irregularly shaped piece which she said was one fen (l/10 of a mu). This plot was about 15 by 15 paces, with two large grave mounds in the middle. I asked who was buried there and she replied, "*Lao zuzu*" (the old ancestors). She quickly ladled the night soil onto the fields. In one part she had planted mixed vegetables. In another, there were newly transplanted white sweet potatoes. The leaves and later the roots of this plant are used to feed pigs. She finished the two buckets she brought and then took her buckets over to the adjacent flooded rice paddy, which belongs to other people, and ladled water into her bucket. This water she then carried over to the dry mounds of freshly planted tubers.

9:50    She began on her third set of buckets, watering the tubers. Luckily it was a cloudy day. I sat on the back of the tomb, and then went around to look at the front. One of the two mounds actually contained two graves: a man and a woman. The man's gravestone had two dragons on it, and the woman's had two phoenixes. There was a sun crowning the middle. There were inscriptions, but I could not read them. The woman's grave was newer. After a few more questions, I realized, as I should have known, that these are Cao family tombs, those of her husband's ancestors. The other, single tomb belonged to the family next door to Mrs. Wu's courtyard, also named Cao. It was their *nainai* (paternal grandmother), she said. The plots that Mrs. Wu cultivated then, which were allocated by the collective, were marked by private graves attesting, in stone, to the possession of this land by the Cao family. Later, I learned that when vegetable plots were redistributed in the early 1960s, long before the reforms permitted the redistribution of rice land, many families claimed plots from the same place their families had originally owned land. My interest in the tombs did not spark much response from Mrs. Wu. After all, they were there every day as she worked around them in the vegetable patch, and squashes were growing over the mound of rocks at the back. But when I pointed to the little altar shelves in front of the carved stone, and asked if they burn incense on Qing Ming (the holiday for remembering the dead) she smiled and said, "Yes, and we give them a little food too." Even though Mrs. Wu is a cadre, she obviously no longer felt that she had to uphold the ideas of the Cultural Revolutionaries, who would have cursed these "feudal survivals."

10:00    She finished her fourth set of buckets, and began the fifth. I sat on the grave mound writing notes, thankful that it was cloudy. Insects were snapping at my feet.

10:10    We walked over to another 3 *fen* of vegetable land on the other side of the road. Mrs. Wu picked some celery-like vegetables and cabbage for lunch, and some green peppers. None of the eggplants were ready yet. There were tomato plants as well. She took about 10 minutes to pick vegetables and then we walked back to the main road and to her house by 10:15 A.M.

10:15    Mrs. Wu stoked the fire, went across the courtyard to hang up the shoulder pole, and took out a light green plastic basket to collect some more vegetables for lunch. We walked out the back lane, past one of the pigsties and the latrine, and went out a back door in the mud wall to another vegetable plot, also about one fen. She picked up some straw that was lying on the patch and put it over some vegetables as mulch to keep them from baking in the hot sun. Then she went into the vegetable patch to pick some *Nanjing dou*, which are large beans. She also picked some *bai shu teng*, yam vines, to feed the pigs.

10:20    She was still picking vegetables. The Nanjing beans were growing up large stakes, three tied together, in about 13 such "tepee" constructions. There was corn planted among the beans. Some of the beans were too old to eat; she would let them dry out and save them for planting. Soon we returned and she went immediately to stoke the fire some more.

10:30    Mrs. Wu went upstairs, using a new outside cement staircase to the second story and I followed her. At the top of the steps was a chicken coop with several chickens in it. The second floor was a large storage room. In the front of the room was a bed on the floor that looked like it was stuffed with straw. Her son slept there when he came home on weekends. In the back was a heap of potatoes on the cement floor, and around a partition was a large bin with two kinds of chaff: bean chaff and rice chaff. She scooped some of each type of chaff into a wicker basket, and then got a little ground corn, went downstairs, and added these to a large wok, which already had yam vines cooking. Then she got some coal dust in a pan from the coal bin across the courtyard, next to one of her pigsties. She shoveled it into her pan and then took it to the fire and added it in little scoops. Then she scooped water from the sink into the wok and stirred with a large ladle.

10:35    Mrs. Wu squatted on a stool in front of the fire in the kitchen. There was straw for kindling piled in the corner behind her. Right then, her daughter was in school. She was in the second year of junior middle school. Mrs. Wu's husband was in Chuxiong, the prefectural town, for a meeting and would stay overnight. Her older daughter would come home for lunch from her job in a tax agency in Lufeng.

10:40  Mrs. Wu squatted at the square table on the porch and began cleaning string beans into a bucket. In the courtyard, there were some turkeys milling about. Mrs. Wu has two middle-sized pigs in the pigsty across the courtyard and two small ones in the pigsty by the latrine.

10:45  Mrs. Wu returned to stoke the fire and stir pig slop. She started ladling the slop into buckets. I noticed how neatly dressed she was despite her farmwork. She was wearing cloth-topped shoes, black trousers, a white, long-sleeved blouse over an undershirt, and a small print blue apron. Her hair was neatly pinned up in the back.

10:50  She had taken the slop buckets to cool by the pig stall and was cleaning up the stove with water from the tap. She swished things from the wok onto the stove top, where there is a little drain that runs down into a bucket below, which she empties down a gutter across the courtyard.

10:55  Clean water was starting to boil in the wok and she started to sweep up the kitchen floor and the courtyard.

11:00  She stoked the fire and returned to cleaning beans, and we discussed her son's marriage options. She commented that her son has a railroad registration and works in another county town. She thought that he would probably have to find a wife there because it's very difficult to transfer a wife's residence registration to that place. I teased her about wanting grandchildren. Her son was only twenty-two and did not want to marry for a few more years. Working for the railroad made it hard to find a wife because there aren't many women in that unit. I asked, if he married and lived in the other county town, "Would the daughter-in-law still come to her *pojia* (mother-in-law's house) to give birth? Is she supposed to come here?" "If she's willing, or else, if she needs me, I could go there to help her. But if her own mother was there, perhaps she could help out, perhaps she would prefer her own mother," replied Mrs. Wu. This did not sound much like the prescription I found in the north, where women were expected to give birth in their mother-in-laws' house. Time would put this attitude to the test (as we see in chapter 7).

11:10  Mrs. Wu washed the rice steamer in a basin of water.

11:20  She washed rice containers. Rice was boiling in the wok. The old woman from the house next door stopped by for a moment. [That house belongs to Mrs. Wu's husband's younger uncle (*shushu*) and the old woman was a stepgrandmother, the second wife (after the first one died) of the grandfather.]

11:25  Mrs. Wu removed the rice, and washed out the wok with clean water several times. It was hot water and boiled right off as she swept it out with a little brush. Then she added some more clean water, put the cooked rice into a bamboo steamer, set it in the wok, and covered it to steam it.

11:35   She washed the celery or bitter vegetable, stoked the fire, adding more coal dust. The sun came out. She threw basins of dirty water out across the courtyard. The rice she cooked will be enough for supper, but she will resteam it.

11:40   She began to tear vegetable leaves into smaller pieces and wash pots.

11:45   She began to cut up a long English cucumber for a lunch dish and chatted with me about her difficult responsibilities as a family planning official.

11:50   She chopped more vegetables added a bowl of leftover rice on top of the steaming rice, and continued to stoke the fire.

12:00   She chopped vegetables quietly.

12:10   She sautéed vegetables, and hot peppers.

12:15   We began to eat lunch, together with Mrs. Wu's daughter, who had returned from her job to eat lunch at home, and my assistant. We ate four green vegetable dishes and three bowls of rice.[31]

12:35   While we ate, a man came to discuss sharing a load of coal that was to be delivered. The man was Mrs. Wu's brother-in-law, her younger sister's husband.

12:40   She added rice water to the pig slop after giving us some rice water to drink for its nutritional properties. Then she started cleaning up.

12:45   Mrs. Wu started feeding the pigs. She squatted by the door of the pig stall. She fed them by ladling slop into their trough, waiting, and filling the trough again. Then, she closed up the pig stall. Her daughter, wearing white high-heeled shoes and new blue jeans with zippers on the ankles and colored embroidery on the hips, began to wash the lunch dishes.

12:50   Mrs. Wu fed the small pigs next to the latrine. She dumped out their old, unfinished food and swept the stall litter to a side gutter by the latrine and went back to the kitchen for a basin of water to flush it down with. While her daughter washed dishes, Mrs. Wu went back to the pig stall. It was raining. Her daughter read newspapers, while Mrs. Wu went inside, washed her feet, and changed to nicer shoes to get ready to go to town on an errand.

This description shows how fertilizing and watering the garden is integrated with cleaning the latrines and stoking the fire, how tending and gathering vegetables for the family combines with tending and gathering vegetables that will be consumed by the pigs, how cooking for the pigs is followed by cooking for the family, how the family meal is followed by feeding the pigs, and how the family courtyard has pens for pigs, chickens, and turkeys, while bedrooms are also used for storing grain and chaff. These tasks form complex daily routines that are ever changing as vegetables need planting, hoeing, staking, weeding, and picking, and as pigs grow and eat more or are sold or slaughtered. A good farmer integrates the work of tending gardens, feeding pigs, and feeding family in ways that make efficient use of time, space, and resources, with considerable recycling of waste products: chaff from rice and beans, yam stalks, and leftovers, with rice water and family wastes going to the pigs and pig wastes going to the fields. The primary technological im-provement affecting this cycle is the installation of running water in the courtyard. Most of the other tools, the buckets on a pole, the hoe, the large wok, and firewood, are traditional. Coal has replaced firewood for most cook-ing in Lu Village Center, since wood is scarce and coal can be delivered to the house by truck.

According to my 1990 survey, the average family cultivated about 0.4 mu of land for vegetables and raised two to five pigs. All but one household re-ported raising pigs.[32] The garden plots are primarily tended by women and sometimes by retired old men. For pigs, the main work consists of gathering fodder and preparing (often chopping and cooking) food for them. In more than 80 percent of the households, only women gathered the fodder and fed the pigs. In the remaining households, these tasks were performed only by men in roughly half the cases, and shared by both sexes in the other half. Gathering fodder and cooking for pigs on average takes 3.4 hours per day (al-though, as seen above, they may be combined with other tasks). Cleaning pigpens, performed about equally by men and women, is infrequent, takes less time, and shows more variance between households. Usually it amounts to two or three days (or half days) per year or, at most, one-half day every two weeks. Obviously, pigs need to eat every day, but some households are more rigorous than others about cleaning up after them.

In Lu Village, pig production takes place entirely at home, with pens lo-cated in courtyards or nearby sheds. So far not a single household special-izes in large-scale pig farming, although no rule limits the number of pigs households can raise. If a household has two sows that produce large litters, they may temporarily raise up to twenty-five, but when the piglets are weaned, farmers sell off most of them, bringing their total down to seven or less. The small scale is probably due to scarce space and local materials for fodder, and a small local market. Pigs are grown without hired labor. They produce income in subsistence and cash, but consistent with the distribu-tion of land in small plots, they are raised in small pens in a labor-intensive fashion.

Village records for 1988 show that 693 households used or sold a total of 1,091 pigs. Of these, 97 were sold to the state, 441 were sold on the market, and 563 (51 percent) were slaughtered and consumed for subsistence, with 592 mother pigs and immature pigs remaining. This suggests that most households (over 80 percent) annually consumed one whole homegrown pig, while around 75 percent sold a pig as well. These figures are consistent with my survey results.

## Farmer Status: Household Registration as Labor Registration

In contrast to the prerevolutionary view of the labor force, Lu Village women today count in official labor-force reports. Since collectivization in the 1950s, women's administrative status as farmers has become explicit and official. No longer is their work disguised or ignored as family labor. Under the revolutionary agenda, village officials began to count women as part of the labor force when they engaged in collective farming. This accounting practice has continued after the return to household farming in the reform period. There is a certain ambiguity about this status, for in China the term *farmer*, or *nongmin*, also designates residential status, with attributes of class and caste attached to it, along with certain entitlements and obligations (Bossen 1995b; Potter and Potter 1990; Zhou 1996). While women in the early twentieth century were not explicitly recognized as farmers, there is no question that today they are thus considered, counted, and counted upon to produce the village's grain quotas. During the collective period, both women and men were required to work under collective management. Today, most village women and men are still registered and counted as farmers, but having the status of farmer does not necessarily correspond to their actual occupation.

Women and men in Lu Village, like villagers across China, usually report their occupation according to the classification imposed by the government system of household registration. This means that they first describe their occupation in terms of the status of farmer (*nongmin*) or nonfarmer (*fei nongmin*).[33] The registration status (*hukou*) of individuals does not, however, describe the actual division of labor. Farmers registered in a particular village are entitled, as a birthright, to contract a share of village farmland and resources, for which they are obligated to sell certain quantities of grain or other crops to the state at nonmarket prices. Nonfarmers, by contrast, include formal workers in state-run industries, officials, bureaucrats, or teachers in government posts. Through the 1990s they were entitled to government housing and welfare benefits, although they might actually live in a village if they owned a house there, and especially if their spouse or children retained farmer status. My 1990 survey showed that 92 percent of the men and 97 percent of the women age eighteen and over were registered as farmers. More men than women achieved the coveted status of nonfarmer (8 percent of men versus 3 percent of women), which, at least in the collective period, conferred the privileges and benefits of the "iron rice bowl," employment security.[34] The complexities of registration and inheritance are examined in chapter 7.

### Declining Farmwork: Men First

Some Lu Village men and women of *nongmin* status practice other occupations, sometimes continuing to help with farmwork. Comparing residential status with actual occupations classified as farming, part farming, and nonfarming in 1990, again shows more men than women engaged in informal nonfarm activities (table 4.8). This pattern was evident in the 1930s, although women at that time were not considered farmers. Similar patterns of men disproportionately leaving farmwork have been reported widely across China since the reforms (Bossen 1992, 1994a; Huang 1990; Wolf 1985; Woon 1990). Lu Village women, like rural Chinese women in general, are more likely to stay in the village and labor on the family plots.

The Chinese system of keeping and changing residence at marriage may produce underestimates of village women's access to nonfarm jobs over time. Sons who gain access to urban employment before or after marriage may maintain their residence in Lu Village (often because they inherited a house or house plot), but Lu Village daughters who gain urban employment are likely to transfer[35] their official residence away from Lu Village (and thus out of my data universe) after marriage, particularly if their husband has housing in town. Women who already have state sector employment or urban occupations are unlikely to transfer their registration to a rural place such as Lu Village after marriage, even if their husband has inheritance rights there. Thus the incoming wives most likely to obtain official residence in Lu Village are those with farm registration. In other words, outgoing daughters and in-coming wives might both be practicing marriage strategies that move them closer to large urban centers, and access to nonfarm jobs.[36] However, the wives coming into Lu Village generally remain within the farmer classification.

Within Lu Village, women are still the majority of the active farm labor force, but like men, they are looking to the market for alternatives. In 1990, 63 percent of the men and 84 percent of the women farmed as their main occupation. By 1997, only 20 percent of the men and 64 percent of the women were primarily farmers. Significant numbers of women had moved into the nonfarming and part-farming categories, and many more men had moved completely out of farming (table 4.8). From 1938 to 1990, the proportion of

**Table 4.8.  Lu Village: Percent in Farm and Nonfarm Work, 1938, 1990, and 1997**

|  | 1938 | | 1990 | | 1997 | |
|---|---|---|---|---|---|---|
|  | *Male* | *Female* | *Male* | *Female* | *Male* | *Female* |
| Primarily farm | 74 | 86 | 63 | 84 | 20 | 64 |
| Part farm | 23 | 12 | 19 | 5 | 21 | 13 |
| Nonfarm | 3 | 2 | 18 | 11 | 58 | 23 |
| Total | 100 | 100 | 100 | 100 | 100 | 100 |
|  | (n = 121) | (n = 121) | (n = 131) | (n = 132) | (n = 90) | (n = 94) |

*Sources:* Fei and Zhang (1945); 1990 random sample of eighty-six househlds; and 1997 random sample of fifty households. Totals exclude unknown, retired, disabled, and students.

women farmers changed little, but the proportion of men working off farm rose. But in the 1990s, Lu Village men continued to leave farming, so that only 20 percent were still primarily farmers in 1997. Women were also leaving farmwork, though more slowly. Not surprisingly, opportunities to leave farming were best for those in the center as opposed to the hamlets. Just under a third of individuals from the center were primarily farmers in 1997, as opposed to three-fifths for the hamlets.[37]

Lu Village conforms to the global trend of a declining proportion of labor in agriculture.[38] The exodus from agriculture is influenced by changes in farm productivity and income as well as opportunities to earn cash in other sectors. What is the relationship between gender and farm productivity in Lu Village? Has farm productivity increased over time? Do women have access to the more productive sectors of the economy?

## Changes in Farm Productivity, 1938 to the 1990s

Changes in farm productivity can be measured in various ways. Here we are interested in the productivity of land and of labor. The productivity of land increases when the amount of grain produced on a given amount of land increases. Rice and broad beans, the main crops in Lu Village in 1938, were still the main summer and winter crops in the 1990s, so we can compare changes in output per mu. The productivity of labor increases when the amount of grain produced for each day of labor has increased. (Like Fei, I have not estimated the productivity of labor or of land in family vegetable plots due to the variety of crops and consumption patterns.)

Despite Fei's efforts to provide detailed information on rice output, the inconsistencies in his reporting and his use of different measures and equivalencies create serious headaches for anyone who works with his figures (see Arkush 1981:299). Without claiming these are finely tuned measures, his estimates roughly suggest the direction and magnitude of change.

Fei estimated the total village rice output by extrapolating from key informants' estimates of yields for different land categories and multiplying by the amount of land in each category. He thus calculated that in 1938 Lu Village produced 21,000 *piculs* of unhusked rice. From the information given, I calculate that the yield of unhusked rice in 1938 was approximately 420 kilograms per mu. Anyone interested in the rather tortuous path I followed in converting output in *piculs* per gong to kilograms per mu is invited to read Bossen (n.d.). Using Fei's labor estimates, each mu required approximately forty-one days of labor for growing rice (twenty-two male plus nineteen female). Dividing output per mu by labor days per mu, we find that each labor day produced roughly ten kilograms of unhusked rice.

Comparing 1938 with subsequent years (table 4.9) shows that productivity of land fluctuated with China's political conditions, dropping during the revolution and the Great Leap Forward and improving little until the 1990s. The productivity of labor (unmeasured between 1938 and 1990) had increased dramatically by 1990 and was roughly 3.6 times greater than in 1938, largely due to the technological changes mentioned above. Of course, certain tasks, specifically rice transplanting and harvesting, still require a great many laborers all at once. With present technology, one could not expect one-fourth as many people to complete these tasks fast enough to complete the work on time. Today, as in the past, some farmers hire laborers from the more remote villages (who lack comparable access to nonfarming jobs) to transplant and harvest for them. Others pursue full-time nonfarm jobs as they become available and take two weeks off to go home and help with the planting and harvesting during the busy season. Thus, if scheduling problems can be solved, Lu Village families allow more members to seek nonfarm work. So far the opportunity to leave has been disproportionately available to men.

The increased productivity of Lu Village farm labor should make farming a desirable occupation. But the economic rewards to higher productivity are offset by official limits on the amount of land a family can farm. Land allocation on a per capita basis means that, with village population growth, each household receives less land than they farmed in the past. Today, farmers have only half as much land per capita as in 1938. Without a market allowing families to buy and sell land, farmers are, in a sense, limited to a part-time job with no prospect for turning it into a full-time profession. Farming, which has long been portrayed as a masculine occupation, is increasingly rejected by rural men as they seek more lucrative opportunities elsewhere. Moreover, what was once portrayed as a path to the liberation of rural Chinese women is increasingly perceived by younger women as a dead end and treated as a last resort.

**Table 4.9.   Lu Village Rice Production**

**a.  Output per Mu and per Person, by Year**

| Year | Area (mu) | Output kgs/mu | Population | Output per person |
|---|---|---|---|---|
| 1938[a] | 960 | 420 | 694 | 581 |
| 1938 | 1,120 | 459 | 611 | 841 |
| 1949 | 964 | 363 | 883 | 397 |
| 1952 | 1,390 | 403 | 776 | 722 |
| 1953 | 1,416 | 455 | 776 | 830 |
| 1958 (GLF) | 1,091 | 380 | 636 | 652 |
| 1959 (GLF) | 1,192 | 248 | 669 | 442 |
| 1960 (GLF) | 1,177 | 316 | 692 | 537 |
| 1961 (GLF) | 1,133 | 284 | 689 | 467 |
| 1962 (GLF) | 1,204 | 314 | 729 | 519 |
| 1978 | 1,245 | 476 | 1,127 | 476 |
| 1980 | 1,266 | 487 | 1,122 | 550 |
| 1984[b] | 2,650 | 426 | 2,850 | 396 |
| 1988 | 2,507 | 492 | 2,943 | 419 |
| 1992 | 2,522 | 569 | 2,983 | 481 |
| 1997 est. | 2,530 | 738 | 3,025 | 617 |

**b.  Labor Days per Mu and Output per Day by Year**

| Year | Rice labor days/mu[c] | Output kgs/labor day |
|---|---|---|
| 1938 | 41 | 10 |
| 1986 | 16 | 29 |
| 1988 | 16 | 31 |
| 1992 | 16 | 36 |

*Sources:* Fei and Zhang (1945:50–51; 1990:62–72, 93), Arkush (1981:299). Qian, Shi, and Du (1995:61–63), for years 1949–1982, refer to only six teams, approximating Lu Village of 1938.

*Note:* For Village annual reports for 1984–1997, output is unhusked rice, converted (from *shijin*, units of 1.1 pounds) to kilograms. "GLF" refers to the years of the Great Leap Forward, when output dropped. Rice output is rounded to 1000 kgs. Village population figures vary slightly from other tables, as population is calculated at different times for production reports and for demography reports. Village production reports separate grain production by spring and fall harvests. Most of the fall harvest is rice. For 1984, I used total fall grain production for rice, since I was not given separate rice output.

[a]There are two entries for 1938. The first is based on my calculations and the second on those of Qian, Shi, and Du (1995). The two calculations are similar for output per mu, but differ notably for output per person. There are three reasons for differences between my figures and theirs:

1. For cultivated land (2,800 gong) they included 400 gong rented *outside the village*. I used 2,400 gong (960 mu), the amount the villagers owned (Fei and Zhang 1945:50) and managed *within* the village (50).
2. For rice output (of 841 kgs) per person they used a low figure (611) for population, the number Fei reported for 1939 *after* many men were conscripted. Using the 1938 population (698) gives 741 kgs per person for 1,120 mu.
3. For rice output, they assumed all land cultivated was "good" land instead of weighting it by quality as I did.

[b]For 1984 and after, village area and population include hamlets and center teams.

[c]1986–1992 estimates of rice labor days/mu are based on a 1990 survey (n = 82). Households averaged 4.5 mu in rice, and contributed seventy-one days of labor for an average of sixteen days per mu. For beans, they averaged 22 labor days for 2.8 mu, or 8 labor days per mu. (The total labor for rice was thirty-one days of male and forty days of female labor. Bean output used 9.8 male and 12.2 female labor days. The average land in beans for seventy-four households was 2.8 mu.)

*Informal migrant farm labor market (1999). At a central intersection in Lufeng, farmworkers from other areas wait to be hired, often in groups, to harvest in nearby farm communities, including those of Lu Village.*

## Village and State in Farm Management: Agricultural Production in the 1990s

Like village officials across China, those in Lu Village, operating as overseers, make systematic biannual reports on agricultural production to the county after each major harvest. These reports, part of a national rural bookkeeping system, show the continuing importance of rice and bean production, with roughly 96 percent of the cultivated land used to grow rice in summer. Nearly all the land is double cropped with beans, wheat, and barley grown in winter, while cash crops include canola oil seed and vegetables (see table 4.6). In 1992, all fifteen teams raised their rice production above 500 kgs per mu, for an average of 569 kgs per mu. The 1997 harvest report showed a tremendous increase in output, with all but one team over 700 kgs per mu and another at 800 kgs per mu. However, these numbers should be viewed cautiously.

An official commented on the declining importance attached to agriculture and explained that three officials (the village party secretary, director, and team accountant) now estimate rather than measure output, because "today the agricultural output figures are given no importance." With land contracted to households, officials no longer manage production and only make general estimates based on land quantity. Each year, they examine the fields to get a clear idea of each crop's condition and, adjusting by adding or subtracting, they calculate overall production. Their annual reports all use this as the main method. (Estimates dropped two digits of precision, making round numbers especially obvious, in the 1997 grain report.) It is unclear, therefore, whether official reports reflect *real* increases in productivity or respond to other motives for reporting high yields.

Even so, technological changes increasing productivity have diffused throughout the population. Village leadership deserves some credit for this (see chapter 9), as do market forces and increased flows of information that occur when farmers assemble in marketplaces. Yet with the state still playing a major role in agricultural planning and pricing, China's farming households resemble tenant farmers with limited scope for management and profit. What farmers produce is still largely decided by the state and mediated by the local village administration through production contracts. Farmers with irrigated land must grow rice as a condition for using the land. Household contracts stipulate that farmers sell a fixed quantity of rice or other specific crops to the state at set prices. They cannot independently decide to grow vegetables for a higher price or trade rice land for some other kind. In turn, the village government organizes the flooding of all the fields, the investments in irrigation maintenance, and also sells agricultural inputs such as seeds, fertilizers, and pesticides at prices set by the state. Carter et al. (1996:20) observe that the national government still promotes grain production while prohibiting grain price increases, thereby favoring the industrial sector over agriculture. In Yunnan, because tobacco has proved very lucrative for the provincial government, Lu Village officials have been pressured to get villagers to raise more tobacco, even though much of the land is not suitable. Villagers have opposed tobacco because it requires much more labor than rice, and the state pays low prices for poor quality tobacco.

In the reform period, China's system of managing village economies has succeeded in increasing production and labor productivity compared to the collective period. Farmers can reap some of the benefits of improved output by selling part of what they produce in the market for higher prices and allocating their labor as they think best. Unlike the collective period, they do not have to show up for work even if there is little work to do. Families have flexibility in deciding their own gender division of labor. The land allocation system, however, prevents households from buying and selling farmland (or use rights to such land), and leaves them with few agricultural outlets for their surplus labor. The system limits many farmers to part-time farming on small plots. To increase their standard of living, Lu Village men and women, like rural populations across China, increasingly look to nonagricultural opportunities.

## NONAGRICULTURAL OCCUPATIONS

One of the great differences between agriculture and commerce is that agriculture never helps a man to expand his wealth quickly but acts rather as a stabilizing factor in rural economics. (Fei and Zhang 1945:289)

Our revised image of Lu Village women's prerevolutionary work as farmers and the continuities in the gender division of labor recommend a careful review of the historical changes and continuities in nonagricultural work as well. How did men and women in prerevolutionary times obtain cash and meet their needs for other goods and services? Did women experience special disadvantages in the market place? To what extent were men and women "earthbound" then and how did their opportunities change in the 1990s? Have gender differences persisted into the present?

### A Village with Inns and Outs in 1938

Fei produced a list of nonagricultural occupations in 1938, which I have modified in table 4.10 to include gender. His original list ignored gender, but his text and terminology sometimes indicated female participation. Interviewing male informants, Fei probably missed some nonagricultural occupations practiced by women. He did not explain whether nonagricultural occupations were individual specialties or household activities performed by several individuals. For instance, "innkeeper," the most common occupation listed, probably included labor by both sexes: providing bed and board for travelers, stabling and feeding horses, and managing income and expenses. To compare men and women, I generated information regarding individuals from Fei's account. Fortunately, Fei drops many hints throughout his text. Like latter-day harvesters, we glean what we can.

First, and most unambiguously, the witch (or seeress, *wupo*) was a woman. This woman, the subject of chapter 5, earned a living and supported her family by performing divinations and a variety of services in the realm of healing, ritual, and advice. Second, it is reasonable to assume that most innkeepers were running a business that involved significant amounts of women's work, since providing room and board were essentially extensions of housework, while providing fodder for pack animals (mules and horses) could involve either sex. Apart from the more menial tasks, for which hired labor or servants (of either sex) could be employed, innkeeping probably involved considerable managerial work for senior women in these households, overseeing food supplies, money, and any servants. Elderly women interviewed in 1996 recalled their own work at the inns in their youth, some as family servants.[39] Women might also have been partners or participants in some

**Table 4.10.   Lu Village Nonfarm Occupations, 1938–1939**

| Occupation | Households (n = 120) (%) | Individuals' estimated participation[a] Men | Women |
|---|---|---|---|
| Innkeeper | 7 | 9 | 9 |
| Grocer[a] | 2 | 2 | 3 |
| Bean-curd maker[a] | 2 | 3 | 3 |
| Carpenter | 2 | 3 | |
| Cold-jelly peddler[b] | 2 | 2 | |
| Blacksmith | 2 | 2 | |
| Druggist and medicine man[b] | 1 | 1 | |
| Medicine man[b] | 1 | 1 | |
| Mason | 1 | 1 | |
| Witch[a,c] | 1 | | 1 |
| Daoist priest | 1 | 1 | |
| Fortune-teller[a] | 1 | 1 | |
| Butcher | 1 | 1 | |
| Wine maker[b] | 1 | 1 | |
| Schoolteacher | 1 | 1 | |
| Cotton comber | 1 | 1 | 1 |
| Total | 26 | 30 | 17 |

*Source:* Adapted from Fei and Zhang (1945:45, table 6). Lu Village then had 120 households, with 32, or 27 percent (difference is due to rounding), represented in his table.

[a]The four households not farming were: one grocer, one bean-curd maker, the witch, and the fortune-teller (Fei and Zhang 1945:45). The fortune-teller was a single male. All others combined farming with the listed activity.

[b]The cold-jelly peddler, wine maker, and medical specialists may also have been women or included women in the household activity. One grocer was explicitly a widow (46).

[c]The Chinese version of *Earthbound China (Yunnan San Cun)* identified the witch as *nuwu.*

household enterprises, such as making and selling bean curd, running a grocery store, making wine, or combing cotton. Various elderly women recalled that they helped make bean curd or bean noodles, and that their mothers operated stores before the revolution.

## Seasonal and Sideline Occupations: Transport and Marketing

In my earlier classification of occupations as primarily farming, part farming, and nonfarming in 1939 (see table 4.8), I omitted intermittent economic activities mentioned by Fei. In Yunnan's mountainous terrain, there was great demand for overland transport. Fei left an unforgettable image of human toil in those times: "We saw, stumbling along the roughly paved paths of the village, lines of heavily laden coolies with lean, hungry faces and in worn, ragged clothing. On their backs they carried huge blocks of salt, burdens beneath which their bodies were bent almost double. . . . These people were the salt carriers, whose job it was to transport salt on their backs from the well to the district town—more than a full day's walk" (Fei and Zhang 1945:41).

Lu Village women as well as men took up the burdens of long-distance and local transport. Women carried salt, coal, charcoal, and firewood up and down the hilly paths, transporting it on foot between source and town markets. This laborious, backbreaking occupation was seasonal, undertaken primarily by the very poor when there was no farmwork. Elderly women interviewed in the 1990s confirmed that they worked as porters in their youth. This was not easily undertaken by women with bound feet, yet as we have seen in chapter 3, such women often performed work where bound feet would have been a disadvantage. Perhaps this speaks to the power of economic need when economic fortunes change. Then again, few *young* women in Lu Village had bound feet in the late 1930s.[40] Though work as a porter was not a coveted occupation, it shows that village women were far from housebound or restricted to their courtyards. Porters were transport workers, using their legs and backs to carry loads over Yunnan's difficult, mountainous terrain. Undoubtedly, men greatly outnumbered women, particularly on long caravans that traveled for several weeks. Unfortunately, Fei did not indicate how many women porters he saw, or how much time they worked as porters in addition to farming. From his account and my own interviews, I merely know that there were more than a few women.

Other women, probably those who were older and wealthier, traded in local markets (Fei and Zhang 1945:110). To earn cash or upkeep, women performed varied activities that Fei noted only in passing. These included raising and selling pigs, buying goods in one market and reselling in another, making and selling handicrafts, and working as servants. Finally, as seen in chapter 3, making cloth and straw shoes and sewing and embroidering clothing were alternatives that landless widows used to support themselves and their children.

The freedom of women to come and go outside the home was clearly associated with occupations such as transport, marketing, and farmwork. This might be perceived as positive in our current age, but Fei clearly felt that it was men who benefited most from the gender division of labor for they enjoyed the leisure of *not* going out to perform manual labor, and of sitting at the tea house and playing music, while women worked in the fields. Fei's impression of leisured men and laboring women applied to the wealthier households. Unfortunately, his generalization was supported only by anecdotes rather than systematic records of activity by sex and age.

## The Wartime Male Labor Exodus

A portrait of Lu Village labor in the 1930s would be incomplete without noting that wartime conditions resulted in a heavy loss of adult men from the village between Fei's two visits. "Nineteen men [were] taken in the nine calls for conscripts up to October, 1939," while many others left the village to pursue war-related employment in government or industry, or to take student deferments (Fei and Zhang 1945:62). There was a net loss of fifty-two men in the sixteen to fifty age group between 1938 and 1939. Others found opportunities in road construction. "In 1939, there were 27 villagers working regularly, and 30–40 were working part time, on the construction of the Yunnan-Burma railroad.[41] The high wages paid for such work was making it hard to hire farm workers for harvesting" (63). Of course, it is often assumed that all the construction workers were male, but in Yunnan, women also work(ed) as unskilled laborers in road and building construction.[42]

## Moneylenders and Rent Collectors

Referring to one family in Lu Village, Fei wrote in *Earthbound China*, "We know of one instance in which this man had to borrow money from somebody outside the family while his mother and his wife were both lending money to others. I wondered at the time why women should keep their purses so tightly closed" (Fei and Zhang 1945:111).

Some women made money from money lending.[43] While not conventionally viewed as an "occupation" in the 1930s, providing financial services and taking risks (then often stigmatized as usury), that is, allocating capital, is today recognized as a core economic activity. Not only does it provide income for the lender, but it provides credit to the borrower. Aside from money lending, my interviews with older Lu Village women indicate that women as well as men used to form credit circles, formerly a common social institution and more recently "discovered" by development planners.[44]

Marxist and Christian theorists and moralists have both traditionally despised money lending as profiteering or usury, because money can be accumulated without manual labor. It has gone unnoticed that this bias may have worked against women, particularly widows, since money lending may have been one of the few avenues of economic support that elderly women had, especially if they could not farm on their own and lacked adult (and filial) children. Although money lending and rent collecting have often been condemned as evils of prerevolutionary society, some elderly women in Lu Village seem to have depended on both (Fei and Zhang 1945:77). Abolition of these activities after the revolution deprived elderly women and widows of the right to receive rent for an income or to use their monetary savings and social knowledge (social capital) accumulated through kinship and local networks to risk making loans for a living.[45] In a rural society without pensions, money lending and rent collecting may have kept some of the elderly from neglect and destitution when they became too old for manual labor. During the Maoist period, however, even to have once suggested that money lending, or providing rural credit, could have positive effects was to risk condemnation as a "rightist," an enemy of the revolution.[46]

## Lu Village Nonfarm Occupations in the 1990s: The Call of the City

A common slogan of the reform period is "leave the soil, not the village" (*li di bu li xiang*). This advice expresses official concern about China's huge rural population. Fearing that massive urban migration will create disruption and political volatility, officials have tried to halt the stampede by emphasizing rural industry as an alternative to farmwork in rural areas. The political strategy of creating barriers and alternatives to urban migration has slowed the process, making it more difficult for rural migrants to gain a foothold in large cities without official registration. The exodus from farming takes many forms, including migration to the nearest county towns and market centers, where villagers may have a connection, through kinship, friendship, school, or village ties, to someone already established. It also includes people who commute from homes in the village, with registration unchanged, to jobs in town. This process is "suburbanizing" the villages located near cities, towns, and road intersections. Commuting becomes easier and the perimeters of suburbia expand as more people acquire bicycles or motor scooters, and as horse-cart taxis, motorized taxis, and regular bus service spread. In the past ten years, Lu Village Center has shown signs of suburbanization with respect to Lufeng, whereas the hamlets lag behind.

During two decades of economic reform the revival of markets has brought rapid changes in access to nonagricultural work and to modern technology. These changes point in the direction of significant social transformation, particularly urbanization, in the future. The villagers, especially those in the center, take advantage of nonfarm opportunities whenever they arise. In 1939, there were few chances to work outside of agriculture, but in 1990 and even more in 1997, the proportion of farmers is waning with economic development and technological change. This process affects the hamlets more slowly than the village center, largely because roads to the hamlets are worse.

Nonagricultural employment for villagers now includes industrial and commercial work, increasingly connected with the market town. Agriculture and raising livestock, taken together as two kinds of farmwork, accounted for 63 percent of gross village income in 1992 (table 4.11). Industry, transport, and construction accounted for 34 percent. These records, based on village farming and enterprises, do not include casual labor (*xiaogong*) undertaken outside the community or informal commerce or services. As a result, village

**Table 4.11.   Greater Lu Village Gross Income by Source, 1992**

| Category | % of total income |
|---|---|
| Crops | 42 |
| (of which, grain) | (37) |
| Industry | 23 |
| Livestock | 21 |
| Transport | 8 |
| Construction | 3 |
| Other | 2 |
| Total Village Income (¥3,618,000) | 100 |

*Source:* Village records 1992.

employment records do not always correspond to information from household interviews, which ask about informal work outside the village as well as "official" occupations.

In the collective period, some laborers from Lu Village were sent to work on outside construction projects (especially during the Great Leap Forward) and in mining. Men were usually selected for such work, leaving a local farm labor force that employed more women. In the late 1980s and 1990s, men were still disproportionately working in external construction (see tables 4.13 and 4.14), but increasingly, construction was organized by private entrepreneurs and not by work teams directly under the village or state management.

Women have made inroads into new industrial and independent commercial occupations in which they were not permitted during the closed economy of the collective period. They worked in over a third of the private enterprises (*getihu*) in 1989 (table 4.12), although official village labor force reports did not reflect this (table 4.13). Between 1990 and 1997, my surveys suggest, opportunities for women increased in commerce, industry, health, education, and government (table 4.14).

New nonagricultural wage work opportunities particularly attract young women under twenty-five, who came of age after the reforms began. Young women have worked in factories (the village plastics and town paper factories, usually on temporary contract), commercial employment (working in beauty salons and restaurants), and government jobs (kindergarten teacher, hospital employee, agricultural technician). Occasionally, young women with a poor education work for wages in road construction or sifting sand from the river for construction purposes. In 1990, only two older women held nonfarm jobs; one operated a feed store with her married daughter in another village and another was a team leader who has served for several decades. In 1997, one of the few middle-aged women doing nonfarm work half the year

**Table 4.12. Greater Lu Village Private Enterprise Households (*getihu*), 1989**

| Individual enterprise | Male | Female |
|---|---|---|
| Commerce (*shangye*) | 3 | 2 |
| Butchering (*tu*) | 2 | |
| Processing local foods (*jiagong*), both sexes[a] | 10 | 10 |
| Metal casting (*zhuzao*) | 2 | |
| Carpentry (*muqi*) | 2 | |
| Brick making (*zhuanwa*) | 5 | |
| Blacksmithing (*datie*) | 1 | |
| Cement plank making (*chazhuan*) | 3 | |
| Plastics (*suliao*) | 2 | |
| Peddling (*shangfan*) | 4 | |
| Repair (*xiuli*) | 6 | |
| Food and beverages (*yinshi*) | 7 | |
| Transport (*qi che*) | 2 | |
| Making bean curd (*doufu*) | | 15 |
| Total private entrepreneurs | 49 | 27 |
| Total households (n = 66) | | |
| Employees (plastic factory) (n = 30) | 6 | 24 |

*Source:* Village director, July 10, 1989.

[a]Ten food-processing households (milling rice, making noodles, drying mushrooms) are jointly managed by men and women. The director amended the list to include making bean curd, specifically done by women in fifteen households. Some figures may be rounded estimates, particularly those ending in "0" or "5" (e.g., bean-curd makers and food processors).

worked in road construction along with her grown daughter. She was divorced and lacked access to better town jobs that would be compatible with her need to farm half the year. Men had better access to formal and informal industrial and construction jobs, and held a variety of other occupations, such as school cook, manager, accountant, and soldier.

**Table 4.13. Greater Lu Village Official Labor Force, 1988**

| | Percent |
|---|---|
| Males (n = 695) | 51 |
| Females (n = 671) | 49 |
| Agriculture | 85 |
| Industry | 2 |
| Construction | 9 |
| Transportation | 2 |
| Commerce | 0 |
| Government service | 0 |
| Health/education | 1 |
| Management | 0 |
| Outside contract work | 0 |
| Total (n = 1,366) | 100 |

*Source:* Village records. Agricultural labor figures must be estimates: out of thirty entries for both sexes in fifteen teams, twenty-three end in "5" or "0."

Table 4.14.  Lu Village Employment (ages eighteen and over) by Sex, 1990 and 1997

| Employment sector | 1990 Male (%) | 1990 Female (%) | 1997 Male (%) | 1997 Female (%) |
|---|---|---|---|---|
| Nonfarming (total) | 15 | 9 | 53 | 22 |
| Industry | 5 | 2 | 10 | 6 |
| Commerce | 1 | 3 | 7 | 8 |
| Mining | 1 | 1 | 1 | |
| Health and education | 1 | 1 | 3 | 3 |
| Government | 1 | 1 | 6 | 3 |
| Construction | 3 | 1 | 16 | |
| Transportation | 3 | | 10 | 2 |
| Part-time farming plus (total) | 17 | 4 | 18 | 12 |
| Industry | 2 | 0 | 1 | |
| Commerce | 8 | 3 | 7 | 7 |
| Government | 1 | | | |
| Construction | 5 | 1 | 8 | 2 |
| Transportation | | | 2 | |
| Artisan | 1 | | 1 | 2 |
| Farming primary (total) | 53 | 78 | 19 | 62 |
| Other (retired, students, unknown) | 14 | 9 | 9 | 3 |
| Total | 100 (n = 155) | 100 (n = 143) | 100 (n = 97) | 100 (n = 97) |

*Source:* Greater Lu Village surveys, 1990 and 1997. Totals may not add up due to rounding.

*Note:* The 1990 sample includes one soldier and the 1997 sample includes two soldiers as government employees. To make 1997 consistent with 1990 in comparative table 4.8 (which used 1990 n = 263), I excluded the thirty students, retired persons, and unknown listed in table 4.14. The percentages for farm, nonfarm, etc. in table 4.14 also differ from table 4.8 because the denominator excludes students, disabled, etc. This is a reasonable way to compare with Fei, for he does not give such information, and treats each household as if it had one adult male and female unless noted otherwise.

*Villagers and outsiders hired at the plastic (garbage) recycling factory in 1989 sorted and washed plastic garbage to be remolded for new products. Several years later, the factory had switched from plastics to other products.*

*Lu Village women selling wild mushrooms in the market town in Lufeng.*

## Rural Industry

Factory employment has grown in the township and the village, expanding the range of opportunities for both sexes. By the 1990s, three small, privately owned factories—a plastics factory, a factory producing metal pots, and a furniture factory—had been established in Lu Village. These employed a mixture of local labor and specialists from outside the region and sold their products outside the community. While the plastics factory had male and female workers, the metal pot and wood furniture factory mainly employed male workers. Since such small enterprises appear, change, and disappear rapidly, it is risky to describe their employees as if there were a stable gender composition.[47] In the county town, a range of other factories, such as a state-run steel factory, an electric battery factory, a mineral water factory, and a scissors factory, provided employment to men and women. By 1999, the state steel factory had closed and some of its employees, with small pensions, were starting small businesses in town. (In 2001 it reopened with fewer workers.)

*A young girl tends the family store, while her mother and father harvest rice.*

Cottage industry in textiles has almost disappeared. While women can still be seen making cloth shoes, knitting sweaters, or sewing outfits at home, no one in the village makes these goods commercially. More and more people buy ready-to-wear shoes and clothes. Plastic sandals, leather shoes, pastel dresses and blouses for women, and white shirts and leather jackets for men are among the many items that increasingly fashion-conscious villagers buy in the town.

## Transport and Commerce

To reach outside markets, village businesses have had to invest in transportation and sales outlets in town. In each case, private owners have brought family members into the business. The son and daughters of two entrepreneurs have worked in the transport and commercial sides of the businesses, rather than in manufacturing. Two daughters have joined a select group of villagers with driver's licenses and drive trucks or minivans to transport goods for the factories. Driver's licenses are expensive in China and in the mid-1990s required about ¥5,000 (U.S.$1,000) for a year of training. In 1996, one daughter had made over fifty trips to Kunming, one hundred kilometers away, and had obviously become very knowledgeable about the "big city." Daughters have also helped mind the family stores in town, again expanding their horizons beyond the village. At marriage, even if they do not inherit land (one entrepreneurial family returned their land to the village because they no longer wanted to farm), they already

*A Lu Village woman drives her horse taxi between Lufeng and Lu Village.*

have valuable skills and experience. It remains to be seen how dowries and in-heritance will be handled for these daughters, but their fathers seem willing to invest in them. In 1999, I learned that a daughter of one successful entrepreneur married at home, with her husband joining her father's enterprise. Of course, these young women are truly exceptional. By chance, one of the major entre-preneurs has only daughters, and the other has several daughters and only one

*A young Lu Village woman with a driver's license drives this minivan for her parents' busi-ness, making trips to Kunming.*

son. Nonetheless, the ability of daughters of the wealthier households to work in long-distance minivan transport challenged gender stereotypes.

The role of Lu Village women in transportation has also expanded for the less privileged. In 1990, the transportation between highway and market town was mainly by horse cab, and the drivers were all men. By 1993, a number of women horse-cab drivers were plying the routes between highway, market town, and Lu Village. By 1996, several young Lu Village women were among those driving these local horse cabs. One, a widow in her thirties with several children to support, invested in the cab as a more lucrative alternative to farming. Thus, Lu Village women, with the revival of a market economy, have also been reviving their prerevolutionary role in transportation. For women and men in transport, the shift from carrying heavy loads on their backs and shoulders to driving horse carts and minivans is dramatic testimony to an increasing standard of living.

Commercial enterprises in the nearby town also offer a growing variety of opportunities for young women, now that bicycles have become commonplace. Since most young women now know how to ride bicycles, and most own them (which was not true in the 1980s), they can live at home in the village and commute to jobs in town. They work in a variety of stores, beauty salons, and offices. Recently, one young high school graduate got a job in a word-processing and photocopy shop in town, one of about a dozen that opened in the late 1990s. She has learned, on the job, to use the computer. This seems, to my eyes, truly revolutionary. I suspect it will not be a decade before many homes in town, and then village, invest in computers. After all, most families now have televisions, stereos, and bicycles.

The transition from heavy dependence on agriculture to increasing reliance on urban industrial and commercial employment is reflected in higher standards of living since the reforms. Village records show that cash incomes rose in the 1980s, although this is overstated due to inflation (see table 4.15). Increased wealth is also reflected in declining household size, from 4.8 to 4.2

**Table 4.15.  Changes in Lu Village Income, 1980s**

|  | *1984* | *1985* | *1986* | *1987* | *1988* |
|---|---|---|---|---|---|
| Households | 594 | 628 | 634 | 650 | 693 |
| Population | 2,850 | 2,865 | 2,882 | 2,912 | 2,943 |
| Persons per household | 4.8 | 4.6 | 4.5 | 4.5 | 4.2 |
| Avg. food grain per person (kgs) | 360 | 389 | 396 | 445 | 409 |
| Avg. annual income per person (yuan) | 258 | 327 | 423 | 473 | 647 |
| Laborers | 1,328 | 1,275 | 1,314 | 1,333 | 1,366 |
| Avg. annual income per laborer | 554 | 735 | 934 | 1,033 | 1,394 |

*Source:* Village director, July 10, 1989.

Table 4.16.    Lu Village Sources of Household Income, 1990

| Income Source | | Number of Households | Average Annual Income/Household (yuan) |
|---|---|---|---|
| Crop sales (75% rice)[a] | | 81 | 993 |
| Livestock sales (92% pigs)[a] | | 81 | 895 |
| Industrial work | male | 20 | 1,177 |
| | female | 4 | 1,105 |
| Handicrafts | male | 4 | 263 |
| | female | 0 | 0 |
| Construction | male | 23 | 643 |
| | female | 2 | 225 |
| Sidelines | male | 12 | 534 |
| | female | 6 | 503 |
| Trade | male | 6 | 1,373 |
| | female | 5 | 578 |
| Transport | male | 4 | 415 |
| | female | 0 | 0 |
| Government wage | male | 8 | 1,402 |
| | female | 1 | 120 |
| Subsidies | male | 4 | 1,723 |
| | female | 1 | 360 |
| Total | | 82 | 2,902 |

Source: 1990 survey. Numbers refer to households reporting that source of income in 1990.

[a]Crop sales are roughly 75% from rice, with the remainder from beans, wheat, and vegetables. Livestock sales are roughly 92% from pigs, using gross income from pig sales. Subtracting pig purchase price (highly variable as, often, households breed their own sow) reduces average household income slightly.

persons per household in the first five years after land was redistributed, as families began to build new houses, allowing the younger generation to separate earlier. In 1992, roughly 60 percent of officially reported gross village income came from farming (grain and livestock, see table 4.11). My 1990 survey similarly showed that household incomes from grain and livestock sales accounted for around 56 percent of average household income (table 4.16), with nonfarm sources of income gaining importance.

## The Child Care Dilemma and Women's Work: The 1930s

Fei did not seem particularly intrigued by the tragedy of high infant and child mortality in Lu Village, and did not discuss child care as a form of women's work. But he was struck by the declining labor supply and depopulation in 1938–1939 as a result both of male emigration and an excess of deaths over births. From spring 1938 to autumn 1939, a period of eighteen months, "there were 26 deaths but only ten births. The ten births were balanced by a like number of infant deaths" (Fei and Zhang 1945:62).[48] High infant mortality may have been due, in part, to the unusual economic difficulties associated with wartime and, in particular, the removal of healthy men from the village through military conscription. Although disease was always a danger, we can also imagine that women, faced with the need to make up for the loss of adult male labor, might have accomplished additional fieldwork by reducing time and effort spent tending their children. Fei did not explicitly consider this when he calculated that women might be able to make up for the loss of male labor in activities such as fertilizing fields, which overlaps with the period of transplanting (40).

Even when there is a marked division of labor by sex, the nature of women's work cannot always be assumed to be compatible with child care. In Fei's time, when infant and child mortality were common, it was probably among the poorest tenant and landless households, where women worked the most, that child mortality was highest. Reporting on two poor, landless households (D and E), Fei described their ramshackle housing and patched clothing, and noted "it is not surprising that, although each family had produced six or seven children, *only one* was alive at the time we were in the village" (Fei and Zhang 1945:94).

In contrast, landowning households A and B, wealthy enough to farm with hired labor, together had *seven* surviving children. Although Fei maintained that *all* women worked in the fields, there must have been differences in intensity and types of work. The family situations in the two wealthier households, A and B, had two adult women (mothers and daughters-in-law) in the household, whereas the women in D and E did not have such help. Fei estimated that the wife in household E worked for wages two hundred days per year, presumably in agriculture (86, 94). The differing work burdens in farming in these four households may well have affected the differential survival of their children. It is likely that children in poor households suffered more often, not only from disease and lack of money for medical treatment, but also from longer periods without feeding and from being left unattended, perhaps locked up at home, where they were more prone to fatal accidents.[49]

## Revolution and Reform Effects on Child Care

How had the dilemma of protecting children and conducting work changed at close of the century? First, infant mortality was now very low, and nearly all women could expect to raise the children they bore to adulthood. The widespread use (and overuse) of antibiotics after the revolution meant that very few babies and children died of illness. At the same time, the family planning policy (see chapter 8) has meant that women have fewer children to care for and, thus, have more time to give each child. Since the early 1980s, each woman has been allowed to have only two children, spaced at least four years apart. However, no major social structural or institutional change has resolved the dilemma of combining child care and work, whether farming or off-farm work, by women. The stories of two women, mother and daughter, illustrate how this problem has been and still is a source of painful choices for women and their families in the revolution and reform years. I summarize aspects of their child-care difficulties here, and resume their narrative in chapter 6, on wealth and poverty.

The first story took place in the 1970s (during the Cultural Revolution). Mrs. Shui described her experience when she had a number of small children and was working as agricultural production team leader in charge of one of the women's work teams in the village. In her husband's family, she had no help from her mother-in-law, for her mother-in-law herself was an invalid. A capable, hard worker, Mrs. Shui was exhausted by the long hours at work and her duties at home with two small children. She asked her husband to substitute for her in calling together the women's team. He did so in order to spare her more work. In the politically charged days of the cultural revolution, this was interpreted as "feudal" behavior, trying to seize power by taking over the women's production team. As a result, he was publicly "struggled against" (shouted at, poked, and humiliated for hours at meetings each evening). Severely shaken and defenseless, he returned home in despair and set off in the night to commit suicide. Mrs. Shui followed him and persuaded him not to abandon her and the children.

This example supports contrasting interpretations of male protectiveness toward wife and children, and of male domination by replacing women in non-domestic jobs. Yet in the context where rural women predominantly breast-fed their babies for at least a year, and therefore needed to be close to them, and of women who lacked alternate child-care arrangements, his actions seem sympathetic. Since this community had no child-care system and since men were also required to work, women relied on mothers-in-law for baby-sitting. If the parents-in-law were dependents themselves (as in Mrs. Shui's case), a woman was too heavily burdened with taking care of elders and children to be able to manage. Women team leaders confided to me that they were always expected to do the hardest work, to try harder and work longer, in order to demonstrate their political commitment and to inspire others. Mrs. Shui faced this situation and found the burdens of team leadership and family care overwhelming.

The second story is from the 1990s (during the reform). A generation later, Mrs. Shui's daughter, Mang, experienced a similar predicament in managing work and children. When I met her in 1990, Mang, one of the better-educated young women, had a two-year-old son and was employed as an agricultural technician for the village. She had married a man in the same village who was employed as an agricultural technician in another village, where he lived during the week. Mang nevertheless lived with her widowed mother-in-law, and her husband returned on weekends. Mang attended meetings and participated actively in village affairs as agricultural technician, often bringing her child with her. Clearly, there was tension between the two women over the distribution of farmwork and child care.

When her son was three or four years old, Mang could not call on her mother-in-law for child care and would sometimes leave her son locked in the house or courtyard alone while she attended to her duties at the team headquarters, about a mile away. Yet after the required interval of four years had passed, she followed the village norm[50] and had a second child, a girl. Thereafter, the tension between the two women led to the unusual step of the mother-in-law leaving and going to live with her married daughter in another village. (People spoke of this in hushed tones.)

This left Mang with no one to help with the farming or child care. In 1996, although her elder son went to school, she still had a toddler at home, and throughout the week no one else was at home to help her with the chores of farming, cooking, and child care. Thus she had no choice but to quit her job as an agricultural technician, greatly disappointed because she clearly aimed for more in life than farming. Although her natal family lived in the same village and prospered in the new, open economy, her own household situation kept her from participating in the modern sector. Mang's mother gave what help she could but was very busy with her son's two small children and with her own household's farming and entrepreneurial activities.

While this is just one case, it represents the classic quandary for young women who have sought nonagricultural jobs but find them significantly more incompatible with child care than farming. Although heavy farming by women in Fei's time may have been associated with high child mortality, today it is not. The labor requirements are lower and medical technology is better. But Mang's child-care dilemma still applies even to farming women. In one of the distant hamlets, I interviewed a woman whose young son had been badly burned on his face and body. Having no mother-in-law, she had locked him in the home while she went with her husband to work in the fields. Her small son had tried to pour boiling water while she was out and badly scalded himself. Despite this accident, she felt she had no choice but to continue working in the fields, leaving her son alone at home.

## Family and Farm at Century's End: Less Binding?

Hill Gates has shown how incompatible women's work and child care can be, particularly for many Chinese women engaged in petty commodity production. She quoted a Chengdu worker who described "locking her young children up when she went to work, and returning every day to a house full of puddles" (Gates 1993:264). She also described the tensions that arise between mothers-in-law and daughters-in-law over child care when women are working in the fields or in outside jobs. In north India, Jeffery et al. (1989) have similarly shown how the family composition of the household (together with or independent of the mother-in-law) has a great impact on women's ability to combine farmwork and child care. Rural communities like Lu Village do not have day-care centers; they just have mothers and mothers-in-law. Women in town, on the other hand, often have access to nursery schools for their children. In Fei's time, heavy farming responsibilities (due to male outmigration) and heavy child-care responsibilities (since women bore more children) probably contributed to high child mortality in Lu Village. Contemporary village women benefit from technological innovations reducing farmwork but find that most forms of off-farm employment are also incompatible with child care. It is difficult to hold employment in the nonagricultural sector unless, like farming, it involves a flexible schedule. There is no question that technological improvements have made women's lives considerably easier, but rural social institutions have not sufficiently changed to resolve the child-care problem. At the same time, however, family planning, as discussed in chapter 8, and formal education have greatly reduced the child-care burden for contemporary young mothers.

While child care continues to impose meaningful constraints on married women as economic agents, the modern economy offers them a greater range of opportunity than they had in the 1930s. One might claim their improved opportunity owes much to the rhetoric of the revolution, which praised women's abilities and brought them out of the house. Conversely, one might claim it follows on the post-reform opening of the market economy, which creates wealth and makes it acceptable for women to participate in new market-oriented activities.

Both arguments are suspect, however. They are based on assumptions about attitudes toward women's work that we cannot, with confidence, affix to Lu Village in the early part of the century. We do not know the early-twentieth-century attitudes toward gender in Lu Village, and whether respectable "femininity" required wealthy women to remain at home. In fact, the lack of any statements pointing in that direction in Fei's study and in the stories of older informants leads me to wonder if the ideal of the homebound woman may have been foreign to this region. What we do know is that, in the 1930s, Lu Village women bore heavy responsibilities for production and child care.

*A child helps at the threshing ground as adults scramble to rake up and cover rice before storm clouds break.*

In agriculture, the gender division of labor of 1990 would not surprise a member of the 1938 community. Similarly, the commuting and seasonal migrations of men and, to a lesser extent, young women to work outside the community continue a pattern that existed before the revolution. Today, however, a greater proportion of these jobs involve some modern technology

*Children play nearby as parents work at the threshing ground.*

and some educational skills, skills which women as well as men are increasingly seeking. Finally, the wealth of the village largely remains in the form of its farmland and houses. Inheritance of land and houses continues in the patrilineal tradition, slightly mitigated by a willingness to include married daughters. Allocation of land to households on a per capita basis offers women a sense of contributing to the quantity of land a household receives, but it does not give them any independent control. Access to land and housing is still bound up in what Hill Gates (1996) would call a "tributary," rather than a capitalist, system. Opportunities for women to accumulate substantial wealth in their own right remain limited, hence marriage and childbearing remain almost obligatory. From these perspectives, the legacy of planned economic changes to the transformation of gender looks relatively minor in Lu Village. At the same time, the growing importance of employment beyond the village for both men and women testifies to the importance of the expanding markets of the reform economy. For many families, the importance of land, at least in small plots, is receding.

## NOTES

1. One hundred and forty *kung* (now written *gong*) are fifty-three *mu*, almost nine acres or 3.5 hectares. Conventionally, 1 mu = ⅙ acres, or .067 hectares. The local term, *gong*, referred both to a quantity of land (that could be worked in one day) and of labor (a day's work). For Fei, 1 mu = 2.6 gong. Today, the conversion used is 1 mu = 2.5 gong. This results in slight discrepancies when using Fei's conversions to mu. I use the 1 gong = 0.38 mu for consistency with conversions in Fei's text, but for the 1990s I use the current standard.

2. Mao Zedong (1990), Fei Xiaotong and Zhang Zhiyi (1945), Xiang Jingyun (1940), and John L. Buck (1937a; 1937b; 1957) examined China's land tenure question during the 1930s.

3. Carter et al. (1996:23–24) analyze land and agricultural reform in China.

4. There were 690 mu in private ownership and 237 mu held collectively (Fei and Zhang 1945:54).

5. The total area cultivated was 2,800 gong, at 2.6 gong per mu.

6. My survey of elderly women showed that before 1949 families had complex patterns of owning and renting out farmland. This remains a touchy subject for interviews, however, since during land reform, landholding information was the basis for classifying and punishing landlords and rich peasants. Most old people, remembering that experience, stated they rented land but denied receiving rent.

7. Many authors state categorically that women in prerevolutionary China had no right to inherit (Potter and Potter 1990:19), yet cases of female inheritance have been documented, with daughters in wealthy families sometimes inheriting lands (Liu Dewei, personal communication) and widows inheriting control over their deceased husband's land, and even selling it (He 1993:26).

8. Greenhalgh (1985) analyzes demography, the family cycle, and class inequality in Taiwan.

9. Qian et al. (1995:52–55) describe land reform changes in Lu Village.

10. These data come from the autumn harvest (mainly rice) of 1992. The total area of cultivated land is slightly less for winter crops (mainly wheat), but the area in village reports of cultivated land changes little from year to year. Village farmland cannot be expanded, since there is no land market, but it can be reduced if the village grants permits to use crop land for construction.

11. In using Fei's data, I convert to units that facilitate comparison. It would be tedious to show how these calculations were performed in each case, so I omit this information unless it involves unusual assumptions. See "Weights and Measures" and the glossary for definitions of the Chinese weights and measures used.

12. The term "layer" highlights continuity with the prerevolutionary land system in which a layer of "subsoil" belonged to one set of owners, often the gentry, who paid taxes to the government, while another layer of "surface soil" rights was in a sense owned by peasants who paid rent and could mortgage their cultivation rights, but who could not readily sell or be displaced from their land.

13. See also Endicott (1989:137) and Zhu (1991:44, 122).

14. Households in certain Henan villages typically have five or more separate plots of land (Bossen 1992), a degree of fragmentation comparable to Henan in the 1930s (Buck 1937a). As in Yunnan, landholdings per householder were larger than today, but yields were considerably smaller.

15. This section draws on Bossen (1991).

16. Varied practices are reported by Endicott (1989:167), Hartford (1985:37), Judd (1994:27), Potter and Potter (1990), Huang (1990:197), Huang (1978), and Carter et al. (1996:24). In my research in Henan and Yunnan, villagers commonly reported contracts lasting five years, with redistributions in 1990 (Bossen 1992) and again in Lu Village in 1995. In July 2001, I learned that policy had changed in Lu Village. In 2000, the year land would have been redistributed if the village had kept to the five-year cycle, there was no redistribution. Landholdings were now fixed "for thirty years," a villager reported.

17. For Huaili, Judd reports the 1984 land distribution was partly per capita and partly based on age and sex, giving one mu to men age eighteen to fifty-five, only one-half mu to women age eighteen to forty-five, and none to those outside these ages. Simon (1994) describes a Zhejiang village where daughters received half as much land as sons, on reasoning that sons would later bring in wives.

18. This is essentially identical to the interpretation of inheritance principles explained by a village cadre in Henan. It is part of official Han culture, but it has not been applied with the same intensity in Yunnan villages I studied.

19. Davin indicates that some provinces introduced family planning regulations that would reward the one-child family with land "equal to that normally given for two children, or where land is short, 1.5 children" (Davin 1985:49). She emphasizes, however, that provincial regulations and benefits promised vary. I did not find such land benefits in the villages I studied in Henan and Yunnan.

20. Zhu Xia reported this information after speaking with village officials in August 1998.

21. The names of parcels of land are all that is recorded about a plot of land in the notebooks; there are no numerical references to its dimensions, other than the total surface

area. Examples of recorded names are Hemp Pear Village, Two Stone Bridge, Big Sluice Gate, Side of the Big Well, Oil House, Central River, and Village End.

22. The revolution was to liberate women by bringing them outside the domestic fortress to participate in productive labor. Thenceforth they would no longer be valued solely for their reproductive and symbolic capacity but would become an integral and equal part of society. This theory has collapsed in two stages. First, in the 1970s critics began to point out that bringing women into the agricultural labor force did not necessarily mitigate gender discrimination, particularly when patrilocal kin groups remained largely intact (Diamond 1975; Johnson 1983; Stacey 1983; Wolf 1985). Second, in the 1990s various scholars have revealed misconceptions about women's work in the prerevolutionary period. Hill Gates (1996), for instance, has argued that women, housebound or not, have always played an important part in the rural economy of China.

23. See, for example, Davin (1975), Wolf (1985), Potter and Potter (1990), and Jacka (1997). Even when they do not specifically cite Buck, many authors repeat generalizations drawn from his surveys. Kate Xiao Zhou states that "although most women in rice-growing areas worked in the fields before 1949, fewer women in the North worked in the fields at that time" (Zhou 1996:27). Potter and Potter, describing "the old 'feudal' order" before Liberation, say only that "poorer women did work in the fields but not as much as they were to do after the Revolution. They spent most of their time at home tending the children, taking care of the household, raising the family's pigs and chickens, and weaving bamboo shrimp traps to earn extra cash" (Potter and Potter 1990:33). Oddly, they do not mention how farmwork in rice was accomplished before the revolution.

24. More recently, Hill Gates's innovative research (1996) on early-twentieth-century women addresses this issue in other parts of China.

25. Boserup (1970) was one of the first to describe the process. Butler describes it in China's Dahe Commune, Hebei Province, at the beginning of the reforms: "most peasants continued to regard agriculture as a dead-end occupation. Thirty years of propaganda glorifying the virtues of field labor seemed not to have altered this view. . . . Men have gradually moved into nonfarm jobs, and women in Dahe now perform 80 percent of all field labor" (Butler 1985:111).

26. Fei's research was conducted during the autumn months: November 15 to December 23, 1938, and August 3 to October 15, 1939 (Arkush 1981:80). Rice is transplanted in spring.

27. Examples of unequal work points are in Davin (1976), Diamond (1975), Judd (1994), the Potters (1990), Stacey (1983), Seybolt (1996), and Wolf (1985).

28. At that time, elections were conducted with a show of hands, not a secret ballot.

29. In 1990, I conducted a broad survey of gender, occupation, and economic activities from a random sample of 86 households in Greater Lu Village.

30. Field notes, June 5, 1991.

31. On this day when my assistant and I ate with Mrs. Wu, the food and quantity were the same as what her husband usually ate when he came home for lunch, thus this work was fairly normal.

32. This is based on eighty-three cases (three households were incomplete for this topic). Village records from 1986 reported 126 mu in vegetable gardens.

33. *Nongmin* can normally transfer registration rights only to other rural villages (as they do at marriage) but not to cities. Many anthropologists translate *nongmin* as "peasant," which conveys subordinated, fixed status rather than entrepreneurial farming. Un-

der Mao, Chinese farmers were more firmly constrained as "peasants" than in the reform period (Bossen 1995; Cohen 1993).

34. The 1990 survey included 155 men and 143 women age eighteen and over. Village farm labor-force records were not based on activity per se, but calculated from the population of official labor age minus those with official nonfarm occupations.

35. Even if they do not succeed in transferring their residence officially, they are likely to lose official status in Lu Village if they marry out, remaining in unofficial, or "black market," status in the town or city where they reside and work, as shown in the section on land rights.

36. Lavely (1991) discusses this marriage strategy with demographic evidence from Sichuan.

37. For Lu Village Center, 32 percent (34/107) were farmers, and for Lu Village Hamlets, 61 percent (52/85) were farmers in the 1997 sample.

38. "The share of agriculture in the total labor force has declined worldwide . . . in all countries, with the median share down from 70 percent in 1950 to 33 percent in 1990" (Mundlak et al. 1997).

39. Harry Franck traveled in caravans across Yunnan in the early 1920s and described women working in the inns (1925:450, 467).

40. Fei described women with bound feet as a normal sight in Lu Village (Fei and Zhang 1945:111). However, interviews with Lu Village women who were adolescents during the 1930s indicate that footbinding had by then stopped in this village, and young women were not having them bound any more at the time of his research.

41. They were probably working on a branch of the railway going northward from Lufeng.

42. Some of the elderly women in my sample reported that women worked on road or railroad construction. At the present, it is not uncommon to see rural women in this area working on road construction crews, although they are a minority. In 1994, I observed women working together with men fixing a road going through a hamlet of Lu Village, and in 1996 I saw women working together with men on a road-building crew just several kilometers south of the main highway (the Burma Road) to Lu Village.

43. Fei wrote of women's commercial activity (Fei and Zhang 1945:48) and of money lending. "A well known moneylender in the town, an old woman, told me that those with money to invest are anxious to lend it because the profits are greater than would be the case if they were to invest in land" (123).

44. Credit circles were common in many Chinese villages (Gates 1996:140). Fei described the financial operations of male members of such circles, noting there were many such circles in Lu Village but not specifying that women also formed them (Fei and Zhang 1945:122). Margery Wolf (1972:223), writing of rural Taiwan, described retired women as "minor financiers, loaning varying sums of money (at good interest) to friends and friends of friends. In many communities the *hue-a* are nearly dominated by women. *Hue-a* are short-term loan associations that meet well the borrowing needs of a community in which everyone knows everyone else and always has." Ironically, current development planners now place considerable emphasis on overcoming the lack of access to credit in rural areas through credit circles, often referring to this as the Grameen bank model. This idea has even returned to China, long after revolution dissolved such groups (Mei Yue, sociologist at Beijing University, personal communication).

45. While I echo Fei's defense of moneylenders in *Peasant Life in China*, he did not consider that this may have been one of the few options open to widows or single women,

where women's ability to purchase land and to farm it independently was severely cur-
tailed.

46. In *Peasant Life in China*, Fei did not denounce landowners and lenders. The sentence, "it is incorrect to condemn landowners and even usurers as wicked persons" (in
which he recognized the demand for rural credit was a need that was not being met by
lending institutions) was used to condemn Fei as a rightist during the 1957 antirightist
campaign (Arkush 1981:96, 264).

47. By 1999, the plastics factory had become a metal smelter, the furniture factory had
closed, and the factory that produced metal pots had switched to simple threshing machines. Village factories were encountering stiff market competition.

48. For sex ratios, Fei's table 3 showed that three boys and seven girls were born, and
four boys and six girls under six died (Fei and Zang 1945: 38), which does not suggest preferential treatment for boys. He did not reveal whether the cause of death was epidemic,
or economic hardship and hunger. Cholera epidemics still swept Yunnan in the 1930s (see
Hsu 1952). Fei mentions malaria and trachoma (1945: 93) in 1939.

49. My life histories in rural Chinese villages suggest that fatal accidents, such as
drowning or falling from high places, were not uncommon. Perhaps when people had
more children, often left supervised by slightly older children, accidental deaths were
more likely to occur.

50. The family planning policy forbids families to have a second child until a four-year
interval has passed. The village norm is to conform closely to the rule and have the second
child immediately when four years are up, if possible. It is rare to find anyone who waited
beyond the minimum period to have her second child or who stopped at one child.

## Chapter Five

# The Wealth of a Gifted Woman: The Shaman of Lu Village

One of the very intriguing, and little noticed, observations Fei Xiaotong made in 1939 was an entry in his table of nonagricultural occupations in Lu Village: *witch*.[1] This occupation, along with those of the Daoist priest, the fortune-teller, and the medicine man, falls outside the usual conceptions of "productive activity," which so captured intellectuals in the early part of the twentieth century. It can be seen as one of those artful specialties that are secretive and include variable mixtures of healing, counseling, chicanery, and bluff, but no measurable product. In Fei's discussion of family incomes, I was immediately struck by two conditions surrounding this "witch." First, she held the only nonagricultural occupation listed, which clearly indicated that the gender of the specialist was female; therefore she must have exercised a degree of economic independence by practicing an occupation in her own right. Second, and most important, Fei described the witch's occupation as "the *top profession*, from the standpoint of *income*" (Fei and Zhang 1945:46, emphasis added). For someone who had combed early ethnographies for specific information on what women did, this was an interesting glimpse of nonstereotypic behavior. But what was most surprising was that an independent female occupation should be described as the most lucrative at that time. Was it really the most lucrative? If so, how did this come to be, given all the impediments to female economic success that pervade the literature on prerevolutionary women?

This chapter is devoted to the subject of the witch, whom Fei also called a seeress, and my efforts to reconstruct her position and history. This individual woman's story merits a separate chapter for several reasons. One is that her story is a fascinating one, an exceptional case that illustrates many of the historical themes of this book. Another reason is that it is a special opportunity to trace the fortunes, over time, of a woman perceived as wealthy and powerful by Fei and to learn how her life unfolded afterward, reaching an age that villagers claimed was over one hundred. Although I never had the opportunity to meet her, I have sought out information about her from a variety of sources. I have tried to preserve some of the flavor of the various contexts in which my information was obtained, for the passage of time and different degrees of familiarity, education, generation, and politics have much to do with the way she is remembered. Her story, as it illustrates shifting perceptions, is a humbling reminder to anthropologists that our sources are often partial and approximate. Finally, this individual case allows me to portray some aspects of the present in my search to understand the past. In particular, it shows some of the relationships among the village, outsiders, and the town, as well as the opportunities and risks faced by a woman in commerce.

## WITCHES AND RICHES

In his description, Fei shifted from the pejorative connotations of the label "witch" to the less censorious term "seeress," again making her gender explicit. The seeress

> is a diviner and serves as a medium between her clients and the dead. She is so popular that it is frequently necessary to make an appointment in order to see her. It is said that a high official in Kunming once sent a car for her but that she refused to visit him. Unlike the carpenter, she has a large measure of control over her market. Likewise, although there is a fixed price for each service, she may at any time exact money from a client by making her demands in the name of a spirit. She need never be unemployed, for she may, at will, inform a villager that a certain spirit is calling for him. She supports her husband as well as herself, and both are able to smoke opium lavishly. (Fei and Zhang 1945:46)

This brief description is all Fei told us about the "top profession, from the standpoint of income." Unfortunately, Fei did not provide enough information about the quantity and quality of her income or the nature of her profession to encourage great confidence in his evaluation. We are not told whether she was paid in goods or cash, what the fixed prices were, how many clients she saw a week, or what services she actually provided. In addition, we learn very little about her. Was she a native-born woman or an in-marrying woman? Was she more educated than other women? Where did she learn her trade? How did she practice it? Who were her clientele? Was her clientele, in fact, steady? What was her relationship to her husband, whom she is described as "supporting"? Did she have children? Did she accumulate wealth? Did she purchase land or do any farming? How did she manage to buck the patriarchal system, which channeled lucrative occupations to males? What was the role of opium in her profession?

Perhaps Fei did not tell us more because he disapproved of her profession. In the 1930s, many Chinese intellectuals believed, along with the Communists, that peasants were overly superstitious and subject to exploitation by unscrupulous charlatans who provided dubious services. Present-day anthropologists would tend to take a more lenient (though not necessarily more accurate) view than Fei and would probably place the "seeress" into the category of shaman, portrayed with respect as a kind of traditional healing profession, offering comfort and counseling if not cures.

## FEMALE SHAMANS FROM A WIDER PERSPECTIVE

In 1993, when I revisited Lu Village shortly after reading Margery Wolf's engaging book *A Thrice-Told Tale* (1992), I had a better notion of the tradition of shamanism in Chinese culture and of the kinds of conditions that might induce a woman to attempt to become a shaman, or spirit medium, as well as those that might prevent her from establishing herself. Wolf (1992:107) reviews the literature describing Chinese shamans, or *tang-ki* (as they are called in Taiwan), and analyzes some of the "job qualifications" of shamans, as well as the ways they obtained income:

> A number of scholars have discussed the means by which spirit mediums are identified in China, and they report pretty much the same set of expectations (Elliot 1955, Jordan 1972, Kleinman 1980, Potter 1974). *Tang-ki* come from modest socioeconomic backgrounds; they are preferably illiterate; they must be sincere and honest; they must display clear indications that a god has chosen them to be his or her vehicle. . . . *Tang-ki*, incidentally, must not charge money for their services, but it is assumed that reasonable gifts will be made by grateful clients. The evidence suggests that in rural Taiwan, few *tang-ki* receive enough in contributions to support themselves without another source of income (Gould-Martin 1978:62–63; Jordan 1972:75).

Wolf's description of the variable means of payment is, of course, quite different from the "fixed prices" that Fei claimed were charged in Lu Village, and the levels of income for female shamans do not appear to be as high as those Fei attributed to the seeress.

Margery Wolf's aim was, in part, to understand why a given woman, Mrs. Tan, who began to act and perform like a shaman, was not accepted as such within her community but was dismissed as crazy. "Had Mrs. Tan become a *tang-ki* in Peihotien, we would have pages of field notes on her subsequent career, for having a *tang-ki* in one's village is a source of considerable prestige (Jordan 1972: 81)" (Wolf 1992: 109).

Two aspects of Wolf's case study of Mrs. Tan especially intrigued me in relation to the woman shaman of Lu Village. One was that Mrs. Tan was a thirty-year-old woman facing acute economic stress, probably the kind that could lead to a breakdown, a suicide attempt, or a desperate effort to seek a solution. She was a young mother of three, with two sons, seven and two years old, and a three-month-old baby. One daughter had already died at the age of nine months (Wolf 1992:62, 64, 68) and her children were "woefully underweight" (20). Her son was also getting into fights and being bullied by the children of the village's dominant lineage, the Lims. Her husband was known in the village as "Dumb Tien-lai" and her seven-year-old son had just reported that his father had taken a sizable amount of money to gamble and lost it, when Mrs. Tan began to behave bizarrely, throwing herself into the rice paddy and possibly attempting to drown herself. During the period of her "crazy" behavior, while the villagers were trying to decide whether this woman was truly becoming a shaman or not, Mrs. Tan made several pleas to leave the village (67, 74). Wolf's field notes are an extremely rich source of information, offering insights concerning Mrs. Tan's need to take drastic action. It appears that Mr. Tan had no property and relied on unstable work as a laborer (20). If Mrs. Tan *had* succeeded in becoming accepted as a shaman, she would have had a source of income. Indeed, in Wolf's account, "Dumb Tien-lai was enjoying the spectacle far too much and talking too openly about how expensive it was for him to have his wife providing *free* advice to anyone who asked for it" (100), implying they should give material gifts. The episode ended on an economic note, when Mrs. Tan's younger sister and mother each gave her money after she failed to become accepted as a shaman, and as Mrs. Tan scolded her husband because he would not go to work (82).[2]

The second aspect that intrigued me was Wolf's analysis of why there are, in general, few women shamans. Mrs. Tan's particular failure to gain legitimacy as a shaman serves as an illustration of more general processes that limit women's alternatives:

> To begin with, her gender was against her. There are respected women *tang-ki*, but not very many of them. *Tang-ki* are expected to be and do things inappropriate for women, and even though the extraordinary circumstances of a god's demand should make it all right, the sheer incongruity between the expectations of a god's behavior and those of a woman's behavior is enough to create misgivings. *Tang-ki*, even when not in trance and speaking with a god's voice, must be assured and competent individuals. (Wolf 1992:111)

Another factor that Wolf considered important in this particular case and in the literature was that the condition of being an "outsider" was not conducive to establishing trust:

As noted above, the Tans were "outsiders" in a Lim village. They had no relatives in the area whose genealogy would vouch for their respectability. . . . [T]he Tans by virtue of their newcomer status remained objects of suspicion and people who were slightly dangerous because they had no family whose face their misbehavior could ruin. (Wolf 1992:111)

In Mrs. Tan's case, not only was she a stranger as an in-marrying bride, but her husband was a stranger. As Wolf said,

Mrs. Tan came to Peihotien a stranger, and a stranger she remained. There was no family to smile or frown, no mother-in-law to approve or disapprove of her behavior, and only a husband who was himself a stranger. Without ties to a family that had an accepted place within the village social system, when Mrs. Tan was no longer a novelty, she ceased to have any identity. (Wolf 1992:115)

Because of these differing views and impressions of Chinese women who take up "visionary arts" as their means of livelihood and succeed or fail to achieve economic success, I approached a number of the older villagers of Lu Village with considerable curiosity to see if any of them could identify and remember the woman whom Fei described as "the seeress" in 1938. I hoped to learn whether Fei was right about her income, and if Margery Wolf's portrait of the female shaman was similar to this example in a village in Yunnan.

My goal here is not to analyze the religious, medical, or psychological dimensions of shamanism but to view it as a particular occupation that, under certain circumstances, may be open to women and to understand what kind of woman seeks this occupational alternative as well as what may make her successful. In the course of seeking to understand the seeress as an economic specialist and shamanism as an occupation, we can also come to better understand other aspects of gender and village organization.

The following material is extracted from my interviews about the seeress of Lu Village, Huang Shiniang, whom I shall call Mistress Huang (where "Mistress" is used as a feminine form of the term "Master").[3] I have edited the interviews slightly to simplify them or remove some of my questions and some extraneous comments that crept into group discussion, from the current whereabouts of married children to recent gall-bladder operations. The text remains close to verbatim discussions that were tape-recorded and translated. I have changed or avoided using the names of those interviewed and discussed.

## HUANG SHINIANG, THE SEERESS REMEMBERED

During a lengthy wedding celebration in Lu Village in January 1993, I had the opportunity to ask a group of elders if they could remember the seeress.

As we took shelter from a light rain in a makeshift kitchen located near the school grounds where the outdoor banquet was being prepared, I spoke mainly with three senior village women and one man. I have tried to preserve the experience of different voices with minimal confusion by labeling them "A," "B," "C," and "D." "A" was the older sister of the village party secretary, in her seventies or eighties, who had married and moved out of the village at age fifteen, although she would come back for visits. "B" was a seventy-six-year-old woman who "married in" to the village. "C" was the wife of the party secretary (in her late fifties) and "D" was the party secretary himself. There were also other people in the kitchen speaking together, and the party secretary, busy with preparations for his nephew's wedding, came in and out. Distinguishing between these individuals is not essential; I preserve the different voices largely to give a feeling for the process by which the seeress was recalled and some of the confusion about her.

Voices

Q    Anthropologist posing questions with help of assistant
A    Elder sister of party secretary, seventy-five to eighty years old, married out
B    Village woman, seventy-six years old, married in
C    Village woman, fifty-six years old, wife of party secretary
D    Village man, age fifty-seven, party secretary

* * *

Q:   *Guma* (aunt), do you remember Huang Shiniang?
A:   I remember her, because I had a son in Chuxiong. He said, "Ma, you go with me and see her." I had been away for twelve years. I came back and she had just died.
Q:   Did she have a husband?
A:   She did not have one. I am afraid her husband died.
B:   She had two daughters.
A:   Two or one?
B:   Two!
A:   At that time, I worked every day in the fields. We did not see each other much. My paternal grandaunt liked to visit with her. Women of their age usually met together in one place. . . . I only went to market, worked, and visited her in the little store. I would greet her and go on. I did not have much contact with her.
B:   At that time, I am afraid she had no husband, ah!
A:   I am afraid there wasn't any. I never saw one. I was a young wife, only fifteen years old, when I married [out to the closest neighboring village].
Q:   Who was her husband?
A:   What was he called? I don't know.
B:   Her man was called Huang Bayang. Her *niangjia* (mother's home), I don't know. So everyone just called her Huang Shiniang! She was called by her

husband's name. Her husband was not an uxorilocal (*shangmen*) son-in-law. He was from Liangguang. With her man, the two *tao lai* (fled) here. Then [around 1937] I was more than twenty years old.

Q:  Do you know why they fled?

B:  I don't know.

A:  At that time, many people were fleeing to Yunnan.

D:  In those days, if life didn't work, you fled.

B:  They fled here. Everyone called her Huang Shiniang. She was a spiritualist; she could *see* [as a clairvoyant] just by looking closely at someone. She would also do egg divinations. She would become dizzy. After a few years, her husband died. Before Liberation, her man just got sick and died. She had two daughters. The older one married out to a place in the south. The second one never came here to her mother after Liberation [1949]. She could not call spirits like her mother. She said, "Everyone says I'm the *shiniang jia's* [the Mistress Seer's] child." She said the fame was unpleasant. When her mother was dying, she did not even know about her mother's condition. Perhaps she did not know, but when she died, she came to carry her; she just carried her and left.

Q:  Where were they from?

B:  Liangguang.

C:  In this area, that is how we refer to Guangzhou. We call people from there Liangguang people.

B:  No, No. She was from Kunming! Yuxi!

D:  They were not from Guangzhou.

Q:  What was their accent?

C:  It was a Liangguang accent.

B:  It was Yuxi, that's how it was. It's not the same.

D:  Yeah, it really is not the same.

C:  You need to go to Guangdong, Guangzhou; then you'll know if it's true or not.

B:  [imitates Huang Shiniang's voice] "What did you come for? What do you want?"

C:  Her accent was like *that*, not like *us*. Also not like Yuxi. [Later, it was decided she must have been from central Yunnan, south of Kunming, on the road to Yuxi.]

B:  When I was more than twenty years old, they fled here. Now I am seventy-six years old. She died about four years ago! She said she was more than a hundred years old! She *was* more than a hundred.

C:  She was ninety something. We remembered she was ninety.

B:  She said she was over a hundred! I say she was about a hundred.

C:  Ninety-eight years old. Some people say that men think years ending in multiples of three are easiest for them to die in: three, six, nine. Women think it's years with two, five, and eight—eighty-two, eighty-five, eighty-eight—that are the easiest for them to die. I say again, if she would have lived two more years, she would have been a hundred.

Q:  Was Huang Shiniang a foreigner?

C:  Her accent didn't seem like it.

Q:  Did they farm?

B:  No, No. Neither of them. When they fled, they just ate these bowls of rice here [I surmise this means she ate rice and eggs that people offered to her, and then did divinations for them from their remains in the bowl].

Q:  What did her husband do?

B:  I don't know. They fled here to us, but did not rent land. They just called the spirits.

C:  She just practiced superstition!

Q:  Did her husband also do that?

C:  Her husband depended on her at this door to eat! The husband ate leisure rice. Everyone called him *Shiniang pojia hanzi* (also *shiniang po de hanzi*, old lady's husband)! Old husband (*Lao guan*), you eat ready-made (unearned) rice!

Q:  Did they smoke opium?

All: No, they didn't smoke.

B:  They lived by looking at someone's eggs; they did not plant paddy, they did not plant dry land. They just specially ate these bowls of rice.

C:  Their monthly income was also satisfactory, not small. Generally in the past, it [what they said] was partly true and partly false. Yet not completely true and not completely false. These rice bowl eaters are all like that.

B:  The egg divination was normal and accurate. She took a chopstick and put an egg on its end. The egg just stood on the end of the chopstick.

D:  If you went to see her for egg divination, you took a bowl of rice and an egg. She ate it but did not finish; she dumped it out and kept it.

C:  After she looked at it, the egg and the rice were given to her to eat, and she was also given money. So she could earn enough with this life.

D:  In one day she could only see a few people.

C:  In one day she could see quite a few.

B:  Whoever went to see her took a bowl of rice, three sticks of incense, and one egg, besides giving her money.[4]

C:  We peasants here, our custom then was to criticize and call names, saying: "*Shiniang po de hanzi* (the old lady's husband) eats idle rice![5] He just eats unearned (*xian cheng*) rice. He just eats unearned food." Just from her family here, the curses started. Her man did nothing, he only specially ate hers.

Q:  When they came here, how old do you think she was?

B:  Big, probably just about ten years older than us. Around ten years older [speaker is seventy-six years old], still not old. I think she was only around thirty-seven or thirty-eight. Her daughters were small. Here, she sought a *mao* (a tenth of a yuan, or a small amount) of money, she also provided for her kids to study, ma! She also raised two kids. At Liberation, when her girl was big, she gave her to be married. Then the second girl did not let her work [practice shamanism]. In the daytime, she did not work, but at night she cured.

D:  Certainly she "cleaned up," but in the daytime she did not *look*.

C:  When people went to seek her, they met her daughter, who criticized them. She cursed them, and made them go away. Certainly then her mother still cured. How could she not be curing? She still had a child [to support]! But she did not dare do it in front of her daughter.

Q:  During the Cultural Revolution, her daughter still didn't let her practice?

C:     In the Cultural Revolution, they did not like it.

B:     Before, they still liked it. It was okay that she practice.

D:     She [the daughter] still depended on her [mother's] income to read books. But in the Cultural Revolution, they opposed these feudal things. She still practiced but it was only at night. At night she would see people.

B:     In the day, how could you seek her? She wouldn't see you. You would take an egg, some incense, and give it to her, then everyone went back. At night she would look and look. The second day you came again, and then she would tell you. If she did not arrange it, if she did not work, how did she live? Her daughter did not pay attention. How did she care for her? Unless the egg was for her to eat, how did she get full? The eggs, she could not eat them all up. She had more than enough to eat.

D:     They gave her small gifts.

B:     They gave her money. In the county, some of them still asked her to see their kids. If the kids were sick with diarrhea, little aches, they would go find her and she would "cure." She gave children names of those completely gone outside to work, ah. She gave children names, the boys were called Ding, Bao. About one or two hundred kids.

D:     If she gave a baby the name "*guai*" (obedient), it was easy to raise.

B:     She called them Ding, Bao, Sheng, Hai, Zheng, just these names.

C:     These types were also ideals. That is to say, she gave the names of obedient children, so they would want to study or go inside.

Q:     Were these small names [nicknames] or big names [formal names]?

C:     They were small names.

Q:     Did she give names to girls as well as boys?

C:     She gave names to girls as well as boys. For girls she just added Xiu ah, Fen ah, Zhen ah; boys were Bao, Zheng.

B:     When the year ended [at New Year's], then we gave her things.

C:     Meat, *er kuai* (rice pancakes—a special Yunnan New Year's treat).

D:     We then gave these things to her.

B:     People sometimes gave her clothes—shoes, pants. People would come and give them to her.

Q:     How did she start to call spirits?

B:     When she came, she just started to call spirits; then one, then another. There were some young people at Zhou Zhengming's father's house, who just went to have her call spirits. They looked, looked to see if it was true or false.

D:     At that time Zhou Zhengming's father was still there! He was still alive!

B:     I am telling you sincerely that if she was false, they would have just wanted to wrap her incense burner and throw it away. After she called the spirit, she went to them and said, "Do you want this person?" They asked, "Did you find him?" She said, "I found him. This person is still sitting in the house, sitting on the platform, he is still smoking tobacco. If you want him to come, just call him to come. Thus, later you do not have this person. This person is alive. You, how could I come and cure you, give me money!" These people smiled and laughed and then did not break her incense burner. So in those early years they did not break her incense burner, for she discovered the person was living.

C:   She only went to call the spirits of the dead to come back. She called the spirits and it was rather true. When she released someone who used to sing, they would come sing; when she released someone who coughed, then they would come and cough.

B:   For example, if you went to release a spirit, she chanted weird words. No one knew what it was about; they waited until she woke up. She took the burning incense and it did not hurt her.

D:   [On one occasion] they wanted to find a living person. But generally, it is the spirit of someone who is already dead. They just called her and made her seek a living person. She then said, "This is a living person, now he's sitting and smoking." She said, "Do you want this person dead or alive?" She fully knew this person was alive, not dead. Then she said, "If you want this person dead, I will tell this person's soul to be taken away, and this person will die!" They wanted to test her. If it was not true, then they would have broken her incense burner and thrown away her rice bowl. The meaning is that when she started, there was a very mysterious special story.

B:   Then they did not make her leave. One by one they started to seek her. Then people from all over came to see her. If two people came to see her at her place, she already knew it. She did not even [need to] see them.

C:   One time my grandmother went to "cure" my father. She called me and I hurried to come in. She grabbed a burning incense and said, "This girl here never calls me." My grandmother then quickly said to me, "Call your grandfather." I was thinking of old *nainai*, how she wanted to call grandfather, but then I did not call. Then Huang Shiniang took a stick of burning incense. . . . She was sitting, with three sticks of incense, like this [she makes a hand gesture] with her eyes half-open, half-closed.

D:   And she called in a loud, loud voice.

C:   Then when you called her, her soul had already gone to find more souls. When you spoke ordinary words to her she did not understand. Whatever family member went to "call," that is the only person she knew. My grandmother went to call my grandfather and I went in. She knew I was *nainai*'s grandchild. Then she called me by my small name, "Xiao Xiu! You call grandfather, ah!" I did not call. Then she lit a stick of incense.

Q:   Would calling spirits make families harmonious?

C:   Sometimes you would ask her about certain disputes. If there was a calamity in the family, if something broke out, she knew how to handle it. Then it might turn out better.

B:   You would watch later, is it better or not? Then she could tell you, ah! If this person could be cured, she could tell you what to do for this person, their later arrangements.

C:   If you called her to come, then she could tell you what time and what day that a spotted snake would come, or that someone came to curse, or that some person came to argue. She spoke out, but still it is correct to dispute [question this]. She could not have seen these things, but still she spoke out about what was going to happen. She could tell you the reasons.

Q:   These days if *po-xi* (mother-in-law and daughter-in-law) have a conflict, is there anyone around to help?

C: Now there are no people of this type. Ordinary people do not speak clearly. These days certain people, just from looking at your hand, can seem to read it like a book. But this was not true originally. . . . This is according to the study of scientific reason. They speak a little at random, and one third of this is true. In the past, two-thirds were true, and only one-third was false. Now only one-third is true and two-thirds are false.

Q: In the past, if there was a suicide (*zisha*), could they tell the truth about it?

C: They could say at what day, at what time, and what ghost came looking for a person—why they wanted to die, or what medicine they ate when they fell dead or drowned. Huang Shiniang told fortunes. She said, "Over there a month ago, you lost something. You must look at the road." She could tell you all about it.

In this group interview, we can see that "C", the party secretary's wife, coming of age in the revolutionary period and with six years of elementary school education, had a somewhat more skeptical view toward Mistress Huang than the older woman, "B," who simply told what she remembered. The oldest woman, "A," did not have much to say, because her memories date to the time before she was married, when she lived close by. As a fifteen-year-old, her understanding of the adults in her home village was very limited and, once married, she had little free time to come home. "D," the party secretary, did not seem very judgmental about Mistress Huang's practice. The group claimed that Mistress Huang and her husband did not smoke opium, contrary to Fei's report. Poppy production had been banned by Fei Xiaotong's time and he did not observe any local poppy fields, but he noted that opium was still available and costly through illegal channels at the inns of Lu Village in 1939. After the Communists took power, opium smoking was much more severely repressed. It is possible that some of the memories of Mistress Huang and her husband may be based on the 1950s, when opium was no longer available, or that the older women had little knowledge of Mistress Huang's visits to the opium den at the inn during the late 1930s if the innkeeper was discreet. Unlike Fei Xiaotong, young farm women may have had little opportunity to become acquainted with the subculture of the guesthouses.

I had another opportunity in 1993 to inquire about Huang Shiniang at the home of the Lu Village women's director (a woman in her fifties, born in 1940), at a time when she had a visitor from town, an older man who was a former policeman. When I asked about the famous seeress who lived in their community in the time of Fei Xiaotong, they had no doubts about who it was. They first began remembering the seeress by discussing the year in which she died, 1988 or 1989. The former policeman used to patrol her street and therefore knew about her family. He used to go to her house to visit, and knew her two daughters. He called her "*Da Ma*," Big

Mother or Aunt, an affectionate, respectful form of address for elderly women.

> I never saw her husband. I am now more than sixty, and I never saw him. At that time, she was alone. Her daughters, Huang Huaping and Huang Huaxian, were both close to me. I often went to her house to drink tea. Every time I came home from the county town I always went to see her. She was one hundred and one years old when she died.
>
> She was a specialist in calling spirits (*guan gui*). When calling spirits she would just release the underworld (*fang yin*). She took sticks of incense, and while shaking and shaking them, she said superstitious things (*mixin*). She could stand up an egg. She could put an egg on its end, standing. This kind of person could even control spirits. Basically, everything she said was true. She spoke superstitions—ah! Also she would look, she would see. The suspended egg, the egg in the rice bowl. She would also stand a chopstick on top of the egg. It seemed like magic. She would do divinations by looking at eggs, she would call spirits and release ghosts from the underworld, she could do it all! In Lufeng she did these things and was rather famous. Everyone certainly went to her. On Sundays, young and old, all of them willingly went to see her. When they went to see her, well, they gave her a little money, sometimes they bought her a little something. She still practiced after the Cultural Revolution, but during the Cultural Revolution she did not dare do it. She was among Lufeng's very famous old people. I also voluntarily went to her house to visit, to eat. She was a person whose basic specialty was to call the spirits. She depended on calling the spirits to earn a living. She also looked at egg symbols. Before Liberation she was in Lu Village. After Liberation she went to the county town and bought a little house, across from the present police station. She later bought a house on a bigger street. In Lufeng, once you bring up Huang Shiniang's name, everyone knows her, including young people. She was famous even in the city.

At this point, I reminded the ex-policeman that Fei wrote that Huang Shiniang had had the highest income in the village because she was very famous, and I asked him if it was true that she earned a lot.

> She did not actually receive that much. Everyone who came brought a little something to give her, a little pastry to give her, or left some money for her. It was according to how much she aroused you, ah! According to how much your heart was moved, eh? You cannot say she asked people for money—twenty or thirty yuan. It was just that if I wanted to go see her, I knew she liked sweets and pastries, eh? So I would buy a few bags and give them to her, that was fine.

Clearly, then, Fei was wrong about her "fixed prices." Her form of income was closer to Wolf's description of "reasonable gifts by grateful clients." To my surprise, when I asked the former policeman to describe Mistress Huang's standard of living he responded not in terms of cash income or savings, as I expected, but in terms of the number of children her daughter successfully raised and the quality of housing her daughter owned. These were clearly important measures of the old woman's success in the eyes of this elderly man. It is also noteworthy that this independent woman, mother of two daughters, *brought in* a son-in-law for one of her daughters rather than send them both out into conventional marriages as daughters-in-law. That would have left her with no heirs and no kin to care for and protect her as she aged.

> From the time when her son-in-law (*guye*) came, he and her daughter had eight kids. Every one of them did well. One works for the Provincial Police Department, there are some in the city, another is in the army. He was adopted (*bao lai*). He is the oldest. Later they gave birth and altogether had eight kids. Her older daughter went far away, I just don't know where. It was the second girl in Lufeng who had eight kids, built a house, and it is a good one. When my mother was alive we often went to visit.

According to the ex-policeman, both men and women equally sought Huang Shiniang. Their reasons echo the kinds of reasons Margery Wolf describes, largely problems of family harmony.[6]

> [She came] when people were sick, or when the family was not harmonious. When there were seven or eight people in a dispute, they would all call spirits and ask people in the netherworld; they would ask the spirits to come and say a few words. The cover next to her head would rise up, she would lift a cover by her eyes, then she called the spirits, and spoke with the voices of dead people. Her voice changed. She would speak with a man's or a woman's voice. Her hand would also gesture and she would recite and speak like your own family. She would do some Daoist incantations. She would sort them out and just tell people. She said she "rose them up." It is said that raising up the dead is deceiving people. Still, sometimes what she said was true. At certain times, she did not know a certain person. . . . [I]t was strange and odd. We both believed and didn't believe in these things. I willingly went there to visit, and she voluntarily saw us. Generally the situation involved only two people; only two people were there, at most at your side was a relative or friend.

When I asked if she could read, he told me she could not. In that respect Huang Shiniang again fit Margery Wolf's profile of a shaman. Since he was a generation younger than the seeress, there was little he could tell me about her entry into the occupation or how she acquired her knowledge and established her reputation in the village.

Because the ex-policeman seemed quite sympathetic toward the old seeress, despite his former occupation, I asked him if he ever went to her himself to ask her to call up spirits. The answer he gave was equivocal. He claimed he did not see her about his own problems, but to pump her for information about "certain conditions." I suspect that the euphemism, "certain conditions," means information that would help him with police investigations. It is unclear whether he believed she obtained information through supernatural means, through her contacts, or through her shrewdness, but he seems to have had some confidence in her as a source of information about people. Nonetheless, one can speculate that the female shaman, who is "quick-witted and alert to the needs of her clients" (Wolf 1992:106) would recognize the advantage of having friends among the police during China's many periods of political turmoil. According to the former policeman:

> I did a kind of work that was incompatible with asking her to call up spirits. I worked for the police. I also liked to go there at times to investigate the outcome of a certain condition, because we in this society need to understand certain conditions. I certainly went there to visit. In your mind, she had this influence. A person with a cold or ordinary illness would not go to see her. Mainly you went if there was no true harmony in the family, if things were agitated or disorderly (seven things with eight heads). For example, if there were some abnormal, serious matters, such as telling someone to die, or that you would burn their house down, or if all their livestock died, or if a person was sick in bed and could not get up—at these times people would seek her. For small things, they would not seek her. If the whole family had no peace and harmony, then you would seek her, and ask her to call up the ghosts, to "see," to do some magical chants, to arrange it. It was just like that.
>
> Her payment was at most a liter (*sheng*) of rice, or she would get some money. In those days her income was not bad. Because here one, there one; altogether it adds up to a lot. He would take a liter of rice, I would take a liter, you take a liter. One day, for example, if ten people came, then she received a bushel of rice. If it is a small city, there are many "conditions." Thus, she depended on this for a living. Her whole family depended on her livelihood. Her son-in-law (*guye*) originally was a Nationalist soldier. After he came here, he became a son-in-law. Then her daughter was just eighteen years old. The man was more than thirty. He was from Anhui. This was before Liberation.

I was unable to find out if Huang Shiniang had learned her profession from her mother. I asked whether either daughter followed the same profession, to learn if the skill was transmitted from mother to daughter, but neither daughter became a shaman. According to the ex-policeman, one of them "used to have a small store. She sewed shoes with someone else. Her daughter's sewing and needlework was very skilled. She sewed beautifully; the shoes were about five *mao* a pair. She sewed them to sell. She is now more than fifty years old." The fact that her daughters did not follow her profession may be due to a system of recruitment based on a "calling," a spiritual crisis or turning point, which the daughters presumably did not experience. However, the revolutionary assault on shamanistic and religious professions as perpetuating feudal superstitions might also have prevented the shaman's daughters from following in her footsteps.

I also asked if there were any other spiritualists left in the area. The ex-policeman and women's director both named one, also dead now. Then, as if they had read Margery Wolf's work, they debated whether or not she was crazy. The ex-policeman maintained the woman could tell fate. But the women's director said she was mentally ill, a lunatic, that the old woman was crazy (*feng feng dian dian de*). Apart from the two older, famous names, they replied that basically there are no seers at present, or at least none with major reputations.

## GIFTS AND WEALTH

*Reasonable gifts* will be made by grateful clients. (Wolf 1992:107, italics added)

Let us now return to questions raised by Fei's brief description and Wolf's multiple views of a would-be shaman. With the information given so far, what can we say about the status of this unusual woman in Lu Village in the 1930s and during her long career in the village, and later the town, until her death in 1989? Was she wealthy? Literate? A desperate woman with an unemployed husband? An outsider with no other means of livelihood? A shrewd and quick-witted woman? An opium addict?

Mistress Huang clearly came to Lu Village as a poor, illiterate woman with two daughters and a nonproductive, propertyless husband. Her husband may have been an opium addict, incapacitated in some other way, or simply lazy, but he did not live long enough for any of my elderly informants to describe him in depth. Early death (nearly fifty years before his wife) suggests he may have been ill for some time. Perhaps he was unable to defend his land claims in his native village.[7] Clearly, he did not own a home in Lu Village, and the family, like that of Margery Wolf's Mrs. Tan, rented their rooms on the main street. The children who taunted him because he was not the family "breadwinner," or more properly because he "ate idler's rice," seemed to be transmitting the kind of scorn that in Chinese accounts is applied to uxorilocal husbands. In this case, villagers describe Mistress Huang as taking her husband's surname, with no indication that he joined her family rather than the reverse. But perhaps the more significant point is that the two of them lacked property and lacked local roots; they were both what might be called internal refugees, a part of the floating population that left their home towns or native villages and sought a livelihood of whatever kind, wherever they could find it. This kind of family would be looked down on as outsiders in most Chinese villages (e.g., see Wolf 1992; Potter and Potter 1990; Fei 1939, 1983). Despite Mistress Huang's economic vulnerability, Fei Xiaotong did not see her as a woman overcoming disadvantage to support her family; he saw her as a woman of dubious legitimacy taking advantage of gullible people. While Wolf suggested that being doubly an outsider may have limited Mrs. Tan, this same condition did not defeat Mistress Huang, who passed the villagers' tests. Mistress Huang may have been simply more intelligent or better trained in the arts of reasoning and calling up the dead, and her husband may also have been somewhat shrewder and a more skilled accomplice than Mrs. Tan's poor husband, "Dumb Tien-lai."

How do we assess Huang Shiniang's wealth? First, we can assume that Fei did some calculations of her income based on some of the standard gifts he was told about, but he did not report this. Given the rapid and uneven price inflation at the time, any estimate based on currencies would be hard to interpret. Yet if Mistress Huang did receive something like a standard of a liter of rice per visit, as elderly villagers recalled, and supposing (as the policeman did above) she received ten visits per day, then she would have been doing very well with ten liters of grain per day. Second, we can compare this to the pre-Liberation wage reported to me by another elderly village woman who recalled earning five liters of grain in seven days by carrying fifty pound loads of coal between towns. This rate of pay, 0.71 liters of rice per day, was higher than one liter for three days, or 0.33 liters per day, paid for farmwork by women, or one liter for two days, 0.5 liters per day, paid for farmwork by men (see table 5.1).

We do not know if ten visits per day is a realistic estimate of the average number of Mistress Huang's clients, as opposed to a maximum seen on a really busy day. Both the shaman and her clients would probably have a tendency to inflate her popularity.[8] If we estimate that she averaged only three visits a day, each time receiving a liter of rice, or a bowl of rice and an egg, as the accounts of egg divination suggest, then she would probably have provided enough for herself, her husband, and two daughters to eat. However, it is not clear she would have had a large, savable surplus, especially when some of her clients seem to have brought perishable cooked rice and egg, rather than durable dry rice.

Unlike farm households, propertyless nonfarming families had to pay room rent and had to buy (or receive as gifts) all foods. Three liters (estimated to weigh 2.55 kgs, or 5.6 lbs) of dry rice per day might exceed the grain needs

**Table 5.1.  Daily Income for Lu Village Occupations, 1945**

| Task | Grain payment per day or visit |
|---|---|
| woman carrying coal | 0.71 liters |
| woman in field work | 0.33 liters |
| man in field work | 0.50 liters |
| consultation by Mistress Huang | 1.00 liter per visit (0–10 visits per day) |

of a family of four, but a surplus would have been needed to meet expenses for other basic foods (vegetables, salt, oil, meat), cooking fuel, clothing and shoes, and so forth. This income would have probably supported the family at a level near the average for the village. If the average number of clients per day were double or triple this, then the business could make the household relatively prosperous by local standards. Gifts in the form of dry grain would be some protection against market price inflation, as nonfarm households lacked a store of homegrown subsistence foods and were more vulnerable to market price fluctuations if they depended solely on cash. Thus it is not surprising that Mistress Huang accepted payment in grain. Yet we may wonder how much or little control she had over the form of payment she received. If she received cooked rather than dry rice by the liter, there would have been no way to preserve, sell, or accumulate it—she would only be able to eat and share it. Fei dismissed the problem of lack of steady clientele by claiming that she could, "at will, inform a villager that a certain spirit is calling for him."

In assessing Huang Shiniang's business costs, we know neither her rent nor her opium costs. Fei perceived eating well, consumption of opium, and avoidance of manual field labor as evidence of wealth and leisure. By these standards, Mistress Huang, then, appeared to be wealthy; she was able to do what local wealthy people did: eat well, avoid field work and manual labor, smoke opium, and consume leisure.

At the same time, we might speculate on the role of opium in her business. Should she be seen as a business woman, and opium as a business expense? Unlike Mrs. Tan, whose attempts to become a shaman in Taiwan seemed to require the purchase of a god to represent the god that was trying to speak "through" her, Mistress Huang probably did not have such accoutrements—they were never mentioned by the people who remembered her. Her direct capital investment was low—nothing more than strange tricks with chopsticks, eggs (brought to her by clients), and bowls were mentioned. Yet the time spent in the opium den at the village inn may have been time well spent in terms of learning the social structure, the conflicts and alliances, the grudges and "skeletons in the closets"—in short, all the useful gossip of the area. One can easily conjure up images of the ways useful information might be gleaned from the travelers and traders who stopped at the inn, and fed their habits and their horses, on their way to and from the Burma Road. People did not remember Mistress Huang as an opium addict, or as a person who was sent away for reeducation through labor—which occurred in cases of severe addiction. However, from the 1950s on, opium would probably have been much harder to get.

Fei's assessment of Mistress Huang as a shrewd, profit-making woman was undoubtedly true in some sense. However, she clearly was not a *wealthy* woman in some important ways that male villagers were wealthy. She did not own or invest in farmland (as far as anyone knew). She did eventually own a house in town, but that purchase (or allocation) seems to have occurred after Liberation, when she was a widow and had acquired a son-in-law. In the form of this son-in-law, she may have had a male ally to help her defend any wealth she could accumulate—although sons-in-laws could also be scoundrels. It may not be sheer coincidence that she purchased a house across the street from the police station. If she stayed on good terms with the police, they could possibly have provided extra safety for her, a widow who was the main property holder, should men attempt to harass her out of her wealth. True, she was an outsider, and therefore in a very weak position, much as Mrs. Tan in Wolf's village of Peihotien. But she passed the villager's tests and succeeded all the same. Still, she was merely a successful professional and not the equivalent of a capitalist or a landowner. One might grant that, until her children acquired other means of livelihood, she lived relatively well, enjoying leisure and avoiding manual labor, yet her income was probably still precarious, or "slight of hand" to mouth. It was often received in subsistence goods, particularly food, and perhaps more easily consumed than resold and invested. Nonetheless, she managed to support her household, to educate her daughters, and to purchase housing. Not being schooled in magic tricks, I can only imagine how she got those eggs to stand on end.

## POSTSCRIPT: THE CALLING

Since shamans and their clients become secretive when the state regards them as subversive or illegitimate, it is difficult to obtain a large enough sample to see if there are significant patterns in the characteristics of those who take up shamanistic activities. Also, a village is likely to have only one or two shamans, and probably at most one of them would be a woman.[9] Lu Villagers claimed there was no one comparable in their vicinity today. The limited comparisons I draw here must be viewed cautiously.

Wolf suggests that the condition of being doubly an outsider may disadvantage women who seek to become shamans. This may be true, but it may also be a condition that drives women into shamanism both as a reaction and a potential solution to their economic precariousness. This may also be true for men.[10] I do not believe it is known whether most male shamans do, in fact, tend to be local rather than outsiders.

I have formed a different (but not contradictory) impression based partly on Wolf's case of Mrs. Tan and my inquiries about Mistress Huang, and partly on my personal encounter with an elderly female shaman-healer, whom I shall call Mistress X, practicing in a village in Henan province. Mistress Huang and Mrs. Tan were both young mothers burdened with small children, married but economically insecure, for apparently their husbands were not good providers and did not own farmland or housing. When I compare these two cases with Mistress X, I am struck by their similarities.

The village shaman in Henan, Mistress X, has acted for many years as the village curer-midwife, eventually ceding her medical clientele to younger women with at least some formal training in birthing and basic health care, but continuing with her other spiritual cures. Like Mistress Huang and Mrs. Tan, Mistress X was married and was a "double outsider" in the village. However, the life history of the shaman in Henan reveals a little more about how a woman might acquire the skills, psychological and technical, to succeed in such an occupation.

Mistress X had town origins and was not only an outsider to the village but an outsider to the local marketing area, from a rather distant part of the province. She had been raised in a temple by landless, poverty-stricken parents—her mother was a wet nurse. At the temple, she observed the techniques of supernatural mediation, persuasion, and otherworldly powers. She, too, was poor and illiterate, earning income as a child by collecting manure in the street. She married a man with no kin and no property. He opened a small restaurant, but after the revolution they had to close it and go to the countryside to work as peasants. During the Great Leap Forward, he died while pushing a cart of manure to the fields. As a widow with two daughters, neither of whom would continue as descendants with claims to village membership, her economic position with no male kin in the village must have been precarious.

She soon remarried in 1960 to another peasant who was living in Xian, having fled there from famine. This second husband had grown up in an orphanage. He had rights to membership in his ancestral village in Henan but had no property. In 1970, hoping for better farming conditions, they went to live in his village, where they had to borrow a house from a nephew.

Desperate to feed her children, Mistress X began practicing curing and shamanism in Xian. An older woman healer, nearing the end of her life, shared her secret cures and chants with Mistress X. In Xian, she acquired brief training in midwifery as well. In referring to her curing "secrets," Mistress X remains very guarded but also sly and suggestive, evoking mysterious knowledge. Like Mistress Huang, she also found a son-in-law for one of her daughters, for she had no children with her second husband. This allowed her to treat the daughter's family as heirs and make legitimate claims upon them for assistance in old age.

The common theme is that each of these women who took up shamanism (or tried to) was a mother with a landless husband facing desperate economic circumstances. Occasionally, women in economic distress are able to draw on shrewdness, and psychological and spiritual resources, to reverse their fate and reclaim a measure of respect and material reward from a society that has very little to offer women whose husbands lack property. This solution for impoverished women is rarely successful, as Mrs. Tan found out. It is intriguing, however, that even in the most inhospitable circumstances facing poor women, human ingenuity may devise services to meet needs that are always present: to understand the present and predict the future, to revive the dead, to cure the sick, to mend unhappy families, and to give hope to the hopeless. This does not seem to be a niche for women of wealth as much as an enterprise for astute women who lack material wealth but possess special "gifts."

I began this chapter with a quest to understand how the seeress could become a wealthy woman. I conclude that her natural gifts, intelligence, and shrewd understanding of human relations brought her material gifts in exchange for insights and counseling. I do not know what other "capital" she brought to her profession, but based on analogy with Mistress X, I suspect that she brought an informal endowment of previous experience around other spiritualists, curers, diviners, religious specialists, or magicians who gave her direct or indirect training. If a woman seeking to become a shaman lacks credibility, if her insights and skills of persuasion are weak, she will fail.

The particular value of a detailed examination of the economic situation of women such as the shaman of Lu Village lies in the exploration of alternatives to the norm. While Chinese rural women in the past are usually presented as farm women, embedded in families, or else as women condemned to domestic servitude, concubinage, prostitution, or destitution, examples such as Huang Shiniang suggest that some women were able to devise different kinds of opportunities. Nonetheless, the occupation of shaman seems to be fraught with ambiguities and dangers, for as Susan Mann points out, "women of low status outside the household were always dangerous. Historically, instruction books for women contained warnings about the 'hags' whose marginal occupations gave them access to the cloistered inner apartments—female physicians, religious adepts, go-betweens, peddlers, nuns" (Mann 1991:221). As an interview with the shaman's daughter later revealed, Huang Shiniang's life contained its share of tragedies.

## RASHOMON IN LUFENG

As in the Japanese film *Rashomon*, which presents three completely different perspectives on a single event, my own perspectives on Huang Shiniang considerably changed after an interview with her sixty-one-year-old daughter,

Huang Huaxian, in December 1996. Some of the speculations above were clarified by this interview, tinged by hatred of the mother, and memories that pertain to the second half of the mother's life, from the 1940s to 1990. I include the account because it further illuminates questions about her wealth and the nature of the family.

It was dark out when my assistant and I tried again to find someone home at Huang Huaxian's address. After much ringing and knocking at the dark four-story apartment block in Lufeng, Huang Huaxian's grown son answered the door and invited us into the building. The door on the front street led down a dark, cluttered passage to the back, where we climbed exterior stairs to the apartment. We were invited in by Huang Huaxian's youngest son, a young man, jauntily dressed in gray wool pants, a white shirt, and loose tie. He led us up to the top floor, where we entered a brightly lit apartment living room on the courtyard side (its lights were not visible from the street) with four other young men, all dressed similarly, with pomaded hair, smoking and avidly playing cards. We were invited to sit down while they resumed their game. Not completely ignoring us, they sent someone out to buy us soda water—which they were also drinking—but stayed intent on their game. The room had many ostentatious consumer goods, a large video TV, a refrigerator, a large modern sofa and chairs, and wardrobes. I have no idea how much space there was in the other rooms of the apartment, but this one was stuffed. After about half an hour, the mother arrived and brought us down to the apartment she shares with a different son. This was somewhat more modest and less aggressively materialistic and fashionable. There we interviewed her. She was a little uncomfortable and cautious but mostly friendly. Obviously, she did not like her mother.

My father and mother were both from Jiangchuan [more than one hundred kilometers to the southeast of Lufeng, toward Yuxi]. They had no land there; they were landless laborers. My mother's feet were originally small feet (bound feet). Later, she slowly, slowly let them out, and then they just became "cucumber feet" (*huanggua jiao*). The bandits (*tufei*) were extremely oppressive in Jiangchuan, so my parents moved away and came to Lufeng County. First they lived in Middle Village, to the north of Lufeng. Middle Village was also a bandit-ridden (*fei feng*) area. In the evening the bandits would come and order us to pay this kind of tax and that kind of tax, and they would still come and force open the door. My mother and father were afraid. So they moved again, this time to Lu Village. Because we were landless, we had no roots, so we moved here and there. My father knew how to make liquor and could do blacksmithing with iron and make silverware (*yinqi*). He could also fluff cotton for making quilts. Some days, if he had too much work, he hired one or two people. One time, a casual laborer was helping my father to purchase cotton, but he took the money for buying the goods and ran away and never came back.

Our family had no land in Lu Village. We even rented our house. I heard my mother say that earlier I had an older sister in Jiangchuan, who was sold at age three to be an adopted daughter-in-law (*tongyangxi*).[11] I never saw her. When I was eleven years old, I once met her husband. He was also poor and wore poor clothing when he came to see us.

My father, in those days, was able to earn a living. When I was eight years old, my father made liquor to sell in Middle Village. He was captured and held for ransom by bandits. They wanted my mother to take money and ransom (*shumai*) him. My mother could not get that much money. More than one month later, my father escaped and came home. He was injured all over his arms and body, pus was running, and he was bleeding. Before long, then, my father died.

When they were burying my father on the mountain, we came back and on the evening of the very same day my only younger brother suddenly got a fever and very quickly, within two weeks, he also died. My mother took a small coffin and put him in it and hung the coffin in a tree (a local custom). Later, she heard people come back and say that they heard a cry from inside the coffin. My mother hurried to call someone to open up the coffin, and when they opened it, they saw my little brother's clothes and coverlet all pulled up toward his chest, his small hands tightly clasping his clothes, his small legs curled up toward his chest.

My mother realized that my younger brother had not yet died when they put him in the coffin. He suffocated when he was in the coffin. My mother was heartsick and went crazy. Her madness was really terrible. She would even break iron shackles when she struggled. She tore up her own clothes, piece by piece, and ate them. Only in this way, was she able to escape death herself. She was like this for almost three years, and then she slowly got better and was not sick.

After my father died, and after my mother went crazy, the Lu Village headman took over our family's pigs, furniture, and everything else, and took it all away. He also took my sister and me to their house, to help his family cook food and take care of the children. Since my older sister and I were too short to cook, we always stood on a straw stool. My older sister studied for two years in Lu Village, and I studied for two years in Lufeng.

When my mother became crazy, she changed and became especially hateful. She became extremely cruel and bizarre. She arranged marriages for me and my older sister. My older sister was married at age twelve, and I was married at eleven.

My older sister was not at all happy with the marriage my mother arranged for her, so she just ate opium and tried to kill herself. But I discovered her. I ran and called to the neighbors next door to come. They pried open her mouth and took soapy water and poured it in, and used a chicken feather to irritate her throat until she threw up, and this saved her life. My mother still wanted to make her marry out, so she married her to a Middle Village man who, like us, was also from Jiangchuan. This man from Jiangchuan was so poor that even the marriage bed's wooden boards were all borrowed. As we relatives went to see her off, we saw they did not even have a place to sleep. That night we just sat on the floor. My older sister did not even go inside; she sat outside that evening with us. The next day, she just ran away with the relatives who had come to see her off, and came back. After she came back, she would not return there. Then my mother almost beat her to death, and still she would not go back. My older sister was smart. When my mother beat her, she just ran away. When my mother stopped hitting, she came back. One month later, it was Liberation. People said, then, that if marriages had been arranged, then people could divorce. So she just got divorced. When the team that conducted the land reform left, that man and his relatives were not happy [about the divorce], so nothing from her dowry was returned.

In those days, I was not as smart as my sister. While I was still going to school, my mother took me from school one day and brought me back, and I saw a man there. My mother said that to help my sister, she found a son-in-law. She waited until I understood—I was already married that day. My mother had taken me from the school and dragged me home to get married; I did not dare say a word, she pulled me by my hair.

After I was married, I still lived with my mother. I was still small and did not even talk with him. When I would see him, I would cry. That old man, my husband, was twenty years older than me. When I was fifteen years old, I started to like him because he was always good to me. When my mother hit me, he would come and protect me, coming between us so that he would receive the blows. We just slowly started to speak together. When we had the first child, my husband proposed that he take me and the baby back to his family, but my mother did not agree. I heard people say my husband's family village was not a good place, so I did not agree; I did not dare go.

My husband was from Hunan Province—the same commune (*gongshe*) as Liu Shaoqi, and also a place not far from Chairman Mao's home town.[12] His family was very poor. He had a lot of brothers and sisters. When he was just ten years old, his father died. Altogether he had six older brothers and one older sister, seven siblings. Over there the practice was, "out of three men, choose one" (*san ding chou yi*), so they took him to be a soldier. The new army recruits then came here to Lu Village. After the army started to leave, he deserted. He was only a new recruit. Then he went to live in the home of a sworn sister of my mother in Lu Village whom we called "Old Xiang." I did not know that the reason she came to my house was in order to arrange a marriage for him into my family.

My family never owned land or a house. During the land reform, the land reform team gave us three *mu* of land. At the land reform, our landlord's family was composed of a single old grandmother and her brother. They called her family's people to come and return money to my family. Her family said they had no rice and also had no money to return. The land reform team then stated that the house was our house.

In Lu Village my family had rented a house, but I do not know how much the rent was. We were outsiders (*wailaide*), so the local officials bullied us (*bendi dangguan de qi women*). First, they took the head tax, then that tax, then this tax. If, like my father, you suddenly earned a lot, they just harassed you and then you had nothing. After my father died, and after my mother was sick, we were still the same. We had nothing. When we moved to town, we did not even have bed boards. We had only a quilt.

When my father was still alive, my mother used to help cure people. When she cured, she cured well. People used to want to bring their children to her, for her to be their godmother.[13]

One or two years after we moved into the city, my husband then came to my house. We started to sell meat. Before Liberation we were poor. My mother bought all our shoes and clothes second hand and then gave them to us to wear.

When I was thirteen, I started to learn how to make shoes and clothes to sell. My husband went to sell meat and I made clothes and shoes for a living. Later the land reform gave us land, and we just did farmwork. I also participated in agricultural meetings. People came and assigned me to go out and work. My mother was too "feudal" and did not allow me to go. She grabbed me and hit me, she tore and ruined my clothes. My mother's temperament was too bad. She hit people. She also wanted a column (stick) of incense on the floor. She made me kneel on the ground, and when the burning of incense was over, then I could get up.

These days my head often hurts. I think perhaps it is because my mother beat me so viciously. She used fire tongs to hit my head. She especially liked to use shoes. She hit my head with fire tongs and sticks. She also loved doing witchcraft. I did not like that. We did not get along well. After Liberation, I went to peasant meetings and I worked in the production team. When they were making the revolution (*hua geming*), I was also a team leader. I looked after the movement, the women's movement. Then I did not see her do those kinds of things. She and I had formed separate families in 1948. I gave her food to cook for herself. But I did not pay attention to her.

I had a paternal grandmother, uncle, and paternal aunt (*nainai, shushu, guma*). I never saw my grandmother and uncle. My aunt had a daughter, and while she was very small my aunt sold her to another village to be an adopted daughter-in-law. They were pitiful and very poor. My own sister was an adopted daughter-in-law in Jiangchuan. I never saw her. In fifty years I have not had any news or a letter. I served as political team leader for two years, then I got sick. I asked not to serve, but the masses did not agree, so I was selected to serve as political team leader for another two years. In those days I hated my mother. I thought, how could she do this type of thing (divining). It was too embarrassing. "I give you money, I send you grain. Why do you still keep doing it?" When my mother was curing (*duang feng*), she did not dance or sing. She could "see things" with people especially accurately. She could know if someone's door was open over there. I do not know where she learned these things.

My mother and father did not smoke opium. My father also did not drink. We had little interaction with the people of Lu Village. At Lu Village, there were horse stations. I remember two families that ran caravan stations. I do not know if men or women ran the horse station or how they divided the work. I only saw the horses carrying salt going into their courtyard.

These last two years we have lived well. I have four sons, four daughters. My last one, number eight, is already twenty-three years old. They are almost all entrepreneurs. The first had work. Later he disliked it because the factory salary was small, so he began to work on his own. My oldest works. My second also works. My third drives a car, and the fourth works together with his father in the same unit, the food company. My fourth also has a photocopying shop. My fifth and my oldest both drive cars. My oldest is in the car team. My eighth is in Kunming. Now we own this house, from doing business. I sold off my previous house. We bought this new house for ¥20,000.

We were the first to do business. We opened a shop and made rice noodles (*mixian*). I made bean curd, sold vegetables and meat. Those first two years, business was good. Although I worked hard, I could also earn a little money. These last two years, business is difficult to do. When we just started we were the only ones making rice noodles, now there are more than ten families making and selling them.

This follow-up interview confirmed the economic precariousness of this household without roots in Lu Village. The wealth that so impressed Fei obviously impressed the local bullies, who simply levied more taxes. The taxing, robbery, and kidnapping of Huang Shiniang's husband were also more likely to be inflicted on a family without strong local kin support. Tragedy followed and the family was broken and impoverished, with the daughters working as servants and married very early to alleviate their economic hardship. The land reform gave the daughter's family a chance to farm, but the orientation toward commercial activities was part of family know-how. Loyal to the revolution that rescued her from shameful poverty and made her a leader, the daughter repudiated her mother's shamanistic activities. She downplayed her mother's success, her economic contributions and wealth— remembering good things only about her father as the support of the family. The daughter's memory of her mother is at odds with the memories of Fei and other old people in some respects. However, the stories about bandits before and during Fei's time are certainly consistent with many other reports of lawlessness in Yunnan in the nineteenth and early twentieth centuries.[14] Like her mother, Huang Huaxian herself relied on commercial activities to achieve success in the reform period. The daughter and most of her eight children are town-dwelling *getihu*, individual entrepreneurs.

As far as I could find out, there is no contemporary equivalent of the seeress active in Lu Village today. However, such roles are being revived in other rural communities in China, as indicated by Seybolt's encounter with a woman shaman and his account of a girl spirit medium (*xiang tong*) in a village in Henan (Seybolt 1996:100, 108). Perhaps they will reappear in Lu Village.

This reconstruction of the long life of Huang Shiniang offers an opportunity to trace an unusual woman's career from the wartime of 1937 to the reforms of the late 1980s. It also offers insights into the changing nature of village and town life, as well as family crises, hardships, and varying family strategies across the revolutionary years up to the present. The themes of selling daughters for adoption, of sworn sisterhood, arranged marriage, uxorilocal marriage, divorce, and suicide, all of which emerge in this account, receive more complete treatment in later chapters on marriage and demography.

## NOTES

An earlier version of this chapter was presented at the University of California, Davis, Department of Anthropology and East Asian Studies, November 30, 1995. It has been revised to include the daughter's interview.

1. Table 6 in Fei (Fei and Zhang 1945:45) has been incorporated into table 4.10. In the Chinese version, *Yunnan San Cun*, "witch" was "*nuwu.*"

2. I have drawn on Wolf's three different ethnographic accounts of the same episode in *A Thrice-Told Tale* (1992). The first is fictionalized but inspired by her field notes. The second is directly from her field notes. The third, an academic article (Wolf 1990) written many years later, is based on field notes and enriched by wider professional experience as an anthropologist.

3. The title "*shiniang*" in the dictionary is translated as the "wife of a master." As will become clear, this was not the meaning villagers attached to it, for they clearly recognized *her* and not her husband as the master of the profession. The term *shiniang* contains both the concepts of expertise, as in *shi*, teacher or master, and female gender, in *niang*. The feminine parallel to the gendered term "master," i.e., "mistress," is ambiguous in English as well.

4. Fei described this payment in the Chinese text (Fei and Zhang 1990). The English text (1945) lacks these details.

5. The expression "eat idle rice" occurs in an article opposing footbinding and female dependency, "An Address to Two Hundred Million Fellow Countrywomen," written by Qiu Jin (Ch'iu Chin) around 1903 and translated for a collection of original sources in *Chinese Civilization and Society* (Ebrey 1981:248). Qiu Jin advised poor women to "work hard and help your husbands. Don't be lazy, don't eat idle rice" (1981:248). Qiu Jin clearly associated small feet with "physical comfort" and "free meal tickets" from men, arguing "can anyone enjoy such comfort and leisure without forfeiting dearly for it?" In the Lu Village context, the situation is turned around. Villagers criticized the husband for freeloading on his wife.

6. Margery Wolf (1992:105) cites Arthur Wolf's study in Taiwan in 1958–1959, in which over half the problems brought to a shaman concerned family members' health, with domestic discord accounting for 16 percent of the female clients. In the accounts of Huang Shiniang, illness seems less important than family discord or misfortune.

7. Fei commented on the sad condition of one such man "deprived of his inheritance by an uncle" who ended up in Lu Village (Fei and Zhang 1945: 59). Donald Attwood (1995), in a stimulating article about competition between siblings for resources in India, analyzes what was surely a general problem in overcrowded patrilineal villages of both India and China. See also Watson (1985).

8. Fei noted that people tended to cite the maximum rental paid, 60 percent of the crop, whereas a series of individual cases revealed that proportions paid in rent varied greatly and were sometimes as low as 33 percent (Fei and Zhang 1945:75–80). Similarly, people recounting what the seer received from her clients may have cited the maximum rather than the mean. Moreover, one could expect that during the busy season few would have time to see her, so her income could drop sharply with few farmers being aware of it.

9. Emily Ahern (1973) seems to have known only one *tang-ki* in her village and referred to only two others in neighboring towns.

10. Scott Simon (1994) examines the family origins of Daoist monks and nuns in Zhejiang. He finds that both sexes tended to be younger siblings such as second sons or second daughters—those who may be squeezed out of inheritance or dowry when a family already provided for its elder children.

11. *Tongyangxi* means, literally, "raised together daughter-in-law." In the first half of the twentieth century, it was common in many parts of China for families to give away their birth daughters and to adopt daughters from other families to raise. Adopted daughters were often intended to become the bride of one of the adopting family's sons. See

Wolf (1972) and Wolf and Huang (1980) on this custom in Taiwan, and Ruf (1998:44, 184) for a Sichuan village.

12. Liu Shaoqi was the first president of the People's Republic of China. Distrusted by Mao, he was imprisoned and denied medical attention; he died of pneumonia in 1969.

13. They would entreat her to *bai ji*, that is, to become a dry mother, or godmother.

14. Fei and Zhang (1945) wrote about having to wait for a safe caravan before traveling from Lufeng to Yi Village [Yits'un]. Accounts of kidnapping also appear in informant's life histories cited later, as well as in numerous travel books. The village party secretary also described rampant banditry south of Lufeng near Yimen that was difficult to control even after the revolution. In the reform period, accounts of banditry in rural areas are still common. Officials reminded me of this when explaining why they did not want me to stay in the village.

*Chapter Six*

# Wealth and Poverty, 1930s to 1990s: Paths to Ruin and Fortune

> Almost at the moment of entering the village, we were introduced to the startling contrast between the two classes who inhabit it: those who do not need to work during the slack agricultural period and those who must work continuously. (Fei and Zhang 1945:41)

The subject of rural wealth and poverty is as important today as it was in Fei Xiaotong's time. In the 1930s, and under Marxist influence, many writers believed that wealth was immoral, implying that the wealth of some accounted for the poverty of others. This view dominated in the first two and a half decades of revolutionary government, when land reform policies first redistributed land (early 1950s) and then collectivized ownership (mid-1950s), removing what Marxists believed was the cause of rural impoverishment and inequality: unequal ownership of private property.

In China's enthusiasm for reform in the post-Mao period, the government slogan "To get rich is glorious" signaled an abrupt reversal of the ideology of the revolutionary years, when the rich were reviled as the exploiters of the poor. The reformers acknowledged that for a country to become rich, some would have to get rich before others. The belief that socialism could bring everyone to a wealthier life, at the same pace, has now been abandoned by the government. Private property, however, has only been permitted in limited, uncertain domains. As we saw in chapter 4, agricultural land has not really reverted to private ownership. Moreover, the large and inefficient state sector, with ownership of many unprofitable industries, remains a major burden for the economy as a whole.

This chapter examines the question of changing village standards of living, and of wealth and poverty, comparing the present with the past as it was represented in Fei's writing. It is important to document the changes themselves

179

rather than merely interpreting the diverse attitudes about them. Nonetheless, these attitudes are important, ranging from jealousy and resentment toward the new (and recovering) rich by the poor, who grew up under the ideology of class struggle of two to three decades ago, to disdain for the poor as lazy and undeserving by those now achieving economic success. The tendency for some of the rich to flaunt their wealth arouses sentiments of envy, frustration, and injustice among the have-nots. People also believe that some have become wealthy through corruption. But in the aftermath of the Cultural Revolution and the violent suppression of the demonstrations at Tiananmen in 1989, villagers' expressions of their attitudes to wealth and poverty lean more to the cautious than the reckless. Recklessness appears when people are drunk, or flare up in anger, for instance, flagrantly boasting or casting bitter family or village quarrels into the language of class struggle, which had been such an effective weapon in the Cultural Revolution. More commonly, people are cautious, as they attempt to conceal or ignore both the wealth and poverty in their midst, seeming to mind their own business.

At present, the government supports a system that allows private accumulation of wealth and gives more free rein to ambition and individual effort than the get-rich-together policies pursued during the years of collectivization. There is no question that China as a whole is far richer, better fed, better clothed, and better informed today than it was from 1950 to 1975, just as there is no question that poverty persists (and has persisted throughout the period of collectives). To say that the current policies will no more be able to *eliminate* poverty than the past collectivist policies is not saying much—it is merely expressing an ideal. The goal of reducing the proportion of the desperately poor is more realistic, and ought to be the yardstick by which development policies are measured.[1] According to the World Bank, "broad participation in . . . reform-driven rural economic growth brought about [a] tremendous reduction in absolute poverty, from roughly 270 million poor in 1978 to about 100 million in 1985, or from one third to about one tenth of the total rural population" (World Bank 1995:1–2; 1992). During the next five years, however, the number of absolute poor remained unchanged at just under 100 million in 1990. This chapter will illustrate what has been achieved in Lu Village and the kinds of situations in which people have been, and are, most vulnerable.

## RESIDENTS, NEW SETTLERS, AND TRANSIENTS IN 1938: THE "ROOTLESSNESS" OF POVERTY

The movement of the landless people to and from Lu Village in pre-Liberation China made an impression on Fei (Fei and Zhang 1945:57). Indeed, in his description of Lu Village, as well as in his landmark study of Jiangcun (Kaixian-gong) in Jiangsu, he pointed out that length of residence and ownership of land within the community were important elements in local stratification; those who lacked recognized ancestors and owned no land were viewed as noncitizens.[2] Fei classified the population of Lu Village into residents, new set-tlers, and wandering souls—a kind of seniority system interwoven with prop-erty rights.

The history of settlement in Lu Village is difficult to reconstruct. Fei's eld-erly informants, probably born in the 1870s, remembered it as a site with only "a few houses," implying the village had grown up in their lifetimes from a rel-atively uninhabited area. However, the family tree of a prominent clan, shown to me by the descendants in 1991, attests to a long history of local Han settlement, going back some twenty generations to a military colony in the seventeenth century. Villagers point out that the school grounds were the an-cestral lands and garden of this illustrious family, granted many generations ago by the emperor for loyal service. The small number of residents that Fei's elderly informants remembered from their youth can be explained by massive depopulation resulting from the uprisings and massacres associated with the Muslim rebellion of the 1870s and the spread of bubonic plague, which was recorded in Lufeng in 1871–1872. Plague traveled, as epidemics generally do, along the same routes as traders and soldiers (Benedict 1996:41–42).

> The greatest damage in western Yunnan was sustained by towns along the road be-tween Kunming and Dali. . . . Death and emigration had greatly reduced the popu-lation of settlements on the Dali plain: before the rebellion the largest villages had some seven to eight hundred families, but in 1877 they had only two to three hun-dred (Gill 1883:250). The towns along the highway to Kunming lay in ruins: in 1883 . . . Zhennan, Chuxiong, Guangtong, Lufeng, and Anning were all in "a very dilapidated condition. In most of them the walls which were breached, had not been repaired; nor within the walls was there any marked indication of returning pros-perity." (Benedict 1996:41–42; the quoted material is from Hosie 1890:140).

The devastation also reached Lu Village, a station on the salt route with many inns. Fei noted that the largest village property holder, the temple of the Lord of the Earth belonging to "all the inhabitants of the village, for whose benefit the income is disbursed," acquired its property "by the rever-sion of the land of many villagers who perished during the Muslim rebellion of 1855–1873" (Fei and Zhang 1945:54). As a result, Lu Village would have been relatively open to migrants in the early twentieth century, but by 1938 resettlement and population growth meant that, at least in the center, the land was all claimed.

Among its 122 households, Fei counted 38 landless households, of which 34 were at least partly dependent on agricultural employment. Half rented land and, so, shared in some of the returns to farm management, whereas the others relied solely on cash earnings. Of the landless households, half (nineteen) were permanent residents but called "new settlers." They were immigrants from other villages of Lufeng (four), other areas of Yunnan (seven), and Sichuan province (eight), although some had been born in Lu Village. "New settlers" became villagers if they acquired land. However, acquisition of land was inhibited by keeping first right of purchase within the kin group, that is, among old settlers. It is unclear whether new settlers were among the beneficiaries of the Lord of the Earth temple's rental income, which included funds for the village school and "gifts at the marriages and burials of villagers" (Fei and Zhang 1945:54).

"Wandering souls," Fei explained, were different from the new settlers, who had some roots in or near the village. Wandering souls were:

> individuals of either sex who are landless and without special skills and who have no roots in Lu Village or elsewhere. They are often drifters, who appear suddenly in the village, work for a while, and then disappear again, though some of them have indeed resided for a long time in the village, alone and outside the stream of community life. They live in the homes of their employers on a hand-to-mouth, day-to-day basis. There were approximately thirty such individuals in the village in 1938, but by 1939 this number had been reduced about one-half. (Fei and Zhang 1945:59)

Fei gave several examples of such people: an itinerant laborer and former conscript, a dispossessed man from a neighboring village, a boy from Guizhou province who got "lost" from the army, and a maid, "a poor girl from a neighboring village, who worked for food, clothing, and shelter only" (60). These people just showed up, or vanished, living where they could get lodging. The seeress, Huang Shiniang, discussed in chapter 5, was among the uprooted who temporarily lived in Lu Village, after fleeing bandits, and moved on to Lufeng town when repeated "taxing" in Lufeng became too heavy to bear.

Permanency, or what one might call "seniority" or "tenure" in the village ranking system, was closely connected to land tenure, and to wealth and poverty. Examples of the poor were individuals who lacked, lost, or could not sustain family life. His two examples of impoverished, but mature, men in the "wandering soul" category both lacked the means to sustain families and lived drab lives of drudgery.

The first man had been away for twenty years, first as a migrant laborer, then as an army conscript, and had once collected money for a temple by pretending he was a monk, until he was exposed. "Too old to work regularly, without a family, and ignored or ridiculed by the villagers, he is living out his last days as a wretched derelict whose only diversion is attendance at the Christian church, where he can get a free cup of tea and join in the singing" (60).

The second example was thirty-year-old Lao Wang, who had come to Lu Village ten years earlier:

> Deprived of his inheritance by an uncle when his parents died in childhood, he is possessed of a stubborn independence. . . . We were especially smitten by the pathos of this homeless, unattached man when we saw him among the guests at the celebration of the harvest moon. . . . Surrounded, as he was, by those who had families and occupied secure, comfortable positions in the community, his lack of stable ties and sense of belonging were most striking. Those around him represented the personification of the goals he strove for, but the expression in his eyes betrayed his feeling of hopelessness. . . . There is little prospect for Lao Wang other than the prolongation of his present kind of life until the end of his days. (60)

Fei also observed poverty where physical disability was a factor: "The blind fortune teller . . . is a destitute bachelor. He is rarely consulted, and he finds it necessary to travel all over the valley to make a few pennies. When I first saw him on the road, I assumed he was a beggar, and only later learned that he was a professional man" (46). He described two other households as "representative of the landless families" who relied on wage labor for a living. Both rented smoky one-room thatched huts *outside* the village gates. Rain caused the roof and part of the wall to collapse in one house, and flooded the earth floor of the other.

Those who lacked land lacked leisure. The landless labored during the slack season when other households had the security of stored grain from the harvest. The term "coolie," in English, comes from the Chinese term "*ku li*," meaning bitter labor. As we have already seen, many of the poor worked as salt or coal carriers on the caravan trails. Fei wrote with passion about the class differences between village landowners, who enjoyed leisure during the slack season, and the landless, who had to work manually for wages.

> An occupation engaged in by many of the poor laborers is the transportation of salt. The neighboring district produces large quantities of salt and supplies a large area, including Kunming. Since motor transport is available only on the public highway, human and animal carriers must be used between it and the wells. In November, 1938, a carrier was paid 80 cents for transporting a 130-pound load. Deducting the cost of his food and lodging for the three days required for the round trip, his wage would be about 20 cents a day. Although this was, at that time, double the pay for farm labor, the task is so strenuous that only extreme poverty and the lack of any other work would induce the villagers to undertake it. It is impossible to work at it continuously. In fact, even a strong, healthy man can make no more than four trips a month. Kong, who was both poor and industrious, had made only six trips the year before; and he then gave up this work completely because he could get enough farm work. Owing to the reluctance of the villagers to serve as carriers, except when circumstances forced them to do it, the wage was increased in 1938 to three times the farm wage. According to information I obtained in 1939, approximately 40 people in the village, including even women and children, constantly carried salt during the slack agricultural period. (49)

The image of these desperately poor, overworked porters straining and staggering along rural roads, smeared black from the black salt and coal they carried, haunts many accounts of early twentieth century China, yet I encountered scenes like it in many parts of China in the 1980s.[3] While Fei commented that even women and children did this work, he wrote no more about them. One of the women I interviewed in the 1990s, Mrs. Gao, described the part of her life when she experienced severe hardship as the daughter of a widow with young children who alternated wage labor on opium farms with work as a coal carrier in the early 1940s. Her family closely resembled the immigrant settlers and wandering souls that Fei described, who came to Lu Village in search of a livelihood.

Mrs. Gao, a Poor Wage Laborer in the 1940s

I was born in Tanghai in 1927. From Tanghai to here is rather far. It takes one whole morning of walking to get there. In the past, Tanghai had no water. There was only dry land. There was no wheat; we planted corn and waited for rain. When the rain came, we planted rice. Rice transplanting depended on rainfall, so we planted late. The rice seedlings did not grow well. In Tanghai, most of the people worked as hired laborers.

My father had died when I was three years old [1930] and my younger brother was just born. When I was young, I went to Lu Village to several landowners' houses to work, *bang gong* (literally, "help" but used for wage work), with farmwork. For food, we depended on helping people. Other people would take us a meal of rice, or a meal of various grains. Whatever they gave, that was what we ate. For helping three days, because we were young, they did not even give one *sheng* (liter) of rice. They only gave a little rice. Oil—we never touched it to eat, much less any meat. We also could not hunt wild hens or rabbits. Those who hunted were big, rich people. If they had money, they could have guns. Other people did not have them.

We had no money to eat pork. In the past, you wanted to raise some pigs for New Year, for on the last day of the year, you paid your debts to other people. Then they led away your pigs. Our family also raised them, but at the New Year we didn't get to eat them. We took them and exchanged them for food. We did not butcher our pigs. People who had money carried off the pigs of those who were lacking. Before, we never butchered a pig. Only after Liberation did we kill pigs. On the evening of the 30th, we would go to the street and buy a little meat—we could not buy more than a little, half a pound. They cut off a bit of the slippery tip; it seemed so small, like the size of a slipper for bound feet. To this day, when I see those shoes, I still laugh about it.

When I was small we used to come to Middle Village to help people, to help them harvest and cut the opium poppy, *yapian*.[4] I was only thirteen or fourteen years old then, so I do not remember clearly. Only now, at times when I go to pick bitter horse vegetable, I still recall that in the past, opium's leaves resembled these. To harvest it, you took the poppy head and cut it. When you cut it . . . well, you could collect black oil by using a curved knife. The landowners followed along together. Harvesting, we took a large level bowl and went back.

Whether planting opium produced income or not, I do not remember. The landowner would pay us with some beans. If there were beans, they gave some beans, if rice, they gave some rice. For three days of work, they gave one liter. When I went back, I carried it home. Later, the landlords—weren't they cunning?—they wanted to take their rice and sell it as a high profit commodity. They wanted to hoard it to sell, and only gave us some broad beans. They rarely gave us rice. Rice, they would lend out at interest. The landlords would lend out one *dou* (decaliter) of rice, and then get five *sheng* (liters) of profit.

Perhaps opium cultivation had changed and had been broken near and around the city, but fifty years ago, I remember we used to plant the fields, just a little past a hill. Then we came to this Lu Village Hamlet just after the revolution. The year we came here, perhaps the second year, opium was still planted. From that year on, then, not even a little was planted.

When people worked in farming, men did the heavy work. For two full days they got a *sheng*. Women worked three days and received a *sheng*. I myself was still small, and did not even get a *sheng*. Women did the transplanting and helped people with weeding and harvesting. Men did the plowing, threshed, and carried the grain. For plowing fields, men got one liter of rice for two days of labor; they did not use their own water buffalo. Our family had no ox or horse. Those years were most difficult.

I was married at age sixteen [1943]. At eighteen, I had a daughter. My husband was from Sichuan province. He came here to work. He possessed a handicraft, the skill of weaving bamboo baskets. At first, when he came to Tanghai, my mother was raising three children. In the village, my family's relative, *da yima* (great aunt) spoke and said there was my mother, alone, raising us three siblings (*jiemei*). My older brothers had been taken off to be soldiers in the time of the Nationalists (Guomindang). My first older brother later ran away from the army, but my second brother just never came back. When my second brother was taken by the army, he already had a son, who lived to age six and then died. There was only the second daughter-in-law who was still alive. Then my older sister was married out to someone.

My mother decided to seek a son-in-law to help out at home. So we then asked the man from Sichuan to come to our house. My great aunt, *yima*, introduced him to our family. He came to our house mainly because our life was hard. When he came to our house, I was only thirteen. He stayed a few years and then we got married. In the past this was called parental arrangement. When this man came, I knew that he would be my husband. He ate at our house, and lived there. As the years passed, he made baskets and this went to pay our debts and to exchange for some rice to eat. He wove bamboo caps to wear and back-carrying baskets until the New Year. When the year was over, then he tied them together and went to sell them for money. He took them to big, rich people's houses and exchanged them for some rice to pass the New Year. In those days, people could not relax, they were always living under pressure.

We used to go to Lu Village, and we would also go and see many high, high mountain cliffs and carry charcoal back to sell. At one market, I would take coal to sell and I would get five liters of rice. I would walk to Military Platform Mountain (Wutai Shan), on the side of Middle Village's Miaomiao Slope—I went there and to many places to carry coal to Lufeng to sell. In one week, I could go two times carrying loads on my back. Some of those rich people bought it for cooking. When I got five liters of rice, then I could live for the week. Each back load was fifty pounds, two trips were one hundred pounds. Really, there was no other way. If it rained, you could not go. If you wanted to plant land, there was no land. We could only go to the street market and buy a few small vegetables to cook and pass the day. We had not a kernel of rice, and vegetables were cheaper. We had no land. On clear days I went to carry coal to get money and come back and buy rice. If it rained, then we could not carry coal, and there was no money so we could not buy vegetables or rice to eat. We did not have enough rice to eat. In the past it was so hard.

Mrs. Gao's memory of her youth makes it clear that the market offered opportunities for women to work picking opium, farming, or carrying loads. What is less clear is whether people were paid by the amount or value of work done, or by wage rates based on age and gender. In opium picking, women and even children might work as fast as men, yet they may have been assigned to and paid according to different types of task, reflecting their gender identity or age. As porters, it is likely that men, women, and children all carried loads appropriate to their own size and strength, and lesser pay for women and children may well have been based on the load they carried. We also learn from Mrs. Gao that poor families were accustomed to moving from village to village, wherever there was work available, since the land in their home village could not support them throughout the year. As a hamlet leader, Mrs. Gao's memories of the past reflect a sensitivity to class differences that might be less evident in other accounts.

Continuing with the life of Mrs. Gao,

In 1948, a year before Liberation, we came to this area, my mother, my husband, and two children. After Liberation, when our older child was four and our second, a son, was just born [Mrs. Gao was twenty-two years old], we were living in a neighboring village. We heard from someone who lives in this hamlet of Lu Village that there was land available here. We wanted land, so we came to this hamlet. Then, the hamlet had only three families. The fields were all uncultivated. At that time, the hamlet had a landlord family—rich peasants. One family was poor peasants. Three others were all about the same. So we all came together here. Now there are twenty-nine households and 129 people here.[5] Today we have a reservoir, and farming is better. Today, in our hamlet there is a [former] landowner. His former life was still not as good as his son's life today.

Thus, due to labor migration experience, Mrs. Gao's family had knowledge of various villages and, during the land reform, they learned that land was available in an outlying hamlet of Lu Village. Land reform, then, allowed some of the wandering souls and coolie laborers that Fei poignantly described to become permanent residents with land rights.

## MRS. YUAN AND THE EPIDEMIC

The life history of Mrs. Yuan illustrates the terrible impact of disease, an influenza epidemic, and family breakdown upon the woman who later became founder of the four-generation matriline described at the opening of the preface. Mrs. Yuan was eighty (she was born in 1909) when I first met her in 1989. I learned her story during various short chats in 1990. In the next few years, her health declined and when I returned in 1994 I learned she had died.

The first time I was married at age fourteen. The marriage was arranged and my husband was fifteen years old. His name was Yuan. My father-in-law and the whole family got sick. The family, six people, all died. The disease was an influenza epidemic (*liuxing xing ganmao*) around 1925.[6] My father-in-law and mother-in-law, my husband, my own daughter, my husband's younger brother and sister all died. A few years later, the Yuan family clan forced me to marry again, this time to my husband's *tangge* (patrilineal cousin). My second husband was a half year older than I. A year after being married, my husband was taken by the Nationalist Army to Lufeng County town to be a soldier. Later, he went to Baoshan (a town in western Yunnan).

After my husband left, my father- and mother-in-law treated me badly. The Yuan family was not good to me because I first gave birth to two girls. One of them died of neglect and the second died at birth. When my first daughter got sick, they gave me no money for health care. If it had been a boy, they would have given it. One time when I was out, they even threw my seven-month-old daughter into a ditch. Only my third daughter survived. Later, my two sons, one at age three and one at nine months, both got sick and died. My three-year-old died of pneumonia and my nine-month-old son died suddenly from an illness affecting his mouth. My husband never wrote to me nor sent me any money back at home. So then I went to the county Yamen to make a lawsuit (*da guansi*) demanding that my husband give me living expenses. This had no effect. In 1945 [when she was about thirty-six years old], he found a second wife (*xiao laopo*, literally little wife) and did not come back.

The Yuan family was not good to me. When I went to court, the Yuan family gave me money worth two *dan* of rice. The Yuan family had two men come into the road with guns (*qiang*); they wanted to kill me. Then my younger brother came to get me, and then I went home. Later, my brother fled to avoid the draft (*duo bing*) and died away from home. I was caring for a four-year-old daughter and a two-year-old son, and was pregnant with an unborn child when I returned to Lu Village [around 1940]. After I came home, people pressured me to remarry (*gaijia jiehun*). But I was not willing to remarry; I only wanted to raise my daughter to adulthood: that would be fine.

After Liberation, because they were afraid to be classified as landlords, my husband's family gave me one *gong* (0.4 mu) of land, but I myself had already received land and a house in my own village, so I gave it all back to my husband's family. My husband's family was then classified as "rich peasants" in a neighboring village.

When I came back to Lu Village with the children [in 1940], I helped people work [for wages]. During the day I did farmwork, transplanting and weeding, and during the evenings I earned money by helping people make clothes and shoes. I would get six liters of rice for six days' work. When I went to people's houses to make clothes, they supplied me with two meals, a pound of rice. When I worked for other people, in one day and a half, I could make a set of clothes. In three evenings, I could make a pair of cloth shoes. In one evening I could make a pair of pants. Sometimes I also went to Middle Village market to buy grain, chickens and return with them to Lufeng to sell, to earn a little money so my daughter could study.

Mrs. Yuan's story shows the heavy toll of disease in the first half of the twentieth century, which wiped out her first family and took a number of her children. Her second family and husband probably felt she was bad luck, especially since her first children were girls. Fei described a similar situation in household C, when a man whose whole family became ill, possibly from malaria, blamed the death of his wife and the illness of everyone else upon his daughter-in-law, "a vehicle of ill fortune," who was also ill (Fei and Zhang 1945:93). The Yuan family's rejection of Mrs. Yuan's daughters illustrates that certain families were adamant in their belief that only boy babies had any worth, a topic that I will examine further in chapter 8.

Mrs. Yuan's account also shows that a single mother could support herself, provided she could obtain shelter. Fortunately, her younger brother provided this shelter, and when he died she may have inherited the house. Mrs. Yuan also gives us a glimpse of the maneuvering that took place at the time of land reform, when wealthy families tried to divest themselves of land in order to avoid classification as landlord or rich peasant by the Communist land reform teams. In a later section, we see how assignment of political labels with reactionary connotations could bring dire consequences.

## THE RICH IN 1938

In 1938, Fei was struck by the differences between wealthy and poor villagers in Lu Village. The rich had better housing, clothes, and food. They could avoid manual labor and they enjoyed leisure. For example, two households, A and B, "enjoy the highest standard of housing, clothing, and food in the village" (Fei and Zhang 1945:92). They had spacious, clean two-story houses; they wore excellent clothing, including long robes for formal wear, silk and expensive materials for jackets for the men, silver earrings for the women, leather shoes and European shirts for the young men. Their cuisine was appreciated by Fei for its abundant vegetables, wine, wheat-cake desserts, and honey (91).

Fei was predisposed to view wealth in this community as coming primarily from landownership, for there was little income from handicrafts such as weaving or other commodities produced in the village. Like many others of his day, he looked for output in the form of tangible goods, not services. As a result, he did not emphasize income from commercial activities such as innkeeping and trade. He concentrated on measuring the incomes that people could harvest from the land, and these incomes were largely dependent on the amount of land they owned or rented or their work as wage laborers. In chapter 4, we examined the distribution of landholdings in 1938 and found that a small number of households (about 8 percent) owned seventeen to twenty-six mu (roughly 2.5 to 4 acres). Clearly this scale of landowning could provide some security but not great wealth. Fei interpreted the "problem" of the rich as one of "whiling away their many leisure hours. For my landlord, who neither works nor uses opium, this is a burdensome problem, which he can solve only by sleeping long hours and by loitering about the church and the teashops" (105).

Fei was idiosyncratic in estimating income from nonagricultural sources such as commerce. Describing two wealthy households, A and B mentioned in chapter 4, he calculated that cash income from surplus grain amounted to ¥185[7] for B. But household B also netted ¥150 through long-distance trade, purchasing oxen for sale in Kunming and purchasing paper in a distant village for sale in Lu Village (85–86). In other words, long-distance trade provided about half the income, or even more if other commodities were traded that Fei did not learn about. This trading was apparently undertaken by the same landlord that Fei described above as loitering, suggesting he possibly used the tea shops as a kind of "trading room" to organize such business ventures. Other examples of commercial activity can be seen from responses to inflation in 1939, when "the rich ex-headman . . . organized a group of his friends to store more than 50,000 pounds of salt, and even the poor laborers bought pigs for later sale in the rising market" (107). Fei's chapter on family finances also suggests that interest on loans could be a significant source of income. As Fei pointed out, these funds were not always borrowed by the poorest; sometimes they were used to finance productive enterprises or to re-lend at higher rates (121).

The rich were the large landowners, but they were also former government officials, former tax collectors, the headmen, or former headmen. Fei provides little information about the ways these positions became lucrative. This is probably because his informants were secretive about avenues to unofficial sources of income through selling favors (e.g., for closing their eyes to opium trafficking) or imposing extra taxes—problems that still exist.

In addition to wealthy landowners and officials, the innkeepers and the owners of caravan horses and mules could earn incomes that seem substantial for the times. As a rough guideline, I estimate they earned three to six times

more than landowner-farming households (with seventeen to twenty-six mu).
Considerable risk was involved with horse caravans, which could succumb to
livestock diseases or bandits. Of course, risks were even greater for landless laborers, who earned roughly one-sixth as much as the landowner-farmers, for
whom a day without work might mean a day without food.

## How to Get Rich

Fei believed that "in a village like Lu Village, where even simple handicraft
industry is not developed, almost the entire burden of the population, both
landed and landless, must be supported by the land" (Fei and Zhang
1945:44). After examining nonfarm incomes, he first stated that "the economy of this type of village is based mainly on the land, which determines the
standard of living of the people" (51). But in a later passage he stated: "Land
breeds no land. . . . [T]he way to wealth lies outside the occupation of farming and ambitious villagers must leave the land (129). He thus recognized
that real opportunities lay outside the village because successful farming was
not profitable enough to allow families to buy more land. The average
amount of land per family was decreasing due to population growth (see
chapter 8). In addition, opium addiction contributed to the loss of land for
some families. Those who were able to buy enough land for a viable farm obtained the money from nonfarm sources.

In 1938, there were about twenty young Lu Village men pursuing activities outside the village: a college graduate, two students, two craft appren-
tices, a tax collector, a driver, an army officer, and twelve soldiers. Fei observed, "It is the hope of all the parents that their children will enjoy a living
better than their own, and they are aware that this hope can be realized only
if the children are so prepared that they can secure better jobs in the town or
city" (129).

Offering an anecdote about a long-indebted family that cleared up its debts
and bought land one year after their son entered the army, Fei noted that the
richest village family had a son who was commander of a regiment, and offered as examples the school principal, the "head of local government, the tax
collector and others, to prove the pecuniary value of political position." The
paths to prosperity thus included education, the military, and political position—all associated with what Gates would call the tributary mode of production, dominated by the state. Yet as we have seen, a number of examples
showed that entrepreneurship and commercial activities, innkeeping, long-
distance trade, and money lending were also ways to get rich.

Fei's budgets and brief family descriptions of five households were selected
to represent a spectrum from wealthy to poor. His outline of their household

economies provided a glimpse into what caused some households to be poorer than others. Fei found class differences in Lu Village based on land and family history. Some families were early settlers and owned land, while others were more recent arrivals or transients lacking landed property and social networks. The system was fluid, with wealthy families losing fortunes for various reasons such as death of expensive caravan mules from disease, opium addiction, or division of land among too many sons. In fact, Fei felt that success sowed the seeds of its own destruction when wealthy families raised more sons than the poor, reducing the inheritance for each son.

## 1938 to the Early 1990s

The economic changes affecting Lu Village between Fei's study and my own are difficult to trace in a systematic fashion. Shifting government policies aimed at reducing class difference and reorganizing production undoubtedly had profound effects on everyone during this fifty-year period. Nationwide political mobilization reached into the remote corners of China, and in Yunnan, places such as Lu Village were caught in the action. After the land reform and collectivization of the 1950s, the two most significant movements were the Great Leap Forward, 1958–1961, and the Cultural Revolution, 1966–1976.

The Great Leap Forward was an ambitious and disastrous government attempt to force the entire rural population of China into huge communes, to engage in farming, damming waters, and conducting massive construction projects, following principles of socialist planning. It is well known today that the Great Leap resulted in a massive famine. For rural populations, poverty and starvation revisited them, despite the promises of a better life after Liberation. (The demographic impact of this will be discussed in chapter 8.) Rural populations are still very reluctant to discuss those terrible times in any detail.

The Cultural Revolution generally had a less serious impact on the villages, but it, too, disrupted lives and investments in education in ways that are still being felt today. These decades of hardship under Communist government were also years in which record keeping was lax, or disrupted. As a result, my account of changes in the village economy leaps from Fei's starting point to the 1990s. After examining some of the quantitative measures of village change between these two endpoints, I present portions of several life histories that provide glimpses into the experiences of poor and wealthy villagers across time. Often, the nature of their difficulties is unstated, or understated, but knowledge of the chronology of China's macrolevel policies allows us to place personal experience into the context of these larger political and economic movements and ponder their impact.

## WEALTH AND POVERTY IN THE 1990S

Sixty years after Fei's study, village economic conditions and the nature of wealth and poverty have been shaped by both revolution and reforms, but many traditional elements remain. Fei wanted to understand why some households become more successful than others. Today, when we ask this question, we also want to know how gender affects prosperity, poverty, and risk. Chinese women experience certain kinds of disadvantages in rural society, but they also share in prosperity and are not alone in poverty. Does a woman's position in society derive from her own achievements or from those of her husband and family? How much do families influence the position of men and women? The dilemma of sorting out the relationship between gender and class has never been easy because of the mysterious nature of the household, the "black box" of economic anthropology, as Richard Wilk (1989) describes it. Interposed between an individual man or woman and the market of opportunity and failure, there are family bonds and kinship. Families and kin groups form a shifting set of relationships that can pull individuals up or down, take them in or throw them out. After analyzing individuals in terms of their economic coordinates, it is necessary to try to peer into the black box to discover how these families behave.

The pace of Lu Village economic development today can be appreciated by placing it in the context of the wider economy of the nation and province. Where does Lu Village stand in terms of the economic standards of the nation? There is no single standard that adequately conveys economic well-being and quality of living. All standards involve simplifying assumptions and different ways of presenting aggregated data. Those who believe tables of numbers bring certainty and firmness will find that many anthropologists consider them spongy; their usefulness depends on getting good ingredients and mixing them properly. Typically, the cooks don't know very much about where and how the ingredients were produced, and how many mysterious "additives" they contain. Anyone who has worked with census data in China knows they cannot always expect everything to add up. Presenting tables showing the macroeconomic changes from different angles is like cutting slices through a marbled cake, where the colors and patterns vary from piece to piece. That said, let's have a taste.

## CASH INCOME MEASURES FOR
## CHINA, YUNNAN, AND LU VILLAGE

China's census reports income per capita but does not report income differences for men and women. Income includes returns from farming, where farmers sell a large part of their grain output to the state, and the salaries of people with formal employment and formally registered businesses. Officials are less able to calculate income from the many informal occupations that are common in the countryside, such as selling vegetables, prepared foods, and grain surpluses in the market, selling and butchering pigs informally rather than at state slaughterhouses, earning wages from casual construction, furniture making, domestic employment, catering, and so forth.

Even with more intensive interview methods, calculating household income and expenses is exceedingly complex, and people are often forgetful or hesitant to report some of their sources of income over the year. People also have vague ways of reporting incomes. Typical answers among Lu Villagers are "more than hundred a month (*yi bai duo*), more than one thousand a year (*yi qian duo*)." (One has to accept the lower figure, since there is no way to take an average of the open-ended "more than.") Recognizing that the methods used are not absolutely comparable, I present official data on incomes for the national and provincial levels and for Lufeng County, followed by my own survey results for Lu Village. Thus, we can arrive at an understanding of Lu Village's relative standard of living.

National censuses present data that are designed to be consistent across regions, whatever the shortcomings of actual data collection. First, we examine the incomes of the rural population of Yunnan Province compared to other provinces of southwest China and the nation as a whole. Provinces of central and west China are generally poorer than the coastal provinces (Carter et al. 1996). Yunnan rural incomes are below the national average but are similar to its neighbors, Sichuan and Guizhou (table 6.1). Data for 1980–1991 show a tremendous increase in income in yuan, reflecting China's growth rates since the reforms, but also overstate the increase unless we take into account inflation. While net income in Yunnan increased from ¥338 to ¥573 yuan between 1985 and 1991 (an increase of 60 percent), these gains were an illusion due to inflation.

Prices had been quite stable in China from 1952 to 1984 (decreasing from 1963 to 1972), but inflation was rapid in the late 1980s until the events of Tiananmen in 1989, slowed briefly in the 1990s, and slowed again in the late 1990s (see table 6.2).

The national price index, measuring the increase for each year compared to the preceding year, shows that prices climbed 62 percent between 1985 and 1990. In 1991, household expenses for food were worth roughly 60 percent or

**Table 6.1. Southwest Provinces and China: Peasant Households' Net Incomes (yuan) per Capita, Selected Years**

| Area | 1980 | 1985 | 1990 | 1991 |
|---|---|---|---|---|
| Yunnan | 150 | 338 | 541 | 573 |
| Sichuan | 188 | 315 | 558 | 590 |
| Guizhou | 161 | 287 | 435 | 466 |
| China | 191 | 397 | 686 | 709 |

*Source:* SSB (1992:308).

Table 6.2.  Consumer Price Changes
for China, 1985–1991 (previous year's
price = 100)

| Year | Price Index |
| --- | --- |
| 1985 | 109 |
| 1986 | 106 |
| 1987 | 107 |
| 1988 | 119 |
| 1989 | 118 |
| 1990 | 102 |
| 1991 | 103 |
| 1992 | 108 |
| 1993 | 119 |
| 1994 | 126 |
| 1995 | 110 |
| 1996 | 107 |
| 1997 | 100 |
| 1998 | 99 |
| 1999 | 99 |

Sources: SSB (1992:235); YPSB (1995:244).
The years 1994–1999 are from Bloomberg
(2001) CN CPI.

more of the household incomes for Yunnan and for China as a whole (table
6.3). This shows interesting continuity with the 1930s. Fei reported that 60
percent of the income in the average Chinese village was spent on food, and
indeed his five examples of household budgets in Lu Village showed food
ranging from 48 to 70 percent of living expenses (Fei and Zhang 1945:51,
87–89).[8] It is generally believed that with increasing wealth, people spend a
smaller proportion of income on food.

Table 6.4 shows the income of Lufeng County, which includes the market
town as well as Lu Village and other villages. These data show that in 1991

Table 6.3.  Rural Households: Household Enterprise Net Incomes and Basic Living
Expenses (yuan) per Capita, 1991

| Area | Household incomes | Basic household expenses | | | | | |
| --- | --- | --- | --- | --- | --- | --- | --- |
| | | Food | Clothing | Housing | Fuel | Tools | Total |
| Yunnan | 513 | 315 | 38 | 51 | 13 | 51 | 468 |
| Sichuan | 520 | 345 | 41 | 47 | 25 | 57 | 515 |
| Guizhou | 425 | 284 | 35 | 23 | 23 | 30 | 395 |
| China | 589 | 352 | 51 | 69 | 27 | 72 | 571 |

Source: SSB (1992:309–11).

Note: Net incomes from household enterprises exclude income rural households earn from collective or
state enterprises. It should therefore primarily reflect incomes gained through family farming. (Net income
in table 6.1 includes income from collective and state enterprises.)

Lufeng County's average income was only 36 percent of that of Kunming City and 20 percent less than the provincial average. The county, then, unlike so many of those that foreigners have been allowed to study, is not disproportionately wealthy and Lu Village is no "model village."[9]

During the reforms, Lufeng has increased its average income per capita but not as fast as the Yunnan average, or of some other counties of south-central Yunnan, and not as fast as Kunming. Two possible reasons that Lufeng has been lagging are its agriculture and transportation. Lufeng grows less tobacco than some of Yunnan's wealthier areas, especially those near Yuxi. Tobacco is Yunnan's most lucrative crop. With a reputation for quality, Yunnan tobacco is in demand across China, where smoking has become a symbol of masculine well-being, despite the warnings of the Ministry of Health. Growing reminders of the success of tobacco are a rash of new skyscrapers and lavish building projects belonging to tobacco companies built in Kunming since 1990.[10]

Lufeng County may also have been affected by the new east-west superhighway between Kunming and the city of Dali in western Yunnan. This highway now bypasses, farther to the south, the market town of Lufeng. I do not know if this had an influence as early as 1991, when the highway was still under construction. When I asked the Lu Village party secretary about the impact of the highway in 1996, he agreed that it had an effect but felt it was not too serious, since Lu Village still has fairly good transportation to the new

**Table 6.4.   Average Income per Capita (yuan), Rural and Urban Areas, Central Yunnan, 1985–1991**

| Region | 1985 | 1988 | 1991 | Percent increase |
|---|---|---|---|---|
| Yunnan Province | 424 | 673 | 1,011 | 138 |
| Kunming City | 1,109 | 1,988 | 2,512 | 126 |
| West of Kunming | | | | |
| Chuxiong District | 453 | 733 | 1,011 | 123 |
| Lufeng County | 523 | 778 | 914 | 74 |
| Lu Village | 327 | 647 | unknown | 98 |
| | | | | |
| East of Kunming | | | | |
| Qujing District | 402 | 647 | 940 | 133 |
| Luliang County | 402 | 639 | 683 | 70 |
| South of Kunming | | | | |
| Yuxi District | 738 | 1,571 | 2,309 | 213 |
| Tonghai County | 514 | 891 | 1,086 | 111 |

*Source:* YPSB 1992, adapted from table 19-4; Lu Village records (see table 4.15).

*Note:* The percent increase for Lu Village is for 1985–1988. I do not have village records of average income per person for 1991. Lu Village income in 1985 may have been especially low due to the employment of more male labor in town. The records show more than fifty fewer laborers in 1985 than in 1984 and after 1987. YPSB (1995:622, table 19-11) reports net income for a sample rural population by county for 1992–1994, showing Lufeng County *rural* net incomes as 709 (1992), 769 (1993), and 937 (1994).

highway, and to Kunming via the old Burma Road, which is now somewhat faster because it is less choked with traffic. Finally, table 6.4 suggests that incomes at district levels (or prefectures, *qu* or *zhou*) are growing faster than counties, perhaps because higher-level administrative cities are generally growing more than county towns.

Turning to Lu Village, my 1990 household survey shows lower incomes than those for the county. Unlike the county, which includes the county town with higher income administrative, commercial, and industry sectors, the village is almost entirely rural. In addition, the incomes I report for Lu Village are exclusively cash incomes. I have not calculated the value of the home-grown grain, pork, and vegetables consumed by all households receiving land allocations, but only their cash income from grain or livestock sold (table 6.5). The incomes of individuals in the center are, on average, about 14 percent higher than those from the hamlets, most likely a reflection of proximity to jobs in town.

By 1997, another survey of fifty households (table 6.6) shows that the average annual cash incomes have increased considerably, even when adjusted for inflation. This is primarily due to the growth of opportunities to earn cash in town or outside the village. What is particularly interesting about this sample is that within the 20–29 age group, although women are only about one-third of those reporting, the difference in cash incomes between the sexes is insignificant (with women showing a tiny edge).

This suggests that more nonfarm opportunities are opening to women. It also points to the importance of education, for some of the women with good salaries have high educational levels and some of the cash-earning young men are working seasonally as unskilled labor for much lower wages.

Table 6.7 gives examples of incomes of men and women with nonfarm employment, taken from the first and fifth (top and bottom) quintiles for men and women. The villagers who earn higher incomes generally work for the government or as entrepreneurs with skills that are scarce (e.g., carpentry, medical education, driver education, and license to drive a car) or access to scarce capital (ownership of a horse cart, access to a cousin's minivan or to an uncle's store). They also engage in these occupations roughly twelve months of the year. In contrast, those who earn low incomes are generally performing manual labor using skills that are not scarce. They perform these jobs for several months a year, contribute to farming, and take available odd

**Table 6.5.   Lu Village Average Income per Person, 1990**

| Unit | Avg. annual cash income (yuan) |
|------|-------------------------------|
| Lu Village Center (8 teams, n = 40) | 572 |
| Lu Village Hamlets (7 teams, n = 42) | 502 |
| Greater Lu Village (15 teams, n = 82) | 534 |
| Incomplete = 4 | |

*Source:* Village survey, random sample 1990.

**Table 6.6.     Lu Village Nonfarm Cash Incomes by Sex and Age, 1997**

| Age Cohort | Men Avg. Nonfarm Income (yuan) | Number | Women Avg. Nonfarm Income (yuan) | Number |
|---|---|---|---|---|
| 50–59 | 4,084 | 10 | — | 0 |
| 40–49 | 2,930 | 14 | 1,973 | 6 |
| 30–39 | 1,892 | 5 | 1,019 | 4 |
| 20–29 | 2,984 | 29 | 3,106 | 16 |
| 17–19 | 1,566 | 9 | 800 | 1 |
| Total | 2,865 | 67 | 2,460 | 27 |

*Source:* 1997 random sample, fifty households (totals based on rounded averages).

jobs during the rest of the year. The annual cash incomes overstate the difference between the first and fifth quintiles because the former tend to work year round. The monthly returns to labor are around 350 to 800 in the first quintile and 100 to 350 in the fifth quintile.

**Table 6.7.     Lu Village Range of Nonagricultural Incomes per Year, 1996**

| Main occupation by sex | | 1996 cash income |
|---|---|---|
| *1st quintile* | *Male* | |
| | Carpentry workshop entrepreneur | 10,000 |
| | County government employee, 787/mo. | 9,444 |
| | High-school teacher, 600/mo. | 7,200 |
| | Minivan driver (maternal cousin's van), 600/mo. | 7,000 |
| | Steelworker | 6,000 |
| *1st quintile* | *Female* | |
| | High-school teacher, 600/mo. | 7,200 |
| | Cadre, county police, 600/mo. | 7,200 |
| | Horse-cart driver, 500/mo. | 6,000 |
| | Doctor (university educated), 500/mo. | 6,000 |
| | Saleswoman (uncle's store), 350/mo. | 4,200 |
| *5th quintile* | *Male* | |
| | Brick factory casual worker, 3 months (450), plus rock breaking, 1 month (300) | 750 |
| | Transport worker, 3 months | 700 |
| | Construction worker, 2 months | 624 |
| | Construction worker, 2 months | 600 |
| | Construction worker, 1 month | 200 |
| *5th quintile* | *Female* | |
| | Brick factory casual worker, 9 months | 800 |
| | Store clerk, 3 months | 750 |
| | Vegetable vender, 1 month | 300 |
| | Seamstress in Lufeng, 3 months | 300 |
| | Wild mushroom vender, 1 month | 200 |

*Source:* 1997 interviews.

Quantitative data about Lu Village provide information about the aggregate population and the place of individuals at various points in time. Other dimensions of village life cannot be easily grasped from this kind of summary. I now examine the lives of poorer and wealthier segments of the population.

## THE POOR IN THE 1990S: WIDOWERS, REFORMED LABORERS, THE OLD, AND THE DISABLED

As explained in chapter 1, in 1990 I used village household registers to select a random sample of eighty households for interviews. However, it was not equally easy to gain access to all households. In particular, the very poor and the very rich households proved more difficult to locate at home and less capable or cooperative in fully describing their economic situations.

The shortcoming of my sampling method is that it assumed that all residents were official residents; that is, registered in the village records. I was told that there were no transient workers living in the village in 1989 and early 1990. By 1991, I knew of some cases, and by 1994 I suspected this category might be growing as new enterprises were spreading. These migratory workers did not have registration in the village (and therefore had no land rights) and usually came without their families, living in housing provided by their employers. When I encountered them, I found conversing difficult both because they were supposed to be working and because they often spoke out-of-province dialects that I do not understand.

Seasonal wage laborers, as opposed to long-term migrants or homeless people, are also an important part of the Lu Village labor force, just as they were in 1939. They still perform farmwork in the peak periods of transplanting and harvesting, and many of them come from the same neighboring villages that supplied seasonal labor before the revolution. This condition is partly due to the environmental differences that affect the timing of farm labor demands. While migrant and seasonal workers play a role in the village economy and tend to have an undesirable position *within Lu Village*, they are not the subject of this study.[11]

### Life Histories

Life histories and other accounts collected from some of the older villagers of Lu Village reveal rich detail about how they fared under the difficult years of warfare and social disorder before the revolution. Some people described the difficult years that followed the revolution as well. In collecting these stories, because of the well-known history of punishing those who appeared critical of the revolution, I did not press for details on the difficulties experienced during the Great Leap Forward or the Cultural Revolution; I did not want people to feel my purpose was to discredit the revolution at a time of heightened political sensitivity to foreign criticism after 1989. Even if individuals wanted to be critical, they could not be sure that local officials would not hear about it and cause them to regret what they had said.

Sometimes, through reconstructing the timing of certain events, it is clear that they coincided with certain political movements. People occasionally elaborated, but I did not encourage them to turn their accounts into political statements. Overall, I believe that villagers felt cautious both about speaking too graphically to a foreigner about some of the hardships they experienced after the revolution, and also about revisiting painful memories— memories that have never been legitimated within the villages by "speaking bitterness" meetings (yi ku hui), like those held in the 1950s to denounce oppression in prerevolutionary China. Many accounts of hardship experienced during the revolution have been written by intellectuals, but the most critical ones have been published by émigrés or by people who are now powerful. Rural people have few protections should their memories get them into political trouble. In later sections (and in chapter 8) I present some accounts of the kinds of conditions people faced and the social and cultural resources they could draw upon in times of hardship.

## Finding the Village Poor

The persistence of poverty in China is inevitably a delicate topic for a government that aimed to eliminate class inequality. In the 1980s, particularly sensitive to political pressures to control Western impressions, China's cadres sought to mask the signs of poverty and misery in their villages. In the 1990s this attitude was beginning to shift, as certain government institutions began to realize that they could not attract major development assistance and loans unless they demonstrated that they had poor people who would benefit (Croll 1995). When my random sample of households to be visited included some that were atypically poor, I found that village associates were quite hesitant to lead me to them, and it often required several attempted visits before I managed at least to meet the family and learn something about their circumstances. Without the use of random sampling, I would have been much less likely to encounter some of the poorer individuals in the village. In some cases, the conditions of poverty and disability made it difficult to conduct a full interview.

What is certain is that poverty has persisted for some people in Lu Village, and that the circumstances may not have changed greatly. One condition

that has changed, however, is that if a person belongs to a registered household in the village, he or she has a right to an allotment of land. This, alone,
however, does not guarantee well-being. Fei observed that, for men, poverty
was often synonymous with bachelorhood. A poor man had difficulty attracting a wife, and without a wife, the quality of life was seen as pathetically
lacking. The same condition seems to apply today. If, for whatever reason, a
man lacks a female partner, his life seems far poorer for it.

## Mr. Hou, Labor Reform, and Lost Time

After many unsuccessful efforts to find Mr. Hou at home, one morning I met
him and he told me parts of his interesting story. In 1990, Mr. Hou was fifty-
six years old and unmarried. The village officials seemed to want me to avoid
him, but when I finally found him at home, I realized it may not have been
strictly because of his poverty but also because of his political history and the
way he had been treated as a landlord's son.

Before the revolution, Mr. Hou attended school to about eighth grade. He
lived in one of the districts of the market town of Lufeng. His parents' family, of about eight or nine people, was classified as a landlord's family because
they had purchased about twenty-four mu (3.6 acres) of land. This was 2.7
mu, or less than ½ acre, per capita. Mr. Hou had been educated in the teach-
ings of Confucius and Mencius, and was a follower of the Confucius-Mencius
Association at the age of sixteen, when Liberation came. When land reform
was carried out in 1952, he and his family were assigned to Lu Village and
their large house was confiscated. In return, they were given two small rooms
(for nine people) in the village and expected to become peasant-cultivators.

In 1953, because of his classical Confucian training or practices, he was
declared a counterrevolutionary (*fandong*) and sent for ten years of labor reform (*laodong gaicao*, known simply as *laogai*) in a southern part of the
province (Mengzi Caoba), where he had to do farm labor. This is the kind of
labor reform described by Harry Wu (1992:175). When he returned in 1963,
Mr. Hou was nearly thirty years old, still under surveillance (*ta shou guanzhi*),
and not a desirable candidate for marriage; he was both poor and one of the
"bad categories" from an ideological point of view. His younger sister, however, did get married. She now lives in Kunming, as a city resident, as do most
of her children, but one son—born at the wrong time—had to keep his residence in the village and become a farmer. This nephew, married with two
young daughters, is unlike other peasants in that he has several hundred
books and reads a lot, perhaps primarily novels.

A solitary, middle-aged man, Mr. Hou did not show outward signs of bitterness as much as sadness. With his nephew, he has at least some kin in the

**Table 6.8.   Mr. Hou's Annual Expenses and Income**

| Expenses | Yuan | Income | Yuan |
|---|---|---|---|
| Fertilizer | 100 | Grain sale | 250 |
| Pigs purchased | 120 | Pigs sold | 500 |
| Fodder and pesticides | 100 | Taiwan uncle | unknown |
| Hired labor (10 days, male) | 60 | | |
| Furniture | 200 | | |
| Food, clothing, household needs | 360 | | |
| Coal | 120 | | |
| Medicine | 30 | | |
| Gifts | 30 | | |
| Total | 1120 | Total | 750 |

village. He lives in small, simple quarters within a larger courtyard occupied by other families. He does most of his own farming, cooking, pig raising, washing, and cooking, but once in a while he gets a little exchange labor, say from the nephew's wife, and he also babysits for her cute little girls. He impressed me as a pleasant and intelligent man, yet subdued. Inside, I suspect he conceals a well of suffering for the years of deprivation he experienced, primarily, it seems, because his family had been somewhat better off. In 1990, I roughly calculated his expenses as ¥1,120 and his income as about ¥750 (see table 6.8).

Life had recently brightened a little for this old man, since an uncle in Taiwan wrote him letters and sent him money (apparently making up the difference between income and expenses). This uncle had not come back, although some elderly Taiwan expatriates have, since conditions were still "not suitable." Perhaps he was Nationalist and still feared Communist hatred. In any case, the former landlord's son received enough money to have a few nice things: a couch, a clean pink plastic cover on his coffee table, a TV, and a bike. He did not seem to fear me but was cautious about the small, protected world he has managed to reconstruct after so many years of deprivation and scorn. His life was not completely miserable and mean, but as an older man he had to do all the hard domestic work and farmwork himself with no one to care for him.

## Mr. Du, the House of "Three Bachelors," and Other Solitary Men

The Du household was located in one of the hamlets that belong to Greater Lu Village. The road was not even good for bikes; it was a double-rutted tractor road with a turn-off onto an eroded path that ran along narrow banks between the irrigation canals for two hundred to three hundred meters. The path had already eroded before the rains that would make it treacherous on the way out. Although there is another, longer road between the village and hamlet, it, too, was still only a tractor road. Approached from outside, this hamlet looked old-fashioned and fortress-like, built in a circle and closed to the outside by high walls without windows. Houses looked inward, not out at the surrounding fields. When Fei described Lu Village in 1938, the center was similarly fortress-like, with entrance gates that are gone today. Unlike the center, where brick and cement construction is beginning to replace mud walls, the process had not started in this hamlet in 1990. Once inside, invited into courtyards to chat, I could not help noticing the more crowded and dirty conditions. The narrow paths between households were not convenient even for foot travel, and there were heaps of manure in the paths. Like most of the hamlets of Lu Village, this one had electricity but lacked running water. It looked less prosperous than the center, and I thought that a woman from Lu Village Center would not be eager to marry into a family here.[12]

In 1990, Mr. Du's household appeared on my list as containing three bachelors. Mr. Du, head of the household, was an old man. Neighbors pointed to a small, completely dark, dungeon-like room, next to some pigsties, and said he lived there. He was not in. It would clearly have been quite difficult to interview him in there. I returned at a later date, and when I finally met Mr. Du, I did not have any success at conversation because he was deaf. But I did learn something about this tragic family from the neighbors, from the younger son, and partly by piecing together information from the household registry. Mr. Du's family consisted of himself (a thrice-married widower) and two sons. Old Mr. Du was born in 1918, in Sichuan, and was seventy-two in 1990. His two surviving sons were born in 1972 and 1975. The older son was in prison for stealing, but according to his neighbors, Mr. Du was very honest.

When we finally did encounter one of the three residents in this all-male household, his poverty was instantly visible in his clothing and demeanor. Although his father, Mr. Du, was not home, a pale, thin undernourished boy stood before us, wide-eyed and speechless, barefoot and in patched blue pants. (It is rare to see anyone go barefoot in rural China.) When he stated his age, fifteen, I surmised that he was probably chronically underfed. There were few questions he could answer, out of shyness and awkwardness in speaking, but villagers assured me "the boy's mind is good." I learned he had never been to school, that he had tried for a few days, but there was no one to cook his lunch. No one in the team had taken the initiative or responsibility to see that the boy was able to attend school. So he stopped going. He had to do the cooking for himself and his old father. His father had indeed lost three wives. The first wife ran away before Liberation. The second died in childbirth with her second child, but neither of her children survived. The third wife, whom he married in 1971, gave birth to two boys by Mr. Du.

Neighbors said she was "fat"—meaning that she appeared to be in good health—but then suddenly she got sick and died in 1983. The second son never attended school because, after his mother died, when he was just eight years old, he had to do both field work and cooking for himself. The family never had meat to eat. All their clothes and a sack or two of grain were donated to them. The boy's older brother was in jail for stealing, and one glance at the poverty of their home made one wonder how anyone could expect him not to steal.

When I returned in 1996, I sought out the younger brother, now a young man of twenty-one. He was unmarried and earned his living through farmwork on his own fields and working for others to earn wages. His father had died a few years earlier. His brother was released from jail in 1995, after a term of about six years. He had been in jail for stealing electric wire to resell for money. This crime is punished severely, obviously to protect the system that brings electricity to the villages. But my assistant reasoned to me, "This was not the crime of a criminal—a greedy person who would steal someone's wallet. It is the crime of someone who is poor, who may get only ten yuan (less than $2) from reselling the wire."

In 1996, I saw that the young boy had grown up and was managing better than I had expected. He worked at casual jobs, here and there, and did his own farming. Between my visits, he had gone to government literacy classes for adults for three months (he showed me his book). He learned to read approximately the first twenty pages of this book, but that is all. Since the government does not pay for more than three months of literacy classes, he stopped attending. He showed me a picture of himself with his brother and maternal cousins. Although they knew him, these cousins never helped him in any significant way.

His former pigsty home is in the same location, tiny, but now improved. It has two stories (a ladder to a room upstairs with a bed). Downstairs he has a table and three tiny stools. He has a picture on the white wall: the wealth god with the words "Wealth God, Bring Wealth" (*Caishen facai*). His elder brother is hardly ever at home. The young man says he does not earn enough money to save to build a larger house should his brother come back and want half of it. His house is only about four square meters on the ground floor and perhaps three square meters above. With a hard floor and whitewashed walls and ceiling, it no longer looks so dismal. His neighbors said that he can now take care of himself; he cooks and wears clean clothes. He is taller than his brother and no longer bone thin. He wears a pair of blue jeans and a modern-style jacket: not a bad-looking young man, shy but pleasant. Maybe he is marriageable, but a girl would have to like him a lot to live in such a small place, only one half of which is his. He says he gets along well with his older brother. In this poor household of two brothers, it would be desirable for one or both of them to marry into a family that could offer more living space.

These cases of unmarried men illustrate a common theme in Chinese analyses of social misfortune. Without women to take care of them, men do not experience an enviable life. As in Fei's time, they are not able to take part in the richness of village life on equal terms, and in their domestic life, without any division of labor, they find it difficult to achieve the same quality of life observed in households with both sexes cooperating. In the case of the children of widowed Mr. Du, we see that there was only a minimal social safety net for the family. The family did not starve, but the sons lacked the domestic support that would have made it possible for them to go to school. As a result, they are permanently handicapped in their ability to seek anything but manual employment in a rapidly changing economy.

## Age, Disability, and Poverty: Mrs. Lu and Her Husband

Mrs. Lu was an old, illiterate woman of seventy-two (born in 1918) when she was interviewed in 1990.

> I was married at age fifteen, by parental arrangement. My husband and I had not seen each other until we were married. After marriage, my work was the same as it had been in my mother's home: I planted fields. My mother-in-law was very terrible. Originally, I did not dare go outside to visit. My husband worked outside driving a horse cart to carry salt from Heijing to Lufeng and rarely came home. My husband, from his childhood, had always worked hard and was very good to me. The two of us never fought. But before Liberation, my life was bitter. We rented land from a landlord [the family of the bachelor, Mr. Hou, described above], who lived in the city. Each year after paying rent, there was not much left. We could only eat gruel made from squash (*nangua*). We could not afford to raise pigs and ate almost no meat. We had barely any clothes. When I bore children, I sat at home for the period of one month and then returned to the work in the fields. Then, the Nationalist army took a lot of soldiers. My husband went outside as a soldier and did not come back for three years.
>
> After the revolution, working in the production team, I did the same field work as my husband. The work was very tiring. In 1958 [during the Great Leap Forward], my uterus fell. To this day it often drops out, so now I cannot do much work. During that time, because I myself was sick, one daughter died of hunger. Working in the production team, I earned seven work points a day. The annual grain ration did not give us enough to eat. We had to buy grain, and life was really bitter. My husband [age seventy-seven] worked for fifty years as a horse cart driver. Now he rarely goes out to drive his horse cart. He is retired and gets a pension of thirty yuan per month [because he had formal employment as a horse cart driver] and fifteen jin (16.5 lbs.) of rice.

When Mrs. Lu was married in 1934, her husband's family provided two sets of clothing, a bed, a sheet, a bracelet, and twenty yuan. Her own family provided a cupboard, a basin, and a quilt. Altogether, Mrs. Lu bore seven children, but four of them, two boys and two girls, died between the ages of three months and a year. While she did not dwell on the famine of the Great Leap Forward, it is clear that the hard labor took a heavy toll on her health and cost her at least one child. Although it is routine to talk about the bitterness before Liberation, clearly the Great Leap Forward years held their own horrors.

These two old people now live together with their forty-seven-year-old second son, who lives and farms at home. They described their son as unmarried, but village records show that he had been married. This suggests that his wife left or something happened to her, but the parents did not refer to it, possibly out of embarrassment. Their second son does most of the farming and also carries firewood and goes to market for the family. With no running water at home, their son hauls water to the house each day. They own no draft animals, but Mrs. Lu raised four pigs and some chickens. Last year, the family ate one pig and she sold three in town. Since they do not grow enough grain, they must also buy some. Over the year, their expenses amounted to about ¥1,085, not counting supplementary rice and other food, for a household of three people. Their income was only ¥360 from the husband's pension and about ¥1,300 from Mrs. Lu's sale of pigs and chickens. Their older son, who served as a soldier, has been married and separated from them for fifteen years and has three children, so he has little to offer his parents. Their daughter also married out and lives in another hamlet of Lu Village. This family has no modern appliances other than two hot water thermoses bought in 1958 and 1962. At night, they watch TV at the home of their neighbors. Although they are getting by, they depend very much on their middle-aged son to farm, and on the pigs that Mrs. Lu raises to sell.

## Mrs. Jiang: Disability and Unity

Mrs. Jiang was born in 1948 and was forty-two at the time I first interviewed her. She had a difficult childhood because her father died when she was eight years old (around 1956) and her mother was left alone raising four children. Mrs. Jiang attended school for four years and is semiliterate. Introduced to her husband by an aunt, she married at age twenty-two and came to live in Lu Village, which is about sixty kilometers from her parents' home. Her husband, age forty-one, had just two years of schooling. When I first met them in 1990, they were coming to terms with a tragic accident. In 1989, while her husband was riding a train in order to engage in trade, his arm was severed at the shoulder. In 1990, they were struggling to keep three children, ages twelve to eighteen, in school without the help of the father, who could no longer do manual work. Mrs. Jiang was doing all the field work, raising pigs, and doing much of the housework. When she was in Kunming Hospital with her husband, students who were friends of their children came to help harvest their wheat. In the slack season, Mrs. Jiang continued to travel to sell clothes and shoes in various markets, buying here and selling there—work that she and her husband used to do together. Their annual expenses amounted to almost ¥2,000 and their income was about ¥1,700. They borrowed ¥100. Although they had purchased a few consumer goods in the late 1980s (a bicycle in 1987 and a washing machine in 1988), they had no radio or television. Their home was dark, poor, and cramped. In the midst of these difficulties, Mrs. Jiang and her husband were struggling to keep their children in school. Their eldest son, age eighteen, had completed high school and was a good student. They had hoped he would be able to attend university, but the pressure for him to quit and replace his father's lost labor must have been great.

I revisited this family over the years and, much to my surprise, they managed to keep their son in school. He attended Kunming Agricultural University and was set to graduate in 1997. Their younger daughter and son only completed eighth and sixth grades, respectively, and helped in the farmwork. Mrs. Jiang still farmed and grew vegetables for sale in the town market, while her husband, with the help of relatives, had managed to get work as a watchman for ¥100 per month. In 1997, their expenses (rising with inflation) were about ¥1,600 for food and clothing; 800 for electricity and fuel; 240 for farm tools, fertilizer, and transport; 400 for medicine and gifts; and about 2,700 for their son's education, or around ¥5,740 for the year. Their annual income was 1,200 from watchman's wages, 600 from the sale of grain, 300 from the sale of home vegetables, and about 700 net from the sale of pigs, or a total of ¥2,800. Clearly, their income is still falling way behind their expenses, unless they failed to report casual income earned by themselves or their young adult children. It is also possible that Mrs. Jiang sells vegetables (or other goods) more than one month per year, as she reported. As their children have grown older and assumed a greater proportion of the work, the family has done better. One sign of success is the TV they bought in 1995.

My visits to this home always showed that, consistent with their budget shortfalls, they were way behind their neighbors in terms of modernizing or expanding their dark, cramped living quarters, and in purchasing modern appliances and furniture. Nonetheless, they managed to make great sacrifices to keep their son in university, and when he graduates, their economic situation should improve. This family managed to stay together and cooperate despite the severe disability of the husband. Their situation was also helped by the fact that they live in Lu Village Center rather than a distant hamlet, where comparable commercial opportunities and employment as a guardian would be harder to find.

## Mrs. Ning: Disability and Division

When I met her in 1990, Mrs. Ning was age sixty-two. Born in 1928 in one of Lu Village's hamlets, she neither attended school nor had her feet bound. Although she had five grown children, she was living by herself, destitute, disabled by arthritis, and fairly deaf. She could not hear us knocking on the door, and a neighbor brought us in. The small house Mrs. Ning lived in was very bare, and she had no one to help her accomplish the daily household tasks that make life difficult for the old and disabled in Lu Village. Interviewing her was not easy, but by speaking very loudly we were able to piece together her situation.

My parents arranged my marriage at age seventeen, before Liberation, to a man I had never met. I was carried here in a sedan chair. He was from a landlord family. He had gone to school and knew how to write. I was from a peasant family.

I gave birth eight times and have five surviving children, four sons and a daughter. I lost one in a miscarriage. My third child, a girl, died at age three of measles and my fifth, a girl, died at age three of a lung illness. The family was poor then, living with my mother-in-law. [Because her husband was the son of a landlord, her husband's family would have been targets of class struggle by the revolutionaries in the 1950s, but Mrs. Ning did not say this directly.]

My husband did not drink when he was younger. When the children were small, there was no money for drink. But the last ten years [coincident with the reforms and the greater use of cash instead of work points and coupons], he has been drinking. My husband now drinks liquor every day and smokes. He controlled the money, so I never knew how much he spent on liquor. He also used to wait until everyone left before he killed the pig, so he could eat meat by himself.

When I became sick and could not work any more, he no longer wanted me. My husband was good to me while I was in the production team, when I was still young and could work. But I have been deaf for ten years, and for five years I have had arthritis. My fingers hurt, so I cannot do much work. It especially hurts to be in water, transplanting. I also raise two small pigs. Because of my arthritis my hands hurt when I put them into water, so I cannot wash the pig food, I can only cut it up. My husband and I have quarreled a lot since I became sick. He often beat me, not only when he was drinking. He began to hit me because I cannot hear.

My husband used to live here, but two years ago he took his things and went and bought a two-room house elsewhere in the same hamlet. Since then, I do not see or speak with him. When he came back home to steal all my things, I was afraid to say anything because he might beat me. But afterward, I got so angry I wanted to die. I even ran to the pond side to throw myself in, but fellow villagers stopped me and made me go home.

When he left me, the leaders in the village office were not called in to divide the household properly, so I would get a fair share of things. He just took the cow, ten chickens, the small stove, the pots, and household tools. He took the grain and the pigs and sold them for about ¥3,000, and then he took all the money. He spent about 1,800 to buy another house and took most of the things out of this house. He took the thresher and the handcart. He also took the radio. He has a bad conscience.

When we divided the land, my husband took the good land and the fertilizer subsidy booklet and left me the poor land. My husband has three mu of land because he also farms third son's land, while I have only 1.2 mu, and my fourth son just plants his own one mu of land. The land he left me is poor quality land. I have no fertilizer for farming. [In formal divisions, the size of land given to each person is adjusted to take into account differences in productivity of land.] Because I have nothing, I refuse to pay the grain tax. When it was necessary for every household to pay ten yuan for road repairs, my husband said I should pay. But I told the team leader that he took all the money and household things, and I have no money to pay. So they made my husband pay.

To farm, I water the fields, but my sister's son's wife and daughters help with rice transplanting. My third son comes back from Kunming to help me irrigate the fields and to organize and pay additional people to transplant. He also comes back for the rice harvesting. The land grows enough to eat, about five bags of unhusked rice, which hold about fifty kilograms each. I still get enough to eat, three bowls a day. [A spartan diet of just rice, less than a pound a day, would be barely possible for her with this amount.] For money, I sold a chicken for ten yuan, and I still have two hens. If they lay eggs, I can buy medicine for my arthritis.

I asked Mrs. Ning about each of her five children only to learn they could offer little economic assistance. Her eldest married son suffers from mental illness, her second son is married out with many dependents, and her remaining younger sons and daughter have migrated to Kunming but have low incomes.

Mrs. Ning's case illustrates several important points. First, it shows how an informally divorced woman eked out a minimal standard of living aided by her children and kin. Mrs. Ning had enough food, but little else. In an economy dependent on a gendered division of manual labor with almost no labor-saving appliances, married life becomes extra difficult when one adult loses the capacity to work. Second, Mrs. Ning's difficult situation illustrates a pattern of rejection that is not rare when a partner becomes disabled (despite the more inspiring case of Mrs. Jiang above). Mrs. Ning's husband became violent toward her as she became deaf and arthritic, and ultimately he left her. Third, even in a family that produced four sons, which in theory should offer parents plenty of security, Mrs. Ning was not very secure. Finally, the mental illness of her eldest son, born in 1954, and the loss of two younger daughters, probably born in late 1950s or early 1960s, may well reflect the famine conditions of the Great Leap Forward, when chronic hunger and malnutrition killed and retarded millions of rural children across China.

## WEALTH IN THE 1990S

In the 1990s, we see cases of fluidity, with formerly poor families doing well. Yet our examples of wealthy families in the 1990s show that some of the pre-revolutionary wealthy families preserved certain advantages, even after they had been dispossessed by revolution, and were able to respond successfully to the opportunities that the reforms presented. Their social and cultural capital (education and business orientation) had not been entirely depleted by the revolutionary decades.

The reform period of the 1980s and 1990s loosened the restrictions that forced all households to share poverty during the 1960s and 1970s. There is now recognizable differentiation among households that are better off, a few reaching middle-class levels by international standards, and others that are quite poor. Compared to the 1930s, people have substantially more wealth at their disposal. Because people are never very comfortable talking about either wealth or poverty, collecting reliable data on incomes and expenses is difficult. As I largely rely on self-reporting, people can decline to discuss their incomes, or they may "adjust" them. I assume that wealthy households usually minimize their incomes to avoid provoking jealousy among their neighbors and certainly would not want to disclose information that, if leaked, might provoke taxation. Jealousy can clearly be seen in the first example below.

### Finding the Village Rich: The Tang Family's Caution

One morning in July 1990, my assistant and I made a call at the home of the Tang family, where I hoped to conduct an interview for my random sample. We were told no one was home. We noted that the house was new and had a nice courtyard with flowers and a big barking dog. (Dogs never failed to frighten my assistant, as indeed they are trained as watchdogs.) Later, the family planning cadre said she had told the family about our desire to interview them, and they had come to her the night before to say they did not want to be interviewed; they then left town to visit the wife's father. The cadre said that this family did not want to be interviewed because they are one of the richest families in town. They did not want to answer questions about their income. She explained that they were "big" landlords before the revolution and now they are rich again. The husband is a construction team boss or contractor (*ban bao zhang*) who earns a lot of money, in addition to planting rice. I did not find out much more about them at that time, but later my assistant tactfully managed to have an interview with them, after reassuring them that they did not have to answer any question that they thought inappropriate. The resulting interview thus avoided the details of their income, apart from farming.

This family consists of Mr. Tang, his wife Mrs. Tai, and three children. In 1990, they cultivated 5.1 mu of rice and a small plot of vegetables and sold three pigs. They said their annual gross income from the sale of grain was ¥2,000 and from the sale of three pigs was ¥1,500. Their annual living and farming expenses amounted to about ¥2,000. Mr. Tang also "sometimes" worked in construction in and around the town. Mr. Tang shared in some farm tasks with his wife, Mrs. Tai, while she took the primary responsibility for the pigs and vegetable garden. Their account of the construction business emphasized the difficulties rather than their successes. In late 1989 and 1990, they experienced a setback in the construction business. They also lost a considerable amount of capital, ¥30,000, in 1989 because they made building commitments for a certain price and the cost of materials went up rapidly with inflation. Then, after the political events of 1989, there was a dramatic slowdown in the economy and few people wanted to build houses, so Mr. Tang was not doing much work at that time. Indeed, the economic slowdown was quite evident across China.

Their previous prosperity from construction was evident, however, in the new house they built in 1986 and the many appliances and tools they had been able to purchase during the 1980s compared to other households. These included a threshing machine, a hauling cart, two bicycles, an electric stove, an electric rice cooker, a washing machine, a sewing machine, a stereo, and a color television. The most expensive of these items was the color TV, at ¥3,200 in 1988. While these items have become increasingly common in the 1990s, they were quite rare in the 1980s, and this family was one of the first to purchase so many. Evidently, despite their success, memories of class struggle, dispossession, and envy still worried them. Villagers told me that this household is probably the second richest in the village, after the factory owner.

## The Cao Family Revival: Failure and Success in Business

The fluidity in family fortunes and the reversal imposed by the revolution is illustrated by the case of Cao, a wealthy man now in his early fifties. The account below mixes Cao's contemporary description with excerpts from Fei and explanatory comments in brackets.

> My father was a respected, capable man in Lu Village. In 1938, when Fei Xiaotong came here, my father's house had thirty mules going to Heijing to carry salt, and he

also built a row of new housing. My father once said to Fei Xiaotong, "This year my family's transport is not going well. The horses are dying."

[Four of the wealthier families raise horses to use in the transportation of salt. A horse carries a load of approximately 200 pounds and requires only two days for the round trip. . . . We find that the owner of 5 horses will receive an average of $4.00 [¥4] a day. Since a horse is worth $100, an investment of $500 is necessary to set up in business on this scale. . . . The high mortality rate among the draft animals is revealed by that fact that . . . during 1938, 23 horses and 15 mules died. Among those that died were 15 animals belonging to a single owner. (Fei 1949:49)]

At that time the Cao family had the money of a big household. A few of the sons quarreled in competing for housing. At Liberation, my family was assigned the label of landlord. Between 1960 and 1961 [the time of the Great Leap Forward], both my father and mother starved to death. I was sixteen or seventeen years old then and had to take care of myself. What kind of work didn't I do! Woodwork, cement work, field work, hired labor, work with pigs, butchering. In 1981, when they began to contract land to households, then I was the first to run out and do it. At that time, doing construction was the most profitable (*zhuanqian de*), so I contracted a construction team. At that time, in all of Lu Village, then, there was only myself and Yang Lizhan (later a factory owner) who were the first to make our families rich. I was the head and he was the tail. In those days, if a person built a new house, the whole village was shocked. When I built a new house, because I had formerly been labeled a landlord, some people said, "Don't look at [envy] him building a house now. Later we will come to live there." [They were referring to the earlier confiscation of landlord's houses for redistribution to poor peasants.]

When 1989 arrived, the Politburo was in turbulence, and some people came and quarreled with me. Because I had been of landlord status, I was very afraid (*hen haipa*). I did not dare to continue making a profit. Then I allowed the contract for the work team to be transferred to someone else. From 1990 on, I have not done anything else. [He had also injured his back while doing construction.] The opportunity, once lost, cannot just come back. Economically speaking, from 1989, when I sold the contract for the construction team to other people, it has been a loss (*chikui*). From the political angle, I think it was correct. I do not worry about how much I can profit. The new day has unexpected turns. Even life perhaps cannot always be protected. If you have a lot of money, you can wait for another use. All my children have left my place in Lu Village. They all transferred from rural to nonagricultural occupation status. For some of them, I spent money to buy them urban household registration. I do not want them to be peasants.

Locally, this family is considered very rich. Cao's wife jokingly calls her husband a "new landlord." This case is especially interesting because it reveals how a wealthy family returned to wealth despite a twenty-year period of class reversal, when their wealth and housing were confiscated and they were assigned to the most despised socialist class, that of landlord. Cao glides quickly over the painful life that the revolution brought to his family during his childhood, noting only that his parents starved to death. I also learned that in 1958 his sister was married (without any dowry) to a man in Kunming mainly so that she could eat, since during the Great Leap Forward urban residents received rations while peasants starved. Undoubtedly, those with "bad family backgrounds" had the least chance of obtaining enough food during the Great Leap Famine. The twenty years of hard work at manual odd jobs show that Cao remade his own fortune once the economic policy again permitted enterprise, but he still felt threatened by fellow villagers who envied his wealth and implied they would confiscate it again.

It is debatable whether inherited "class" advantages from the prerevolutionary period permitted this man's family to rise again, or whether he earned his wealth through his own efforts. Clearly, Cao's inherited advantages did not include material wealth, special educational opportunities, or parental support. This leaves childhood socialization within the family, despite the public opprobrium he would have experienced in the village, to explain how class advantage might have survived the revolution and enabled him to make his family wealthy again. This advantage may well have been the value his family placed on education. Cao completed nine years of schooling. This was about as high as a villager could go in the 1950s and was certainly more than the average villager completed who dropped out earlier to work. Individual motivation, willingness to take risks, good timing, and hard work contributed to his success, but better education was probably a factor, too. The family preference for nonagricultural work is clear. Cao's daughter received a college education (fifteen years) and is currently working in a government office. His two sons only finished ninth grade, like himself, and both work as salaried drivers, resuming the earlier family specialization in transport, mules replaced by cars. Only the wife, in her fifties, dedicates herself to manual labor, doing most of the farming. She grows rice, beans, and vegetables and raises pigs. She hires labor to help her with plowing, transplanting, and harvesting rice from their 1.6 mu of contracted land.

Cao and his wife spent ¥40,000 yuan on a new house in 1984 and ¥5,000 on their daughter's wedding in 1995. Their current cash expenses are estimated at about ¥7,400 per year. The cash incomes of the two sons totaled ¥7,368. Additional income comes from the home-grown grain, vegetables, and pork that they consume, as well as the sale of pork, which nets over ¥1,000 more per year. His wife takes the major responsibility for the farming and pig raising. Cao currently produces no direct income, although the amount he has saved or invested in other forms is unknown. The next major expenses he faces will be for the marriages of his sons, but they themselves are earning enough to save for their weddings and would be attractive prospects to young women of Lu Village. Most likely, however, they will marry women with nonfarmer status.

## "Official Success" Biography (January 1993)

Below I present parts of a speech given by Mr. Shu, a Lu Village entrepreneur, explaining his successful career. He gave this speech to discharged soldiers who were ending their service and returning to civilian life. The purpose was to encourage them about their return to farming status and to allay their concerns and discontent, if they were not given urban registration upon their discharge. The author printed up and distributed the speech.

> Rely on the party's good policy for the overall development of agriculture, industry, and commerce: An example of hard work that brings wealth

Leaders, Comrades:

My family lives in this township, in Greater Lu Village. I am now fifty-seven years old, of Han nationality. In 1955, I was recruited into the army and in 1958 I was discharged and returned to the village. These years, following the party line, guided by its general and specific policies, and resulting from industrious manual labor and help and support from all levels of government leadership, my household economy has experienced a very big change. Starting from a household that was in extremely difficult circumstances, living in a poor, one-room village house that was not even twenty square meters, I have expanded into a farming, industrial, commercial, and animal raising diversified, developed, and productive household.

When I came back from the army in 1958, I was sent to work in the Chuxiong Casting and Forging Factory. Three years later, my father had lost his sight in both eyes, while my mother's legs were suffering from rheumatism so she could not walk, and my younger brother died from encephalitis. Because of these kinds of difficulties, my wife and I had to resign and leave our state factory jobs[13] as workers and come back to the old village hamlet to assume the burden and heavy responsibility for raising and nurturing the family. . . .

Particularly, under the guidance of the Party Reform Open-door Policy, step by step I promoted a diversified economy.

1. I set up an individual woodwork manufacturing factory, a furniture store, with seven people working, with a production value in 1992 of ¥136,750, paying an annual tax of ¥6,771, and an industrial-commercial management fee of ¥4,169, and a net income of ¥67,710 [about U.S.$12,200].[14]

2. I contracted 7.2 mu of land, with an annual grain production of 7,200 kgs, or production of 1,000 kgs per mu, for a production value of ¥5,000. Apart from paying government service of 998 kgs, I can sell 1,000 kgs of rice for a cash income of ¥1,100.

3. Last year we raised seven pigs. We sold three of them for an income of ¥1,987 and kept four pigs with a value of ¥2,500.

4. We contracted an apple orchard, with an area of two mu and, under the guidance of the township-village scientific technicians, I grafted new varieties of pear trees; this year, some of them already bore fruit, for an income of ¥400.

After many years, we two people, husband and wife, through industrious, hard work, scientific management, and the labor of our two hands, achieved a total annual income of ¥43,487 [about U.S.$ 7,828]. This is an average of ¥6,212 [U.S.$1,118] per person for the whole family of seven people. We have achieved an affluent life and have stepped into a small, healthy occupation. In 1990 we also built a new residential structure, with cement-tile floors and an area of over eighty square meters, at a building cost of ¥50,000.

In the spirit of the party's Fourteenth Congress and to satisfy the conditions of Lufeng's market demand and customers' consumption levels, I plan to introduce a new style of furniture using Hong Kong-Australian production technology, importing it to the Lufeng market. Now, I have already applied to the County Land Office to buy three hundred square meters of land, to expand and to build a woodwork factory and furniture store.

Leaders, Comrades, the foregoing explains how I have gained a little success in these recent years. In days to come I need to continue diligently striving for still greater economic results. Thank you everyone!        Dec. 20, 1992

Mr. Shu's public statement of success should be compared with private interviews with his wife, Mrs. Shui,[15] presented next. Mr. Shu omitted the years from 1961 to 1968 from his account. This was a time when the household experienced difficulties due to the Cultural Revolution. Also, he did not describe the family division of labor, which includes himself supervising the hired craftsmen, along with his son who is learning furniture making, his wife who takes responsibility for raising pigs and for performing and organizing the field work, his two unmarried teenaged daughters who work in the stores, and his daughter-in-law who shares the responsibility for field work, pig raising, and child care with her mother-in-law. His wife's life history fills in some of the details, showing that, indeed, the path to wealth was not an easy one.

### Mrs. Shui's Story

I was born in 1944. My home village was about fifteen kilometers from the county town and about fifty-five kilometers from Kunming. My parents both farmed paddy. They were poor peasants and those were difficult times. I only studied to the fourth grade, because my family was very poor. My father was an opium addict. I started to work in a factory at age fifteen.

My mother could not endure life with my father—it was extremely bad. My father smoked opium, and my *nainai* was rather mean to her. My mother could not endure it, so she left when I was only a little over a year old. She abandoned us. My mother went to help my aunt, who had a little variety store in a town.

At that time, my mother had two living children. My older brother had died because life was difficult. When my mother left, my older sister, barely twelve, cared for me. . . . After Liberation, my father finally managed to give up opium when the government gathered up all the addicts and made them stop smoking.

My older sister took care of me until I was thirteen or fourteen [1956–1957]. Then she married out, so there was only my father and me. There was no way to manage the household, except by myself. Then my father obtained this later wife. . . . When my stepmother came, she did not care for us and was not good to us. . . . There was no way to study, so I only studied to fourth grade. You see here, this hand of mine? It was all by myself that I used to cut horse fodder to sell.

*The Great Leap Forward.* When I was fifteen, I left home and became a worker. At that time, I still did not own any pants. I wore my father's old shirt, a long shirt that covered my bottom. It was 1958. Those were the most difficult years [of the Great Leap Forward]. It was the most tragic, the most difficult time. Meeting society. . . . (She paused and wept at the shameful memory of having no pants and leaving home to work outside the family.) Also, we were semi-mountain district people, so it was even more difficult.

When the factory started they sought workers, but only from age eighteen and up. I was not quite fifteen years old and I thought I could pass as eighteen. So I went. I did not know this destiny was no good either. I "passed," and then I did well for a while. I worked just three years in industry [to 1961], and then I "got off the horse" again. Old Shu [referring to her husband] and I then worked in a car workshop. I wanted to quit industrial work. I just went to work there for a while and then I left. But at that time there was nowhere to go. Because "Old Shu" was close to me, I revealed these kinds of things to him. When I went to Chuxiong to work, I also came to see Lu Village, to see its farm paddies. Seeing that it was very flat and level, I agreed to come here with him. I quit industrial work and came back to his village.

*Marriage.* I married him in 1961, when everything was a mess [referring to the nationwide famine conditions produced by the Great Leap Forward] and I wanted to quit work. I had thought perhaps I could go back home, and yet there was no place to stay, no temporary lodging. So I thought, and I figured . . . I could go, I reckoned then I could go down [to the village with him]. I was seventeen when I married, but it was still not satisfactory. In 1962 I bore the oldest child, my oldest daughter. I do not remember exactly when the others were born. I bore them too close together. We did not know birth control methods [contraception]. I only breastfed my oldest daughter for eight or nine months, and then stopped—I did not have any milk. Those years I bore them too close together, the children were troublesome, and it was hard. My health was quite bad. Ah!

*Hardships in the early 1960s.* We were back only a very short time when Old Shu's father lost vision in both of his eyes. He was a blind man. Then his mother, when cooking at the mess hall [during the Great Leap Forward], had to dig a ditch . . . and broke her foot so she had to crawl. Old Shu's younger brother, the same age as I was, got encephalitis and died.

After I married here there was violence. They watched the place, it was a very strict time. I went to find my mother to seek her help. . . . I, too, was a mother, pregnant with my second child. My mother-in-law was terrible. It was then that I understood women's difficult place. I went to find her . . . [living in a remote mountainous area]. I realized that this old woman, my mother, was pitiful, carrying such a big basket, her head extended, not upright. How could I go into her house? I could see that my mother's life had not gone well. How could she have gone to that kind of place? Seeing her, did I not hold her head and cry painfully a lot? Did we not care for each other? After a few days there, I came back.

I have always missed and thought of my mother, but there was no choice. Her life was miserable. I had had to take care of two sets of old people. My father had no son and, although my sister and I left home, he still depended on us to support him until he died in 1960. On my husband's side and on my mother's side there were old people needing my care, and altogether I had five children. How could I help her? I never returned.

*Doing capitalism: raising fowl.* My family has always had difficulty and sadness in one form after another. When I planted some vegetables to sell, they said I was practicing capitalism. I was the first in this village to raise ducks. I was only doing a household sideline to see if I could help the family out of its difficulties. I was the first to raise water ducks. After I raised them, everyone in the village saw that I made money, so raising ducks became popular. Everyone started to raise them. When they did, then I stopped because it did not earn money anymore. In 1961 I raised water ducks. In 1963 I started something new again, raising early chickens—a special breed of small chickens. Someone from Xishuangbanna [a county in the southern, tropical part of Yunnan] came here and spent money; the price was rather high. I thought: this was something new. When I did something early, one step ahead, it was good. Whenever I succeeded, it soon became widespread and then I stopped. Once I started to raise big geese. Everyone in this village including the office wanted to buy the eggs. They all came here to buy, and again the idea spread, so again I stopped raising them. Then, I tried again, first to make repairs and then we started to make furniture.

The public and private accounts of Mr. Shu and Mrs. Shui allow us to glimpse the history of a household that has become wealthy. Starting poor, this couple faced setbacks due to family burdens and public policies, yet they finally managed to develop a successful business and prosper. They have not become ostentatious. They dress in ordinary clothes and are generally very busy with different aspects of their business; they still raise rice, beans, and pigs, although the ¥67,000 net income from the furniture business dwarfs the ¥4,000 that comes from agricultural pursuits. They dedicate time to civic affairs (such as the performances described in chapter 9) and maintain friendly relations with village and township leaders, generating good will and, very likely, good business.

These examples of families that managed to become wealthy during the reform period show certain similarities. Starting essentially without material capital, their legacy from the Maoist period, they each brought together a working husband and wife in good health, a commercial orientation, and some nonagricultural experience. While the husbands' construction-related enterprises account for the wealth that differentiates these households, the wives concentrated on the farming, pig raising, and other activities, which would have buttressed the family efforts to accumulate start-up capital. Mr. Shu's statement explicitly credits that partnership when he says, "After many years, we two people, husband and wife, through industrious, hard work, scientific management, and the labor of our two hands, achieved . . . an affluent life."

# CONTINUITIES AND CHANGES IN WEALTH AND POVERTY

In the 1990s, certain structural conditions associated with poverty in Lu Village are similar to those in the 1930s. First, the position of outsiders remains marginal. Migrants cannot establish themselves in Lu Village because membership is granted for descent or marriage. Those who migrate to the area in search of work have typically left their families behind and lived without the benefit of their own family life. Moreover, they have no possibility to gain access to land in Lu Village. Outsiders who marry someone in the community are able to gain access to land through their spouse, but as we shall see in chapter 7, they can still experience disadvantages if they lack local kin support.

Second, single people are handicapped. Men who miss the opportunity to marry during their prime find it difficult to find anyone who will marry them. A man over thirty is considered an old man by the young women who are still unmarried, and nearly all village women are married by the age of twenty-five. Single individuals and single-sex households have a hard time achieving the efficiency of a household economy where men and women each specialize in different kinds of work and cooperate. Men or women who are single due to widowhood or divorce may get a second chance to marry if they are not very old, but they usually have to settle for someone equally needy, widowed or divorced, with additional children to support. Children who lose a mother or a father are likely to grow up poor, as did Mrs. Shui in the 1950s and the son of Mr. Du in the 1990s.

Finally, physical disability and illness remain a major cause and outcome of poverty. Fei described the blind fortune-teller as a most unfortunate man, but in the 1990s the man with one arm, the woman with severe arthritis, and her son who is mentally ill face poverty, which is mitigated only by the extreme efforts of family members to support them and the intermittent and much less adequate aid of neighbors and the village government. In family histories, a toll of deaths and mentally retarded children appears to coincide with the difficult years of the Great Leap Forward, when poverty meant, not just a lack of material conveniences, but daily hunger.

When we look at the conditions that confer wealth, there has been somewhat more change. In the past, wealth was primarily inherited. Those whose families settled early in the valley (or those who survived the depopulation caused by plague and the Muslim rebellion) owned large amounts of land and passed this advantage to their children. In Fei's time, there were relatively few self-made entrepreneurs, although innkeeping and trading contributed to the income of those who owned land. Mrs. Huang, the seer, was one, but since she lacked kin support in the village, her enterprise was heavily taxed and she could not retain wealth. Other paths to wealth were educational and military careers, both of which might lead to accumulation of wealth outside the community but were highly competitive. Education required a degree of ability, tested in examinations, but it also reflected preexisting family wealth that made it possible to pay tutors and release children from farm labor in order to study. Military careers (and banditry) in Fei's time offered opportunities to excel in the use of force, including plunder and extortion, albeit at high risk.

Today, inherited landownership cannot account for different access to wealth, since land is still distributed on a per capita basis. Social and cultural capital are important factors. This capital comes in the form of education, special skills, and social networks. Literacy and knowledge of carpentry, construction, commerce, and the regional geography of markets have been important to Lu Village's entrepreneurs. To some extent, cultural capital has been handed down within families, despite the severe efforts of the revolution and Cultural Revolution to reduce all families to an equal footing. Even during the collective period, those who had completed elementary education and attained literacy were so scarce that, when they were not punished for their background, they were likely to be called on for jobs requiring record keeping, learning, or other skills.[16] In the reform period, higher education was likely to open the doors to job assignments in urban or state enterprises, which also carried the benefit of urban household registration. In the more open market economy, skills in literacy, communication, and computation have undoubtedly aided those who started independent enterprises.

In sum, the contemporary system has smaller inherited advantages and a degree of fluidity, enhanced by nearly universal access to public education. Even if their parents are illiterate, most children have the opportunity to succeed in school. However, appreciation of the value of education seems to be stronger among families that were educated before the revolution. In the next generation, moreover, wealthy families will increasingly be able to pay for better educational resources and continue on to university by paying their way rather than depending on government subsidy. This will help the wealthy to retain some of their advantages for succeeding generations.

In the 1990s, building construction is more important than it was in the 1930s, and contractors do well. In the 1930s, there were also large construction projects, not of housing or factories, but of roads, railroads, and mines. In the 1990s, one can see continuity in ownership of transport systems (horse caravan to minivans) as a means of increasing wealth. Some of these activities may require good political connections. One woman of Lu Village Center, whose husband is an outsider and handicapped by a bad back, commented on the continuing gap between rich and poor by charging that, after decollectivization, the leader of her team took possession of and used property of the collective. She pointed to his house and said, "Look at his house, so great. He sold things belonging to the collective and built this house." She paused and said, "My parents were poor in the past. We have no powerful relatives or friends. So we are still poor now." Neighbors say that this woman belongs to one of the poorest households in her team.

The image of gender that emerges from these accounts is one in which men and women have depended heavily on one another for survival and success, particularly in the agrarian economy. When men lost the opportunity to marry, or lost their wives through death or disability, they did not prosper. While I encountered no cases of women who did not marry, women clearly also suffered greatly when they lost the labor of their husband through death, disability, or divorce. To a large extent, their well being depended on the age, capabilities, and loyalties of their children and kin. These conditions show continuity with the past. In the reform period, with the opening of commercial, construction, and town-based employment, young people have increasing opportunities to seek individual wage work. These opportunities have been more common for young men, including low-skilled construction workers, but educated young women are increasingly seeking and finding jobs in town. Town employment can be significantly more rewarding than farmwork, but it does not have the capacity to generate wealth comparable to that of the most successful entrepreneurs. To date, the most successful households, however, have risen on the basis of men's entrepreneurial specialties in construction-related businesses, where rising incomes have stimulated demand. These businesses involve larger amounts of capital and risk, and although they may have relied on women's farming and pig-raising contributions to accumulate capital and benefited from more direct collaborations in the business, they are clearly associated with the entrepreneurial and technological skills of the men. Women have operated small businesses and stores but have yet to develop their own large, profitable businesses hiring nonfamily labor. Clearly, some Lu Village women have succeeded in getting urban jobs and residences, allowing them to improve their standard of living and leave farmwork behind. However, it remains to be seen if Lu Village women will make inroads into the emerging entrepreneurial class through businesses that they control and manage.

Overall, Lu Village in the 1990s is considerably wealthier than it was in the 1930s, the 1950s, and the 1970s. This is difficult to demonstrate in quantitative terms because the forms of money and prices are different. But looking at general indices of the standard of living shows that these are relatively good times. We recall the statement of one woman that even a landlord of the past does not live as well as his son does today. We also note that all villagers have access to electricity, and many have televisions, bicycles, and running water. Nearly all of them have ridden on buses or trains, if only to go to a hospital in the city. Some of the other obvious places to compare well-being are in an analysis of demography, which measures the effect of poverty on children, and in a comparison of marriage gifts, such as dowries, today and in the past. As we shall see in later chapters, both of these show considerable gains over the past.

## NOTES

1. The United Nations' *Human Development Report* (1994:97) shows China as one of the world's top ten performers in 1980–1992 in terms of absolute increase in the Human Development Index (HDI) value, which is based on gross national product, life expectancy, and education.

2. A similar situation occurred in prerevolution Guangdong, where outsiders were treated like a permanent class of slaves (Potter and Potter 1990).

3. This arduous labor, described to me by C. Y. Hsiang (Xiang Jingyun) recalling the carriers along the Burma Road in Yunnan in the 1940s, as well as by Harry Franck (1925), is not only a prerevolutionary memory. In 1985, I witnessed similar backbreaking labor by a long stream of lean, wiry men who, hour after hour, climbed up and down an enormous cliff with sacks of heavy coal on their backs, doubled over and sweating, loading barges on the Yangtze River. Above were bleak cement buildings with many tiny rooms, presumably the barracks for these coal miners and porters. A more dismal, "nineteenth-century" scene of manual toil could scarcely be imagined. Even in large cities, such as Chengdu and Sichuan, I often saw lines of straining men shouldering, pulling, or pushing huge loads, such as cement telephone poles or logs thirty or forty feet in length, along the road with the help of wheels but no motor power.

4. When Fei visited Lu Village, he reported that opium had been eradicated as a crop, although there were still many opium addicts in the village who purchased opium at a local inn.

5. In citing these figures to me, this woman, a team leader, can be assumed to be accurate, because she has known everyone for years. Yet even here the number of households that she cites and the number in the official registry book are different. She has more households, and less total population, reflecting, I would expect, her greater knowledge of de facto divisions and departures.

6. See Benedict (1996) for an excellent study of the bubonic plague in Yunnan.

7. Fei used the dollar sign for yuan, which varied from four to twenty to the U.S. dollar in 1938–1939 (Fei and Zhang 1945: see footnote, 46).

8. The calculation for household A, the richest, with the lowest proportion spent on food, rises from 31 to 48 percent if household income does not credit the subsidy of 120 yuan given by the clan for the son's university education.

9. This should be compared to villages studied by the Potters (1990), Huang (1990), and Huang (1989), as well as Fei's restudy of Kaixiangong (1983). Model villages, with incomes above the provincial average, were also studied by Judd (1994).

10. Yunnan Province is China's largest tobacco producer, with about 20 percent of the nation's crop (SSB 1992:363).

11. It is possible that migrant workers and seasonal workers have comparable homes and living conditions in their home villages, but while working "outside," they are likely to accept lower-quality living conditions in order to bring home more cash.

12. In my interviews, one woman of Lu Village Center married a man from this hamlet, whom she met in school. He was illiterate, while she had a grade five education. This case, involving marriage to a worse place and to a less-educated man, was unusual. Lavely's analysis (1991) of marriage patterns in southwest China (Sichuan) shows women tend to marry toward urban places. The household registry lists gave little evidence of people from the center marrying out to the hamlets.

13. The significance of leaving a factory job is that workers with state sector employment enjoyed an "iron rice bowl," meaning employment security and many benefits, such as health care, housing, and urban food rations.

14. In 1992, ¥1.00 (FEC) equaled U.S.$0.18. Foreign Exchange Certificates were the official exchange rate for Chinese yuan to foreign currency. The black market rate for Chinese *renminbi*, which is now the sole currency, would have been 30 to 50 percent lower.

15. Although I use Western forms of respect (Mr. and Mrs.), I want to preserve the contemporary Chinese custom whereby a woman keeps her natal surname after marriage. Children usually, but not always, take the surname of their father, so Mrs. Song refers to the married daughter of Mr. Song.

16. He Liyi's biography (1993) illustrates this.

# Chapter Seven

# Marriage, Household, and Gender: Keeping Sons and Daughters

Even a woman who contracts a matrilocal marriage is considered only a temporary link in the chain of patrilineal inheritance. (Fei and Zhang 1945:66)

Patrilineal joint family systems which obtain in one variant or another in a continuous belt of agrarian societies stretching from China across South Asia and the Middle East into Eastern Europe and North Africa, present the extreme examples of consistent, thoroughgoing male bias. . . . Moreover, in the East and South Asian societies where marriage is exogamous, the bride moves not only to the groom's family but to another village or town altogether, where she has no connections and her social knowledge is no longer of use. (Skinner 1997:59)

Today, [in China] . . . patrilocal marriage is rarely identified as problematic and there is no longer any significant effort being made to promote matrilocal marriage. (Jacka 1997:98)

## MARRIAGE: EXPECTATIONS AND EXCEPTIONS

The pattern of residence after marriage is considered an important diagnostic for gender inequality, intimately related to inheritance practices and property rights; all three obviously contribute to the political economy of gender. The forms of marriage that anthropologists refer to as patrilocal or matrilocal are influenced by norms for the inheritance of land and housing by sons and daughters. In patrilocal marriages, which are typical for most of China, sons are the heirs to family land and daughters marry out to join their husband's household. The couple resides where the man's parents live, often living in a joint family at the start. In matrilocal marriages, land passes to daughters and the couple resides where the woman's parents live. Uxorilocal marriage, an awkward term for residence with the wife, describes the situation where land normally passes through the male line (father to son), but in particular cases passes to daughters who remain "at home" and bring in a husband to continue their patriline. The daughter is viewed as an intermediate heir in a lineal system that retains its focus on father-son property transmission.

Patrilineal descent, patrilineal inheritance, and patrilocal marriage are hallmarks of the Chinese family. Chinese kinship is famous for recording patrilineal genealogies, tracing descent through fathers and sons, and ignoring the whereabouts of daughters' descendants. Daughters are expected to marry exogamously, that is, marry out of their natal village, leaving their own patrilineal family to join their husband's. I arrived in Lu Village expecting the kind of "thoroughgoing male bias" that anthropologist William Skinner referred to in the opening quote. But as I pointed out in the preface, Lu Village did not strictly conform to the expectation of patrilocality with exogamous marriages for women. After my initial surprise at discovering that the party secretary belonged to a twice uxorilocal household with a four-generation female line, I gradually learned Lu Village indeed has, in some ways, a more flexible approach to family and gender than official Han patriarchal models and stereotypes imply. More specifically, uxorilocal marriages are fairly common in Lu Village, and there is considerable emphasis on cognates, kin who are related on the mother's side.[1] As we shall se, Lu Village families have experienced many political and economic changes since the 1930s, but marriage residence patterns retain their distinctive characteristics.

## MARRIAGES IN THE PAST

Fei described the exceptional marriage practices of Lu Village, under the heading "Matrilineal principle," as follows:

> Instances of the matrilineal principle in marriage can be found anywhere in China, but it is normally operative only as a temporary solution when the deceased owner has no male successor. In such a situation, the daughter will take a husband into her father's house, so that she may have children to perpetuate the family line. This is the case in Lu Village, *but here a daughter who has brothers may also remain in her father's house after marriage and share her brothers' privileges.* Yet such an act will certainly be regarded as contrary to the traditional spirit of patriliny, and the brothers will be loath to tolerate such an encroachment by their sisters upon their full rights of succession. (Fei and Zhang 1945:112–13, italics added)

To illustrate the practice of uxorilocal marriage in Lu Village, Fei gave the example of Uncle Zhang, who took his mother's surname. Uncle Zhang's mother had been a very capable person, who gave her parents much assistance in the management of their farm. A bachelor named Song, who had brought some money with him from Dali when he came to the village to live, was taken into the Zhang house and married to the eldest daughter. The daughter was given a share of Zhang's land, and the couple [Uncle Zhang's parents] later acquired more than 10 *gong* by themselves. As long as they lived, they enjoyed fairly amicable relations with all the members of Zhang's house; but when they died, the brothers demanded that the land be returned. Uncle Zhang, who is still unhappy about this unfriendly action, told me that he could have refused them, since he had never taken his father's name. Bearing the name Zhang, he was entitled to inherit the land from his mother's line. However, he felt that the maintenance of good relations with his uncles and cousins, who were influential persons in the community, was worth more than the land; so he yielded to their demand. (Fei and Zhang 1945:113, converted to pinyin orthography)

Uncle Zhang's parents did not fit the expected uxorilocal pattern where the bride's family had no male heirs and the groom was poor (260). Uncle Zhang's mother had brothers, and his father had money, if not land, in Lu Village. The next generation demonstrated the fragility of an agreement to pass land to a sister. Her heir, Uncle Zhang, was squeezed out by his cousins.

While uxorilocal marriages interested Fei, traditional patrilocal marriages were clearly predominant. Fei illustrated the investment that parents made in the marriages of their sons, and generally discussed family management, landownership, and kinship in terms of patrilineal, patriarchal models. However, he did not cover marriage in much detail. For instance, he did not mention the sale and purchase of women as wives, later a key topic in Communist Party discourse criticizing the marriage practices of the "feudal past."

The majority of Lu Village marriages undoubtedly took the form of negotiated arrangements between parents of both parties in which a woman's parents usually considered, among other things, their daughter's well-being and maintained contact with her after marriage. Some arrangements, however, were much closer to the "sale" of a woman or a girl.[2] Women who were sold lacked a dowry and kinfolk who retained a responsibility for them (Watson 1981:239–44). They were likely to occupy a very subordinate position in the household. One such marriage story, told to me by a lively old woman in Lu Village, deserves consideration.

In 1991, seventy-year-old Song Ailin described interesting aspects of her early life and changing family circumstances. These included kidnapping, the sale of women, nameless girls, polygyny, and uxorilocal residence. Her family story begins with the traumatic events of her childhood and takes us to the present.

My father was kidnapped by bandits in the mountains and held for ransom. My *nainai* (father's mother) did not have any money to give them so she sold her daughter at age twelve for ¥360 yuan (in old Yunnan silver coins with a picture of a dragon) to a local family. She gave the money to the bandits but they said it was not enough. The bandits still did not give my father back. So my *nainai* also sold her daughter-in-law (my mother) to another man in the village. That man was a widower who had a crazy daughter. My mother was still a young woman then and later bore another daughter, who was my younger sister. At that time, I could still encounter my mother in the village.

Then I myself was sold by my *shushu* (father's younger brother). It was not my loving *nainai* who did this to me. My first husband's family was poor; they had no land. As tenants, they gave two-thirds of the crop to the landlord. I did day labor in the opium fields. As a twelve-year-old daughter-in-law, I was still not mature. I had no periods yet and did not understand anything about sex, nor did my husband, who was only two years older than I was. [It's unclear whether they actually slept together.]

My *popo* (mother-in-law) was not good to me. She would scold and criticize me because I didn't know how to do much yet, and my *popo* had a lot of work with other younger children and was still a young mother herself. Then, my husband, just a boy at age sixteen and still in school, was kidnapped by the Nationalists for the army. They wanted him because he was tall. They kidnapped him three times. The first two times he came back. The last time, he did not return, and my life was unbearable. I was then sent to town to be a servant in a doctor's house and worked there for two years taking care of children. I worked from early morning until dark and then came back. They sold me several years after he was kidnapped—when I was about seventeen, for ¥360 of paper money, to my current husband in Lu Village.

In my *first* interview with Song Ailin, before I knew her well, she did not mention her first marriage and merely explained that she met her (second) husband when he came to work in her village. She implied they married willingly, because neither had any parents. This did not seem completely inconsistent with her later use of the term "sale" to describe her transfer from the family of her first mother-in-law to that of her second husband, for in those days people did not transfer from one household to another without such economic transactions.

As a child, they gave me no name: they simply called me "Xiaohuan" or "Small Exchange."[3] Later, when I was with a bunch of girlfriends without names, we gave each other names. That's when I got the name "Ailin."[4] The other girls, like me, had not attended school so had no personal names. My father's surname was Song.

My second husband was a tenant and skilled craftsman. He also had no parents, so he paid for me himself. But he already had a wife and supported his wife's mother as well. The four of us lived together. The first wife's mind was slow, although she was not mentally ill. She could do farmwork, and cook, and routine things, but she could not solve any problems. Also, all her children died. After I arrived [as the second wife], the first wife still bore three more children, who all died. There were two girls who died as babies and a boy who reached about five years old and fell from the second floor of the house and died about five months later. The first wife also still had a five-year-old girl from before my arrival, who also died, plus other earlier children died. I got pregnant and bore a child who died at age one. Later, I gave birth again.

When my second child was born, the mother of the first wife died. The other wife appreciated what I could do for her, and we did not hate each other. We lived to-gether for a long time. The first wife died only a few years ago. I called her "*Jiejie*," or older sister, and she called me "*Meimei*," younger sister. My children called her "*Dama*" (Big Mother). When my older son separated from our house, he took care of her (the first wife, his stepmother) until she died a few years later.[5]

When the revolution came, we were first labeled "*funong*," or rich peasants, even though we owned no land, simply because we were friends with the landlord. A year later, another classifying team came through and we were classified "*zhongnong*," or middle peasants. [This status did not carry the same stigma and punitive conse-quences.]

In 1958, the time of hunger, my husband, who is tall, was starving and swollen from malnutrition [fixed rations were given to all adults, regardless of size]. The party secretary helped him by bringing him the cooking water from someone who made bean curd and by getting him extra coupons for sugar, oil, and things from the cooperative. That's how he survived.

Neither of us [now in their seventies] is literate but all our children have studied to eighth grade or beyond. We decided that education was a great opportunity, so we lived cheaply, wore old clothes, and scrimped to be able to save for the children's education. We told our children that we wanted their lives to be better, and so they must study hard, and they did. Half of them went through upper middle school (high school) and the others all completed eighth grade.

As adults, the better-educated children (the sons and a daughter) found white-collar occupations, and those with eighth-grade education became workers or farmers. Because their sons were not farmers, one daughter be-came a farmer and married uxorilocally. This daughter lived with them, first using the empty room of her brother, and later a new section she and her hus-band built. In the early 1990s, the family courtyard was shared by the old couple, plus the families of their son and daughter, their spouses, and their children. In the mid-1990s, the eldest son built a new, modern house (¥30,000) located on a separate lot near the paved road. Ailin frequently went to Kunming to stay with a married daughter, a worker with official res-idence (*hukou*) there. Her family life, despite its tragic beginning, seemed happy and successful.

It surprised me that this polygamous marriage survived so many years of revolution, when marriages were legally required to be monogamous. I origi-nally thought the polygamous relationship endured because there were sim-ply no other kin to take care of the possibly retarded first wife and the village would have had to support her if they divorced. As far as I could tell, the vil-lagers quietly tolerated a man who had a second wife to help him care for the first, run a household, and raise children.[6] The relationship between the two wives seemed more cooperative than competitive. I wondered if this was true even in the early years or during the famine, but I was impressed that the first wife survived the famine and lived to old age. Ailin, sold and resold as a girl, worked hard and forged ahead in the collective period, and in old age was a lively grandmother, still strong and full of character, living with children and grandchildren around her. In later interviews, however, the image of family and marital happiness dimmed.

One day years later, I finally asked Ailin when we were alone about the tolerance for polygamy after the revolution. She filled in the blanks in a surprising fashion. She had not easily accepted her marriage to her current husband. Negating the harmonious relationship she had previously described, she now spoke of forced sex and violent beatings, and she pointed to deep scars, showing how her second husband beat and kicked her. In her revised narrative, she explained that after the revolution, when the new Marriage Law took effect, she divorced her second husband with the help of a woman representative from the Women's Federation (an outsider).[7] She lived alone for nearly two years, leaving her older children with their father while keeping the younger one and renting a separate place to live. However, her husband did not leave her alone and repeatedly broke into her home and assaulted her. She became pregnant again and went to the authorities, but they told her they could not protect her and advised her to return to live with him and raise her children. Because she had no choice, she returned reluctantly and bore more children. Officials, far from tolerating polygamy to protect the first wife, apparently failed not only to enforce the law against polygamy but also to support a woman's right to divorce.

To compound the tragedy, Ailin's first husband, who had been conscripted, did not die in the war. He finally returned and discovered his mother had sold Ailin to another man. The two of them still had feelings for one another. Ailin's two husbands fought, but the second husband won. Her first husband was beaten and put in jail for six months. Many years later, she saw him again shortly before he died. He had married and had children. He asked if her husband still beat her. "No," she said, "the children are grown now, so he no longer beats me."

After hearing this story, I saw how she avoided her elderly husband and realized that she had always done so, but that I had paid no attention to it. A strong character, she has survived and raised capable children who are filial to both parents. Of course, her feelings toward her second husband, a respected man, were undoubtedly complex. As shown in the account of the seeress, there are many sides to all human relationships. It is difficult to judge events of a half century ago by the standards of today. At the same time, we must not ignore the pressure for many women to hide their feelings under the cloak of patriarchal family harmony. Ailin's story of personal suffering reveals both certain prerevolutionary "feudal" practices and the difficulties women had in realizing some of the basic rights the revolution promised them.

## MARRIAGE AND MOTHER-DAUGHTER
## TIES: UXORILOCAL RESIDENCE IN THE 1990S

The expression for uxorilocal marriage that is most often heard in Yunnan is "*shangmen,*" which might be translated literally as "at the gate" or "at the door." This expression seemed potentially offensive or unpleasant to my urban assistant, who used it in low tones to avoid embarrassing people.[8] When I tried to elicit more information about its connotations, she squirmed uncomfortably at the thought of a man approaching the gate this way—almost as if referring to a burglar, an invader, or an unwelcome visitor violating the defensive sanctuary of the patrilineal home. Yet when the term came up in interviews with villagers in other villages of Yunnan, they showed no obvious discomfort with it and even used it matter-of-factly themselves, without resorting to whispers. In Lu Village, an expression often used to describe the contracting of such a marriage is "*zhao guye,*" which translates as "seek a son-in-law" and perhaps has less-negative connotations. This is quite comparable to the term used for contracting patrilocal marriage, "*tao xifu,*" meaning "to ask (or beg for) a daughter-in-law." Both terms emphasize the role of the parents in finding partners for their children.

My very first two interviews in Lu Village in 1990 turned up uxorilocal marriages that had occurred in families with both daughters and sons. Both are completely Han in their ethnic background and one revealed conflict between sons and daughters over family resources. The condition shared by these first two cases was that the mothers were widowed early and had older daughters who married and stayed in the home to help raise the younger siblings. As in the cases of Mistress Huang and Mrs. Gao, described in chapters 5 and 6, teenage daughters could be kept home to help their parent or parents attract adult male labor to the family. This was most likely to occur when parents were ill or disabled, or when a woman was widowed and had other young children to raise. But the following cases, along with previously described examples of Mrs. Song's daughter (above) and the party secretary's family (preface), show that uxorilocal marriages occur under a wide variety of circumstances.

### Widows, Daughters, and Siblings

An Juhua is age thirty-seven and uxorilocally married with three teenage children. She lives in a courtyard shared with her mother, but mother and daughter do not get along well. Juhua was the oldest daughter. Her mother was widowed at a young age with three small children. When it was time for Juhua to get married, her mother persuaded Juhua to marry uxorilocally to help the mother raise the two younger brothers, and Juhua agreed. Also, when money was short, Juhua and her husband borrowed ¥2,000 to support the family.

Now, Juhua's two younger brothers are both married and living in the same crowded courtyard (also shared with two unrelated families). One is living with his mother and the other lives separately. Both brothers have turned against their older sister and her husband and want them to leave. They will not help pay back any of the loan that was borrowed to support them before they divided the family. Juhua's mother has also turned against her daughter.

Juhua's husband was born in the same county but in a different village district. He served as a soldier for six years in the north. He is a capable, hard-working man and if they were not paying back the loan, they would be doing well enough. But in the meantime, Juhua is very unhappy, living in conflict with her natal family next door. I noted that, when asked about people she exchanges labor with in rice transplanting, she did not mention her mother or brothers.

In this family, patrilineal inheritance is obviously not simply sustained by fathers who favor their sons. Here, a mother and jealous, resentful brothers seek to drive their sister out in a struggle involving limited family resources (particularly housing) and responsibility for debts. Because there are two brothers opposed to their elder sister and her husband, they have some power in the dispute. My assistant said that if they went to the court over this issue, however, the court would support the daughter's right to inherit. But getting people to live together in peace is hard for the court to achieve.

Mrs. Bei is sixty years old. As in the previous case, Mrs. Bei's father died early, making her mother a young widow. As an older daughter, Mrs. Bei stayed home to help raise younger siblings, and her mother found her a husband for an uxorilocal marriage. Mrs. Bei eventually inherited her father's house. Now she is a widow and lives with her unmarried thirty-year-old son, who became mentally retarded after childhood encephalitis. Her two daughters and other son moved out at marriage, but one daughter, whose husband works in another province, returns with her child for extended visits and runs a bean curd business with her mother, rather than stay in her husband's village while he is away. This may mean she is a candidate to inherit her mother's house and possibly the burden of care for her brother.

While the lack of male heirs is usually seen as a condition for uxorilocal marriage (as mentioned by Fei), the presence of older sisters with a lot of younger siblings to care for is another fairly common pattern. The following case illustrates this as well.

Mrs. Fang was the second daughter in a family with six children. She explained that she and her older sister married uxorilocally because her parents needed help with the younger children. Now at home there are two married younger brothers and one younger sister still unmarried. Family property consisting of the house and courtyard was divided between the two older sisters and the two younger brothers. Presumably the younger sister will marry out.

## The Ming Family: Two Generations with Uxorilocal Marriage

Old Mrs. Ming was the only daughter in a family with one son. Her father was an only child, one of the descendants of a famous official some eighteen generations back. Old Mrs. Ming's only brother died at age thirteen. As she was the only surviving child, her parents arranged for her to marry "at home" (*zai jia*). Her husband officially joined her family (*shangmen*) and changed his surname to Ming. He came from a slightly more mountainous district to the northwest, about five kilometers from Lufeng. Together they had seven surviving children, two sons and five daughters. The eldest was a son, born in 1942, followed by two daughters, a son, and three more daughters, the youngest born in 1969.

The eldest son took the Ming surname and got a state sector job as a teacher. His residence registration was transferred out of the village to Lufeng. The eldest daughter, Ming Jiexing, born in 1944, did as her mother had done and married at home before she was twenty. Her husband also changed his surname to Ming. With an age gap of twenty-five years between Ming Jiexing and the youngest sister, Ming Jiexing and her husband obviously helped a great deal with the work of raising the younger siblings, until the last one married in 1989. Five of the remaining six children (four daughters and a son) now live in Lu Village and the other daughter lives in the next community on the road to town. All five daughters took the Ming surname, but the second son took the original surname of his father.

Not only does the Ming family have two generations of uxorilocal marriage, but the daughters show a high rate of village endogamy. Several of them live very close by (almost next door) and interact daily. Visiting among the many sisters and aunts and their children is always a pleasant experience. The house inheritance was divided between the eldest son (who lives in town), the eldest daughter, and the younger son. These families live in an old-style, two-story house with rooms sharing a single courtyard. Ming Jiexing had four children, three girls who took the Ming surname and a boy who took his father's original surname. Her two older daughters were roughly the same age as the two youngest daughters of her own mother, Old Mrs. Ming. Unlike the first case described, this extended family was living together in harmony, with a great deal of cooperation and good humor. One interesting aspect of the family was that two of the sisters and a niece all had husbands working in the same financial institution in town. The family as a whole was shifting from reliance on limited farming resources to cooperation in obtaining occupations in the expanding urban sector.

These accounts suggest that older daughters were kept at home to baby-sit for younger siblings. While the burden these daughters shared included child care, it also included growing food and earning work points for the family. One older daughter reported, "My housework included watering the vegetable fields, carrying water, cooking, feeding the pigs, and taking care of my younger brother and sisters, and in the busy season, I transplanted rice and planted beans."

## Older Sisters with Younger Siblings

Comparing Lu Village to a village in southern Yunnan, Fei and Zhang wrote: "In Lu Village there are more cases in which the better-class farmers follow the matrilocal system of marriage. This may be due to the fact that in Lu Village the women take greater part in farm management, so that for the continuity of the family enterprise there is greater interest in trying to retain the elder able girls in the house" (1945:260). The following case illustrates that the desire to retain female labor still affects marriage strategies and that parents still play a major role in deciding the kind of marriage their daughter will have. There are social advantages for women in uxorilocal marriages, but as we have seen in the case of Mistress Huang's daughter in chapter 5, these are not necessarily the arrangements the daughters would choose themselves.

Mrs. Bing, born in 1964 and one of the younger women in an uxorilocal marriage, was sixteen when her parents arranged her marriage in 1980 to a man from another area. He was thirteen years older than she was. She said her parents arranged the marriage because the family lacked labor power: her brother was only seven years old at that time. Because her family was poor, a man with better qualities did not want to enter her family. She was forced to accept the man her parents liked. Her husband came from outside the village but within the same county. Her marriage was very simple, involving none of the economic transactions described later in the chapter: "Then the two of us went to do casual labor, earn money. We bought a set of new clothes, and then we got married. We did not have anything." When her brother grew up, they divided the household. This family remains poor today because, with a bad back, her husband cannot do heavy work outside or much of the work at home and in the field. His disability places a heavy burden on her. She said if he could work hard at home, she would be happy to earn money outside. Her husband needs a light job because of his sore back, but because he has no relatives and friends in Lu Village, he cannot find such a job there.

## An Only Child

Mrs. Li, age forty-one, had no siblings and therefore married "at home" at the age of twenty-one, in 1976. Her husband is from the same village and both of them are farmers. Together they support her seventy-three-year-old widowed mother, who lives with them. When Mrs. Li and her husband married, neither side had money to contribute to marriage expenses. She and her husband jointly manage household money.

The cases above give some sense of the frequency and diversity of uxorilocal marriages in Lu Village. Uxorilocal marriages in Lu Village have occurred under a variety of circumstances. In some cases there were no sons, in some cases there were, but they were too young. In some cases, the sons left for better jobs and parents turned to their daughters for support and sharing the work of farming. While Lufeng women who marry at home are still in the minority, they are much more frequently encountered than in the north Chinese villages I have studied.

## THE POLITICS OF RESIDENCE

Government control over household registration (*hukou*) also has an effect on marriage strategies. In some cases of uxorilocal marriage, the husband lives and works in a setting where women are scarce or where there are restricted opportunities for women. It may be difficult to obtain a wife unless the husband agrees that she can stay with her natal family. The next example involves a miner. He has formal worker registration and his wife has rural registration in Lu Village. Because the government limits urban migration by limiting access to nonagricultural registration, she would be unable to hold a formal job or enjoy urban benefits if she went to live in the mining community with her farmer registration. Nor would she be given land to farm there, although she is allowed to keep land in Lu Village. In marriages where the household registration of husband and wife are mixed (nonagricultural and agricultural), the nonagricultural registration cannot be extended to the spouse. It is like a nontransferable form of citizenship. Only one child can inherit it, when the parent retires. (Increasingly, however, nonagricultural registrations can be purchased, as I discuss later.)

## Marriage to a Miner

Mrs. Mai is a middle-aged Lu Village woman married to a coal miner who is from a nearby city (Yipinglang) and lives at the mine. Her husband never transferred his registration to Lu Village, because he has nonagricultural status, which is considered superior. Household registration regulations do not allow her to change her status to his, so she remains in her natal village and farms an allotment of land for herself and her children. Her husband comes home two months a year. Her three children all bear her surname and are registered in Lu Village. Mrs. Mai never attended school, because there were a lot of siblings in her family. She inherited her house from her father, and it was divided into three equal sections between herself, her older brother, and her younger sister.

## THE UXORILOCAL PATTERN

In 1990, with a population of 2,943, Lu Village as a whole maintained the importance of uxorilocal marriage that Fei observed five decades earlier. My analysis of registration records for all adults of Greater Lu Village showed that 22 percent of the women have uxorilocal marriages.[9] The rate for men is slightly lower but still nearly one-fifth (table 7.1).

I cross-checked these findings with my interviews based on a random sample of eighty-six households drawn from all fifteen teams of Lu Village. The sample offers strong support for a pervasive high rate of uxorilocality, with 24 percent (twenty-one out of eighty-six marriages) belonging to the uxorilocal category.

## PATRILINY AND PATRILOCAL MARRIAGES

The emphasis given above to uxorilocal marriages should not obscure the fact that patrilineal and patrilocal marriages remain the dominant practice in

Table 7.1.   Lu Village Marriage Types (adults ages eighteen and over)

| Marriage type | Males Percent | Females Percent |
|---|---|---|
| Uxorilocal | 18 | 22 |
| Patri/virilocal[a] | 76 | 73 |
| Neolocal[b] | 6 | 5 |
| Total | 100 | 100 |
| | (n = 666) | (n = 761) |

*Source:* village household registration records (fifteen teams) of 1990.

*Note:* Table excludes adults who were unmarried, widowed, divorced, or transferred out. It includes only cases where the marriage and residence registration information seemed clear on the basis of family names and birthplaces. Less than 1.5 percent of the female and male marriage types were incomprehensible.

[a]These are households in which a couple lives in the husband's village and defines themselves as members of his family, whether or not they maintain joint household budgets with the parents.

[b]Neolocal households reside in a new location, independent of the parents of either spouse.

Lu Village. Since these aspects of Chinese family organization have been amply described for many of China's villages, I devote less attention to their internal dynamics here. Lu Village patrilocal marriages are broadly similar to those found throughout China.

## The Patrilineal Roots of the Family Tree

Being interested in the strength of patrilineal ideology, in my interviews I often asked if families had a "family tree" (*jiapu*). Most families responded that they were poor and therefore had no family tree commemorating illustrious ancestors. They indicated that family trees were concerns of the rich and powerful. It is difficult to know whether this was strictly true, or whether people were recalling the repression of the Cultural Revolution, when such signs of ancestor worship and class origin would have been severely attacked. Eventually, however, I was given a copy of a family tree document written about the most illustrious family in village history. This fifty-three-page document includes text describing an ancestor who achieved imperial office during the Ming dynasty and a patrilineal family tree tracing the links between men who shared this ancestor. Despite the repression of the Cultural Revolution, interested family members attempted to reassemble the family tree from the surviving fragments of information collected by senior members in the mid-1980s. For some descendants, this illustrious ancestry is still a source of pride and inspiration.

Clan groups today are clearly not as strong as they were in Fei's time, when there were numerous clans with clan lands, trust funds, and ancestral halls. Overt expressions of clan solidarity are much muted compared with the past. But patrilineal family organization is still very much a part of the social landscape and kinship structure. Stone grave markers attest to ancestral plots of land, and portraits of deceased parents are often hung high on the walls of the main family room. Many people burn incense to honor their ancestors, at least on special ritual occasions.

## Marriage Distance and Kin Support

Comparative studies of family systems have shown that marriages that keep women close to their natal kin offer women advantages of access to land, protection, and greater longevity than systems that require them to live among strangers.[10] As a result, measures of distance from a woman's natal kin, whether in kilometers or in the time it takes to reach her mother's house, become an indirect measure of social support for women.

In uxorilocal marriages, women remain in their natal patrilineage, along with all or most of their children. Marriage distance for these women is zero.

In a patrilocal marriage to someone from the same village (village endogamy), the marriage distance between a woman and her natal kin is also
close to zero. Patrilocal marriages that remove women greater distances from
their natal kin groups are believed to be more detrimental to women.

The pattern of marriages in Lu Village (table 7.2) shows that more than
half (55 percent) of the women married and live within one kilometer of
their natal family. For men, the rate was much higher, 92 percent. Only 8
percent of the married men moved their residence more than one kilometer
after marriage. Although the majority of both men and women benefit from
close kin, men in general are clearly at an advantage. At the other end of the
marriage distance scale, marriages that require people to move more than
twenty kilometers from their natal kin are examples of "distant exogamy."
Distant exogamy accounted for only 9 percent of the women and 4 percent
of the men in Lu Village in 1990. These outsiders, whether first or second
generation, are the individuals, like Uncle Chang or the seeress, Mrs. Huang
(in chapter 5), who are most likely to be bullied or dispossessed by those with
kin support.

## ASK FOR A DAUGHTER-IN-LAW (TAO XIFU), OR GET MARRIED (*JIEHUN*)?

The conflict between old and new attitudes may be illustrated by Mrs. Niu's
account of her son's recent wedding.

> My son and *xifu* (daughter-in-law) married more than ten days ago. They are both
> high school teachers. The *xifu*'s parents are also high school teachers. Recently, the
> wife's parents spent ¥50–60,000 to buy a small piece of land to use to build a three-
> room house. Because the land is close to the high school, they look forward to their
> daughter living nearby. They do not want us to say "ask for a daughter-in-law" (*tao
> xifu*). When we used the expression "ask for a daughter-in-law," they said it was not
> correct to say "ask for a daughter-in-law"—it was "get married" (*jiehun*). They said,
> "Our daughter was raised the same as a boy. Also she will not live with you here."

**Table 7.2.  Lu Village Marriage Distance**

| Marriage type | Women (%) | Men (%) |
|---|---|---|
| Local (0–1km) | 55 | 92 |
| Nonlocal (>1km) | 45 | 8 |
| Distant exogamy (>20 km) | (9) | (4) |
| Total | 100 | 100 |
|  | (n = 106) | (n = 106) |

*Source:* Village survey 1990.

While the house was being built, the *xifu*'s parents helped build the house, and in the evenings they came here to eat, every day for more than two months.

Mrs. Niu was clearly stung by the attitude of the daughter-in-law's parents, which stressed that their daughter was not marrying into a joint family. The bride's parents no doubt were trying to limit the authority of her in-laws, in part to ensure that their substantial investment in the house plot not be claimed later by Mrs. Niu's family, rather than their daughter.

One of my good friends in the village, unmarried when I first met her, had discussed the difference between *niangjia* (mother's home) and *pojia* (mother-in-law's home). She told me after her marriage, "You were right, even if you have a very good mother-in-law, it's never the same as being with your own mother." This young woman lived on weekends with her husband in an apartment in town and during the week at her mother-in-law's house, because it was close to the village school where she taught, but she frequently visited her own mother's house, which was located between the two.

## LONG-DISTANCE MARRIAGE AND EMIGRATION

In a system of patrilocal residence, women may view marriage as their one big opportunity to improve their lot in life by moving to a more prosperous place (Lavely 1991; Croll 1994). But when women contract marriages to men from distant places, there is extra concern about their safety. Cases of deception, abduction, and sale of women appear in the press and suggest that there is a particular pattern of trafficking in people linking southwestern Yunnan Province to northeast China. For instance, Jacka reports that:

> One of the effects of the increased bride-price payment has been, just as the CCP [Chinese Communist Party] previously feared, the maintenance and reinforcement of the view of women as commodities bought and sold by patrilineal families. This is most starkly illustrated by the abduction and sale of young women as brides. According to one report, almost 10,000 women and children are abducted and sold each year in Sichuan alone. (Jacka 1997:62)

We see in this passage the conflation of sale by parents and abduction by strangers. Although brides may have little say in either case, at least in the former case parents may have had their daughters' interests in mind. In a similar vein, Honig and Hershatter state:

> The practice of selling women from the south to villagers in the north was apparently widespread. Although [news] coverage of kidnapping did not explain the reasons for a south-north axis, most cases seemed to involve women from poor, remote

regions of the south being transported to northern villages where they were too poor to attract local brides. . . . Local governments in the south also expressed concern about the outflow of women from their region. A report in the *Yunnan Daily* stated that every day in 1982, five or six cases of women leaving the area were reported to the Dayao county court. From January to March, the report continued, "some 750 married and unmarried women have left the county for Shandong and Henan provinces, of which 60 percent are not old enough to marry and about 10 percent are married women. More than 95 percent of these women had gotten married without proper registration." Some cases did not involve south-to-north migration: abductions were also reported from Sichuan and Hubei to Henan, from one part of Zhejiang to another, and from Hubei to Guangxi. (Honig and Hershatter 1989:289–90)

These two reports suggest that southwest China supplies women to poor areas of central and northeast China where marriageable women are scarce, and that women have no agency in the process. In official reports, the processes of emigration and of underage and unregistered marriages are fused with the concern over abductions. Yet in reality it is difficult to separate the involuntary from the voluntary migrations. In Lu Village, a small percentage of women do move out to distant provinces such as Shandong (roughly two thousand kilometers from Yunnan, six days by train). And while a few men and women in Lu Village came from Sichuan (most before the revolution), there are no cases of Shandong brides coming to Lu Village. The local pattern of marriage migration does seem consistent with the northeastward flow of women. There is a tendency, however, to conflate the net flow of women between regions with sale and abduction rather than with voluntary migration toward the more prosperous provinces of China.

In 1996, I raised the subject of Lu Village women who have married out to distant provinces with a young woman shopkeeper, uxorilocally married, who has excellent knowledge of Lu Village's young adults. She said,

More than ten women of Lu Village have married out to Shandong. First, one woman married and went there. She later came back and sought other local young women to marry out to Shandong. The young women who went were introduced (*bei jieshao*) to local Shandong men. If one man is not satisfactory, then they introduce another; if they are satisfied (*manyi*), then they marry. There are another four or five who married out to mountain districts of Zhejiang Province. Of those who marry outside the province, some marry well, some not so well. There was one rather stupid girl who married to Shandong and got a good husband who was nice to her and didn't make her do hard work. Ironically, another smarter and very capable (*nenggan*) girl married out to Shandong and got a lazy (*lan*) husband. The two sets of parents went to see them. The parents of the clever girl were not happy at what they saw. They were hurt.

This statement makes it appear that women voluntarily went to Shandong to seek a better life through the marriage market. It does not sound as if they were abducted or "sold" by their parents seeking the highest bride-price. They may, however, have been deceived about the qualities of the men they selected. This problem exists in all marriages, but for these Lu Village women, the more serious problem is that they are far from any kin support, and there is little tolerance for divorce in rural areas.

We also see that Lu Village parents want to know if their daughters are living well after their marriage. They do not forget them once they marry out, although it is very difficult for them to do anything to help a daughter who lives so far away. Once I had a chat while walking down the road with a sixty-year-old retired team leader. He has five children and two are daughters who married far away: one to the province of Shandong and the other to Meng-hai, a distant county in southern Yunnan. The Shandong daughter, husband, and two-year-old son had recently come back for a thirty-day visit. I asked him about the view that some women are deceived into marriage in the east.

> My daughter was not deceived into marriage. She went there willingly to get married. We had traveled there to visit friends, an old army buddy of mine. I had a god-daughter (*gan nu'er*, or fictive daughter—a status given the children of very close friends) who had already married there. She introduced my daughter to the man that my daughter married. She married into an area of Shandong famous for its apples. She and her husband contract an orchard. I think their income is okay. She came all the way here by train—six days of travel—to go to her younger brother's wedding and for Spring Festival. Her husband and two-year-old are here with her.

Another parent of a daughter who married a man from Shandong described the arrangement as follows:

> My daughter took care of my daughter-in-law's son and took him out to the street to play. There she got to know my son-in-law. The son-in-law is from Shandong and was serving as a soldier. When he was demobilized (*fuyuan*), he stayed at our house for one month, and then took our daughter back to Shandong. Their house is a five-room brick house, and her mother-in-law treats her like a daughter. My daughter comes back to visit each year. She has two children, both girls, and still wants to have another.

These statements, of course, come from the parents rather than the women themselves. Yet they show that expensive cross-country visits take place between these particular daughters and their parents. These are important signs that these particular daughters have not been abducted or sold as "commodities."

By suggesting that not all daughters who end up in Shandong have been abducted, I do not mean to imply that kidnapping and the sale of women and girls as brides and of small boys as heirs is not a serious problem in China today. There is indeed interprovincial trade in women. Authorities from the township branch of the Women's Federation in Yunnan Province have made trips to east China to try to locate and retrieve young women whom they think have been kidnapped or enslaved, but were not very successful.[11] However, I was unable to obtain any specific information pertaining to Lu Village. In north-central China (Henan Province), I have interviewed women from China's southwest who had been abducted through deceit and sold into marriage by intermediaries, and one who had her daughter kidnapped. It is possible that, from shame, some of these women never tell their parents what actually happened to them.

## MARRIAGE COSTS AND WEDDINGS

The preceding discussion of long-distance marriages leads to the question of how to distinguish the marriage market from the market in women. How easy is it to distinguish between marriage costs, in the form of bridewealth and dowry, and selling women into marriage against their will? I encountered this problem of interpretation in the preceding account of Mrs. Song, the old woman who was twice sold in marriage. The second time she may have been willing to marry the man who bought her, for she had been hired out as a day laborer by her mother-in-law. If she had remained with her mother-in-law, her status would have been that of a childless young widow. The sale was a way of arranging marriage for a dependent who was of reproductive age. Elizabeth Sinn's description of Chinese women in nineteenth-century Hong Kong resembles older women's accounts of practices in Lu Village and the surrounding area in the 1930s.

> The idea that every woman in China must be owned by someone was especially prevalent. . . . Another feature of Chinese society . . . was that almost every social arrangement—betrothal, marriage, concubinage, adoption, servitude—was professedly based on a money bargain. Given his absolute power over members of his household, and the right of holding property in persons, the patriarch's right to sell his children was unquestioned. Even the temporary pledging of a wife, concubine or daughter to another family for domestic servitude was not interfered with by the law in China, regardless of the penal code. This gave rise to the general belief that people could be traded, a belief held not only by those who purchased and sold, but by the object of sale as well. The use of the term *ming mai*, meaning open, legitimate purchase and sale (of persons), with written documents confirming the transactions, clearly indicates the wide acceptance of the system. It is said that until the foundation of the People's Republic in 1949, China had one of the most comprehensive markets for the exchange of human beings in the world. (Sinn 1994:142)

In the 1930s, wedding costs were a major household expense. Fei briefly described a family, normally thrifty, who spent lavishly for the wedding of their son. He noted that wedding costs could exceed the annual family income and place the family in debt, so some men could not afford to marry (Fei and Zhang 1945:103). He pointed out that these heavy expenses, concentrated for the wedding ceremony, were partly for a general renewal of household furnishings. He did not refer to bridewealth (*caili*), the negotiated monetary gift from the groom's family to the bride, as "buying" the bride. In fact, he did not refer to it in Lu Village at all.

## MARRIAGE TRANSACTIONS IN LU VILLAGE

The idea of free-choice marriage is accepted in contemporary Lu Village, but women's accounts of their marriages show that they often exercised their choice by accepting or rejecting candidates selected by their parents. Even in cases in which couples met on their own, they always engaged a "matchmaker," or one or more intermediaries, who spoke to both sets of parents and negotiated an agreement on behalf of the young couple. These matchmakers tended to be friends or relatives, rather than paid professionals (I did not encounter any cases of payment in Lu Village). The terms of the marriage include the type of marriage, whether standard patrilocal or uxorilocal, and the amount of money and goods that the groom's and bride's families will give to the young couple. Tables 7.3 and 7.4 below show the kinds of contributions in money and goods that Lu Village brides and grooms received from their parents. This information is presented by decade to identify times when goods and money were scarce and the Communist Party disapproved of marriage transactions. In the early revolutionary decades, such transactions were often condemned as wasteful or as the purchase of a bride.

Table 7.3 shows that in patrilocal marriages the groom's side normally provided the bed and most of the quilts and sheets. None of the brides' families contributed beds, but they gave other furniture, such as cabinets, tables, and washstands. Among the more personal items, most grooms provided clothing and, often, shoes. Sometimes the brides also provided shoes.[12] Jewelry and wristwatches were rarely given until the 1980s and were more often given by the groom's side. Modern items such as bicycles, sewing machines, and washing machines did not appear until the 1980s and were given by either side. For uxorilocal marriages, there were some differences (see table 7.4). The bride's side contributed more heavy items, such as furniture: bed, cabinets, tables, and washstands; but the groom's side gave more quilts and sheets. Only one of the uxorilocal grooms (marrying endogamously) contributed money, but none of the uxorilocal bride's families reported a monetary gift to the groom's family.

The tables show that in Lu Village both families contribute furniture and clothes, although items differ according to gender and marriage locality. The list of contributions does not suggest that marriages have been one-sided transactions in which the groom's family buys a bride, but it is difficult to estimate the expenses of each side, because the process commingles them. In some marriages in the past, the groom bought cloth that the bride later sewed into the clothing or shoes, which became part of her dowry. Similarly, money given to the bride's family might be used to make furniture for her dowry.

One of the standard components of marriage transactions is a monetary gift, called "caili," presented by the groom's side to the bride's parents at engagement.[13] The caili is normally used to purchase goods that the bride will bring with her as dowry (jiazhuang). If it is used in this way, it can be considered "indirect dowry" (Goody and Tambiah 1973). Table 7.5 shows the value of caili for sample marriages from the 1930s to the 1990s. The bride's parents generally add to this amount in preparing the dowry, but the amount they contribute is not subject to negotiation and is not explicit; it is up to their discretion and ability.[14] Nonetheless, brides' parents usually come close to matching the caili, or even exceed it, when they help daughters prepare a dowry. Indeed, the display of dowry given to a daughter is an important opportunity for parents to earn prestige for themselves and their daughter.

## 1997 Cost Estimates

The comparison of the net costs of getting a son or a daughter married can indicate whether daughters are seen as a greater economic burden to their families than sons (as is often claimed for India). If there are major discrepancies in the costs of sons' or daughters' marriages, this would theoretically enter into parents' family planning and sex preferences. In order to estimate whether marriage was more expensive for the groom's side or the bride's side, I used various methods to collect information on the amount of money spent by each side and the net costs to each family. The information was not always complete or unambiguous, but it provides a rough idea of the costs of marriage.

The goods the bride brings with her to the groom's household are not the only wedding costs. Feasting relatives and fellow villagers have become another major expense for both sides. Both families usually invite guests to feasts in their own villages. These feasts are, of course, a major expense, with increasing numbers of guests invited in the reform period, but it is difficult to estimate the net cost to the host family, since most such feasts also collect monetary contributions from the guests that may cover a large part of the cost. The number of "tables" (each table serving about eight to ten guests) invited by both the groom's and bride's kin was roughly comparable in each period.[15]

**Table 7.3.  Patrilocal Marriage Contributions by Category: One or More Items Provided by Groom's Family and Bride's Family**

| Groom's family | 1930s (n = 3) | 1940s (n = 2) | 1950s (n = 6) | 1960s (n = 13) | 1970s (n = 17) | 1980s (n = 17) | 1990s (n = 6) | Total (64) |
|---|---|---|---|---|---|---|---|---|
| Bed | 3 | 1 | 6 | 11 | 16 | 16 | 6 | 59 |
| Cabinet/table | 3 | | 1 | 7 | 3 | 7 | 6 | 27 |
| Quilt | 2 | 2 | 5 | 11 | 15 | 14 | 6 | 55 |
| Sheets | | | 2 | 1 | 9 | 4 | 1 | 17 |
| Washbasin | | | | | | | | 0 |
| Clothing | 3 | 1 | 6 | 11 | 16 | 15 | 6 | 58 |
| Shoes | | 2 | | 1 | 4 | 11 | 2 | 20 |
| Jewelry | 1 | | | | | 8 | 4 | 13 |
| Watch | | 1 | 1 | | | | | 2 |
| Bicycle | | | | | | 1 | | 1 |
| Sew. machine | | | | | | 3 | | 3 |
| Wash. machine | | | | | | | 1 | 1 |
| Money | 2 | | | 7 | 8 | 13 | 5 | 35 |
| Guest tables | 2 | | 3 | 8 | 15 | 17 | 5 | 50 |
| **Bride's family** | (n = 3) | (n = 2) | (n = 6) | (n = 13) | (n = 17) | (n = 17) | (n = 6) | (64) |
| Bed | | | | | | | | 0 |
| Cabinet/table | 2 | 1 | 4 | 7 | 15 | 13 | 3 | 45 |
| Quilt | 2 | 1 | 1 | 2 | 4 | 13 | 3 | 26 |
| Sheets | | | 1 | 1 | | 1 | 1 | 3 |
| Washbasin | 2 | 1 | 1 | 4 | 1 | 11 | 3 | 23 |
| Clothing | | | 1 | 2 | 9 | | | 12 |
| Shoes | 1 | | 2 | 3 | | 3 | 1 | 10 |
| Jewelry | | | | 1 | | | | 1 |
| Watch | | | | 1 | | | | 1 |
| Bicycle | | | | | | 3 | | 3 |
| Sew. machine | | | | | | | 2 | 2 |
| Wash. machine | | | | | | 2 | | 2 |
| Money | | | | | | | | 0 |
| Guest tables | 2 | | 3 | 8 | 17 | 16 | 4 | 50 |

*Source:* 1990 survey.

**Table 7.4.  Uxorilocal Marriage Contributions by Category: One or More Items Provided by Groom's Family and Bride's Family**

| Groom's family | 1950s (n = 4) | 1960s (n = 4) | 1970s (n = 8) | 1980s (n = 5) | Total (n = 21) |
|---|---|---|---|---|---|
| Bed | 1 | | 2 | 2 | 5 |
| Cabinet/table | | | 3 | 1 | 4 |
| Quilt | 1 | 1 | 7 | 5 | 14 |
| Sheets | 1 | 2 | 6 | 1 | 10 |
| Washbasin | | | | | 0 |
| Clothing | 2 | 2 | 6 | 4 | 14 |
| Shoes | | | 1 | 1 | 2 |
| Jewelry | | 1 | | | 1 |
| Wristwatch | | | | 1 | 1 |
| Bicycle | | | | 1 | 1 |
| Sewing machine | | | | 1 | 1 |
| Washing machine | | | | | 0 |
| Money | | | | 1 | 1 |
| Guest tables | 1 | 1 | 6 | 4 | 12 |

| Bride's family | (n = 4) | (n = 4) | (n = 8) | (n = 5) | Total (n = 21) |
|---|---|---|---|---|---|
| Bed | 3 | 4 | 5 | 4 | 16 |
| Cabinet/table | 2 | 3 | 3 | 2 | 10 |
| Quilt | 2 | 3 | 3 | 5 | 13 |
| Sheets | 1 | | 2 | 2 | 5 |
| Washbasin | 1 | 3 | 1 | | 5 |
| Clothing | 1 | 1 | 3 | 2 | 7 |
| Shoes | | 1 | 1 | 3 | 5 |
| Jewelry | | | | | 0 |
| Wristwatch | | | | 1 | 1 |
| Bicycle | | | | | 0 |
| Sewing machine | | | | | 0 |
| Washing machine | | | | | 0 |
| Money | | | | | 0 |
| Guest tables | 3 | | | | 16 |

*Source:* 1990 sample survey.

Interviews conducted in Lu Village in 1997 asked people to estimate current marriage costs for the *caili* (bridewealth) given by the groom's side and the *jiazhuang* (dowry) given by the bride's side.[16] The average estimate for dowry was 2,762 yuan, and for *caili* it was 2,121 yuan. For all *but one* of the estimates, the estimated value of the dowry was 1.5 to 2 times that of the *caili*.[17] Although expenditures on dowry are clearly higher than expenditures on *caili*, local use of the term *jiazhuang* seems to include both the gifts from the bride's

**Table 7.5. Money (caili) Given from Groom's Side to Bride's (averages by decade for those reporting such monetary gifts)**

| Years | Number | Average (yuan) |
|---|---|---|
| 1930s | 2 | 185 |
| 1940s | 0 | — |
| 1950s | 0 | — |
| 1960s | 7 | 72 |
| 1970s | 8 | 139 |
| 1980s | 13 | 315 |
| 1990 | 5 | 393 |

*Source:* 1990 sample survey.

parents and gifts indirectly funded by the *caili* contributed by the groom's parents. Most of my efforts to ask about "net" costs to the bride's family ended in confusion because people are not accustomed to speaking of it that way.

There have been many debates about the significance of imbalances in marriage costs for gender relations. As we can see here, the process of spending on marriage is complex and almost seems designed to mute some of these direct comparisons. Moreover, marriage costs are significant and are generally comparable to the annual incomes that men or women can earn through non-farm work (chapter 4). Marriage costs also appear to be well below the costs of the new housing that families strive to provide for the new couple at, or after, marriage. What is most significant for Lu Village women, however, is that they have not become commodities, traded from one patriline to another, and they have not become family liabilities, requiring enormous dowries in order to get married. They certainly are not treated the same as their brothers, but their parents and siblings care enough about their well-being to provide them with substantial dowries and to maintain relations with them. I did not encounter evidence that Lu Village daughters were married off "to the highest bidder in order to make enough money to pay for wives for their sons" (Honig and Hershatter 1988:96), although there is evidence that parents and daughters alike were interested in men who could earn a good living.

## WEDDINGS

I now briefly describe several different weddings I attended. In no case did I attend them from start to finish, for the whole procedure lasts several days. Each wedding provides an opportunity to observe the interaction between two sets of kin and to gain different insights into marriage decisions. For a patrilocal marriage, the wedding generally includes a feast and public display of dowry at the home of the bride when the groom and his entourage come to get her.

Then she travels with the groom and her own attendants from her village to his village. Guests in the groom's village are assembled to watch the dramatic entry into the courtyard and house, which is accompanied by firecrackers. The dowry is also brought ceremonially to the groom's house. There is usually a brief, unrehearsed marriage ritual directed by a master of the wedding, with bowing to the ancestors, and then the feasting begins. The major preoccupation for the many hours to follow seems to be consumption of the feast. Many tables of guests are fed, and snacks of happiness candy and sunflower seeds are served. The bride and groom must serve everyone wine and tea, while the guests chat. There may be hired musicians, but there is usually no dancing. The next day, similar feasts are held, before the bride's kin and escorts depart. Usually, after three days, the bride and groom return to the bride's house for another, smaller feast. There are many permutations of the script according to the distance between the bride and groom's houses, their economic circumstances, and the local customs of each village.

## A PATRILOCAL MARRIAGE IN 1990:
## MR. MIN'S SON'S WEDDING

The wedding was held in the rainy season, because the date was auspicious. Due to rain, the family moved everything up a few hours (weddings are not run by the clock, I learned) and I came too late to see the bride arrive at the

*Lu Villagers enjoy a wedding feast served at the team threshing ground.*

groom's house with her entourage. The bride came from a village about fifteen kilometers to the west. She and her escorts walked the whole distance, about three hours, because the train near their village does not go to Lu Village. They did not bring the dowry in a truck because of the rain. It would come later, when the weather and the road dried up. When they arrived in Lu Village, they gathered in someone else's house before completing the ritual trip to the groom's house.

When I arrived, people were sitting inside the house in two rooms, just finishing lunch. I presented my gift, a bedspread, and entered a room where I met members of the groom's family: a sister of the groom's mother from Yuxi, a city to the south (a five-hour bus ride), who came without her husband but was accompanied by a grandson; another sister from Anning, a city to the east, toward Kunming (a one-and-a-half-hour bus ride); an older sister who lives in Lufeng town; and a brother who lives nearby. They were fairly urbane people and not afraid to talk to me. The family of the groom's father and mother seem to favor distant marriage.

Soon I saw the groom, who was scurrying around in a nice western suit, nervous, sweating, trying to serve his guests. His hair seemed wet, probably from pomade or gel. He was twenty-nine, the oldest son of the family. Like his father and younger brother, he had eight years of schooling. He had been away in recent years, doing casual labor in construction. He offered us candy, as is the custom. I also met the matchmaker, a woman from the bride's area. This was her first match. Someone joked that the woman next to her had made six matches so far, saying that after death she can turn into a cat, which is supposed to be the best thing. The matchmaker was talkative but much more rustic than the host-groom's family.

Later, I was shown through the adjacent room, where men were playing cards, and into the new marital bedroom, freshly painted and with an expensive new double bed and a new desk. In the adjacent room there was a very luxurious new wooden display cabinet, around eight feet wide and eight feet high. These were the main items presented by the groom's side. The groom's younger sister gave them a desk lamp, hand made in the local idiom of gluing small medicine bottles (leftover from the penicillin used to inject pigs) into a lamp stand and sticking something colorful into the bottles.

I was led to the bedroom and introduced to the bride, who was wearing a gray pantsuit, not yet the bridal color of red, and looking stressed. Gradually her entourage shuffled in; they were very rustic and dressed like country people; they were afraid to talk to me (they probably had not seen a foreigner before). Some of them could barely understand the groom's kin, who spoke a more standard version of Mandarin. My assistant guessed, by accent, that some of the women accompanying her were Yi minority women, though the bride herself was Han.

The bride's escorts were in alien territory. I asked about the bride's natal village. They told me it was somewhat more mountainous (almost a synonym for "poorer" in local thinking) but mainly grows the same crops; they gather mushrooms and plant a little tobacco (but do not seem wealthy for it). The bride had fixed her hair into a tightly curled permanent. She tried to get over her discomfort and be courteous, but she was shy and hid her face at times. She had two *bang niang*, or bride's helpers, probably sisters or classmates from her village.

The bride was the fifth of five girls and had two younger brothers. Among the bride's party were her four older sister's husbands. The sister's husbands seemed more sophisticated than the bride's female kin and companions. The bride's parents do not come to the wedding feast at the groom's house, but her siblings can come. It would seem highly improper for her parents to come. Thus, the bride has some protection and companionship to start but no one to challenge the authority of the groom's parents. I asked the bride how long she would stay before she returned to visit her mother's home, *niangjia*, and she said a week or a month, depending on what her mother-in-law told her. After the marriage, she would return to help out at her *niangjia* when the busy season work at her husband's home was finished.

Asking the story of their courtship, I learned that the groom had been working and living for over half a year on a construction site in the bride's village, and that's how he came to be introduced and got to know her. The bride's parents had come twice to visit the groom's house, and the bride possibly came more often. From my household interview, I realized there was more to it than this. Mr. Min, the father of the groom, was born in a village near the bride's in 1931. His old friends knew the bride's family.[18]

My assistant and I observed that the bride was getting a good deal—a family with a nice house, a village in a good location, and a husband from a more sophisticated family. She was neither particularly beautiful nor rich or well-educated, but my assistant pointed out that she was young, twenty-one, giving her value against the groom's assets. The groom, on the contrary, at twenty-nine was considered old for a groom. He had come back home to farm his family's land, after earning money outside. He had two younger siblings, a sister, age twenty-four, and a brother, eighteen, still at home.

The groom's mother was at home attending guests, while his father was at a reception hall preparing the feast. Eventually, we left the bridal chamber and the bride changed into a new outfit of clothes that were not exactly red, but a rather rust-colored blazer. Both bride and groom wore red ribbons and a red flower. I did not see or hear any official marriage vows or statements made at the home or in the hall (maybe it happened very fast). We were offered the traditional *xi tang*, or happiness candy, and sunflower seeds by the bride and groom together. You are supposed to take candy in pairs, or even numbers, to bring good luck.

We later trooped through the mud and drizzle over to the high school, where the bride and groom had preceded us, and there they greeted us at the door with more seeds and candy. At the entrance, guests passed a table where a scribe wrote down who brought what or, especially for the dinner, who gave how much money. This was also done at the house by a man near the main door.[19] At the reception there were many tables, perhaps ten in one room and ten in another. We were served a dinner with many dishes, quite a few of them fatty meat. Fried and breaded pork fat with sugar on it was one dish; there was also duck, sliced beef, silver-ear mushrooms in a hotpot chicken broth, fried broad beans, cabbage, bean noodles, pork dishes, etc. The bride and groom came to each table offering a drink to guests and we drank to their happiness. My assistant wished they would soon have a son (laughingly telling me that is probably what they wanted to hear). Tomorrow, there would be further meals for the groom's and bride's kin, before the bride's kin returned home in the evening.

The following year I learned the bride had been six months pregnant when they married, and that she had given birth to a boy. My assistant teased the bride's mother-in-law about being lucky to have a grandson. I was told they had legally registered their marriage months earlier and scheduled the ceremony later to have a convenient date.

In 1993, there were two weddings scheduled on the same day—an auspicious even-numbered date—and I was invited to both. I did my best to spend some time at each. The Meng family was calling in a son-in-law (*zhao nuxu*) for their eldest daughter, Liuhua. Laixi, the young man she was marrying, came from a poorer area, about thirty kilometers away.

## AN UXORILOCAL WEDDING: THE MIRROR IMAGE

Locally, people say that an uxorilocal wedding, "*zhao guye*" or "*zhao nuxu*," is just the mirror image of "*tao xifu*." Indeed, the terminology they use is similar, and the bride with her escorts goes to his village to bring him back. In town, people who had heard about this particular wedding told me that on alighting from the car, both bride and groom should race to the house and whoever gets there first will rule the roost. Due to long morning interviews, I did not see the bride return with the groom from his village, but I saw the minibus that transported his kin.

When I got to the courtyard where the wedding was held, the groom was already in the house, but this time I would get to see the vows and the bows.

The courtyard had lots of people milling about, expectant witnesses who would soon be invited to feast. Friends led me into the house, where a crowd was packed into the living room with new furniture. On one side were seated the groom's kin and attendants. I was given a seat on the bride's side. I took some pictures of the bride and groom in front of the new bureau and then, suddenly, without warning, a ceremony began. A commanding voice, belonging to a man who acted in village plays, began to announce that the bride and groom should bow (*bai*) to the older generations, to their parents, and to each other. Standing before the new cabinet furniture with mirrors, a TV set, and four lighted red candles, they bowed to her ancestors, to her parents, and to each other. This bow involved only the head and shoulders; it was not like the kowtow (*ketou*) I have seen in the north, where people touch their foreheads to the ground.[20] It was quickly over if that was "it." But of course, "it" is the whole series of rituals—the bows, the offering of happiness candy by the couple, the serving of food (by helpers), the pouring of wine (by the couple), and so forth. In a later wedding, in 1996, I learned that families hire a "master of ceremonies," who tells everyone what to do as the wedding ceremonies proceed, but even so, it seemed chaotic, and one could easily miss some of the rites.

The in-coming groom was young and dashing in a spiffy black double-breasted suit with a gold pin on his lapel. His black suit and leather shoes conformed to an international Western male dress code; it was not distinctively Chinese. The bride was dressed up in a bright red pants-suit, her hair coiffed in a high bouffant with colorful sequins sprinkled through it and encased in a net. She also wore, suspended from her neck and inside her coat, a chain with a large, round shaving mirror, about five inches in diameter, that was quite visible. The mirror's purpose is to "*bixie*," or repel evil. The bride's red clothing, mirror, pants, and hairdo conformed to local Chinese standards for brides—the color red for happiness, but not, as of 1993, a dress for femininity.

The groom brought several suitcases, some thermoses, and kettles as his "dowry." It was far less than women usually bring, but it was visibly piled on the side of the room. The parents of the groom, as for a bride marrying out, normally do not attend the ceremony in the bride's home when their son marries out. Usually, only the siblings, *jiujiu* (uncles, or mother's younger brothers), and other relatives come with the bride or groom. In this case, the younger sisters and brothers, and an old *nainai*—mother of the groom's mother—came. The groom's parents both died in the 1960s; he was raised by other people, so there would have been no parents to attend his wedding in any case. Much of the afternoon was then preoccupied with serving a feast to the guests.

The evening of the wedding, a crowd of local and out-of-town guests stayed with the couple in their new house to "play" and perform folk music. The warmth of the crowd and bright lights were welcoming compared to the cool night outside. The villagers who could sing or play music were packed shoulder to shoulder on one side, while the visitors, including those who came to send off the group, were packed against the opposite wall. The bride moved about, serving her guests candy, sunflower seeds by the handful, and tea. Four men played the *erhu*, the two-string violin, with spirit, while village women and men sang old favorites about girls planting rice and the peculiarities of the gods in a temple. Villagers entertained themselves and the guests until late into the night. Although I had quite a few friends in the room, as the only foreigner, I felt overwhelmed by the strong familiarity among the local villagers running through their musical repertoire. I realized that the companions of the groom felt equally overwhelmed in a village of strangers made even "stranger" by a foreign woman sitting among them as the festivities continued.

## A PATRILOCAL WEDDING FEAST

The same day as the wedding described above, I had to rush to attend the wedding of the party secretary's nephew. This wedding took the classic patrilocal form, asking for a daughter-in-law (*tao xifu*) to come to the groom's house. The bride comes from a village sixty to seventy kilometers from Lu Village, toward Kunming.

I again arrived too late to see the disembarking and running into the house. But I was taken to see the new house. People sat there for a while, with kin of the bride. Before long, everyone left for the threshing ground behind the school. At the threshing ground, there were 250 to 300 villagers plus the kin of both families seated on the ground or on small benches. Layers of fresh green pine needles were systematically strewn about the ground in large circles, to make "tables" for eating and places for sitting that are "clean"—neither dusty nor muddy.

Guests sat and waited while helpers steadily delivered large trays with bowls of about ten different steaming dishes to each group. Some groups, but not all, were age and sex segregated. Old ladies sat together. I was at a mixed table, but women usually sat next to each other and that way avoided the smoking men. The food included pork dishes, fresh fish, chilis, lotus root, vegetables, sweet sticky rice (eight treasure rice, *ba bao fan*), and sweet potatoes. At the feast, the kinsmen of the groom hustled about, making sure everyone was served and had pine needles to sit on. Huge stacks of rice bowls were washed. Cooks prepared big vats and woks of food, with stacks of bamboo steamers piled over the wok. The many guests sat happily on the ground for more than an hour, while trays of steaming dishes and bottles of spirits were steadily delivered to them. The lively outdoor scene resembled a Breughel wedding.

Most of the guests wore normal everyday clothing, not what we might call "Sunday best." Those who dressed up were the bride, groom, and their kin. The bride was dressed in a pea-green pant suit and a pink blouse, with her hair in a bouffant style. The groom wore black. They had to go around to all the circles of guests and serve sweet wine to each person.

After dinner, as it got dark, the groom's senior kinfolk, reunited by the wedding, organized themselves for a large family photograph. A sister, the oldest of many siblings at more than eighty years of age, sat in the center. Five brothers stood at the back, each with his wife in front of him. Having taken such family photos before, I knew that they would arrange themselves somewhat like a three-dimensional patrilineal family tree. But here was their aged and beloved elder sister in the center and here, too, was the uxorilocally married brother, still united with his patrilineal kin.

*At a send-off feast for a Lu Village bride, dowry goods are piled outside.*

## A BRIDAL SEND-OFF FEAST

In 1996 I was invited to a wedding-departure feast in Lu Village. A family was sending off their daughter to marry a man in another county. The bride's family had prepared a feast and invited many guests to celebrate their daughter's marriage. There was a registry book for the guests, where the amount of money they donated for the feast was carefully recorded. They awaited the arrival of the groom and his party and set off firecrackers when he arrived. The young woman's dowry included a four-piece sofa, a suitcase, a coffee table, an electric kettle, a thermos, a chest, a tea maker, an electric rice cooker, a washstand, a fifty-kilogram sack of rice, quilts, sheets, pillows, and pillowcases. These goods were all assembled in the courtyard before being loaded onto trucks bound for the groom's village.

The fashions for this wedding had already changed from those of the early 1990s. The groom wore a gray suit, white shirt, and tie, and his hair was well oiled and had colored confetti in it. The bride wore red, but the former pantsuit fashion had now given way to a long dress. She also wore a white silk jacket over the dress. Bridal femininity had moved another notch toward Western gender conventions, with their white dresses, but these were also the symbols of Chinese urban youth culture. The older villagers who attended had not changed so drastically as the young. As to ceremony, a man had been hired to organize things and direct people. Nonetheless, the party secretary and my assistant were privately concerned about the groom's lack of ceremony toward the bride's parents; he should have bowed to them.

The groom came from a larger town, closer to Kunming, about an hour away by car or bus on the improved highway. The story of how the bride and groom met is novel for Lu Village. They met on their own less than a year earlier, when they both began taking the expensive driving course required to get a license. Since men or women who can drive cars have good earning opportunities, this evidently seemed like a good match to both sets of parents. The bride and groom were already buying a minivan with which, presumably, they would begin to earn their living when they moved to the groom's village. The investment in driving lessons for a daughter is a very new and practical endowment. While this may seem dubious based on the low proportion of women drivers in other provinces, in Yunnan, women drivers of taxis and trucks (there are still relatively few private passenger cars) have been fairly common since the early 1990s. In chapter 4 we have already seen that two other young women in Lu Village have obtained driver's licenses.

## THE WOK WARMING RITUAL

Wedding ceremonies are not the only rituals (and expenses) that have to do with setting up new households. One day on the road, a small procession of people passed, walking from town toward Lu Village, carrying an object wrapped in red and some bundles, but not a large quantity of goods. A villager told me that this was a ritual called "warming the wok bottom" (*shao guo di*), which is celebrated when a daughter's household is divided from that of her mother-in-law or sisters-in-law. At this time, her natal kin organize a procession to her house at which they give her pots and cooking supplies to help her establish her own independent kitchen, because she no longer depends on her mother-in-law. "Warming the wok" refers to breaking in a new pot, one that is clearly hers—making a separate life-cycle ceremony in the career of a married woman. It is not the agnatic kin of the husband who offer this kitchen "capital" to a woman; the gifts are mainly provided by her natal kin and friends, usually organized by her mother. The woman who explained this had held the ritual for her own married daughter.

Although I had not previously encountered this ceremony in the literature on Chinese rituals, people in other parts of Yunnan had heard of it.[21] A very similar ritual was described by Yan as far away as Heilongjiang in northeast China, on the Han-Manchu frontier, where the villagers called it "*wenguo*" (literally meaning to "heat the cooking pot"):

> Traditionally, this was a small-scale, domestic celebration and involved only the closest relatives and best friends. The gifts presented in this situation were cooking utensils and food (raw or cooked). And the host provided the guests with tea and cigarettes—no banquet was provided nor was a gift list kept. This was a typical *xiaoqing*, or minor rite of gift exchange. (Yan 1996:58)

Small-scale though it may be, this ritual is another demonstration that a woman's *niangjia* usually maintains relations with their daughter after she has married out. It counters the common belief that women's families only make a one-time dowry contribution to daughters who marry out, and are no longer economically involved with them. Most life rituals, not just marriage, involve gifts and economic transactions.

A third occasion for gifts to a daughter is the birth of a child. This set of gifts is called "bamboo rice" (*zhu mi*). This is when the woman's family gives sacks of rice to the new mother just after birth, in addition to giving gifts for the baby. Although I did not witness this in Lu Village, it was certainly also a well-known custom for a woman's mother's family to send large quantities of fresh eggs for her to eat during her confinement. I had seen these processions in other Yunnan villages. These customs show the persistence of ties with a woman's natal kin after marriage. As seen in the preceding description of weddings, women's natal kin, especially her siblings, present gifts to each other's grown children when they get married.

Funerals are obviously another important ceremonial occasion. The family of the deceased holds a large feast, and the guests who come to eat bring paper money and food for the deceased. A woman showed me a red silk cloth, large like a bedspread, that was carried to the cemetery when her mother was buried. The paper things were burned there, but the many gifts of cloth were brought back and kept to give to her children. It was not clear whether all invited guests brought them. The funeral for this woman's mother had a lot of people, forty tables, or nearly four hundred people.[22] This type of ceremony, which included burning paper money for the deceased, clearly comforts the survivor. But while this is the custom, my friend explained that she herself does not believe in an afterlife, that she "might run into a ghost at night."

## FAMILY DIVISION AND INHERITANCE

In 1993, I interviewed Shu Lingqiao about inheritance, because her family had been developing a lucrative business. She is the second of four girls and also has a younger brother.

Q: Do you think your parents will give you an inheritance (or property)?
A: No, they will not give me any. The property is theirs. If a daughter goes to work with them, then they give a salary.
Q: Will they give all the property to your younger brother?
A: Yes, they give it all to younger brother. They will not give to my younger sisters. I do not think that they will give them anything. Here they traditionally give to the girl only if she fulfills the obligation of taking care of the old people, but this only goes smoothly (*heng shou*) if there are not many sons. Also, girls cannot go and compete for it. I cannot go back and say I want it. Although the government says girls and boys are the same, there is tradition—from feudal society to today, it is still the same. It is still the custom: girls cannot go back and demand the inheritance unless they call in a son-in-law—then they can ask for it. When girls marry out—under these conditions, they cannot come back and expect anything.
Q: You married nearby. Every day you can go home and care for your parents. How is this type of "marrying out" different from "calling in a son-in-law"?
A: You can perhaps say there is no great difference. But it was decided that we "marry out," ah! We cannot plan on getting the family's property, we cannot compete for it. My older sister often comes to help. Whenever it is busy, she helps them like that. When there are not enough hands for the farmwork, she also goes to help. She does not go to work in the store for she doesn't have

enough education. My younger sister lives at home with my father, and she works in the store. Marrying out is one's own decision, it is not tainted with these economic questions. We are afraid that later we may not be able to get along (*chu*) properly. Problems may arise. If the girl's life is not good in some way, her parents would still help her a little. *Niangjia* still is concerned about its daughter.

Q:   Your parents "worked hard and prospered." The money is already enough to divide among five kids. Do you think they could divide it equally to give you?

A:   I think it is not possible, because we are an independent household that has gone out. If my two younger sisters call in a son-in-law to our family, then they could. That could happen.

This conversation did not compare the value of the dowry Lingqiao received at marriage and later gifts to the entitlement of her brother. The dowry is sometimes considered a daughter's entitlement in lieu of real estate when she marries out; by facilitating her marriage, dowry also advances her claims upon her husband's estate. But I was struck by the thought that one out of five children would get the lion's share of the inheritance in the family, and that daughters who married out early, before the family prospered, would get much less. However, plans seem to have shifted with time.

In 1996, Mrs. Shui (Shu Lingqiao's mother) gave her point of view:[23]

These children have not experienced any serious difficulties in life; they have not experienced hunger. They have it good in every way, but it is not inside their heart to think of these things. . . . They really think they will always be well off. We have not told them how we old ones suffered in the old times, or they would suffer. However when it comes to work, it is certainly us two old ones earning the money. . . . Ah!

These houses are a problem. We only have one son, and perhaps there will be no problems until we divide the family. We only want a big [joint] family in order for everyone to be free of worry. In the future, we will divide the house. My son does not want to divide, but the *xifu* does. Our two younger daughters are studying. What if they do not test into school? They might not be willing to marry out. If not, will they want to live here? We are not able to say that "you are a girl so you must marry out." We could also ask for a *guye* (son-in-law) for one of them who would come back and live here. But if we ask a son-in-law to come back here, then that can bring contradictions: a son-in-law versus a son. We speak from our old hearts: our son and daughters are everything. Yet this is only for their younger sisters—*meimei*—to decide. We cannot decide it. When we think of needing a hand, it's good to have a joint household. Yet this is very difficult. I speak from experience. We may need to separate.

Once you separate, gossip multiplies. My husband has not realized this. He is working to build their house. Now their children are small. They need me to take the lead. Later, when the kids are grown and I am old, it will be necessary to do things and I will not be able to move. Then, my daughter-in-law can make household decisions herself. This family's business is ours. Right now we still have a little money. Later it will be time to give the property to them. It will be their burden.

Later when we can't work and someone gives us something to eat, that will be fine. I do not have many needs. But when young people are lazy, it does not work.

My old man says, "How can he dare not help me! If he does not help me, I will sell the house!" And I say, "What happens if you and I withdraw? You have a son and daughters. If you sell the house, what can you give? Even if you cut the price in half, you would still have no one who dares to buy it." I say, "It doesn't matter. If the girls leave home, it is good; if they stay home, it is also good."

In 1996, Mrs. Shui and her husband had recently carried out the division of their household. Their only son and his wife, who had been married several years and had a small child, decided they wanted to separate. Mrs. Shui said the reason was that her daughter-in-law, Chunli, wanted to manage the household money herself. Chunli presented an ultimatum: either we divide the house or there will be a divorce. Mrs. Shui was disturbed and found her daughter-in-law's attitude hard to understand. She said that whenever Chunli wanted money, they gave it to her, for medicine, a doctor for the child, and so forth. They had wanted to stay together with their son and his family and depend on them in old age.

The son also wanted more independence from his father. Instead of working directly in his parent's business, he now drives a truck long distances across the province and is making good money. His mother is worried because he has started to gamble money in town. She is afraid that in some gambling places he will start to eat "white wheat" (*bai mian*), the local expression for drugs. Yunnan is well known as a drug smuggling route between Burma and Hong Kong, so there are plenty of opportunities. Mrs. Shui felt that as long as her son remained under their control, they could restrain him; now, she is afraid that her daughter-in-law will not have sufficient power to do so. His sisters are clearly unhappy with their brother's social behavior now. He has friends who are a bad influence and he stays out late. He has already been discovered in town in a hotel with another woman and gave a poor excuse when he did not come home one night. Mrs. Shui concludes that she will not worry about him any more (*bu guan ta*); his wife is the one who has to do this. "Maybe she is happy now," she said sadly.

The parents' plans for division of their property have shifted with these changes in their son's behavior. Originally he was to be their principal heir, inheriting the house and business. Now, they have given the truck (conservatively valued at ¥50,000) to their son, and he is obliged to pay them ¥20,000. They gave him the large older house, while they live in a smaller, earthen house, surrounded by their factory, with equipment scattered all around. They have two courtyards, and some of their courtyard land is reserved to their third and fourth daughters, if they want it. If they do not need it, they can give the empty land to their brother, or sell it. The third daughter is a student and the

fourth has recently become a driver of their minivan. Their older two daughters are married out nearby. The parents have kept a large, new two-story
house for their old age and for whichever child cares for them when they are
old. Right now, this house is used for the business. They plan to continue their
business for another ten years or so, and then they will depend more on one
child than the others.

The division agreement was conducted with the supervision of the village
administration, and copies of the agreement were made and given to each
child. Chunli's mother then came to "warm the wok" and gave her a lot of
goods. Mrs. Shui thought this was done to make her and her husband lose
face, since they had given their son and his wife, Chunli, a lot of things.

It is unclear whether this saga illustrates shifting attitudes about gender in
this household or in the larger society, which is changing so rapidly with
commercialism and materialism, or whether it merely reflects disappoint-
ment in a son. Nonetheless, the investments in the last two daughters, in
higher education and in driving lessons, are quite a shift from the first two
daughters, who were married after lower middle school (eighth grade).

## LU VILLAGE NAMES

Names contain useful information about social relations. Anthropologist Rubie Watson illustrated how, in the past, Chinese names often reflected gender
inequality. Men were likely to take or receive more names over their life cycle,
as they entered school or pursued a career, each name adding to their luster. In
contrast, few women attended school or received any distinctive personal
name. Sometimes girls lacked distinctive names, or their names signaled son
preference, as when they were named Zhao Di, or "lead in a younger brother."
In Lu Village, however, I encountered no girls with names like Zhao Di.

### Generation Names

In Lu Village, it is normal for families to give the same generation name (usually the middle name in traditional naming systems) to both sons and daughters, whereas in more orthodox patrilineal regions, these names are often reserved for sons.[24] Virtually *all* of the households, both patrilocal and
uxorilocal, for which full names are recorded (on occasion only informal
names were provided for small children) showed this pattern. In one household, it was observed that two daughters received a *different* generation name
from their two brothers. In general, however, sons and daughters shared the
same generation name if they shared the same surname and, in at least one
case, even shared the generation name when the surname was different. This

clearly differs from the expected patrilineal model, where generational relationships among females are unlikely to matter. For instance, Judd, who studied three villages in Shandong Province, reported, "daughters *may* be, although *usually are not*, given the same generation markers as their brothers (Judd 1994:56, italics added). Similarly, describing a village in Sichuan, Ruf wrote, "Whereas brothers and male cousins within a descent group shared a common generational name (*hang*), sisters and female cousins usually did not. Girls were usually given generic names, such as Suzhen ("Plain Treasure") or Shufen ("Gentle Fragrance") that were common through the Baimapu area" (Ruf 1998:179, n. 7).

The proximity of a large proportion of women to their natal kin, and the fact that generation names have been given to daughters, suggests that women's relationships to each other, as sisters and cousins, are important. This is consistent with the cooperation that kinswomen offer each other in mundane tasks as well as on ritual occasions. When women need help for transplanting rice, they often call on their sisters. When their children are married, their sisters come to contribute gifts. Of course, sisters can fight and compete with each other here as anywhere else, but there is clearly a use for sisterly relationships among women in the economic and social life of Lu Village. I discovered an unexpected dimension of sisterly relationships when I learned about the funeral of a friend's mother.

## SWORN SISTERS AND GODMOTHERS

Before the revolution, although Fei wrote nothing about it, people sometimes became "sworn sisters" (*da jiemei*, or *da zimei*) or "sworn brothers" (*bai xiongdi*). My friend's mother belonged to a group of ten sworn sisters. Her mother was the tenth. At the time of her death, there were only four left: one in Kunming, one in a village to the north, and two in Lu Village. I was unable to interview any of them, so I only learned a little about them from their adult children.

> You knew my mother—she died just after spring festival. She was sixty-four years old. Mainly, she had borne too many children, fourteen. Since she died, I am not very used to it. I go down the street and often think my mother is still there, sitting by the main door. You also knew her. But now she's no longer there. Often when I go there I still want to open the door and look and look for her. I suddenly feel she is still sitting in the doorway.
>
> When my mother died, several aunts, my mother's sworn sisters, came and wept. Altogether, she was one of ten sworn sisters. There was older sister, second sister, third sister. I call them all "Aunt" (*Yima*). I don't know the far away ones. In Lu Village and a nearby village, I still have Third Aunt and Fourth Aunt. In another

village there is Seventh Aunt. I always called them *Yima*. Since we don't call older people by their names, I can't recall their names. Third Aunt is now about seventy years old. In Kunming there is still another one, old number seven, or old something, who also had eight real sisters.

When my mother was alive, these aunts often came to my mother's house to visit, to cook together and eat together. Then they would go back home. Their children came to the house to play. When I got married, she invited them as guests. They got along very well. My mother was good at sewing. When their clothes wore out, she'd help repair them. When my mother died, they were deeply grieved (*shangxin*); they wept. One said, "Before if I ever needed something, she would look after it here; now where can I go?" Now, my two aunts here are old, they don't go out. Some are dead. Fourth Aunt's older son lives in the village. I call him *Gege*, older brother. [I tried to see his mother, but she was out of town, and her son had no information to add]. I don't know when they swore sisterhood (*jiebai*); I don't even know their husband's names. Both husbands died early, before Liberation. The women were not real relatives; originally, they were unrelated. They were just girlfriends who liked to be together and decided to become sisters. The oldest became older sister, according to age. I don't know how they planned it, or how they came to enact it. Some went to live elsewhere when they married. I only know there were ten sisters.

There are few women of that generation left, and no else could tell me more about sworn sisterhoods before the revolution. Seventy-year-old Song Ailin, for instance, said, "I had no sworn sisters like some of the others. If you were poor in childhood, you could not do that, because you could not afford to eat meals together." Her daughter, about thirty-five years old, also had no sworn sisters, but she said she did have a group of good women friends. We recall, however, that Mistress Huang, the seeress described in chapter 5, had a sworn sister in Lu Village.

Another form of fictive kinship found among women is that of "*ganma*." *Ganma*, a term like godmother, is different from *yima*, the term used for aunts by the children of sworn sisters, although both refer to a relationship between women friends. There can be only one godmother, not a group, and she is chosen in relation to a particular child. The *ganma* is chosen on the basis of *adult*, not childhood or adolescent, friendship. One village man estimated that about half of the people have godmothers. This relationship is thus common, but not obligatory. Why did this relationship, and not sworn sisterhood, survive into the present? Perhaps a one-on-one relationship was viewed as less politically suspect than sworn sisterhoods or brotherhoods, which were associated with triads, or gangs, in the past. The younger generation in Lu Village knew about sworn sisterhoods only in the limited way that my friend did, or else because they had seen them portrayed in the movies. It was from the movies, for instance, that they had the idea that sworn sisters and brothers had to use blood and alcohol as part of the ritual.

## DIVORCE AND ADULTERY

As in most of China, divorce is quite rare in Lu Village. In my 1990 sample, out of 198 people who had been married, there were only four people who had divorced, and each of these had remarried. In the period I was there, I tried to get information on the outcomes of divorce, but it was not easy to find cases. The following one was described to me by one of the women cadres.

> This year there was a couple, over forty years old, who got divorced. They have two children. The older one is more than twenty, the younger in the teens. The man's manner (*zuofeng*) is bad; he often beats his wife, Weixian. The woman's eye is almost blind from being struck. Both the children decided to go with the man since he gives them money. Weixian has been left alone. Now she has gone away to do casual labor. The man has also gone away to do casual labor. The children live alone with their father's mother. Weixian has land in the village, so in the busy season she comes back to plant it and stays at a woman friend's house to sleep. When they got the divorce, the court decided that her husband had to give her ¥300 as her share of the value of their one-room house. They only have a one-room house for division among five people. Her share was about ¥300, but up to now he has not given it to her.

The story behind the divorce is that the man had another woman. The other woman was also married, and her husband first claimed Weixian as his wife, and then beat her when she refused to swap partners. The poor woman has been beaten by both men, has lost her children and her home, and has not even received the ¥300 the court awarded her.

Zhang Lidu, one of the few divorced women in my interview sample, gave a brief account. She divorced in 1992 at the age of forty-four. Lidu said she married of her own free choice in 1964, when she was sixteen years old. In 1992 she divorced her husband because of his bad habits: he loved to gamble money and had too many debts. She now lives with her youngest daughter, age twenty. Her older son and daughter have each married out. The impoverishment caused by her husband's gambling meant that the family was unable to contribute any money to the son and daughter's marriages in 1992 and 1996. They were able to provide no meal, only tea, for their quests. She and her daughter earn a living by farming and doing manual labor, working on road repair.

A third case of divorce was attributed to the wife's adultery while the husband was away working for most of the year. In this case, the husband wanted the divorce and kept the daughter. The court divided the house and the woman remained in the same team as her ex-husband, because that is where she was officially registered. Both parties eventually remarried, bringing in new partners from outside the village. The man married a widow and lived in his parents' household, while his ex-wife first rented and then built a house.

Divorced people of either sex may be considered undesirable as marriage partners, so when they remarry, it is often to a widow or another divorced person. I encountered one family in which a man and woman, each previously divorced, had married each other and had a blended family with three of his children and two of hers. Although Lu Village has few cases of divorce and remarriage, some people break away from unhappy families in more tragic ways.

## SUICIDES

I did not plan to include suicide within the purview of marriage and family relations, yet when I encountered a number of accounts of female suicides, I was reminded of Margery Wolf's (1975) remarkable analysis of women and suicide in China. Wolf showed that, unlike European countries and Japan, where men have higher suicide rates, Chinese women's suicide rates were as high as men's. Chinese women's suicide patterns also differed from men's in that women's suicides peaked in early adulthood, around age twenty to twenty-four, then dropped steadily to age thirty-five or so and did not rise much until age sixty. By contrast, men's suicide rates showed a less dramatic rise at young adulthood, leveled off through the reproductive years, and peaked in old age. These observations hold true for more recent studies of Europe and China as well. In 1990, the median suicide sex ratio of males to females was 2.8 for twenty-six European countries, whereas in China it has been 0.9 in urban areas and 0.8 in rural areas (Zhao et al. 1994:45–46). In 1989, for the twenty to twenty-four age group, more than twice as many suicides were committed by young women as young men.

Wolf correlated the high rates of women's suicide with their changing position within the family. In particular, she associated the high rates for young women with the stress of leaving home and entering a new family at marriage, where they are expected to work hard and bear children. Wolf believed that bearing a son within a patrilocal household, or marrying uxorilocally, were both conditions that would offer young women some protection against suicide. As women bore children, their status would improve until challenged by the entry of a daughter-in-law at their own son's marriage. For women over age forty-five, Wolf linked rising suicide rates to the revolt of the young against the mother(-in-law)'s authority. This was most likely to occur in joint families when a son began to transfer his loyalty from his mother to his wife and the wife resisted her mother-in-law's authority. While the cases I encountered do not perfectly support these conjectures, they were consistent with the general view that domestic life in joint families is associated with a high incidence of suicide by women, particularly when women have few opportunities to leave and live independently outside the family. The most critical times for women seem to occur when there is more than one set of adults or near-adults vying for power in the household.[25]

## Meihuo and Jizhu

I interviewed a young woman in a large household with many brothers. She had high ambitions for her education and wanted to delay marriage. She talked about the problem of "big male chauvinism" (*da nanzi zhu yi*). Later I learned this young woman had had an older sister, Meihuo, who married patrilocally within another Lu Village hamlet and had committed suicide several years earlier. The story was that Meihuo had quarreled with her husband. Meihuo was living at her mother-in-law's house at that time. After they quarreled, she drank insecticide and died. Meihuo left a baby boy of six months, who died a year later of unknown causes. Meihuo's younger sister had heard that relations between Meihuo and her husband were "not bad," but she was too young at the time to understand a great deal. According to the view that giving birth to a boy gives a young woman higher status, Meihuo ought to have been doing well in her marriage. The strains in her family must have come from other sources. In this same household, I learned about another suicide. A young sister-in-law had an older sister, Jizhu, who committed suicide. Jizhu had also been a young mother, with a fifteen-month-old daughter. It was thought Jizhu committed suicide because Jizhu's husband was away from home a lot. He accused Jizhu of having an affair while he was gone. Jizhu had been uxorilocally married in order to help her mother raise younger siblings.

I discussed suicide with three young village women ages nineteen, twenty, and twenty-five and asked them why young women commit suicide by drinking poison. They talked about social pressure and the criticism against any woman who gets a divorce or who has an abortion when she's not married. One young woman mentioned a classmate, a high-school girl, who committed suicide by taking sleeping pills when she was pregnant and the boy let her down. I asked why the classmate did not get an abortion, since they are so common in China. She answered that people at the hospital would demand identification (*zhengming*) and approval from the village officials, and the woman would probably have to pay a fine. Later, when I asked women officials about this, they said it was not true, that you did not have to give your name and (if you did not run into anyone you knew) you could have it done secretly. I do not know which version is true, but even if the young women

are misinformed, their great fear of social condemnation over sexual trans-
gressions affects their actions.

When I asked why *young* women so often commit suicide, these young
women assured me it was because society condemns any sexual independence
on their part. They felt that no one understands them and their problems,
and that there are no solutions if they make a mistake and fall into a com-
promising situation, either before or after marriage. They said they do not
give each other such support. While young women have friends at middle
school, after graduation they all separate. After marriage they are more isolated if they marry out. Yet Jizhu, mentioned above, was married at home; she
was not a daughter-in-law living in a new home. It seems likely that damage
to her sexual reputation was a major factor.

## Meibang

Another case of suicide encountered in my interview sample involved
Meibang, a woman in her late forties, mother of five young adult and late-
teenage children. Her husband had once served as a soldier and cadre. Neither one of them originated in the village. Before she died, Meibang got angry because her husband did not go to help her with heavy labor, particularly
with the job of carrying fertilizer out to the fields. They fought for several
days. She drank insecticide and died. With the daughters married out, the
husband lives alone with his two unmarried sons. This example did not involve a conflict with in-laws, but it was a household with two generations of
adults, or near adults, and there was conflict over the distribution of work.

A case with a similar family structure was described by a daughter-in-law
who joined the family after it happened. After her husband's mother and father quarreled, the mother took poison and died. This occurred when her
husband's father and mother were about thirty-seven and thirty-four years
old, respectively. They had three sons and a daughter, who were then ages six
to fifteen. I did not discover if they were living with the husband's parents at
the time, but the mother had been born in another administrative district
and probably had no kin nearby.

## Lin Wujia

In an extended interview with an older woman, I asked again about the sensitive subject of suicide. She first replied that she had heard of one in a neighboring village, explaining that "in the past, things like that indeed happened
with landlord's children," referring to the practice of tormenting the children
of parents with bad class backgrounds in the early years of the revolution and
during the Cultural Revolution. Then she told me about the suicide of an

older woman relative in her hamlet a few years earlier; this case had little to do with class politics and much to do with family politics.

> In our team there was old Lin Wujia. She was living with her younger son, Shen Buhui. The younger son's wife, Duohua, talked a lot. She scolded and scolded the old woman. The older son, Shen Buyao, was also controlled by the daughter-in-law. The mother had said, "Shen Buyao, I'll come with you at your house." But the older son said "There's no way." She then returned to her younger son and complained to him, but the daughter-in-law again scolded and scolded her. Lin Wujia then thought there was no way out (*bu tong*). She still went out to cut beans, and came back but did not eat. Then she went away. Lin Wujia, alone, took a small piece of rope and went upstairs and then hung herself. She was about sixty-five when she died about five years ago. She died that morning. These modern people! It just seems like old people have suffered to help them in vain (*bailala*); there was no feeling sorry for this old mother.

The old woman who told me this story was having some difficulties of her own with her son and daughter-in-law; her sympathies were with the older woman.

While each of these cases is unique, three of the five suicides that occurred within Lu Village were women in joint households with two generations of adults. The two others had many children and several unmarried young adult or teenage children at home. In addition to these cases, I learned of two other specific cases of female suicide but did not have an appropriate opportunity to get background information. I was only told of one case of an unmarried young man, about age eighteen, who committed suicide in recent years, but none of his family members were in my sample. These few examples seem large in the context of a community of roughly three thousand people (indeed I encountered more cases of female suicide than divorce), but standing alone, this information cannot be used to support any generalizations. Village records do not record suicides separately from other deaths, and I chose not to probe further upon this sensitive subject by direct questioning lest I appeared to be seeking only the negative aspects of village life. Recent information on national suicide rates suggest, however, that the conditions that lead to high rates of female suicide, particularly among rural women, are still widespread in rural China.[26] In one of the theatrical performances by Lu Villagers, discussed in chapter 9, a woman threatens to kill herself by drinking poison, one of the techniques most often used in rural areas.

## CARE OF ELDERS

Westerners and Chinese sometimes criticize the West for neglecting the elderly. Critics juxtapose Western institutional arrangements with the ideal of the harmonious Confucian family, where the elders depend on their children for support. The prescriptions about the young caring for the old are often repeated in rural China. But the following observation from the nineteenth century shows that Chinese in real life have long had difficulties in supporting the elderly and living up to Confucian ideals.

> Theoretically the Chinese do attach great importance to respect for elders. . . . Sons do also provide for aged parents; but as far as my experience goes, little real love or respect enters into the performance of this duty, which owes its origin less to real feeling, than to the Chinese law of inheritance, which besides dealing with the succession of property, confers on the head of families certain powers and privileges, which they hold and exercise towards their families until death. Indeed, nothing is more glaring than the indifference, and even cruelty, often practised by children towards their aged parents, whose dependent condition is generally taken advantage of, to show to the world how good they are in providing for their parents; thus making a virtue of necessity, at the same time that they make the poor old folks (as long as they can work) mere household drudges. (Cooper 1871:427–28)

Cooper made these comments while traveling from India through Tibet, northern Yunnan, and Sichuan to Chungking.

In the 1930s, Fei presented few images of older men and women in the family; there were only six people over age seventy. He noted that many people continued to work into their fifties and sixties (Fei and Zhang 1945:38). He also reported (102–3) a large expenditure for a "long life" celebration for a wealthy old woman, organized by her sons, but he largely ignored the burden of supporting the elderly in poorer households.

In contemporary Lu Village, a patrilocally married woman described arrangements with her husband's parents as follows:

> My old *gonggong* (father-in-law) divided and went to live with the older son. *Popo* (mother-in-law) lives together with us. In our village, the father often goes with the older son, and the mother with the younger son. My relations with Popo are normal. They are good, but the "good" does not go that far. . . . With Popo it is not the same as talking with your own mother and father. If Popo is at home, I am afraid to talk. Even when I should speak, yet I do not speak.

In this case, the burden of the elder generation was lessened by splitting up the parents between two married sons.

A prosperous older woman expressed her concerns about old age and the burden of supporting two parents as follows:

> The old want a certain property. If we are old, we must keep some property. What happens if our daughter says, "I do not want to marry out, I want to stay at home," and then we find a son-in-law? If a son-in-law is at home and there is conflict between him and our son, then do you separate? If you separate, do you go to live by

your daughter or by your son? If we both go with the son, the burden is heavy on him. . . . Or, you may say, "I would like to live with my daughter." But perhaps she cannot say yes; maybe her husband will be the one who decides. How do you decide to live with them or not? In the village they say, "Don't build a big house; go build a second house (*er fang*)." That is also hard, really hard. In the village this problem is real. There are some people who raise five or six sons, and they seem to like their parents when they are small. When they grow up and you are old, then they do not take care of you! Each one shirks and gives the burden to another one. Not one wants the old one.

The division of parents among sons and daughters is not uncommon in Lu Village. In one case, a family shares sections of a courtyard with the parents in their seventies. The old mother lives with an older son and daughter-in-law while the old father lives with an uxorilocally married daughter in the same courtyard. The old mother has been bedridden for many years, and her old husband helps daily to feed his sick wife. By splitting the responsibility for the parents between two households, but staying together in a single courtyard, this family seems to have found a viable solution to care for the elders.

I did not encounter the practice of rotating (*liulun*) the care of aged parents among different siblings as I did in many villages in north China. People in Lu Village have heard of this system and know what it is, but they do not find it practical. As we have seen, sometimes old parents may separate, one living with and cared for by one child, and the other living with and cared for by another child. But one woman cadre mocked the idea of an old parent, in a month of thirty-one days, being left "straddling the wall" on the thirty-first, when one child says "Time's up" and the other says "Not until tomorrow." She said it was not considerate to the old folks to have them continually moving between one household and another, without a permanent home.

## PROLIFERATING HOUSES AND SHRINKING HOUSEHOLDS

One of the ways that Lu Village families have changed since the 1930s has been in household size. Fei showed that average household size in Lu Village dropped from 5.7 to 5.0 persons in the space of a year, 1938–1939, due to military conscription and male emigration. Fei counted 122 households, defined as units that kept accounts and ate together. In 1938, officials gave him a much lower number of 95 households—an average of 7.3 persons per household (Fei and Zhang 1945:19, 38). The discrepancy shows how household size may reflect differences in reporting in response to government policies. In the late 1930s, taxes were levied on a household basis rather than per capita. This encouraged families to delay formal division, even though informal division had taken place.

In the 1990s, average household size for Greater Lu Village dwindled to only 4.2 persons per household.[27] One important reason for the decline is the government's family planning policy, limiting couples to two children, which will be discussed further in chapter 8. Family planning policy indirectly encourages families to underreport their children if they surpass the two-child limit or fail to observe the four-year spacing rule, but hiding "surplus" children today is probably every bit as difficult as hiding them from conscription in Fei's time. The then current land allocation policy had an opposite effect, encouraging households to register all legitimate members if they want to get land. The land policy also allowed young married couples to separate their shares of farmland from the parents, since land was owned and allocated by the village, not the parents. Thus, early independence from the parents did not risk loss of land inheritance as it did in prerevolutionary days.

Why are smaller households preferred? Just as it was difficult to motivate everyone to work hard for the collective, Chinese families have probably always found it hard to manage their members in joint households. As Fei observed,

> When a new daughter-in-law is introduced into the house, the old unit becomes unstable, for the new member, having had no previous relations with the group, will not easily adjust to the older members. Such an economic unit can be maintained only by an equal sharing of duties and privileges among the members who are no longer united entirely on the basis of intimacy and altruism. . . . New relationships which develop must, almost of necessity, be based upon self-interest and will be incompatible with these pre-existing patterns. To build a smoothly functioning economic unit on such a basis is a difficult, if not impossible, task. (Fei and Zhang 1945:115)

In the current reform period, holding the family together is less obligatory. Early separation is an important sign of the growing autonomy and prosperity of young couples, for it redefines the relationships between the young bride and her mother-in-law, between a young man and his father, and between husband and wife. Early separation encourages the *jiehun* rather than *tao xifu* model of marriages, as discussed above. Late separation reflects the poverty and dependence of the young, who are unable to accumulate personal resources (even in rich families) to build a home of their own, while parents are reluctant to relinquish wealth and power. The trend toward smaller households, then, can be seen as a growing opportunity to escape from the rigors of joint household management, where conflict between family members over authority and the division of labor can cause great animosity and anguish. More and more young people are able to renegotiate their relations to their seniors. The consequences of this shift may be increased vulnerability for old people, particularly in households that depend on farm labor for much of their income.

In the reform period, the shift toward smaller households has occurred across Yunnan Province and China as a whole.[28] In Yunnan, average household size dropped from 5.2 to 4.5 persons between 1982 and 1990 (YPSB 1991:4). In the 1980s and '90s, increased wealth fueled home construction, while the family planning policy contributed to fewer and more widely spaced children. The next chapter, on demography, describes Lu Village family planning and its gender implications.

In summary, in showing how it differs from the stereotypic Han marriage and family system, I am reluctant to argue that Lu Village represents a pattern that is widespread across Yunnan or, on the other side, that it is unique to Yunnan, or to just one valley of Yunnan. The marriage practices found in Han areas of Yunnan to the west of Kunming City do seem different from those found in the Han areas to the east of Kunming City.[29] It is unlikely that these differences are simply a result of different degrees of Han assimilation toward the minority cultures. I suspect that differences are also related to the economic and political histories of different regions, including differences in the household economy that have led to quite divergent roles for women and men. The history of farming and domestic textile production, as well as military disturbances and migration, have shaped different regions and villages such as Lu Village. The marriage practices observed in Lu Village, both by Fei and by me over fifty years later, illustrate that, in China, what is "normal" is far from universal. At the same time, there are aspects of Lu Village family life, such as high female suicide rates and declining family size, that are shared with most of rural China.

## NOTES

1. The importance of ties to affines, or a woman's natal kin, and particularly her *niangjia*, or mother's home, has been emphasized by Judd (1989, 1994), and Watson (1985).

2. James Watson (1980) examines forms of slavery in prerevolutionary China. Maria Jaschok (1994) documented female slavery in Yunnan in the 1930s. See also the account of Huang Shiniang in chapter 5.

3. This implied she could be exchanged for something else.

4. She was already married to the first husband at the time.

5. In traditional China, the first wife, if barren, could demand to adopt the child of a second wife or concubine. See Chang (1991) for an example of the first wife's intention to exercise this right.

6. This was not a subject I could easily pursue without causing discomfort to the family and officials.

7. Although illiterate, she was aware of the marriage law "*hunyin falu*" and the new right to dissolve arranged marriages that were not consensual.

8. Fei and Zhang wrote that this type of marriage "is always considered something of a disgrace" (1945:260).

9. Household registration books record for each family the surname, personal name, age, sex, education, place of birth, date of immigration or emigration, and death. The registration books are not always up to date or perfectly accurate, but they are a reasonably good record of village membership. I was able to check anomalous cases with villagers.

10. On the relative merits of endogamous and exogamous marriage for women in patrilineal systems, see Agarwal (1994:317–18, 330–31) regarding women's property rights and Skinner (1997:77) and Wolf (1975) for mortality.

11. The township director of the Women's Federation told me that they had about ten cases where letters were not returned. The Women's Federation representative and the police traveled to Anhui and Jiangsu provinces to look for two women from Lufeng township but did not find them. Usually, the director said, either the conditions are worse in the areas the women have been taken to or the husband is old or immoral. The husbands pay ¥4,000 or ¥5,000 to the matchmaker to arrange the marriage. Some goes to the parents and some to the matchmaker, and sometimes, if he is caught, the husband demands the money back. The director also explained that

> The custom here is that a wife's parents can visit her, and if she is not happy, she can come back. But outside the province, it's not like that. They lock her up inside. They don't go through the formalities of transferring her residence but treat her as their *"jiali de ren"* (a person inside their household). This problem peaked in 1989 and was less severe in 1990 and 1991. We have worked on youth education.

When I asked about the difficulty of tracking down lost daughters, the township director said that everyone clams up when "outsiders" (*waidi ren*) come and ask questions, and that the village women's director is powerless and sometimes colludes in the deception: "If she did do anything about a captive wife, she would be scorned by her fellow villagers. They usually keep the woman in the house until she has born a child and then they begin to let her out to go to the market later on." She cited one girl, age eighteen, who married a man in Jiangsu—she'd met him in Lufeng county and returned with him. She discovered it was very poor there, so she later came home but had to leave her son behind. If her forty-year-old husband comes to get her, it will be hard for her not to go back.

12. For example, in some cases, the groom gave clothing and shoes to the bride's parents, and she made clothes and shoes for his parents.

13. The *Pinyin Chinese-English Dictionary* (Beijing Foreign Languages Institute 1988:62, 326) translates "*caili*" as "betrothal gifts (from the bridegroom to the bride's family); bride-price." The dictionary gives as an example: "reject the old custom of accepting betrothal gifts." "*Jiazhuang*" is translated as "dowry or trousseau."

14. Yan, examining bridewealth and dowry in Heilongjiang, observed that "there is always a socially accepted standard for the bridewealth, although the standard itself is constantly changing; in contrast, individual families have to make their own judgments about how lavish the dowry should be and what kinds of gifts will be given as dowry" (1996:189–90).

15. Using just the cases where figures were reported, the average in the 1980s was twenty guest tables (218/11) for the woman's side and twenty-two tables (336/15) for the man's side, with the average number of guests slightly higher in 1990.

16. These estimates were for the "going rate" rather than for specific marriages. Some people had no idea. Others, with recent marriages in the family, gave a range.

17. This is based on the first sixteen interviews of the 1997 interview sample (n = 50). Of these interviews, there were eight estimates for dowry and seven for bridewealth. In

calculating averages from the estimates that were given as an upper and lower range, I took the midpoints.

18. Mr. Min was the son of an uxorilocal father; both he and his father took his mother's surname. He received a good education for his generation. He served in the army for five years and later worked for the railroad. Then the county government sent him to work in Lu Village because they needed an educated person there. It is also possible that, as the son of an uxorilocal father, he may have felt his claims to inheritance in his mother's home were weak and could be contested.

19. My young assistant from the city felt this was rather materialistic, but I have seen this practice at most rural weddings. Yet this was not like the weddings in Henan, where the clan flag is flown over the table. Yan (1996) examines village gift lists in detail.

20. The film *Small Happiness*, directed by Carma Hinton, offers a good example of the forehead-to-the-floor type of kowtowing at a wedding, where the bride is repeatedly pushed down as the names of her husband's ancestors are read out loud.

21. A woman friend from Kunming also knew of this ritual.

22. The price of the feast in 1991 was about ¥800, while medical care for the dying mother at the hospital cost ¥1,000.

23. This statement is a condensed and paraphrased portion of a rather long-winded statement.

24. Anthropologist Myron Cohen suggests the practice of giving generation names to daughters may well be a post-1949 practice found across China, not only in the southwest. My village data from Henan suggest he is partially correct, although there are differences *in the degree* to which this system has been adopted in different locations. Further checking, however, complicates the pattern with a historical dimension. My assistant in Yunnan reported seeing a family tree belonging to her mother's family in which prerevolutionary generations of Han in southern Yunnan included daughters' names, and these daughters had generation names. Another similar bit of prerevolutionary genealogy comes from a more illustrious family, that of Deng Xiaoping, in northern Sichuan (his ancestors were originally Hakka migrants from Jiangxi or Guangdong during the Ming dynasty). Deng's sister and three half-sisters all shared the generation name Xian with Deng, whose formal name was Deng Xian Sheng (Salisbury 1992:28–29).

25. Here we may also recall that the daughter of the seeress in chapter 5 tried to commit suicide by drinking opium when the mother was forcing her into an arranged marriage when she was still a teenager.

26. CBC radio (November 1, 1997) reported that "more than 300,000 young women commit suicide in China every year—more than double the rate in Canada and the U.S." Zhao and Lester (1997:85) reported that, in rural regions, the suicide rate for females was 47 per 100,000 population per year in 1989, whereas it was only 23 for males. This rate was equaled and surpassed by both men and women in the groups ages fifty and above.

27. In 1988, Lu Village Center (eight teams) had 1,680 people in 410 households, an average household size of 4.1 persons. In the hamlets, average household size was 4.5 persons. The hamlets are more dependent on the land for income and slightly poorer than families in the center. They may therefore delay division of the family. Young couples in the center can more easily work for wages and transport construction materials on paved roads, so are more often able to build a new house at marriage and divide family assets shortly thereafter.

28. Decreased household size has been reported for many regions of China, north and south. For ethnographic discussion see Harrell (1993:81), Johnson (1993:134), Friedman et al. (1991), Greenhalgh (1993), and Jacka (1997:56).

29. William Lavely is currently working on the demographic features of eastern Yunnan. A study on reproductive health (Wang and Li 1994) describes households of Luliang County, 136 km east of Kunming.

## Chapter Eight

# Demographic Change, Family Planning, and Sex Preference

As to infanticide, it would be the part of prudence to speak of it in a whisper, lest the Chinese should overhear, and ask whether in our own country mothers are not sometimes driven to murder their offspring by an overwhelming dread of shame, or the fearful consequences of bastardy? (Lay 1843:60)

For many centuries immigrants from various parts of China have flowed into the frontier provinces and settled themselves in the fertile plains. They carried with them the traditional ideology of filial prosperity—of having many sons—which, in Yunnan, must have been as effective as elsewhere in China in bringing the population up to the saturation-point in a short time. (Fei and Zhang 1945:11)

It has been difficult to ascertain the scale of female infanticide during the reform years. It has been periodically referred to as a problem in the Chinese press, and is an open topic of conversation in China, where everybody has their story of either seeing for themselves, or knowing somebody who has seen an abandoned female baby alive or dead. (Croll 1994:202)

When I bore my first girl at the hospital in town (around 1988), there was a baby girl abandoned in the latrine. Later, a doctor at the hospital gave her to a sister who had no baby. It was very expensive to get her registered—six or seven thousand yuan. (woman of Lu Village, 1996)

In 1990, when I spent my first summer visiting families in various hamlets of Lu Village, my assistant and I were occasionally accompanied along the hamlet paths by the village family planning officer, who offered to help me locate outlying households in my sample. One day, we bumped into a married couple who had a small baby girl with them on their bike. With warm smiles, the family planning officer patted the baby and asked about her. Much to my surprise, we learned the baby had been adopted by the couple, who had been unsuccessfully

273

trying to have a baby for seven years. The family planning officer chatted with the couple about the baby but also observed that the woman was now pregnant. She then paused to fulfill her obligations as an official. She reminded the woman that, now that she had one adopted child, she would only be allowed to bear one child herself, instead of two. The discussion that followed included mention of the "spacing" between the first adopted child and second unborn child, and the advice that she should agree to be sterilized after this second child was born. The family planning officer told the couple that if they did not get sterilized after their natural child was born, they would be fined. The couple seemed to think that was not entirely fair. After a few moments of clarifying the rules, we went on our way. This encounter was friendly and did not produce any overt animosity. The family planning officer told me the baby girl had been given to them by strangers in Kunming for about ¥300. I pondered the feelings of the woman who had adopted this baby. She probably felt entitled to give birth to two if she were able. Village officials exert inescapable pressure to comply with government policy within their domain, but opportunities for migration and exchange permit people to find "black market" solutions to family reproductive goals.

## DEMOGRAPHY, ANTHROPOLOGY, AND REPRODUCTIVE DECISIONS

Demographic policies, as a field of political action aimed at increasing or decreasing population growth, are always controversial. In 1979 China adopted a one-child family planning policy, offering rewards to those who complied and penalties to those who did not. The original one-child policy met with considerable resistance and was relaxed to a two-child policy for rural populations and ethnic minorities. This government policy was in effect throughout the 1980s and has been ever since, with varying degrees of intensification and relaxation in enforcement in different years and in different regions, and it has had a major impact on China's birth rate (Banister 1987; Greenhalgh and Li 1995; Hall 1997; Zhou 1996). Demographer John Aird (1990) emphasizes that it is a coercive policy.

The Chinese state policy collides head-on with the Chinese family, whose ideology and rural economy, as Fei noted in the quote above, have long valued high fertility and many sons. Beneath the family planning policy lie important questions about gender, about women as reproducers, and about girls as the less-desired sex. The government presents and promotes the policy as a gender neutral policy for increasing output per capita by reducing the growth in population. According to the government view, as Greenhalgh and Li point out, if female infanticide occurs, it is because traditional cultural values survive into the present. In policy implementation and outcomes, however, gender is inescapable. Demographers have identified the problem of missing girls and analyzed quantitative data, but the complexities of the household economy and family life, where millions of individual reproductive decisions are made, call for greater anthropological attention (Coale and Banister 1994; Greenhalgh and Li 1995).

Anthropologists typically make little use of demography, but the combination of demographic and ethnographic studies can provide valuable insights as well as a powerful check on speculative interpretations and explanations. Demographic studies can indicate whether aggregate patterns of birth, mortality, health, and family size are linked to aggregate cultural, social, and economic patterns of behavior; they can balance the influence of individual emotive examples by showing whether similar situations are common or rare in the population at large. In return, anthropologists may be able to show demographers how quantitative data are sometimes misreported and misinterpreted, and why theories of demographic change may be inconsistent with the ways people actually think and behave.

## HISTORICAL PERSPECTIVES ON GENDER PREFERENCE

The controversies surrounding China's population, its one-child policy, and its missing girls can all be examined in the microcosm of Lu Village. Demographic evidence at the national, provincial, and township levels reveals and locates lopsided sex ratios, but village-level case studies can further identify where, when, and why the pressures that promote discrimination against girls become stronger or weaker. In Lu Village, the evidence available from Fei's time and from the revolutionary period helps to establish the kinds of demographic patterns that took hold before the Communist regime and before the one-child policy came into force. The revolutionary decades did not emphasize birth control, but the contemporary reform period brought the birth planning policy and birth control into force nationwide. Family planning decisions today are, of course, taken in response to contemporary policy, but they also incorporate local values, knowledge, memories, and experiences.

As with the analysis of footbinding in chapter 3, local social history and economic conditions can help to reveal why sex ratios are more imbalanced in some regions than others, and to understand which factors contribute to strong gender preferences and difficult moral choices between boys and girls. State policies and development planners who address demographic questions on a large scale often fail to understand why and how people make choices in the context of their own experiences and values. To what extent are sons preferred in a place like Lu Village? How does its demographic history influence its current demographic profile?

As the first of the quotes opening this chapter shows, awareness of the problems of overpopulation in China predates the revolution (Dikotter 1995:116–21). Fei identified overpopulation as a problem in China well before the Communists took power and long before the controversial one-child policy was implemented. In his economic analysis of Lu Village, one of the key factors leading to a decline in resources per capita was the growing population, which made it necessary to divide family resources among too many heirs. He argued that the pronatalist ideology and practices of rural families led to the impoverishment of their descendants.

Observing Lu Village in the late 1930s, Fei argued that, by having many children, families were decreasing the share of land inheritance of each of them, resulting in downward mobility in the next generation for those who were reproductively successful and raised several sons. With a growing population in the village as a whole, the size of farms in Lu Village was decreasing, so that the largest farms in the 1930s were considerably smaller than the largest farms of the preceding generation. Fei reasoned that, even if land were redistributed from rich to poor, there would soon not be enough land due to population growth. He did not explicitly recommend birth control measures, however.

There is little information about birth control practices before the revolution.[1] Apart from abstention, or "sleeping apart," as an old-fashioned prepharmaceutical option, many historical sources refer to infanticide as the most common way to rid the family of unwanted children. Such historical accounts emphasize the gendered nature of this selection; female infanticide predominated. References to female infanticide in early-twentieth-century China pop up all over, but they are like archeological artifacts out of place. The location, timing, and circumstances are rarely provided. Indeed, those who resorted to infanticide (which was illegal) did their best to cover their tracks and leave their dead or abandoned babies in someone else's backyard. The accounts of female infanticide were sufficiently current in the late nineteenth century that Archibald Colquhoun, on his travels across south China (including Yunnan) in 1883, wrote as follows:

> During the day, a horrible sight came floating by close to our boat—it was the body of a newly-born child. Far from exciting any pity or compassion from the boatmen, it seemed to offer them great amusement. As they noticed us looking at it, to our amazement they jokingly called out, "Chow, chow (food, food)." It is almost incredible that human beings could find it in their heart to jest on such a subject. The person who usually performs the murderous act is the father of the child. Midwives and personal friends generally decline it as being none of their business and as affording an occasion for blame or unpleasant reflection in future years. Generally the mother prefers that the child should be given away instead of being destroyed. Sometimes, however, the parents agree to destroy, rather than give away, their infant daughter, in order to keep it from a life of poverty or shame. (Colquhoun 1883, 1:237)

Colquhoun did not specify the sex of the corpse that caught his attention but used this as an occasion to launch into a familiar narrative about how infanticide is "usually" performed in China. This information evidently came from various unnamed interpreters (Western and Chinese) who were prepared to generalize about what other people did. While there is widespread agreement on the practice of female infanticide in prerevolutionary China, the secretive nature of its performance and the lack of identity of the parents and victims mean that there is no reliable information on the regions or class of people in which it was most common and most accepted, and those in which it was rare. There is therefore little information about the kinds of social and economic circumstances that enabled people to choose different alternatives.

One alternative to female infanticide that still rid the family of unwanted girls was abandonment or sale. In Kunming, Christian missionaries in the 1930s and 1940s had established two homes for abandoned girls (of older ages): the home for slave girls and the home for blind girls (Smith 1940; Jaschok 1994). Background information on these girls (who were old enough to tell their story) showed that they were often sold into domestic slavery as small girls when one parent died and the other could not maintain them or when the father was an opium addict. The girls had been mistreated and abandoned by their owners once they became incapacitated for domestic work due to physical abuse or illness.

Prerevolutionary Yunnan Province certainly shared the problems of excessive population for available farmlands and for maintaining productivity levels in some regions. Female infanticide, abandonment, and sale were clearly practiced. But that does not mean they were evenly spread across the province or that all of its subcultures had reasons to discriminate against girls. Indeed, the willingness to practice female infanticide has often been associated with the Han, in contrast to the aboriginal minority groups in the province. Lest this be taken as yet another reason for foreign anthropologists to selectively find fault with the dominant Han culture, I cite a remark about infanticide made to anthropologist Margaret Swain by a minority Sani woman in Kunming. "The Han kill their girl babies, while we Sani kill both our boy and our girl babies."[2] The statement leads us to wonder whether the way people carry out their family planning or infanticide decisions is also an ethnic marker, but it does not give the Han a monopoly on infanticide.

Yunnan has always had a great deal of cultural variety, not only among its aboriginal (ethnic minority) populations, but also among its Han settlers, who migrated from different provinces, at different times, and settled in areas where economic resources and ecological conditions varied. The Han are not as uniform as usually assumed, and Lu Village represents one pattern found among the Han in Yunnan.

Fei's account focused on adults; he did not describe reproduction and infant mortality, much less the topic of infanticide or abandonment. As an easterner

from the Lake Tai region, he may have brought assumptions about Han gender values to Lu Village, but he did not present evidence that girls were unwanted. Anecdotes of female devaluation and local sayings expressing female
inferiority and uselessness did not crop up in his account as they have in so
many other ethnographic reports on rural China.[3] Was that just an oversight,
or did his silence mean that preference for boys was less salient in Lu Village?

Tracing Lu Village demography to Fei's time allows us to look more deeply
at the relation between economic and political institutions and family patterns of reproduction and survival. The historical perspective reminds us that
larger conditions such as war, plague, famine, and migration have effects on
local demography and on family aspirations. These conditions may distinctively effect particular age and sex groups in the population. What gender
patterns appear in the demography of Lu Village prior to the revolution?
What hints can we glean from Fei's population data about the value and vul-
nerabilities of sons and daughters, men and women? Did Lu Village data suggest higher mortality for infant girls? How reliable were the data and what
kinds of distortions and events might have affected them? Who survived?

## LU VILLAGE DURING THE WAR

When Fei conducted research in 1938 and 1939, the population was unstable
due to the Anti-Japanese War (World War II). Fei relied on the census data
provided by the headman of the *shang*, a Nationalist administrative level between the county and *bao* (ideally a unit of one hundred households). The
headman conducted the enumeration of population in 1938 and knew the
adults in each family well. The 1938 census included absentees whose families
remained in the village but not those whose families were absent. Fei believed
the census was fairly reliable for population but not for the number of households, because villagers understood that taxes were levied on households. Elders
cleverly kept their families together (or did not register family divisions) for cen-
sus-taxation purposes. Thus, the official count of households was 95, but Fei's
count gave 122 households, suggesting some 27 families were wily tax evaders.[4]

Official figures on population were affected not only by fear of taxation but
also by conscription. The war produced the dramatic drop in adult male population that Fei recorded between the 1938 village census and his second
visit in 1939. The resident population fell 12 percent, from 694 to 611 people, in 1939, primarily due to an exodus of adult men. The sex ratio for the
total population dropped from 107 to 92 males per 100 females. Military conscription and labor migration of men between ages sixteen and forty accounted for most of the population loss (Fei and Zhang 1945:38). Thus, Lu
Village dramatically changed from a community with surplus male labor to

one with a shortage over the course of a year (see table 8.1, below). The indirect impact that the war had on family livelihood and community life was severe. This one statistic, so easily passed over, hides a number of family tragedies, some of which surfaced in the life histories of Lu Village elders who lived through those times and recalled the losses of their brothers or husbands to forcible conscription.[5]

The loss of men due to the Anti-Japanese War does not, however, just reflect a moment in China's history or a one-time experience affecting these villagers. The formula "out of three sons, take one," mentioned by the daughter of the seeress, Mrs. Huang, in chapter 5, refers to the practice in her husband's home province of Hunan.[6] This was the kind of formula that imperial and national armies often used to recruit young men from peasant households without completely destroying the tax-paying, grain-producing family economy. A family, then, had to take military conscription into account when considering how many offspring they desired. High mortality could take about half of the children, on average. Of the few surviving sons, a family had to be prepared to sacrifice one or more to army recruiters.

Even if large national or warlord armies did not take sons, local-level feuds and lawlessness meant that families needed sons prepared to defend the household against bandits. Many people in Lu Village who told me their life histories[7] and other stories revealed that bandits were rampant in Yunnan in the early part of the twentieth century. Indeed as we have seen, warfare and bandits were a common theme in nineteenth- and early-twentieth-century accounts of travel in Yunnan (Colquhoun 1883; Smith 1940). When the Muslim rebellion (1856–1873) devastated many towns and villages in western Yunnan, Lufeng town and Lu Village were among those suffering major de-

**Table 8.1. Lu Village Population Changes during the Anti-Japanese War, 1938 and 1939**

| Age | March 1938 | | | October 1939 | | |
|---|---|---|---|---|---|---|
| | *Male* | *Female* | *M/F x 100* | *Male* | *Female* | *M/F x 100* |
| 0–10 | 92 | 79 | 116 | 88 | 77 | 114 |
| 11–20 | 65 | 50 | 130 | 51 | 49 | 104 |
| 21–30 | 72 | 52 | 138 | 54 | 49 | 110 |
| 31–40 | 54 | 57 | 95 | 39 | 51 | 76 |
| 41–50 | 33 | 37 | 89 | 23 | 33 | 70 |
| 51–60 | 28 | 42 | 67 | 25 | 41 | 61 |
| 61+ | 15 | 18 | 83 | 13 | 18 | 72 |
| Total | 359 | 335 | 107 | 293 | 318 | 92 |

*Source:* Fei and Zhang (1945:38), adapted from table 3. The March 1938 data were collected by the headman, and the October 1939 data were collected during the second visit by calculating immigration and emigration for each household. Fei noted that this method was probably not completely accurate, "especially for the children" (1945:37).

struction and depopulation. These memories and experiences, passed down through grandmothers' storytelling, could well have inspired families to want many sons to defend themselves. They may also have contributed to a reasonable expectation that sons of military age would probably suffer higher mortality than daughters, for without minimizing the horrors of military rape, capture, and pillage, traditional warfare usually selected men as agents and victims, producing higher (direct) male mortality than female.[8]

## Age and Sex Distribution 1938

The age distribution of a population outlines the economic burdens felt by young and mature adults. It shows the numbers of young children and elderly parents whom they are expected to support. The sex distribution of a population reflects a variety of variables linked to gender—patterns of employment, parents' sex preferences for children, maternal mortality rates, military casualties, and different rates by sex of mortality from accidents, violence, hunger, illness, or suicide. Marriage and work patterns that lead to migration in or out of the community also affect sex ratios in the local and larger society.

The age and sex distribution for Lu Village in 1938–1939 showed the population was very youthful, with 41 percent (286/694) under the age of twenty-one in 1938 and 43 percent (265/611) under age twenty-one in 1939 (table 8.1). Women were bearing and raising many children during this period, and children, especially girls, were working at an early age, since few of them attended school. By 1939 the Anti-Japanese War had produced a striking loss of male population, evident in all age groups from eleven to fifty (see table 8.1). This loss was primarily due to military conscription and male emigration, with only four deaths reported for males under age forty. I have no way to estimate how many men ever returned from their military service, but life histories suggest that many did not come back and probably died.

Among children, the total number reported for the 0–10 age group showed slightly more males, but the sample is very small; this kind of variation could occur by chance. Fei's record of births and deaths (from ages zero to six) between 1938 and 1939 shows ten births and ten deaths (Fei and Zhang 1945:38). Four more girls than boys were born and two more girls than boys died. Again, these small numbers are inconclusive regarding son or daughter preference for the prerevolutionary period. Fei commented that he did not have great confidence in the data for the children. Also, it would not be surprising if his male informants remembered boys somewhat better than girls. The hints that daughters may have been at a disadvantage are weak, especially compared to the much stronger evidence of male dislocation due to the war. Indeed, if Fei's 1938–1939 data are correct, the war may have been taking its toll on infants and children, since deaths equaled births, clearly an abnormal situation, or population growth would not be a problem.

In listening to life histories, I was alert to signs of son preference (or indifference) in Lu Village, although I did not introduce the topic, out of concern officials might decide I was out to shame their village. Also, I did not want to hear formulaic answers about the evils of the "old society" (*jiu shehui*). The only direct evidence I encountered was the statement of Mrs. Yuan, already quoted in chapter 6: "The Yuan family was not good to me because I first gave birth to two girls. One of them died of neglect and the second died at birth. When my first daughter got sick, they gave me no money for health care. If it had been a boy, they would have given it. One time when I was out, they even threw my seven-month-old daughter into a ditch. Only my third daughter survived."

Mrs. Yuan's statement offers vivid testimony to an antigirl prejudice in her ex-husband's family (who were residents of Lufeng town, not Lu Village). Such sentiments have certainly been recorded for many parts of rural China in the prerevolutionary period, but this family may have been unusual in the local cultural context of Lu Village and surrounding villages. More information is needed to confirm that this was a common village attitude.

As an alternate source of information, I turn to my 1990 survey of the reproductive histories of older Lu Village women, to see if their reports are consistent with the male surplus in Fei's tiny and somewhat unreliable sample, and the one account of female infanticide in Lufeng. Figure 8.1 reports the number of children either living or, if deceased, who lived to at least age twenty-one. My sample for mothers in their seventies and eighties (born before 1920) is also very small. It includes only 16 children for 4 mothers. These children averaged 1.7 sons and 2.2 daughters per woman. The next age group of 7 mothers in their sixties (born 1921–1930) reported 35 children, with an average of 2.6 sons and 2.4 daughters each. Taken together, the 11 women born up to 1930 reported 51 children, of whom 26 were girls and 25 were boys. This obviously is not evidence for son preference in Lu Village, despite the attitude of the Yuan family of Lufeng. The 14 mothers in their fifties (in 1990, born 1931–1940) raised 55 children, with an average of 1.9 sons and 2.1 daughters each. The oldest of these women might have begun their reproductive careers a few years before the revolution, but most of their reproductive lives belong to the revolutionary period, after 1949. There is no evidence for sexual preference as the revolution began.[9]

Similarly, in my 1996 Lu Village survey, 50 women age 55 and up (born in 1940 or before) reported a total of 226 living children, with a sex ratio of exactly 100. These same women, reporting the children who died, lost 52 sons and 45 daughters. Adding together living and dead children, we get a total of 165 boys and 158 girls born to these women, for a sex ratio of 104, which is quite close to the 105 to 107 rates that one expects without intervention.[10]

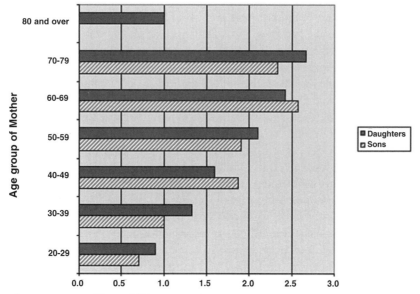

**Figure 8.1.   Lu Village Children Raised by Sex and Age Cohort of Mother**
*Source:* 1990 Lu Village Survey. *Note:* Average number of children raised, including all living dependent children, and any other children who lived to at least age twenty-one.

The limited population data available for Lufeng County (encompassing Lu Village) in the prerevolutionary period is inconclusive.[11] Little information on infant and child sex ratios is available for other rural communities in Yunnan in the prerevolutionary period. Chenggong County in central Yunnan (about 20 km south of Kunming) showed equal infant mortality rates for males and females from 1940 to 1944.[12] Nonetheless, just as footbinding varied in different parts of Yunnan, the intensity of son preference could have diverged in similar ways.

## THE REVOLUTIONARY PERIOD

It is difficult to get official demographic information at local levels for the years from 1950 to 1980. National census data and data on the survivors from earlier periods can be used to reconstruct some understanding of demographic changes. In broad outline, the demographic literature on China shows that the early revolutionary period in the 1950s was marked by rapid population growth, or a kind of baby boom. This was followed by a national catastrophe, the famine caused by the Great Leap Forward (1958–1961), with another recovery baby boom in the mid-1960s. There was some family planning and lower fertility in the mid-1970s and a great intensification of state-imposed birth control in the 1980s and 1990s (Banister 1987:352–53; Coale and Banister 1994; Greenhalgh and Li 1995). Similarly, Lufeng County reported population growth to 1958, but during the four-year period of the Great Leap Forward, deaths outnumbered births. From 1962 to 1964 the birth rate reached more than forty per thousand, dropping slowly thereafter, and more precipitously in the 1980s under the birth control policy (LCG 1997:99–100). These trends are generally reflected in the age distribution of Lu Village population (see figure 8.2).

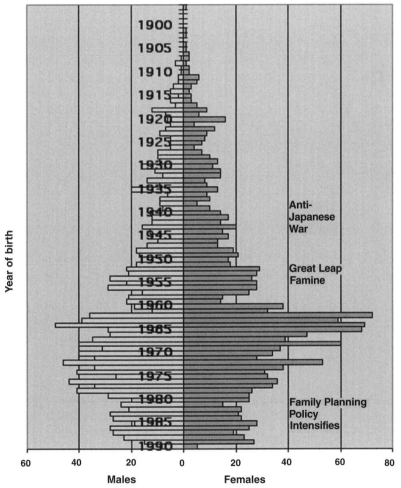

**Figure 8.2.   Lu Village Age-Sex Distribution (1990) by Birth Year**
*Source:* 1990 Village Registration.

## The Great Leap Famine

The Great Leap Forward was a massive collectivization campaign that is now remembered as the Great Leap Famine. This disastrous mass movement left its deep indentations marking infant and child deaths from starvation in all subsequent age-sex bar graphs for provinces all across China.[13] The number of deaths reported for Lufeng County more than doubled from 1957 to 1958, as the death rate shot up from fifteen to fifty-one per thousand (LCG 1997:97–100). In Lu Village Center, the population, which was 776 in 1952, dropped to less than 700 during the four "lean" years and did not surpass 700 again until 1962 (Qian et al. 1995:133). Starvation disproportionately hit the very old and the very young. The pinch experienced by the elderly quickly disappeared from the data, for the top of the demographic pyramid naturally narrows to a point as the elderly die off. Famine or no, the elderly would have soon died of other causes in subsequent censuses. The loss of infants and small children remains visible into the twenty-first century. As very few of the children born from 1958 to 1960 survived, their age cohort remains smaller than those that preceded and followed. It is noteworthy that boys as well as girls were missing from those years. There is no clear evidence at the national or provincial levels that son preference offered infant boys any better protection against starvation.[14]

The story of the Great Leap and its impact on China's rural populations has been documented and described elsewhere (Becker 1996; Smil 1993:80–81), and some of its effects were encountered in the case of Mrs. Lu in chapter 6. Here I present the way one couple candidly described what happened to family relations during the famine. Both husband and wife suffered loss of a parent who starved during the famine. In each case, it was the parent who had "married in" who died: in one case the uxorilocal husband and in the other the virilocal wife. Even though this is just a single example, it suggests that for men *or* women, life in the home village may offer more security against famine. At the same time, sibling rivalry can be intense: the woman's father's brothers and one of her mother's sisters both were willing to squeeze their siblings out of economic resources.

Mrs. Zhao (born in 1950)

Before Liberation, my mother's family (*niangjia*) had no land. We only worked for other people to earn a liter of rice. There were four girls, no brothers. My father was from Luoci and married into his wife's family (*shangmen*, or uxorilocally). Because he married out (of his patrilineal family), the kinsmen in his own family deceived him. He had several brothers. They all got land, but they did not give any to my father. My mother had a stepmother. When my mother brought in a husband, the stepmother got angry about this. My mother's older sister had also brought in a husband. This older sister did not like my mother. She often hit her and criticized her.

In 1958, the time of the Great Leap Forward, when I was eight years old, my father and then my two-year-old sister died of hunger. My mother took care of my older sister, me, and my younger sisters. My older sister attended school up to eighth grade. I only went to second grade [her education was interrupted by the famine and loss of her father]. During the Great Leap Forward, adults could only eat one hundred grams (two *liang*) of grain and children only seventy-five grams. There was not enough to eat. My husband called this the "Great Bowl of Thin Gruel" (*da guo xi fan*, making a wry comment on the Great Rice Bowl, *da guo fan*, a slogan promoting communal kitchens). In order to let us get enough to eat, my father died of starvation.

My husband's mother also died of hunger during the Great Leap in 1959. In Lu Village, everyone ate communally. They ate thin gruel that was mainly plain water. They also ate tree roots and used them to make pancakes. In some places we were not even allowed to dig tree roots. Some cadres also skimped on our rice. Many people died of hunger. When my husband's mother died, he was ten years old. His mother gave her own food to the kids to eat. After his mother died, his father was caring for three children and living with his grandmother, who was over one hundred years old.

Mrs. Zhao and her husband each recall how, as a child, a parent gave up food in order for the children to live. At the same time, the sacrificing parent who died (one male and one female) in each case was the outsider who had married into the family and the village.[15] "Outsiders" might also apply to villagers whom the revolution treated as pariahs due to their bad class background. One middle-aged villager whose father was classified as a landlord explained to me that his father died in 1958 during the Great Leap Forward when he was taken away to build a water reservoir. Needless to say, Lu Village has many examples of people who starved during those years, and it would be interesting to reconstruct the local impact of the famine. But even in 1996 many people were still uncomfortable about openly admitting their losses due to this planning failure. I was unable to collect systematic data on how many adults in Lu Village died during the Great Leap Famine, but it is possible to detect the impact on infants and young children by taking note of the relative paucity of villagers born from 1957 to 1959 (figure 8.2).[16]

When I looked for local evidence of differential child mortality by sex as a result of the famine, I found no indication that Lu Village sons fared better than daughters. The village has no records from that time, so the main evidence comes from later census and population reports that show the sex ratio of living adults who were born from 1955 to 1960 (ages twenty-five to thirty in 1990). Examination of the sex ratios of adults from a later period, however, does not rule out the possibility that differential mortality by sex after the famine might have evened out earlier imbalances. It also does not indicate how many people found partners from other communities. An equal sex ratio of thirty-year-olds also could have been achieved by attracting marriage partners from other areas. Figure 8.1 above, however, shows the average number of children raised to age twenty-one by Lu Village mothers ages 50–59. (Mothers who were 20–29 in 1960 in the midst of the famine would have been 50–59 in 1990.) The sex ratio of children raised by women in that age group does not differ in any significant way from the sex ratios of children raised in other age cohorts. In view of common beliefs about Chinese son preference and sex choice when parents are limited to only one or two children, this is surprising. It implies that parents did not selectively starve their daughters in order to feed their sons during the Great Leap Famine.

## THE REFORM PERIOD:
## BIRTH CONTROL AND RISING SEX RATIOS

The intensified national birth planning policy in the reform period has had a major impact on the demographic profile of Lu Village, as it has across China. Demographers use the "crude birth rate" to refer to the number of births per thousand people. Before the revolution, in 1929–1931, demographers estimated the crude birth rate for China as a whole at forty-one per thousand, while local studies from the 1930s give crude birth rates ranging from forty-eight down to twenty-five to thirty per thousand in different regions (Barclay et al. 1976; Banister 1987:5). In Lu Village, the crude birth rate was roughly twenty-eight per thousand in 1938 before the revolution but by 1992 had dropped to only thirteen per thousand.[17] The transition was not particularly smooth. The *Lufeng County Gazette* shows that the county crude birth rate rose to a high of forty-six per thousand in 1956, dropped drastically to a low of nine during the Great Leap Forward, and soared back to over forty per thousand from 1962 to 1966, before dropping gradually to about twenty per thousand in 1979, just before the state's strict birth control policy was introduced (LCG 1997:99).

After 1980, the crude birth rate in Lufeng County fell still further, vacillating around fifteen per thousand from 1980 to 1987 (LCG 1997:100), while the rate for the nation declined to around twenty per thousand in 1984 and remained low under continued government pressure. A decade later, in 1994, the birth rates for both China and Yunnan Province had stabilized at about eighteen and twenty-one per thousand, respectively (SSB 1995:384; YPSB 1999:65). By 1998, China's birth rate had dropped to sixteen and that of Yunnan to twenty per thousand (SSB 1999:113). The birth rate for Chuxiong Prefecture (containing Lufeng County and Lu Village) was below the national average at seventeen per thousand, though still not as low as the rate of 14.5 in 1998 for Lufeng County (Banister 1987:352; SSB 1995:384;

YPSB 1995:73; YPSB 1999:65; LCY 1999:346). As a rule, Lu Village and the surrounding area have had lower crude birth rates than the provincial or national average.

There are always doubts about the accuracy of official statistics. Rumors that cadres report fake figures to impress higher authorities are common in China. One individual I spoke to went so far as to say that the cadres were doing just as they had in the Great Leap Forward, when they inflated grain production figures.[18] Even so, the birth control policies have clearly had an impact. But what has been their effect on gender? Has limiting the number of children had an impact on sex preference in Lu Village?

## Lu Village Sex Ratios

Records from Greater Lu Village showed a very equal population sex ratio of ninety-nine males per one hundred females in 1988, followed by a decrease in the proportion of males to ninety-six per one hundred females a decade later (see table 8.2). In 1988, Lu Village Hamlets had a shortage of women, but in 1998 they had a slight surplus. Lu Village Center consistently had a

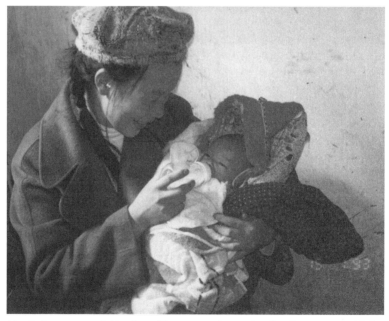

*Married out to a neighboring village, a mother makes her first outing with her newborn daughter, after the traditional one-month postpartum rest, to return to her mother's house for a feast.*

Table 8.2.    Lu Village Households and Population by Team, 1988 and 1998

| Lu Village | Households | Total population | Males | Females | Sex ratio M/F x 100 |
|---|---|---|---|---|---|
| 1988 | | | | | |
| Center teams 1–8 | 410 | 1,680 | 817 | 863 | 95 |
| Hamlets teams 9–15 | 283 | 1,263 | 649 | 614 | 106 |
| Total | 693 | 2,943 | 1,466 | 1,477 | 99 |
| 1998 | | | | | |
| Center teams 1–9 | 440 | 1,776 | 860 | 916 | 94 |
| Hamlets teams 9–15 | 348 | 1,382 | 686 | 696 | 98 |
| Total | 788 | 3,158 | 1,546 | 1,612 | 96 |

*Source:* Village records of basic conditions for 1988, and township records collected in 1999.
Teams range in size from 28 to 121 households.

*Note:* The 1988 village report showed a population of 2,943 with 2,891 farm members and 52 nonfarm members. To make these data comparable with Fei's, the first eight teams can be grouped together as an approximate equivalent to Lu Village in 1938. The remaining seven teams now under Lu Village administration were not covered in Fei's original study. Ninety-nine percent of the village population are Han. In 1998, the minorities were twenty-four Yi and six Bai.

surplus of women. This difference might reflect asymmetrical marriage strategies of women in the two areas. Women in the center may be reluctant to move farther out. By choosing uxorilocal marriage or marriage endogamous to the central area, they could avoid moving to the less convenient hamlets, whereas women from distant hamlets may also prefer to marry men in the central area.[19] Because forms for recording emigration and immigration data for the villages do not specify sex, it is difficult to test this hypothesis.[20] Of course, differential survival rates of men and women are also at work here.

A balanced or low sex ratio for the total village population might suggest that a community does not practice female infanticide, abandonment, or other forms of discrimination against its girl children. However, imbalanced sex ratios in childhood can be offset by adult behavior. More men or women may migrate for seasonal or permanent employment. In Yunnan, men often emigrate for mining and construction employment. In China's patrilocal marriage system, women typically emigrate from their home village at marriage. Thus, a community that raised few daughters could restore balance by bringing young women in as wives or employees or by exporting male labor. As we have seen historically, warfare or other political conditions might also suddenly deplete the male population, eliminating any preexisting surplus of males.

Examination of sex ratios at birth and in early childhood can indicate whether there is a gender bias in infant and child survival. The biologically expected sex ratio at birth is around 106 males for every 100 females. The births reported in my surveys of women of different ages from 1990, 1996, and 1997 provide limited evidence because the samples of women in particular childbearing cohorts are small, but they can be used to check for consistency with the officially reported statistics. As discussed earlier, my 1996 survey of fifty older women showed exactly equal sex ratios for living children born in the prerevolutionary period. For births in the 1980s, my 1990 sample survey of eighty-six households showed that there were fifty living children (twenty-four boys and twenty-six girls age ten and under) born to seventeen women. From this group of mothers, only one child died, a seven-day-old male. In contrast, my 1997 survey of fifty women ages 20–55 showed that from 1990 to 1997 only thirteen women bore children, altogether twelve boys and three girls. Due to the success of the birth control policy, the number of births is too small to be significant, but the rising sex ratio is consistent with the most recent official reports of Lu Village births.

The official records for Lu Village birth sex ratios are intriguing but must also be interpreted with care because the samples are small. In 1992, Lu Village recorded an equal number of boys and girls born, at nineteen of each, for a sex ratio of 100, below the expected sex ratio. Table 8.3 reports the sex of all the babies that were born and registered in Lu Village from 1995 to 1998. This table presents a contrasting picture. A total of 107 boys and 92 girls were born, for a birth sex ratio of 116 males per 100 females, well above the biologically expected ratio of 106. In 1997 and 1998, a total of ten more boys than girls were born out of eighty-six recorded births. These higher sex ratios are within the range of variability normally found in small samples. Indeed, most of the imbalance in the last two years is accounted for by just eight births in team one. It is too early to draw firm conclusions about gender bias in Lu Village, even though the small samples from the survey data and from official reports recently favored boys.

It is unlikely that babies born in the community were not registered. In 1999, the village headquarters had a large public meeting room. Running the length of the back wall was a large blackboard listing the names of all those eligible to become pregnant that year, along with those who gave birth. Birth quotas are a very public matter. Women would have to migrate outside the community for a birth to go undetected, and officials are prepared to hunt for them if pregnant women disappear to have a clandestine birth. While it remains possible that officials sometimes "doctor" the data or that some girl babies are unregistered, so far I have encountered no direct evidence of this in Lu Village.

Recently, pregnant women have been able to go to the town hospital where, for a fee, they can inspect their fetus using ultrasound technology. Even though it is officially prohibited to provide sex determination services for the purpose of aborting a fetus of an unwanted sex, it seems likely that this occurs. In 1999, I saw a new imported ultrasound machine (purchased a year earlier and comparable to the current technology in Western hospitals) in the

**Table 8.3.   Lu Village Births by Sex, 1995–1998**

| Team # | Total population 1998 | 1995 M | 1995 F | 1996 M | 1996 F | 1997 M | 1997 F | 1998 M | 1998 F |
|---|---|---|---|---|---|---|---|---|---|
| 1 | 190 | 0 | 2 | 2 | 3 | 4 | 0 | 4 | 0 |
| 2 | 173 | 2 | 0 | 0 | 3 | 3 | 3 | 0 | 1 |
| 3 | 189 | 1 | 1 | 2 | 1 | 2 | 4 | 2 | 1 |
| 4 | 193 | 6 | 1 | 2 | 1 | 0 | 0 | 1 | 1 |
| 5 | 151 | 2 | 2 | 0 | 2 | 1 | 0 | 1 | 1 |
| 6 | 121 | 1 | 0 | 1 | 0 | 1 | 1 | 1 | 1 |
| 7 | 279 | 1 | 5 | 4 | 2 | 4 | 1 | 3 | 2 |
| 8 | 480 | 3 | 2 | 1 | 5 | 3 | 3 | 3 | 2 |
| 9 | 263 | 3 | 2 | 5 | 2 | 2 | 2 | 2 | 2 |
| 10 | 104 | 1 | 1 | 0 | 2 | 0 | 0 | 1 | 1 |
| 11 | 143 | 0 | 2 | 1 | 1 | 1 | 1 | 0 | 0 |
| 12 | 131 | 1 | 1 | 1 | 1 | 0 | 1 | 1 | 1 |
| 13 | 155 | 1 | 1 | 4 | 1 | 0 | 2 | 1 | 0 |
| 14 | 308 | 4 | 2 | 5 | 2 | 1 | 2 | 1 | 1 |
| 15 | 278 | 3 | 3 | 2 | 3 | 2 | 1 | 3 | 3 |
| Total | 3,158 | 29 | 25 | 30 | 29 | 24 | 21 | 24 | 17 |
| Sex ratios[a] | | 116 | | 103 | | 114 | | 141 | |

*Source:* From the 1998 village plan (*guihua*). Births are from village family planning registration records.
[a]Sex ratios are males/females × 100.

county hospital being used by a young woman and her husband to look at the fetus. Ultrasound technology is not entirely new in Lufeng, for hospital staff told me they had previously had a different machine for about ten years. The old machine could be used to see the basic position of the fetus, but little more. The new ultrasound machine makes a great leap in technological capability. It easily allows sex determination at eighteen weeks and as early as sixteen weeks for a skilled person, still early enough for an easy abortion.[21] Abortions are routinely performed in town at birth control clinics and hospitals under the urging of officials who must keep births within their quotas. It would be easy to have an ultrasound for about forty yuan, or $5.00, and go for an abortion at a different clinic. Indeed, Chu Junhong (2001) reports the widespread use of ultrasound B-scans for sex determination and sex selective abortions among a sample of 820 married women of rural central China.

## Suspicious Sex Ratios: Comparing Township and Village

Table 8.4 shows the aggregate township birth sex ratios over a period of eight years (1983–1990), giving the breakdown for all village districts that belong

**Table 8.4.    Township Births by Sex, Year, and Village District, Including Greater Lu Village, 1983–1990.**

| Village District | Total | | Birth Sex Ratio[a] (M/F × 100) |
|---|---|---|---|
| | *M* | *F* | |
| A | 50 | 61 | 82 |
| B | 100 | 79 | 127 |
| C | 53 | 57 | 93 |
| D | 274 | 244 | 112 |
| E | 211 | 191 | 110 |
| F | 263 | 279 | 94 |
| G[b] | 9 | 10 | 90 |
| H | 223 | 214 | 104 |
| *Lu Village* | *218* | *172* | *127* |
| J | 84 | 83 | 101 |
| K | 111 | 111 | 100 |
| L[b] | 8 | 4 | 200 |
| M | 79 | 80 | 99 |
| Total | 1,683 | 1,585 | 106 |

| Year | Lu Village Samples | | Birth Sex Ratio[a] |
|---|---|---|---|
| 1983–90 | official records | (n = 390) | 127 |
| 1980s | random sample interviews | (n = 51) | 96 |

*Sources:* For 1983–1990, Lufeng Township Police substation, governing Lu Village and twelve other administrative villages. Data through December 31, 1990, was collected in June 1991. For the 1980s, a random sample of eighty-six household interviews was conducted in 1990.

[a]Sex ratio means males per one hundred females.

[b]The township administration subsequently combined these village offices with larger ones.

to the same township as Lu Village. It shows Lu Village had a suspiciously high aggregate sex ratio of 127 (males per 100 females) based on a sample of 390 births. However, with enough samples, by chance, there will always be some that are quite far from the average. In this case, the probability of getting a sex ratio so far from the average in a sample of 390 births is about one in thirteen, or almost 8 percent of the time.[22]

The total of township births (1983–1990) in table 8.4 shows that the births recorded for all twelve communities taken together matched the biologically expected birth sex ratio of 106. This suggests that the high and low sex ratios for the different communities, including Lu Village, were evidence of random variation. Given enough small samples, many groups will look suspiciously biased. The fifty-one children born during the 1980s (drawn from my 1990 interview sample) had a sex ratio of 96, which for living children dropped to 92 since one boy died in infancy.

The variations in sex ratios over different periods and sample sizes can easily be taken to support different interpretations, as is very evident in table 8.4. In the most recent years the township exhibits elevated birth sex ratios (table 8.5). Yet random variation in small samples means that it is possible to select particular years that look terrible for girls and others that are not so good for boys. To make interpretation more difficult, the period 1995–1998 saw the township sex ratio reach 114, up from 106 in the previous decade, while the Lu Village sex ratio dropped from 127 to 114 in roughly the same period. These contrasting trends defy simple interpretation. Although the next to last year of the century, 1998, showed a high sex ratio, over 140 in both the township and Lu Village, only longer-time series data and larger samples can determine whether this is a random variation or a significant trend.

In the context of China's demographic patterns, concerns about rising sex ratios are warranted because the national numbers are so large, but in the case of Lu Village and the surrounding communities, one finds considerable fluctuation, suggesting less consistent bias, or perhaps a weaker, intermittent son preference. A gender bias that appears intermittently is rather difficult to imagine. Attitudes are not generally turned on and off like tap water. The inconsistent data naturally lead to an effort to find just such a "handle"—a way to turn on and off behavior that leads to a shortage of daughters. One proposed handle is government policy and its varying intensity.

**Table 8.5.  Township Births and Sex Ratios by Year**

| Year | Number of Births | Sex ratio[a] (M/F × 100) |
|------|------------------|--------------------------|
| 1983 | 353 | 115 |
| 1984 | 386 | 100 |
| 1985 | 342 | 111 |
| 1986 | 412 | 112 |
| 1987 | 442 | 114 |
| 1988 | 485 | 93 |
| 1989 | 445 | 100 |
| 1990 | 403 | 112 |
| 1983–1990 | 3,268 | 106 |
| 1995 | 540 | 124 |
| 1996 | 517 | 98 |
| 1997 | 491 | 99 |
| 1998 | 431 | 143 |
| 1995–1998 | 1,979 | 114 |
| All years | 5,247 | 109 |

*Sources:* 1983–1990, Lufeng Township Police substation, governing Lu Village and twelve other administrative villages. Data through December 31, 1990, was collected in June 1991. Data for 1995–1998 was collected in September 1999. The total number of male births was 2,737, and the number of female births was 2,510.
[a]Sex ratio means males per one hundred females.

The impact of policy on birth sex ratio can be examined indirectly with annual birth reports. Research from Shaanxi Province suggests that annual variations in birth sex ratios may reflect changing birth control policies and, in particular, the intensity of government enforcement in different years (Greenhalgh and Li 1995). This theory predicts that, in years when strict policy enforcement reduces the number of births, the sex ratio will rise as people insist on having a son. Conversely, in years when enforcement is lax and more births are allowed, more people will be willing to bear or keep daughters, thinking they can have a son later.

Surprisingly, this theory did not receive support from my village and township data. Neither the annual aggregate township sex ratios nor the annual village sex ratios (see tables 8.5 and 8.6) showed a significant correlation with the number of births per year.[23] Although I do not have precise information on the timing of strict and lax policy enforcement for the different levels of government in the village, township, and province, the available data do not suggest that years of fewer births, taken as a measure of strict birth control enforcement, produced disproportionately fewer female births or evoked a preference for sons. The dearth of daughters suggested by the data seems to respond to other factors.

**Table 8.6.   Lu Village Births by Year (1983–1990, 1992, 1995–1998)**

| Year | Number | Male | Female | Sex ratio (M/F × 100) |
|---|---|---|---|---|
| 1983 | 52 | 27 | 25 | 108 |
| 1984 | 40 | 25 | 15 | 167 |
| 1985 | 50 | 24 | 26 | 92 |
| 1986 | 53 | 33 | 20 | 165 |
| 1987 | 52 | 31 | 21 | 148 |
| 1988 | 52 | 31 | 21 | 148 |
| 1989 | 46 | 19 | 27 | 70 |
| 1990 | 45 | 28 | 17 | 165 |
| 1983–1990 | 390 | 218 | 172 | 127 |
| 1992 | 38 | 19 | 19 | 100 |
| 1995 | 54 | 29 | 25 | 116 |
| 1996 | 59 | 30 | 29 | 103 |
| 1997 | 45 | 24 | 21 | 114 |
| 1998 | 41 | 24 | 17 | 141 |
| 1992–1998 | 237 | 126 | 111 | 114 |
| Total all years | 627 | 344 | 283 | 122 |

*Source:* Township police substation and village reports.

*Note:* Data are missing for 1991, 1993, 1994. Figures were collected on different field trips (1991, 1993, 1999), and locating records required negotiation. Earlier years' figures were not always as accessible as recent years. Gaps reflect the spacing of my visits and were not caused by an intention to suppress particular years. The total of 627 births comprised 344 males and 283 females for the available years.

Is the dearth of daughters evidence of the death of daughters? Have the villagers in this township physically discriminated against daughters through sex-selective abortion, female infanticide, or abandonment? These are not questions one can ask with the hope of getting straight answers, so one hopes the numbers will give clues.[24] The fact that the birth sex ratio varies considerably, sometimes near the expected level of 106 and sometimes above or below, does not allow us to draw a firm conclusion, even when the most recent data point toward discrimination. It is possible that villagers or village accountants have at times underreported births to stay within their family planning targets by omitting girls and registering sons. Given the biases embedded in the policy of land inheritance discussed in chapter 4, it is easy to understand that registering a son is akin to registering a family's long-term claims to village land. But it is also possible that new opportunities to view the fetus with a high-quality ultrasound machine in the nearby town hospital allow women to choose abortion if they are not carrying a son. A preference for sons, which may not be strong enough to overcome an aversion to infanticide or abandonment of a girl child once she has been born, may nonetheless be strong enough to permit abortion of a female fetus at an early stage, once early sex determination becomes possible.

The search for evidence of sex discrimination through local demographic data yields important and challenging findings. It also provokes further questions about the relationship between state policies and gender relations, as well as the meaning of the village-level data from which the national data are constructed. Village demography offers new insight into the complexity of this relationship.

In Lu Village and the villages of the surrounding township, the fluctuating and ambiguous sex ratios point to a shortage of girls in recent years. If there is human manipulation, is it due to *drastic* measures such as abandonment of baby girls, female infanticide, and sex-selective abortion, or to *moderate* decisions to delay reporting an infant girl, to give her away, send her to relatives, or sell her to outsiders for adoption? The finding that this township of Yunnan generally had lower fertility and lower birth sex ratios than most of China prompts us to ask how some regions manage to resist the pattern of the mainstream. Will such resistance persist even when villagers have easy access to ultrasound machines? We know that the new technology coupled with abortion can give couples more turns in the biological roulette that selects daughters or sons, but it is even more important to know how village gender preferences are shaped, when and how they take root, how strong they become, and when and how they disappear.

## Lu Village Family Planning Work

Even before the reform period, family planning was an important concern for women of Lu Village. Mrs. Shui (introduced in chapter 5) described her problems with controlling her fertility during the 1970s as follows:

> At first when they started family planning, it was only superficial. It did not spread. After my fifth child [at age thirty-five], I firmly decided I must have the operation. If I hadn't, I could still have had two or three more! My periods were still heavy. I was afraid another could have been born. And how would we have lived? I was always bearing a child again—after only a few months. Anyhow, you cannot take precautions. If you say something, they find it hard to listen [referring to her husband or men in general]. These male comrades—three or four months [after the birth], and they are like this. Ah! Two or three times [of sexual intercourse] and again you have another child. This condition is just so terrible. You are driven to death! In three years, I had two kids. If only I had been sterilized that year, when the family was still being struggled against so much.
>
> Old *Popo* (mother-in-law) would not permit it; she said, "How could you do something like that! A person's body is a person—it is not a pig that you can go and castrate (*qiao*). I will not allow you to go and do it." My old man was afraid to go and do it himself—afraid that it might harm his health. He personally would not go and do it. I was always concerned. I said, in any case, if I do not get this operation, I cannot manage.
>
> At that time there were some people who used an IUD, but some of them failed. Some people are not accustomed to it; they can get dizzy, complain of waist and back pain. This condition, to again be like this [pregnant], would drive you to your death! Ah! How can you live?
>
> I thought a lot about going for the operation. It would simply hurt all at once. In those years we were raising pigs. I said, "this year we won't kill the annual pig, we won't eat pig, we will take the big pig and go sell it." I then got some money and went to Chuxiong City and did the operation. In response, my old *Popo* popped her veins and gossiped wickedly; her words were harsh and evil.

Mrs. Shui was sterilized in 1979.

The national family planning policy was in force in Lu Village by the 1980s, as were ways of evading it. Mrs. Gou, a thirty-five-year-old woman in 1990, had two daughters, ages four and two, when she became pregnant with her third child in 1979. The two daughters were both born in a hospital, but for the third, she gave birth at home with a midwife. Her third child was a son, but according to the government, he was a "surplus" (*chao sheng*) child. Her family was fined and had to pay 250 kgs of grain each year for eight years. Mrs. Gou said if she had not been sterilized in 1980, the fine would have been even higher. Mrs. Gou's household was considered to be one of the two or three richest families in the village, her husband having earned money in construction. They could afford to pay the fine.

In 1991, the Lu Village family planning officer related how she becomes informed about untimely or over quota pregnancies and has to persuade and accompany women to have abortions, to reward those who comply and punish
those who break the rules. The strategies of families without sons can be seen
in some of the cases she described, but we also see that some Lu Village residents are willing to adopt daughters. Below are some insights into her work.

A twenty-four-year-old woman of one of our hamlets is six months pregnant with a
second pregnancy, but the separation between the births is only two years. There is
a fine of ¥100 for every month less than the required four years. This can add up to
a fine of over ¥2,000, so she is afraid. Yesterday, the woman originally agreed to go
to the hospital for induced labor (*yin chan*). Since she does not know how to register and take care of the formalities, she requested me to go with her. In the end, she
once again did not go. Perhaps she still has not decided.

I often go among the masses to hear if anyone can tell me who is pregnant; everyone knows. This work is really not easy. It evokes hatred (*tao de hen*). The majority
know the policy and think about it; a minority may threaten to retaliate (*bao fu*). In
another village district, someone cut down the tobacco plants belonging to a family
planning worker. Here, this kind of situation has still not occurred. The majority of
our male cadres also support me.

We have another woman who already has two daughters. Last year she had an induced labor abortion, and this year she is pregnant again. Tomorrow, I will request
her to go to the hospital for an induced abortion. The team has done a lot of work
to persuade her, to mobilize (*dongyuan*) her to get sterilized. The team offered to sub-
sidize her with ¥100 and to reimburse the operation expenses. But she did not agree.
She thinks sterilization can later affect her health. Then she would not be able to
go to the fields and work. Her family life is difficult, so she is only willing to use an
IUD. She and her husband are poorly educated, both around third grade. Her husband is a local person, whereas she is from another village. When she was pregnant,
she did not even know it. She waited until she went to the hospital, after two
months had already passed. The hospital does not do manual abortions after eighty
days, so then you can only wait until four and a half months have passed and then
induce abortion with saline solution. In general, there is a fine of anywhere from
¥2,400 to ¥25,000 for a third birth. For rich "¥10,000" households, the amount is
not fixed, since the main thing is not to let them give birth. In Lu Village, seven
years have passed without a third birth. We have only had to fine people for births
that are too close (less than four years apart). Last year, they fined two people. One
was fined ¥2,500.

In one Lu Village hamlet, a woman adopted a girl. It happened like this: a couple
came from outside the province, because they had two girls. They came to Lufeng
town to do business, and the woman got pregnant a third time. They were afraid
people would see her, so the woman would only go out at night. Later, they had another girl, so they gave her to the Lu Village Hamlet family with no children. Family planning officials from town came to investigate. Neither side admitted it. So the
government started to say maybe the people from out of province killed the baby.
Then they confessed. Later, they confiscated the nonresident family's possessions

and closed down their store in town. The girl baby has been adopted by the family in our hamlet. Later, the woman who adopted her gave birth to a girl. Since she had two children, she declared she would not give birth again and got sterilized. They did not fine her.

Two neighboring village district offices have more families with one-child certificates than we do. In Lu Village, last year one woman had a daughter and then got sterilized and got the one-child certificate. The township awarded a ¥1,500 yuan subsidy for this.

The examples above illustrate that some families with two girls may keep trying (although the family planning officer insisted to me that the woman who kept getting pregnant was just ignorant, not that she was still trying for a son), others are willing to get sterilized after two or even one daughter, and some are willing to adopt daughters. The family planning officer's account also illustrates how the "black market" in children operates. Some families, for whom a son is obligatory, will travel great distances to hide an illegal pregnancy, hoping to bring back a little boy as a fait accompli. I have not heard of any cases of Lu Village families who did this, however.

Family planning policy has continued to be strictly enforced during the 1990s. According to one woman, 1996 was a special year in that many women in Lu Village were sterilized. Policy required that all woman under the age of forty-five with two children be sterilized. This was done in the hospital. One of the women who was sterilized at that time said that, afterward, she did not feel any discomfort; she recovered in a short time. In general, Lu Village women spoke of birth control in a straightforward, matter-of-fact way, without moral overtones or religious discourse. This does not mean, however, that they did not experience anxieties about abortion and sterilization operations (which they voiced) or regret about lost pregnancies (which they did not voice).

A 1997 random sample of fifty women (all under age fifty-five years at the time of the interviews) provides information on current family planning practices in Greater Lu Village.[25] Taken together, these fifty women had experienced 147 pregnancies, with 116 live births (of whom nine died, six boys and three girls) and thirty abortions (the outcome of one pregnancy was unclear). Thirty of the women had used an IUD at one time, and sixteen of the women had been sterilized: seven sterilizations were performed in the 1970s, one in the 1980s, and eight in the 1990s. Here are some of the comments women offered about their birth control experiences.

I had one saline-induced and one manual abortion. After I bore two sons, I got pregnant again. When you give birth too soon, they induce abortions. The higher-ups (*shangmian*) did not permit a third child; they checked everyone. They didn't allow you to take a peek and see if it was a boy or a girl, so I do not know. After the saline abortion, I got pregnant again, so I went for another abortion, and then I got an IUD.

We were married for fourteen years before I bore a son. When I bore my older son, there was gossip. They said I was lying, that I didn't really bear him. They said he was adopted. I had only planned to have one child. Later, I did not like this idle talk (*xianhua*), so I got pregnant again and let them see. Was I telling the truth or not? Did I adopt him or not? When my older son was two years old (around 1990), I got an IUD. I had it removed when he was four and got my periods again. After two years passed, I got pregnant with my second son. After I gave birth, I got an IUD again and find this method convenient.

[A woman with three sons and numerous miscarriages and abortions gave this statement.] When birth planning began, there was a medicine to eat, but eating the medicine is not suitable; you can bleed without stopping. So then I did not dare eat it, and I got an IUD. After they put it in, after more than twenty days, my period came and I bled for eight days. They put it in a third time, and the IUD was really bad. I walked so many wrong roads until at age thirty-eight I finally got sterilized.

In 1987, they put in an IUD. It never failed. But in 1995, "those above" wanted to sterilize, so then they did this operation. Three months later, they took out the IUD. This is the higher-ups' policy. All who have borne two children and are age forty years and younger must undergo sterilization.

When I bore my older daughter, one year later I had an abortion. When I bore my second child in 1988 [a boy], they put in an IUD but put it in badly, and I got pregnant again, so I had another abortion. They then put the IUD in again, and this time [1992] put it in right. Then they called us once again because policy calls for us to be sterilized. Now I am sterilized. They already took out the IUD. To be a woman is too much trouble (*tai mafan*). First it's this way, and a little while later, it's that way.

A woman with a baby boy of one year and three months stated she wanted another child, a girl. She has had an ultrasound B-scan (*B chao*) to see if the IUD was in. They have used an ultrasound two times to check her.

Two times I got pregnant and had abortions because the IUD fell out and I didn't know it. With the IUD, it's only use is to have another abortion. The third time, they put it in right, and it's there up to now. [This woman is about forty and wants no more children.]

After I had a son, I had no periods. As a result of not knowing, I got pregnant again but had not reached the required waiting period before having the second, so I had to have an operation. After that, they put in an IUD, and it was working. But after about a month or so, I lost it. I still had back aches (cramps), so I started to take pills. When the second birth spacing time period ended, then I could stop taking pills. I gave birth again, and after the second one, then I took pills until 1995, when I got sterilized.

In 1979, when I got sterilized, you were permitted to bear three babies. When I got pregnant with the fourth, then I went to the hospital and got sterilized. Before I was sterilized, I had borne five children. I did not raise two of them, because they died as babies.

These statements, and others not included here, indicate the frequency with which methods, such as the IUD, failed and "out of plan" pregnancies occurred, were detected, and aborted. A number of women stated they were sterilized in the campaign of 1996.

This examination of the demographic changes and birth control practices in Lu Village allows us to understand the ways gender and reproduction are enacted and shaped in a particular cultural and economic setting. At the same time, it is important to identify those features that may be relatively rare in China and those that are widespread.

## County Authorities Report Success

The *Lufeng County Yearbook* sums up the family planning work for 1998 as follows:

> At the beginning of 1998, the prefecture sent down the targets: the number of births had to be controlled at 6,200 or less, the planned birth rate was to be above 96%, the birth registration rate was to reach 100%, and the application of contraception had to reach 90%. In reality, the results were as follows: in the whole year there were 5,858 births, . . . the rate of contraception was 94.48%, and the number of births was 342 less than the target. The special birth certification rate was 99.04%, the application of contraceptive technology reached 96.31%. For the whole year there were granted 3,687 first birth permits, and 2,139 second birth permits. (LCY 1999:346)

The yearbook also reports that of 82,246 married women, there were 70,882 using contraception. Sterilization accounted for 31,108 and intrauterine rings (IUDs) accounted for 37,889. In 1998, there were 2,111 cases of sterilization and 1,850 cases of "remedial measures," presumably abortions, representing a decrease of 479 from the previous year (1999:347). As we have seen, these dry, matter-of-fact reports attest to a high degree of intervention into the personal lives and bodies of village women.

## Population Sex Ratios in Yunnan and China: Numbers Games or Excess Female Mortality?

How typical is Lu Village? The population sex ratios in Lu Village need to be interpreted within the context of changing patterns of Yunnan Province as well of the nation. In 1953, Yunnan had a low sex ratio of 97 males per 100 females (see table 8.7). The shortage of males was probably due to high male

**Table 8.7. Yunnan and China: Population Sex Ratio Changes and Discrepancies, 1949–1998**

| Year | Yunnan | Year | China |
|------|--------|------|-------|
| 1953 | 97 | 1949 | 108 |
| 1958 | 100 | 1959 | 108 |
| 1969 | 100 | 1969 | 105 |
| 1979 | 100 | 1979 | 106 |
| | *One-Child Policy comes into effect* | | |
| 1989 | 104 | 1989 | 107 (106) |
| 1994 | 106 | 1994 | 107 (105) |
| 1998[a] | 107 (102) | 1999 | (104) |

*Sources:* SSB (1995:354, adapted from table 4-1). This source is based on annual Public Security reports. China's figures in parentheses are based on the 1990 census and the 1994 one-per-thousand sample surveys. Table 4-5, 358–373, has sex ratios for China's provinces over time, based on police reports.

    SSB (1999:111, table 4-1). The one per thousand sample survey of 1998 was based on a "stratified, systematic and cluster probability sampling scheme enumerating 1.24 million persons." Note that "data after 1990 are estimated on the basis of the data collected from the sample surveys on population changes. The data of other years are data collected from the residence registration" (1999:110). This yearbook reports Yunnan's lower sex ratio of 102, in parentheses above, for 1998, table 4-4, 114–115.

    YPSB (1999:63, table 4-1). The footnote to table 4-1, "Chronology of the Whole Province Year-end Population," explains, "from 1983 onward the total population was based on a sample survey for estimating numbers, and group indices (*fenzu*) were estimated according to annual population statistic reports." This explanation is somewhat confusing, but suggests that the groups, male and female, were estimated from the residence registration, or Public Security reports, as suggested in the national yearbook.

*Note:* Sex ratios are males/females × 100. Figures in parentheses are based on annual 1/1,000 sample surveys, while other figures are from annual police reports.

[a]SSB (1999:114–115) showed Yunnan's total population as 41,995,000 with 21,239,000 males and 20,756,000 females. YPSB (1999:63) showed Yunnan's population as 41,438,000 with 21,390,000 males and 20,048,000 females.

casualties in the Anti-Japanese War and civil war of the 1940s. The sex ratio rose steadily in the 1950s, reaching 101 in 1958, and dropped back down to 97 in 1961–1962, after the Great Leap Famine, suggesting that more women than men survived the famine in Yunnan. The sex ratio rose again in 1963 and stayed stable from 1964 to 1979 at around 100, indicating roughly equal numbers of each sex.

In the reform period, Yunnan's sex ratio began to rise, coinciding with the government's new policy of limiting births. In 1980, it rose to 102. By 1990, it was slightly over 105, and by 1994, it had reached 106 (Yunnan Province 1991:4; 1992:96; 1995:70). The population of Yunnan is large enough that an increase of this magnitude is significant if the data are accurate. Unless interprovincial migration or biased reporting accounted for the shift, these data would be consistent with the revival of son preference and the possibility that parents were getting rid of daughters in order to try again for sons.

In the 1990s, however, some evidence suggests that rising sex ratios may be an illusion, at least in part. Recent discrepancies in the reported population

and sex ratios suggest that there may have been significant distortions, particularly since the one-child family planning policy was instituted in 1979.
The discrepancies are so large that in one report sex preference appears to be
growing, and in the other it appears to be almost nonexistent (table 8.7).

The population of Yunnan in 1998 is available in two different official
sources, which evidently use different methods of calculating population.
The *Yunnan Statistical Yearbook* reported a sex ratio of 107 males per 100
females, while figures in the *China Statistical Yearbook* for 1999 gave Yunnan a sex ratio of only 102. This is a huge discrepancy for a provincial population of over 41 million. The *China Statistical Yearbook* reported Yunnan's population was roughly 557,000 higher than reported in the Yunnan
yearbook, but with 151,000 fewer males and 708,000 *more* females. Possibly, the smaller male population in the *China Statistical Yearbook* omits military personnel, who were included in its national but not its provincial
population totals (SSB 1999:114). The much larger female population
recorded in the *China Statistical Yearbook*, however, suggests that not all females are being recorded by the method used in the *Yunnan Statistical Yearbook*. A similar but narrower discrepancy in sex ratios also appears in the
national-level census reports. The figures for China from the one per
thousand survey, in parentheses in table 8.7, show lower and more equal
sex ratios in the last decade.

So are the sex ratios of Yunnan and China rising or not? The conflicting
data seem to be derived from two different methods: one uses the one-per-
thousand sample surveys of the national population, and the other uses annual police reports using household registration data supplied by village officials. The annual police reports are constructed by local officials who have a
conflict of interest. They have an incentive to underreport population because they are charged with population policy enforcement and want approval from higher levels of government. At the same time, parents want to
make sure that their sons are registered, but they may avoid registering
daughters in order to try for a son. Thus, Yunnan's rapidly rising population
sex ratios may be partly an illusion created by annual village reports.

In contrast, the one-per-thousand population surveys are independent of
the reports made by local officials. They may include people who are not registered with public security. These surveys obviously use a smaller sample to
estimate total population, but they may avoid gender bias from, say, unregistered daughters or wives. If the problem of Yunnan's missing females was the
result of widespread underreporting of female births rather than female infanticide, we would expect to find a more normal sex ratio of around 102 for the
population as a whole.[26] This is exactly what the 1998 one per thousand survey reported. Whether Yunnan's actual sex ratios have risen to 107 under the

birth planning policy is difficult to determine using indirect evidence and demographic inference; the degree of excess female mortality remains in doubt.

In contrast to Yunnan, China has historically recorded high sex ratios (see
table 8.7). At the time of Communist victory in 1949, the national sex ratio
was high at 108 males per 100 females, and it stayed stable until 1959.
China's sex ratio dropped to 105 in 1962 (suggesting that, in the nation as a
whole, more men than women were lost to the Great Leap Famine) and remained there until 1969 and then rose gradually to 106 in 1979 and to 107
in 1989 (SSB 1995:354).

National public security data suggest that female mortality declined relative to male in the 1960s but rose in the 1970s and 1980s and stayed high in
the early 1990s. Since 1982, two sets of population figures have been published, one based on public security (*gong an*) reports, and the other based on
the national census and sample surveys. In 1994, the two sources displayed
significant divergence, with the police reports giving a sex ratio of 107, and
the census data showing only 104.5 males to females (SSB 1995:354).[27] The
discrepancies here are similar to those with the Yunnan data. Nonetheless,
the national sex ratio has been consistently 105 and above, typically much
higher than that of Yunnan Province and Lu Village. Unfortunately, the di-
verging sources for the 1990s leave us in doubt as to whether China's sex ratios are rising or falling.

## Birth Sex Ratios

During the 1990s, reported birth and early childhood (ages 0–4) sex ratios
have been abnormally high and disadvantageous for girls both in Yunnan at
110 and in China at 118, with the data for China showing a steep rise between 1990 and 1995 (table 8.8). In rural areas, the birth sex ratios rose even
higher. In Yunnan, the 1991 birth sex ratio climbed to 123 males per 100 females for rural births, compared to only 92 (showing a surplus of girls) in city
and township districts (YPSB 1992:104; see table 8.9).

**Table 8.8. Yunnan and China: Birth and Early Childhood Sex Ratios (1990, 1995)**

| Age | Yunnan 1995 | China 1990 | China 1995 |
|---|---|---|---|
| 0 | 110 | 112 | 116 |
| 1 | 110 | 111 | 121 |
| 2 | 111 | 110 | 121 |
| 3 | 110 | 109 | 119 |
| 4 | 111 | 108 | 115 |
| 0–4 | 110 | 110 | 118 |
| 5–9 | 108 | 108 | 110 |

*Sources:* NPSY (1997:26, table 1-2); ACWF (1998:34, table 1-18).

**Table 8.9.  Yunnan Sample Survey Births by Sex and Region, 1991**

| Area | Male | Female | Sex ratio (M/F x 100) |
|---|---|---|---|
| City and town | 56 | 61 | 92 |
| County | 681 | 555 | 123 |
| Total | 737 | 616 | 120 |

*Source:* YPSB (1992:104, table 4-14; 1991: investigation sample survey). This source does not specify the fraction sampled, but it seems to be about 1.6 per thousand.

China's 1994 population survey shows that in city, town, and county (rural) areas, the proportion of males has been rising in younger age groups born since 1975 (table 8.10).[28] For ages 0–10, the urban population has sex ratios that are well above the biologically expected level of 106, but the town and county are even more unbalanced. The sex ratios for the town and county populations have shot up since 1990, with towns surpassing villages in their sexual imbalance in the youngest age groups. Demographers Ansley Coale and Judith Banister (1994) argue that these rising ratios are due to sex-selective abortion.[29]

Here again, it is difficult to determine whether these high ratios signal an increase in females aborted, in female infanticide, or in abandonment or adoption, or if they mean that people are not registering daughters. Most likely all of these occur, yet it would be useful to know the relative proportions of each because the consequence for girls differ drastically. Even the most benign of these possibilities, failure to register a daughter's birth, suggests that these daughters will later face discrimination in access to official services provided by the government, particularly schools.

## Death Sex Ratios

The degree of bias against girls is also reflected in the death rates of infants and young children, assuming that these are reported with some degree of

**Table 8.10.  China: Population Sex Ratios by Age Group and Type of Region, 1994 (sex ratios over 107 are shaded)**

| Year born<br>Age group | 1975–1979<br>15–19 | 1980–1984<br>10–14 | 1985–1989<br>5–9 | 1990–1994<br>0–4 |
|---|---|---|---|---|
| Region | | | | |
| City | 105 | 108 | 110 | 110 |
| Town | 104 | 111 | 113 | 125 |
| County | 106 | 107 | 109 | 117 |
| Total China | 106 | 107 | 110 | 116 |

*Source:* SSB (1995:6–7, table 1-3). Based on a national population sample survey of 752,431 people, or 0.00063 of the nation's population, from all provinces in 1994 (SSB 1995:3). County populations are predominantly rural. *Note:* "County" includes most rural areas (villages).

accuracy. In most societies, males experience higher infant and child mortality. Higher male infant mortality is thought to be due to the biological vulnerability of boys at birth, while most likely a mixture of cultural and biological factors affects the survival of young children thereafter. Worldwide statistics on infant mortality rates for 227 countries show that more infant boys died than infant girls in nearly all developed and developing countries. The one major exception is China.[30] In 1999, China had an infant death sex ratio of only 78 boys per 100 girls. In that year, it is reported that 100,297 more female infants died than males out of a total 815,431 infant deaths (USCB 1999: table 8.11). In Yunnan and in China in general, there appears to be "excess female mortality" in the youngest age groups, particularly in the first year of life, when mortality is highest (table 8-11). Comparing the change from 1990 to 1995 in China as a whole shows that death sex ratios are falling below 100, which means that female infant mortality is increasing relative to male. It is unlikely that these data are biased toward overreporting female infant deaths. If the death records are accurate, this evidence supports the view that, under the family planning policy, infant girls are at risk.

Table 8.11. Death Sex Ratios by Age for Infants and Young Children: Yunnan and China (available years) from Sample Surveys (shaded cells suggest excess female mortality)

| | Yunnan | | | China | | | |
|---|---|---|---|---|---|---|---|
| Age | 1990 | 1995 | number, 1995[a] | 1990 | 1994 | number, 1994[b] | 1995 |
| 0 | 113 | 93 | 485 | 97 | 84 | 417 | |
| 1 | | 100 | 46 | | 92 | 54 | |
| 2 | | 116 | 26 | | 92 | 25 | |
| 3 | | 144 | 22 | | 122 | 20 | |
| 4 | | 200 | 24 | | 100 | 14 | |
| 0–4 | | 99 | 603 | 98 | 87 | 530 | 95 |
| 5–9 | | 132 | 58 | 147 | 275 | 45 | 137 |

*Sources:* NPSY (1997:34, table 6-1; see explanation on p. 1); ACWF (1998:37, table 1-21) for 1990 and 1995; SSB (1995:66, table 1-18). The table in SSB (1995) shows a death sex ratio for ages 0–4 (from 1/1,000 sample) of 87 (n=530) and a death sex ratio of 275 (n=45, 32 males and 12 females) for ages 5–9. A supplementary table (SSB 1995:333) shows the infant mortality rate per thousand, male and female, for 1990, for China and Yunnan. China's infant mortality rate of thirty-three is less than half that of Yunnan at seventy-one per thousand.

*Note:* Death sex ratios (males/100 females) differ from death rates by sex, which compare male deaths to male population and female deaths to female population in a given age cohort. See SSB (1995:66).

[a]The figure for Yunnan 1995 is from a 1.06% population sample (NPSY 1997:1).

[b]The figure for China 1994 is based on 0.63/1,000 survey (SSB 1995:3). The sample numbers rather than extrapolations are given here (SSB 1995:66, table 1-18).

The one percent and 0.63 per thousand survey data on infant and child mortality have relatively small samples because mortality rates are low, but the results still point to a bias against infant girls. Because infant deaths are so rare in small populations like Lu Village, and because available village reports on population change do not report age at death, it is not possible to check if female infant mortality is rising there as well.

## SUMMARY

Despite the many social, economic, and political similarities with other Han villages across China, the population sex ratios from Lu Village and Yunnan Province have been consistently lower than the nation's. Data from my Lu Village sample survey on birth and child sex ratios up to 1990 did not reveal excess female mortality, but official reports gave higher birth sex ratios for the 1980s than for the 1990s, with both decades higher than normal. Larger data sets from the township, however, reversed the trend over the two decades by moving from normal to high birth sex ratios. The inconsistency in the signs of son preference in Lu Village and the township contrasts sharply with the quantitative and qualitative evidence for reduced fertility as a result of the state family planning policy. During the 1990s, Yunnan's population and birth sex ratios seem to be rising, yet major government sources provide conflicting information. Finally, survey data on infant and child mortality by sex for Yunnan and China show that, in recent years, infant and baby girls are at greater risk of death than boys.

Because I found no evidence of female infanticide or more female than male deaths at early ages in my own interviews and conversations, I am reluctant to deduce that Lu Villagers resort to killing or neglecting their infant girls. It would not surprise me, however, to learn that ultrasound technology was beginning to be used for sex-selective abortion. My conclusion, then, is not that male preference is absent, for Lu Villagers share many of the same political institutions that favor sons elsewhere in China. Rather, I think that it is less firmly embedded. During my 1999 visit to the village, I encountered a former cadre whose daughter had married at home about six years earlier. I asked if his daughter had children, and he replied that she had two, both girls. Surely if anyone had the knowledge and means to practice sex-selective abortion, this would have been such a case, yet such a decision was not taken. Ideally, candid conversations about this topic could provide better answers, but in China, as elsewhere, actions that defy public policy and moral values are not easily discussed.

Taking these findings together, the demographic evidence from Lu Village and its township seems less disadvantageous to girls than that for China as a whole. Yet at the beginning of this century, Lu Village, Lufeng County, and Yunnan may all be converging toward the greater Chinese pattern with its persistent demographic profile of high population sex ratios, high birth sex ratios, and high female infant mortality. Even so, it cannot be assumed that all villages respond in the same way, with the same intensity, and at the same pace to national institutions and national policies. The threshold at which families manifest son preference seems to be different from place to place and even family to family, depending on their own local cultural and economic traditions. In some areas, there may be a consistent view that female infanticide or abandonment is acceptable, whereas in others these options may be rejected, while actions such as giving away, selling, fostering out, or not registering a girl may be condoned. The threshold of intervention may also be changed by something as simple as the introduction of a better ultrasound machine, which can shift a difficult choice regarding life and death to the other side of a moral line if the fetus, unlike the child, is seen as disposable.

My view that Lu Village sets greater value on its daughters than do villages in other parts of China emerges from considerable struggle with the official statistics, my own statistics, and my interactions with villagers over the years. It is also based on qualitative evidence of a weaker form of gender bias in the historical data. Any such assessment is, of course, provisional. Different methods and sample sizes make firm conclusions hazardous. Keeping these caveats in mind, I suggest that Lu Village represents an alternate expression of Chinese culture responding to local and historical conditions. Such alternatives are undoubtedly not unique to villages in Yunnan and are certainly not characteristic of Han villages in *all* parts of Yunnan. Indeed, Yunnan villages have often received migrants from other parts of China, and these individuals have brought with them their own notions about gender and the value of sons and daughters. They have also responded to local conditions of farming, trade, technology, and political authority, which all contribute in various ways to shaping gender within the family, village, and society.

The most recent indications of rising sex ratios are disturbing. Do they demonstrate the strength of pressures toward convergence in rural China? If the most recent high birth sex ratios turn out to be more than random variation or underreporting of females, it would signal that Lu Village and perhaps rural Yunnan more generally were succumbing to the dominant culture and adopting the more inflexible forms of gender discrimination that endure in many parts of rural China. This is, indeed, a pessimistic view. A more optimistic view is that development brings counteracting pressures—urbanization in particular. While inward- or backward-looking parts of rural society may cling to the importance of sons, other parts of rural society are adopting urban styles of life and preparing for a more mobile, knowledge-based future society in which sons may lose their special value and parents may lose their grip on sons.

This extended examination of gender through the lens of village demography illustrates the value of looking at population changes where they can be compared to known social, economic, and political contexts. This is particularly useful when changes can be examined over time. Reviewing Lu Village demography from the 1930s to the end of the twentieth century illustrates the importance of reduced fertility and infant mortality in relation to gender and development, as well as the impact of coercive state birth control policies and new technologies associated with reproduction. Although reported birth sex ratios show rising proportions of missing baby girls in China, the mixed evidence for Lu Village suggests that girls may have been somewhat better protected here than in other regions. The most recent data, pointing toward a convergence with the rest of China, show the urgency of better understanding these gender dynamics.

## NOTES

1. Discourses about sexuality in the prerevolutionary period describe retention of sperm (while engaged in sexual intercourse) as a male strategy for preventing depletion of energy. While these ideas could have a contraceptive effect if successfully implemented, evidence is lacking about the extent to which these beliefs were shared by the uneducated rural population or about their effectiveness (whether in terms of contraception or preservation of male vitality) among the elite that espoused them. See Dikotter (1995), Baker (1979), and Gilmartin (1994).

2. Margaret Swain, personal communication.

3. Baker (1979), Buck (1957), Gamble (1954), and many others draw on such sayings.

4. Fei did not specify whether these 122 separate households had formally divided their property with their heirs or simply had juniors living or cooking in separate buildings.

5. For example, recall the story of Song Ailin in chapter 7.

6. The popular 1998 Disney movie *Mulan*, based on an ancient Chinese folktale, illustrates the long history of the danger of conscription to Chinese men.

7. See chapter 5, the life of "the seeress," Huang Shiniang.

8. I insert the term "direct" here to indicate that men primarily kill men in warfare, but the aftermath of disease, famine, and dislocation raises indirect mortality for the entire population.

9. Note that higher male differential mortality will reduce the number of surviving sons in a "natural" sample, especially for older women.

10. A sex ratio of 105 to 107 is generally accepted as the range for naturally expected sex ratios at birth in European and Asian populations (see Miller 1981:40; Aird

1990:137). In Canada, the sex ratio for children 0–4 was 105 in 1999 (Statistics Canada, CANSIM, Matrix 6367).

11. The history of Lufeng County sex ratios is shown below. Obviously these data, much affected by *adult* patterns of migration, conscription, war casualties, and various reporting biases, cannot be taken as reliable signs of *child* sex preference affecting mortality during this period.

Table 8.12.    Lufeng County Population and Sex Ratios, 1857–1987

| Year | Number | Sex ratio |
|------|--------|-----------|
| 1857 | 53,690 | 110 |
| 1919 | 148,947 | 109 |
| 1938 | 152,289 | 99[a] |
| 1943 | 136,528 | 97 |
| 1949 | 187,287 | 100 |
| 1953 | 195,762 | 95 |
| 1964 | 241,376 | 105 |
| 1982 | 362,974 | 105 |
| 1987 | 372,486 | 105 |

*Source:* LCG (1997:103–104), tables 4-10, 4-11.

[a]Figure for 1938 was printed as 108.9, but corrected here to 98.6 based on other
  data in the table, and in table 4-1 on p. 97.

12. Chengong County, with a crude birth rate of 24.9 per thousand population, had an infant mortality rate of 212.1 per thousand live births for males and 211.1 for females (King and Locke 1983:378 in Banister 1992:168).

13. See the *Population Atlas of China* (Population Census Office 1987).

14. Coale and Banister (1994) analyzed China's national census data and fertility surveys for evidence of "missing females." They report that the impact of the Great Leap Famine is seen in the disproportionate loss of older female children, but not infants. While the number of children born during the famine years drastically declined for both sexes, it is unclear why the sex ratio of infants born during those years should be more equal than that of older children.

15. G. W. Skinner's analysis (1997:77) of a large set of Japanese villages supports the general interpretation that exogamously married members of a couple experience earlier mortality, particularly if the senior in-law of the same sex had a long life. Thus, daughters-in-law had shorter lives if their mothers-in-law had long lives, and uxorilocally married sons-in-law had shorter lives if their fathers-in-law were survivors.

16. Figure 8.2 was constructed from 1990 data on all registered residents of Lu Village. The smaller number of people born in the late 1950s was still evident in age distribution of adults (and in the shortage of people in their thirties) in my 1997 interview sample.

17. The 1938 estimate is based on Fei's data. This relatively low birth rate is consistent with information from other parts of Yunnan. A rate of 25 per thousand was reported for 1940–1944 in Chenggong County, in central Yunnan (Banister 1987:79). Lufeng reported a birth rate of 22 per thousand for 1953, the first year with data after the revolution (LCG 1997:99).

18. Jasper Becker published an article in the *South China Morning Post* (March 31, 1999) concerning a six-year-old orphaned girl who survived a flood in Pai Zhou County, Hubei. Crying on Chinese Central Television, the girl said she feared her four siblings had drowned. This revelation of a family that had three daughters and two sons drew national attention to the fact that population figures are often fudged. Becker quoted Hubei's party secretary, Jia Zhijie, in the provincial People's Congress as saying "some cadres have been reporting fake figures and exaggerating their achievements."

19. This agrees with Lavely's observations about female marriage migration in Sichuan (1991).

20. I have often wondered if the categories for immigrants and emigrants were kept deliberately vague by not recording sex, so that category totals could be balanced and discrepancies could be adjusted in local population reports.

21. I visited the hospital with a U.S.-trained obstetrician who provided me with an assessment of the capabilities of the Japanese-made ultrasound machine. This is consistent with Chu (2001:269).

22. This is a fairly high probability that the result was due to random variation. I used the two-tailed test and the formula $Z = x-np/\sqrt{(npq)}$ or $\mu/\sigma$ (the population mean over the population standard deviation).

23. Regressions testing the relationship between annual number of births and sex ratio yielded no significant correlation for either the village or the township.

24. Kay Johnson's study (1998) of informal adoptions in China shows methods that might be used.

25. The sample is not perfectly random, for two cases drawn from the most outlying hamlet were omitted due to the difficulty of getting there in bad weather; two randomly selected cases from the center were substituted and may produce some bias toward the center. The sample was planned to include fifty households.

26. Coale and Banister (1994:460) note, "In the 1990 census, the recorded ratio of males to females was 1.066; a normal sex ratio at birth and normal differences in survival would have yielded a ratio no higher than 1.02. Female mortality evidently has been abnormally high in relation to male mortality in China."

27. The census data sex ratio for the total population has been dropping since 1986, when it was as high as 107. The census survey data (with higher population counts than the public security data) may include girls and women that have been omitted by public security (China 1995:4, 354; China 1996: 4).

28. Over these two decades, birth planning policies became stricter, particularly for urban residents (Li 1994).

29. The rise in sex ratios, first in the towns and later in the rural counties, coincides with the spread of ultrasound technology (Coale and Banister 1994:475), as already noted for Lu Village.

30. U.S. Bureau of the Census (1999) statistics show that, of 227 nations, only China, North Korea, Bhutan, and Papua New Guinea report higher infant mortality rates for girls than for boys (infant mortality rates are also higher for girls in the Isle of Man, Jersey, and Macao, where the numbers are so small that the ratios are insignificant). See also Coale and Banister (1994:460).

*Chapter Nine*

# Politics and Political Culture

The traditional saying, "To be promoted in political rank is to become richer and richer," appears still to be true. (Fei and Zhang 1945:130)

Today, the cadres are all rather male supremacist, *zhong nan qing nu*, in their thinking. Now, when they choose cadres, they only choose young men. The new team leaders are all selected by the office. In four recent cases, the old team leaders retired, and the officials chose the new team leaders. [Whispered:] They were not elected by the masses. Please take care of these things that I have said, for I am a little afraid. I am going now. (Lu Village resident)[1]

For most rural women, it is far easier to deal with their husbands or fathers than to deal with local cadres, who are nearly all male and are not family. The family economy is patriarchal, but it was double patriarchy under the collectives. (Zhou 1996:207)

## WHERE CADRES MEET

Every administrative village in rural China has some kind of building complex, often with dull rectilinear architecture, that reminds villagers of their links to higher levels of government. In Lu Village, the administrative headquarters is located on the main street, close to the center point of the elliptical village settlement. A two-story cement building, in the severe socialist style, it dominates the main street. On the broad front step, clusters of old men dressed in blue cotton and with grizzled faces and gnarled hands often gather for intense games of chess or cards. A storefront for selling agricultural supplies opens onto the street, and a narrow driveway leads into the interior courtyard. From the second-floor balcony, you can look down on the street life below.

311

Inside on the ground floor there is a courtyard, storage space, a meeting room, and both a men's and a women's latrine (only one of which is usually open and in working order). The interior courtyard is large enough to hold village meetings and has a plain stage, or platform, that can be used for rehearsals for cultural performances. The building also has running water, electricity, and facilities for cooking for large groups, as well as tables and chairs. Upstairs are various offices for the cadres, or village officials, and a large meeting room. Meetings of smaller groups take place upstairs. The offices have wooden desks, chairs, a few cupboards, and stacks of papers. In the larger meeting room, chairs and coffee tables line the perimeter, leaving an open space in the middle.

During the 1990s, the symbols of austerity were being replaced by symbols of prosperity and fun. The village government added a large, new second-story meeting room, reached by a grand circular cement staircase in the middle of the courtyard and thus symbolically breaking away from the rectilinear designs of Mao's day. By 1993, the office had purchased a television and a video attachment so leaders could watch videos in the office, although there was still no telephone and no photocopier. In 1999, a small health post was operating from a room off the courtyard.

Like most guests, I was brought to this site when I first arrived. It is a place I revisited each time I came to Lu Village. I attended meetings and banquets (and parked my bicycle) in this building complex; I also hand-copied village reports there and sometimes just came to chat with friends. It was both imposing and familiar, depending on your position in the village. In my many visits there, I never witnessed any real conflict within its walls, although during the Great Leap Forward and Cultural Revolution, there must have been a very different atmosphere. Before I describe some of the political activities and actors found there in the 1990s, I will review the political structure in Fei's time. As with the household economy and family organization, Lu Village exhibits a mixture of continuities and changes.

## FORMAL GOVERNMENT IN THE 1930S

The political organization that Fei described in Lu Village in 1938 was the *baojia* system, which dated back to the Qing dynasty. According to historian Jonathan Spence, the *baojia* system required community mutual responsibility within the judicial structure.

> A *bao*, a group of 1,000 households, consisted of 10 *jia*, each of which contained 100 households. All Chinese households were supposed to be registered in *jia* and *bao* groups and supervised by a "headman" chosen from among their own number on a

rotating system. These headmen were expected to check on the accuracy of each household's registration forms, which listed family members by gender, age, relationship, and occupation, and to ensure local law and order. The headman also supervised community projects such as dike repairs, crop watching, or militia operations. (Spence 1990:125)

As Spence described, the Nationalist government relied on a "household responsibility system similar to the old Qing *baojia*. In time, the community groupings were supposed to elect headmen and councils; in practice, these officials were appointed from above by the county magistrates" (1990:368).

Fei did not specify whether Lu Village headmen and councils were locally elected or appointed. His brief outline[2] suggested that the headmen were appointed, but he did not identify those who had the powers of appointment. The units called "*jia*" seem like antecedents for contemporary teams, or small organizations, which in the 1990s had about fifty households each. The higher-level organization, the *bao*, was similar to the present-day village administration of Greater Lu Village.

The ninety-five officially recognized households of Lu Village . . . comprise 9 *jia* of the fifth *bao* . . . of the district. Two other villages—one of 3 *jia* and the other, populated by . . . recent immigrants from Sichuan, of 1 *jia*—are included in this *bao*. As might be expected, the political dominance of the villages varies with their numerical dominance. The headman of the *bao* is always selected from Lu Village, and the village of 3 *jia* provides the vice-head, while the immigrant village has only a *jia* head, with no representation in the *bao* government. (Fei and Zhang 1945:97–98)

Without outlining village political posts in any detail, Fei mentioned a village headman, a vice-head, as well as a tax collector, and a "principal of the public school (who is an official in the eyes of the people)" (Fei and Zhang 1945:65, 130). To resolve disputes over land, villagers went to a magistrate (a higher official presumably located in Lufeng) who kept records of court decisions (79).

The formal *baojia* system was charged with implementing and enforcing the policies of higher levels of government. However, many local affairs were conducted through nongovernmental village associations such as the Temple of the Lord of the Earth, whose rental income was used for public services, and other associations responsible for maintaining the water system. Foremost among the responsibilities of the formal village government was the collection of taxes and the maintenance of land registry books in each village. Taxes were used to pay for public security and military services, irrigation, village education, the census, a public granary, and a system of subsidized loans. In addition, households were subject to corvée labor demands for building the Burma Road or other public construction (99).

Public education was a responsibility of the village government. Fei took note, however, that few parents took advantage of the opportunity. "When we suggested that our landlord's twelve-year-old daughter, who was completely illiterate, should be sent to school, her mother explained that she would not be able to keep the house going without her daughter's help. The children in poorer homes have even less opportunity to go to school" (130). Those who obtained education in Fei's time were mainly young men from well-to-do families.

The complete absence of women from Fei's description of the political system stands in sharp contrast to the appearance of women throughout his economic analysis. Lacking any evidence to the contrary, I believe that Lu Village women had no direct, formal role in the political hierarchy. Like the imperial examination system, which excluded women, the Nationalist government and its local branches in the *baojia* system seem to have excluded women completely. That was to change dramatically with the Communist revolution.

## VILLAGE GOVERNMENT IN THE 1990s

The current governing body of Lu Village is composed of two groups. The executive committee, a core group of eight officials, works out of the central office. The larger village council includes the executive committee plus the team leaders from each of the fifteen teams, a total of twenty-three members who meet periodically.[3] Like villages across China, Lu Village also has two streams of leadership: the Communist Party and the village government. In theory, these are distinct, but the two overlap considerably, so that many members of the village government are also members of the party.[4] Together these leaders are responsible for organizing agricultural production, allocating land for farming and housing, managing the irrigation system, and providing information about new technologies, fertilizers, and pesticides. They are also responsible for enforcing the birth control policy, rewarding model families, managing the local school, helping with the census, and entertaining political visitors. Members of the executive committee act as the liaison with the township and higher levels of government by implementing policies and providing regular reports of economic activities and population changes.

The village cadres' scope of activities has shrunk considerably from the pre-reform period. From the 1950s until decollectivization, the cadres were responsible for organizing the entire population into production teams and supervising production as a collective endeavor. They had to assign tasks to the village workforce in agricultural and pastoral activities, award and record daily work points for different kinds of tasks, keep track of equipment and output, and later, distribute rewards. Cadres supervised the work and, after the harvest, paid out shares of the total village output on the basis of work points. Villagers received income partly in grain and partly in cash, and the village government delivered grain to the state as required.

In the reform period, under the household responsibility system, the village leaders no longer supervise daily labor. This responsibility has returned to the individuals within the household. After selling a contracted amount of grain to the state at fixed (low) prices, households are allowed to keep their surplus production and sell it on the market if they choose. Cadres can still call the villagers to meetings, but they no longer call people out to work in the mornings. Each household can once again work at its own pace.

Cadres continue to exercise important roles in agricultural production, however, through the allocation of resources. Cadres manage the water system, the building and maintenance of roads and dikes in the fields, the distribution of subsidized fertilizer and pesticides, the purchase and storage of the harvest, the purchase of pigs, and payment of quotas to the government. They must make sure that farmers have opportunities to learn about new seeds and pesticides and know when and where to buy fertilizer and plastic for their fields. The village government calls meetings throughout the year to announce and explain plans for irrigation, canal maintenance, fertilizer and pesticide use, and new strategies for planting. At the end of the harvest, the village council meets to assess performance and any difficulties encountered. Cadres also keep detailed records of all types of team and household production, distribute booklets to farmers regarding the fulfillment of their contracts to sell grain to the state, and pay villagers for grain they delivered as contracted.

One day when I was sitting in the village office copying some information given to me by the treasurer, a middle-aged farm woman came into the treasurer's office with a receipt and presented it to him. He promptly opened his cash box and counted out a large sum of money. He was paying her for crops sold to the government. I found it interesting that a woman came to perform this transaction with the treasurer, indicating that not only do women do much of the farmwork, they also have the right to collect the cash income themselves, without sending a man to act as household head.

## Team Differences and the Selection of Leaders

The role of team leaders in the reform period has been reduced now that they no longer control labor or agricultural surpluses, but some villagers believe that differences in economic performance between teams can be traced to differences in team leadership. One man who was working in town explained that he belonged to team "B," which was not as prosperous as team "A." The reason it was less prosperous, he believed, was that the leader of his team had served too long and was too old. The differences arose, he said, even before the household responsibility system. Team A had a younger, more capable leader whose management was better, so their agricultural surpluses were greater. As a result, the members of team A had more cash on hand for investing in town enterprises once that became permissible. Team B still has not caught up because, lacking capital from farm surpluses, it has been taking them longer to get into commercial enterprises. This interpretation attributes commercial investment to greater farm yields, aided by good leadership.

## Selection of Leaders

Township party authorities select the party branch secretary, the most powerful position in the village. As in most villages in China, his authority clearly exceeds that of the formal village director. The other seven committee members are theoretically selected by the team leaders. The team leaders are, in theory, elected by their own team, but if these leaders make no serious mistakes, they continue to serve for an indefinite period. Village leaders said that the fifteen team leaders were all elected by their teams. The first time there was a village election was in 1984. Some new leaders have been selected since then. In commenting on his own team, one villager implied that the team leaders were chosen "from above," as if they were not elected by team members. There is no easy way to confirm the differing accounts of the election versus appointment of team leaders. One possibility is that elections were a "pro forma" ritual in which preselected leaders were merely ratified. I surmise that in some cases they were elected and at other times they were appointed, but that once they began to serve, they might serve until death, disability, official retirement age, or "mistakes" put an end to their career. (To be fair, this power of incumbency is not very different from what we observe in the U.S. House of Representatives.)

The director, assisted by the vice-director, is responsible for village management. The accountant and treasurer keep track of changes in village population and production. The technician, a position that is not common in other villages, disseminates agricultural technology to the farmers. The family planning officer has the duty of enforcing the family planning policy, and the women's director is responsible for any matters concerning women.

## Age and Gender

Men clearly predominate on the executive committee, although village government is no longer exclusively male, as it was in prerevolutionary days. The executive committee and team leaders are mostly middle-aged men. In 1990, men held 83 percent (nineteen of twenty-three) of the council leadership positions (table 9.1). Among the seven paid executive committee positions, men occupied the highest positions—party secretary and director—as well as those that managed the village economy. Two of the three positions that women held dealt specifically with women's matters and with family planning, which in implementation is perceived as women's domain, since the vast majority of technological interventions are performed on women. Neither of these women exercised direct authority over men. The technician was paid to transmit technical information, but she did not have power over

**Table 9.1. Lu Village Leaders: Executive Committee and Village Council, 1990**

| No. | Position | Age | Sex | Education | Years of service | Years of military service | Location |
|---|---|---|---|---|---|---|---|
| 1 | Party secretary | 52 | M | 4 | 26 | 5 | center |
| 2 | Director | 31 | M | 8 | 6 | 4 | center |
| 3 | Vice-director | 34 | M | 6 | 6 | 4 | hamlet |
| 4 | Records | 29 | M | 12 | 6 | 6 | center |
| 5 | Treasurer | 43 | M | 9 | 6 | | center |
| 6 | Family planning | 40 | F | 6 | 6 | | center |
| 7 | Technician | 26 | F | 9 | 3 | | hamlet |
| 8 | Women's director | 51 | F | 6 | 9 | | center |
| 1 | Team leader | 33 | M | 5 | 6 | | center |
| 2 | Team leader | 58 | M | 6 | 16 | | center |
| 3 | Team leader | 50 | M | 6 | 24 | | center |
| 4 | Team leader | 50 | M | | 21 | | center |
| 5 | Team leader | 71 | M | | 34 | | center |
| 6 | Team leader | 45 | M | 9 | 18 | | center |
| 7 | Team leader | 59 | M | | 24 | | center |
| 8 | Team leader | 35 | M | 8 | 2 | | center |
| 9 | Team leader | 40 | M | 4 | 3 | 2 | hamlet |
| 10 | Team leader | 36 | M | 9 | 2 | | hamlet |
| 11 | Team leader | 41 | M | 9 | 2 | | hamlet |
| 12 | Team leader | 35 | M | 9 | 12 | | hamlet |
| 13 | Team leader | 61 | F | | 24 | | hamlet |
| 14 | Team leader | 26 | M | 9 | 2 | | hamlet |
| 15 | Team leader | 45 | M | 9 | 2 | | hamlet |
| | Average (n = 23) | 43 | 83%M | 6 | 11 | | |

*Source:* Village records and interviews, 1990.

**Table 9.2.   Gender and Political Participation in Selected North Chinese Villages**

| | Village Committee | | Party Membership | |
| Village | M | F | M | F |
|---|---|---|---|---|
| Zhangjiachedao, Shandong | 5 | 0 | 44 | "several" |
| Qianrulin, Shandong | 5 | 1 | 30 | 3 |
| Huaili, Shandong | 5 | 0 | 34 | 1 |
| Half Moon, Beijing | 5 | 1 | 15 | 0 |
| Houhua, Henan | no data | no data | 34 | 6 |

*Sources:* For Shandong, Judd (1994:78–81); for Beijing, Chance (1991:43–45); for Henan, Seybolt (1993:101).

villagers' incomes or resources. Nonetheless, the presence of three women on a committee of eight gave Lu Village women a relatively high profile in village politics. It was enough to raise them above token status and allow women to feel comfortable at village meetings. This can be compared to many other villages that anthropologists have studied where women have a much more marginal role (see table 9.2).[5] Indeed, among the team leaders, men have a near monopoly, with fourteen out of fifteen leadership positions.

## Cadre Education and Experience

On average, village cadres in 1990 were forty-three years old, had six years of formal elementary school education, and had served for 11 years. Four cadres were illiterate, eight had completed some primary school (four to six years), ten had completed lower middle school (eight to nine years), and only one completed upper middle school (twelve years). Only seven of these leaders had served for less than six years. Five men had military experience and four of these ex-soldiers were on the executive committee.

The women cadres' age and education levels were very similar to the men's[6] but for their lack of military experience. Previous military service was almost insignificant for team leaders, with only one man having served in the army. But the predominance of ex-army personnel in the village executive committee suggests that military training and (paid) political office go together, possibly because higher authorities believed this was an important qualification. Such men, trained in following orders, have had experience beyond the village, and have often received additional literacy and technical instruction. Military experience also gave them access to a wide network outside the village.

In 1990, the executive committee and team leaders included a small group of "old hands," including the party secretary, who by 1996 had served in that position for thirty-two years.[7] In general, educational achievements were higher for younger cadres who have served shorter periods of time. All of the illiterate leaders had served more than twenty years, whereas those who had served six years or less had an average of eight years of education. Like the older men, the one woman cadre who served as team leader for many years in one of the hamlets was illiterate, while the young woman technician with three years of service had nine years of education.

For village women, the achievement of three positions out of eight on the committee and one out of fifteen among the team leaders was clearly a long way from gender equality but far better than the complete absence of women in government in the past. It was also better than many other villages in China, where women occupied no positions at all or have been confined to the sole position of women's director.[8]

In the 1990s, leadership changes indicate that women have not been able to expand their role in village leadership. The original eight positions on the executive have been reduced to six (see table 9.3). The man currently serving as agricultural technician used to work as vice-director. When they cut his position, he did not serve for two years. Mrs. Mang, who formerly served as agricultural technician, resigned for reasons described in chapter 4, and the former

**Table 9.3. Lu Village Leaders in 1998**

| | Position | Age | Sex | Education | Years of Service |
|---|---|---|---|---|---|
| 1 | Party secretary | 45 | M | 9 | 1 |
| 2 | Director | 48 | M | 6 | 4 |
| 3 | Accountant | 36 | M | 12 | 14 |
| 4 | Treasurer | 51 | M | 9 | 14 |
| 5 | Family planning-women's director | 48 | F | 6 | 14 |
| 6 | Agricultural technician | 46 | M | 6 | 10 |
| 1 | Team leader | 34 | M | 9 | 6 |
| 2 | Team leader | 50 | M | 6 | 7 |
| 3 | Team leader | 57 | M | 8 | 35 |
| 4 | Team leader | 52 | M | 6 | 25 |
| 5 | Team leader | 35 | F | 9 | 1 |
| 6 | Team leader | 52 | M | 9 | 25 |
| 7 | Team leader | 26 | M | 12 | 1 |
| 8 | Team leader | 42 | M | 9 | 9 |
| 9 | Team leader | 35 | M | 9 | 1 |
| 10 | Team leader | 45 | M | 9 | 8 |
| 11 | Team leader | 48 | M | 6 | 4 |
| 12 | Team leader | 46 | M | 6 | 1 |
| 13 | Team leader | 45 | M | 6 | 2 |
| 14 | Team leader | 34 | M | 9 | 7 |
| 15 | Team leader | 51 | M | 6 | 20 |
| | Averages (n = 21) | 44 | 90%M | 8 | 10 |

*Source:* Village records and interviews.

vice-director eventually took the position. The two positions of family planning official and women's director were combined into one, when the older
woman retired and a younger one being groomed for the position was forced to
resign. Thus between 1990 and 1998, women's representation on the executive
committee fell from three of eight (38 percent) to one of six (17 percent).
Among the team leaders, the one long-serving old woman was replaced by a
forty-five-year-old man, after she went blind around 1996. An older man was
later replaced as team leader by a thirty-five-year-old woman who happened to
be the younger sister of a woman who served on the executive committee. The
net result was that there was still one woman among the fifteen team leaders.
In addition to the shift in gender composition of the leadership, educational
qualifications increased slightly and the length of prior service decreased
slightly. Of the six executive committee members in 1998, four were holdovers
from 1990, showing a high degree of continuity in service.

## The Communist Party

The village branch of the Communist Party is the other main source of political power within the village. The proportion of women party members is
considerably lower than that of men, as it is in most Chinese villages. My
random sample of households in 1990 included nine male party members and
no women members. According to one woman council member, a party
member herself, there were about twenty women party members in the village, nine of whom lived in the center. Later, a more detailed report revealed
that in 1990, out of seventy-five party members, only thirteen (17 percent)
were women. In 1997, the number of party members had grown to ninety-
one, with eighteen (20 percent) women. Obviously, the party made an effort
to recruit new members, including women, during the 1990s. Communist
Party branch committee members and team leaders meet to report on each
small group, or teams', conditions. Every party "small group" (*xiaozu*) meets
once a month; they study articles from government publications, recruit new
members, make awards to outstanding party members, and support government policies.

The creation of roles for women in village government has loosened the
male monopoly on village leadership positions. But the concerns of the leaders
have also shifted. In the 1930s, the state played no direct role in reproduction,
as it does today, and military security was a far greater preoccupation for leaders; China was at war with Japan, and local men were subject to conscription.

Since prerevolutionary days, when women were excluded, women have increased their political presence in Lu Village government and participate in
party politics, even though men continue to dominate both. Some of this

change is due to the radical demands for female participation during the revolutionary years under Mao, and some is due to the reform government's ongoing efforts to manage both farming and family planning, which require government to deal with women. In the early 1990s, I attended a variety of village meetings. These included a meeting with the women's representatives from all the teams and meetings of village leaders to review production and land reform. Based on my field notes, I offer the following accounts of some of those meetings as a way of illustrating different facets of village government, as well as contemporary women's participation.

## The Annual Meeting of Women's Representatives, 1993

The cadres told me that there was to be a meeting of the women representatives of all the teams to start at noon in the administration's meeting room on the second floor of the new building. But it was now 2:00 P.M. and the meeting had not started. There were only about ten women present. One of the experienced women leaders introduced me to her niece, her younger brother's daughter, who was attending the meeting. Four of the women present were stitching together cloth shoes, while two others were knitting. Finally, the Greater Lu Village women's director started the meeting to review the year's work. After the meeting began, three men entered: the party secretary, the village head, and the accountant. There were now twelve women leaders and three male officials, plus me and my assistant.

### *"Develop the Economy!"*

The party secretary spoke second, slowly and rather softly, sometimes mumbling so that only certain emphatic words stood out. He spoke at length about the usual political themes, punctuating his remarks with good socialist words like "collective, united" (*jiti, zongji*). He praised the women's work and household production as "fairly good." He noted women's work raising pigs, mentioning that his own household raised many pigs, and that this work depended on the women. He also referred to the scientific methods of farming disseminated by the village administration.

The women listened quietly but not very attentively, most of them with their heads down and their hands working at something. There was only a little whispering. Their general attitude was similar to that of people sitting through a long sermon at a religious service, with a bit more rustling and inattention. I had the impression most people were attending out of moral obligation, not great interest, and that what they found interesting was contained in the gossip passed back and forth between the clusters of two and

three women dispersed around the room. One woman representative, formerly a team leader, arrived late with her daughter, currently a member of
the village council. The party secretary ignored the inattention and went on
talking. He continued to review the importance of women's farmwork, economic planning, and family planning; of the bean-curd businesses run by
women; and, citing production figures, of the hamlets that produced tobacco during the preceding year. He discussed the three types of grain they
produced and the prices for them, locally and in other cities. Then he compared production changes over the last ten years and talked about goals for
the year 2000.

By 2:30 P.M., the women looked dazed as he continued to talk about agricultural work. He was almost done, adding the phrase, "We need women's
support to develop the economy, isn't that so?" Then he spoke a little more
about the problems of building the new office and the lack of a (women's) latrine. Throughout his speech, his tone and style were modest and reasonable;
he neither boasted to nor intimidated his audience.

*Family Planning*

Once the party secretary and the two other men excused themselves, the
woman in charge of family planning started to talk animatedly, with other
women interjecting and responding. The atmosphere in the room changed and
the women went from being listeners to talkers. They began calling out the
names of different women and counting up the births. There were eighteen
"second births" and more than thirty births overall. Each team leader went
through each of her team's births, referring to particular individuals, not by
name, but by kin terms such as "brother's wife" (*xiongdi's xifu*). Some would ask,
"Which *xifu*? Which daughter-in-law? I do not know her name." Among the
representatives attending, I noted that two sisters were representing different
teams. Another woman leader's son had married a daughter of one of the two
sisters. I wondered how many kinship ties and affinal links I would find if I
knew the others better. The representatives discussed second births for some
time, reviewing the names of women and their babies for each team. This
meeting had become a discussion of women, by women, concerning their right
to bear children. These were the regulators. In a sense, the women representatives have replaced the traditional mother-in-law's concern with regulating reproduction.[9]

One woman talked about those currently entitled to have children, her
daughter-in-law included. Someone's child had died, so they could permit
three births in her team. There was lots of banter as they hurried through the
lists for each of the fifteen teams. The hamlet representatives reported their
births, and the family planning officer recorded the information in a little red

notebook. One woman crossed the room to sit next to the family planning officer to discuss privately a particular case. There was no discussion of policy itself, merely implementation of the requirement to record and plan births. By the end of the meeting, they had determined who could have babies in the coming year. This involved thirty or more households and eighteen second children. Each month, throughout the year, they would register the births.

The family planning officer left the room and the women's director spoke again. She talked about the fines the village charged for extra births. She then turned from family planning to production and care of the old. Next, she discussed crops and the details of growing beans, wheat, and rapeseed. "The rapeseed plants are taller now." I admittedly found this part of the meeting dull, but the details of producing these crops are, in fact, "women's things." The director kept talking fast, and I got lost in local details as they discussed raising pigs, chickens, the price of pigs, and prices in general. The women's director recommended that they grow more tobacco, because prices were high.

## "Five Good" Awards

The next subject of the meeting was the awarding of "Five Good" household awards. The women began discussing whose households should receive the "Five Good" awards, an honorific marked by a special tiny metal plaque placed on the doorway of quintessentially (pardon the pun) "good" households. It was now 3:30 P.M. and the meeting was in chaos; only thirteen women were left, and most were chatting in pairs while a leader went around and took down the list of women recommended for the Five Good awards by each of the team representatives. My assistant and I asked the women near us what these "five goods" were, and they could not remember. After thinking for a while, they said: "good family planning, good neighborly relations, good child education. . . ." At this point, they thought they should go to ask the leader, but we said they should not interrupt her. If the five goods were part of a national standard, then they would be the same as those listed by Judd (1994:278), which (paraphrased) include admonitions to be good in the following ways:

1. love socialism and the collective, and be law-abiding
2. dare to reform, be innovative, and fulfill tasks
3. develop strengths, work hard to prosper, lead in helping others
4. practice family planning and teach children
5. respect the elderly, care for the young, be democratic and harmonious within the household and with the neighbors.

The representatives seemed to put names forward spontaneously, if not arbitrarily, as "good." They did not refer to the five formal criteria but used other, informal criteria, such as whether or not their local women's representative felt they were managing their household affairs well. Finally, when one of the women leaders read out the names of the award-winning households, they were all women's names. I could not avoid thinking that these sounded like "Good Housekeeping" awards, that they maintained a traditional sphere for women. But good housekeeping in Lu Village means a lot more than interior decorating and recipes. Good housekeeping means managing household production, reproduction, and human relations. I do not have the impression that these awards actually meant much to village households, except as a sign that the local cadres approved of them. All the same, the women leaders seemed to feel that managing the household well was an important job deserving recognition.

I observed that the fifteen women representatives who attended the meeting were all wearing dark-colored brown or blue pants. Their shoes were either cloth shoes or rubber boots. They were only beginning the fashion revolution that by 1996 would have even the elderly women cadres experimenting with brighter colors and floral prints. The meeting finally dispersed around 4:30 P.M. No one was paying attention anymore anyway. During the whole meeting, three things happened and four people dealt with them. They heard a pep talk, they reported on births and set birth quotas, and they selected good households for annual awards.[10]

## The Annual Production Review

I also witnessed the Annual Production Review, a cadre meeting concerning the teams' agricultural production over the course of the year. In the afternoon, the township director came to the village and explained the conditions for transplanting tobacco; he talked for three hours. Everyone just listened. Lu Village grows very little tobacco, but the provincial government promotes it because it generates so much provincial revenue.

The day before, every team leader reported production conditions and the party representatives from each team reported their activities. For example, that year, the water regulation was well done and the transplanting was very fast; they finished it in only fifteen days. They used chemicals to get rid of weeds: also an improvement. They also again adopted the "narrow strip" (*tiao zai*) rice transplanting method and the planting went fast. They said that the "go with the wind" (*tong feng*) style of planting was also good, because the kernels ripened well. These two methods were explained as follows.

Earlier, planting was done by groups of several women making rows together at the same pace. Now, they used a line and divided up the plot into several segments, and each transplanter did one segment, going back and forth by herself. This was said to be faster. They did the same amount and they still did it together, yet it seemed like a way for the fast ones to be held up less by the slow ones and to see more clearly who did what—although they did not state these reasons themselves. Second, they used to plant rice rows perpendicular to the wind direction, so that the rows faced the wind like armies. Now, they planted the rows in the same direction as the wind, so the wind blew through the rows; this was less likely to knock the plants over and cause crop losses.

These experiments in transplanting management were surely of interest to farmers, but what I found most interesting was evidence of the village and township governments' ongoing contributions to farm management. Although they no longer directly supervised labor, they exhorted people to manage their work in particular ways. Why should they continue to take such a great interest? Under the Household Responsibility System, the village government was still the underlying owner of the land. The officials at the village and township levels wanted to achieve high agricultural output because they depend on the village farms and enterprises for revenue.

### Irrigation and Cooperation

When these farming techniques were being explained, I asked a cadre about the reason for cooperation in planting. Why did teams of women work together instead of alone? The answer was that if one person planted only her own fields, all by herself, it would not coincide with the needs for water control. The water control system, which involves scheduled flooding of different fields at different times, requires coordination and cooperation, because farmers must transplant each field quickly while the water conditions are right and then send the water down into the next field. Originally, I supposed that the need for an evenly ripening crop was the reason for teamwork in transplanting: it would be more efficient to go out and harvest a crop that ripened all at once. That may be a factor in cooperation at harvest time,[11] but the coordination required by irrigation also imposes constraints on the time allowed for transplanting. In this way, heavy reliance on an irrigation system for farming rice favors systems of local social organization and kinship that allow recruitment of lots of labor for peak times. Cadres organize the distribution of water between villages, teams, and particular fields. One result is the system of interhousehold exchange labor and intervillage hiring seen in chapter 4.

## A Production Team Meeting

One of the team meetings I attended was held at the team threshing ground. Holding a meeting at such a place is a common practice, as each team has its own common threshing ground and buildings to store agricultural equipment. On this occasion, the leader was inside the building, slowly reading an announcement that most people could not hear. People told me they were fined three yuan if they did not go. If they did attend, they received a ticket to turn in later to confirm attendance. Each household sent one representative, but if a household had more than four mu of land, they had to send two representatives. There were seventeen men and twenty-four women attending the meeting. The leader was reading an essay on the responsibility system. Most of the women were knitting or sewing shoe soles, as usual. Some women were cleaning vegetables, while the men were idle, or smoking, and children ran about. There were at least six small children at the meeting. The leader read very haltingly, making it difficult to comprehend. After about half an hour, he finished. Then another man read the first two pages of the new household responsibility contract booklet out loud for those who could not read. The booklet was titled "Agricultural Contract Agreement." It listed the name of the household head, the village name, office, and cooperative society (*hezuo she*), or team. Then followed the date and two pages of specific regulations. On one page there was a modification of the older booklets, which only listed quantity of land. The new booklets had a column where the *name* of each piece of land and its area were to be recorded, with blank spaces for production quotas to be entered on the right-hand column.

Next, the team leader talked about transplanting methods. About 80 percent had used the new method. The team leader encouraged everyone to strive toward higher production. The treasurer then spoke, and after discussing whether they had planted too close together or too far apart, he praised the team for good, fast transplanting. He explained that for maintenance of the water canals, they had hired and paid for labor this year instead of drafting village families to do the work. Then, instead of pesticides (*nongyao*), he encouraged team members to discuss and to try the new, recommended scientific methods, and urge others to try them. He then reported on the recent village administration meetings.

I noticed that when the leaders spoke about general topics, the audience chattered, but when they finished the general introductions and got down to specific matters, people were less bored. Some of the women were holding sleeping babies, the woman next to me knitted a red sweater, several of the children yawned, and a seated man inhaled tobacco smoke through his two-foot-long bamboo water pipe, making long gurgling sounds, while the leader repeated the phrase "develop the economy" (*fazhan jingji*), the mantra safely reiterated at so many village meetings.

The leader recommended that villagers try certain varieties of pigs and certain production strategies. He discussed the low prices for local pigs and recommended raising mother pigs or selling piglets. He noted the low grain prices this year and recommended that people not rely too much on grain, but that they do other things as well, such as make bean curd, do a little business or trading. As he spoke, some people shouted back comments or occasionally made jokes. The talk then shifted outside the building to several male leaders who were in the center of the threshing ground. They asked the crowd for suggestions and encouraged them to share information on problems and successful efforts. The leaders also took attendance and gave out red tickets to confirm attendance. Two men raised the issue of a dispute over a wall. One man built a wall to protect his courtyard fruit tree, and his neighbor complained that the wall robbed his sunlight, so he knocked it down. The two men may have fought. Now they brought it up in the team meeting, and the team leader promised that on Friday he would go look at it and see who was right. Another problem was that an old man in his seventies (*laoguan*) had a mentally disturbed son but no children to care for him. The man used to be a soldier for the Nationalist Army and came to Lu Village as a married-in husband. I did not hear the response to this problem, but someone raised it because they felt the man needed to be supported and wanted to know how the team proposed to do it. However, the meeting was already breaking up and, in the commotion, I could not tell if a decision was made.

This team meeting illustrated some of the challenges and successes in organizing farmers to solve problems of production and living together. The team is clearly charged with both production activities and general neighborhood government. Leaders have problems in keeping the interest of community members who remain passive until an issue arouses them, much the way citizens in my own community respond to local government. Team members clearly do have opportunities to obtain useful information and to raise their concerns, but they do not always want to take time to participate. Sometimes they send their junior or retired members to the meetings, just to avoid the nonattendance fine. The leaders and followers at these meetings are neighbors, and leaders must maintain peace and productivity among their constituents, whether elected or not. My impression is that they made sincere efforts to do so, and villagers did not seem overtly dissatisfied; they seemed to merely weigh the value of attending meetings against the other things they would rather be doing.

*Lu Villagers attend a hamlet team meeting at the threshing ground to discuss land redistribution. Women stitch cloth shoe soles and shoe tops, with small children nearby.*

## A Hamlet Land Redistribution Meeting

In late July 1990, toward the end of my fieldwork that year, the process of land redistribution, or readjustment, as villagers call it, was beginning. I attended an organizational team meeting in one of the hamlets on a Tuesday morning when the villagers were informed of the process and discussed the issues. Who would give up land and who would get more? Families that had experienced a loss of members would have land subtracted from their holdings. These included families with members who died, daughters who married out, or offspring who had gained permanent work and household registration outside the village. Families that increased their membership would gain new plots of land. This occurred when they brought in new wives or bore children. Team leaders conducted this readjustment in accordance with family planning regulations so that families that had not paid their fines for "out-of-quota" births (*chaosheng haizi*) would not get land for those children.[12]

As we approached the hamlet by foot, along the dirt path, I noted that this gathering involved the usual waiting about and chatting. Team members met in the mud-brick team building off the threshing ground, bringing their own chairs or straw stools to sit upon, and bringing their knitting, cloth shoe-sewing materials, and children. As they waited, some people drifted in and out of the building, while others clustered outside in the dusty clearing with ground flecked with straw; they were surrounded by the fields and the familiar sights and smells of country life.

At the first organizational meeting in this hamlet, the proceedings did not flow very smoothly, for a new leader was just learning the ropes. The people attending the meeting were mainly women farmers, with a small proportion of men. The young leader read off the new list of household membership for each household, to make sure there was agreement from the members, and made a few corrections. This took a lot of time. Then the leader explained that they would have to gather up their booklets and make decisions about who would give up what piece of land or receive what piece. I saw the booklet in which he kept the records—some families had as many as sixteen small pieces of land scattered all about. Then, after some confusion, the young team leader (and a former leader who was guiding him and half-trying to run the rather disorganized meeting) decided to pick representatives for about six to ten households each, to help make these decisions. Of the six representatives selected, one was a woman. The meeting was then adjourned. No further meetings were held in the team for the next three days, but meetings were held in the office, where all these representatives met with the Lu Village executive committee officials to decide on divisions. This process was not concluded when I left the village.

## WOMEN CADRES

The revolutionary years of official rhetoric promoting gender equality may have had some impact in Lu Village, but there are many instances revealing unequal treatment in the political sphere. For instance, the village women's director surprised me with the information that she was the only cadre from the main office without a regular salary. She received two yuan every time they called a meeting but, otherwise, was not on the payroll. In the township, she said, there were fourteen women directors, but only four had specialized positions. The ten others, who were not *tuo chan*, or withdrawn from production, had no salary. The women's director primarily supported herself from her farmwork and raising pigs at home. She had served as a cadre for more than thirty years, beginning as a team treasurer (*kuaiji*) and team leader (*duizhang*). From 1971, when she entered the party, until the reform began in 1979, she was a team leader. She was one of three women who were serving as team leaders during those years. She has been the women's director for many years and also used to take care of family planning. In the old days, she said, the men used to laugh at this work. Now they take it more seriously, because the government places great importance on it.

In several cases below, I describe individual women and men who have served as village cadres. These examples, along with others presented earlier

(see Mrs. Shui and Mrs. Mang in chapter 4), give a fuller picture of the challenges facing village leaders.

## A Long-Serving Hamlet Leader

Mrs. Gao was one of the early women leaders after Liberation. Her story conveys some of the flavor and tensions arising from her political experiences in
a small hamlet.

> At the time of Liberation, I was more than twenty years old. The "Four Cleans"
> campaign had started. At first, when land reform was carried out, we had only a few
> families in our team. There were three main families in our hamlet and three lead-
> ership positions. The mother of the current vice-director of Lu Village was serving
> our hamlet as storekeeper (*baoguan*), a man from another family was bookkeeper
> (*kuaiji*), and I served as team leader (*duizhang*). We had more than sixty people and
> we managed well, but I had no experience. Later, another three families came and
> the team became harder to manage. I had invited other families to join our team.
> They came, but they were crafty. They caused a lot of strife. It became so disorderly
> and they made us so angry we could not stand it. Early on, there were only these six
> or seven families. Then the children grew up and divided their households and the
> population grew.
>
> The team leader, storekeeper, and bookkeeper were all elected positions. Every-
> one met, and they voted by raising their hands. The bookkeeper had to be literate—
> he had a little schooling, but the storekeeper and I were both illiterate. They asked
> me to be storekeeper but I refused, because I was afraid to deal with economic mat-
> ters; I had no contact with economics. The storekeeper received the output and
> came back to the threshing ground. I could not do it because I was not literate. I am
> a person of small courage. In those days, the team leader led the work in the fields
> and mainly carried out the farm production. In those times, we really suffered and
> worked hard in the fields. The early years were the hardest; we suffered but it got
> better. In the evening, night after night, we worked with the other people. Today
> we have none of that kind of accounting, but at that time it was very important.
>
> After land was redistributed to households, they didn't want the previous leaders
> and elected new ones by a show of hands, and I continued to serve. The election
> was to see who they wanted most. Since the storekeeper's husband knew a craft, he
> wanted to concentrate on the family's food and manage the land; he did not want
> to serve. In the past, women team leaders were more numerous than today. There
> were women leaders in two hamlets and one team in the center. Only I am still serv-
> ing. As soon as I leave, then there will be no women team leaders. Lately, many of
> the leaders have been changed.
>
> In the past, when we served as team leaders, we offended some people. Now, these
> people still hate us. Earlier, landlord and rich peasants caps were adopted [to iden-
> tify those with bad class backgrounds]. Some people's sons and daughters remember
> this in their hearts. When we served as team leaders, how many of us offended
> them? Now when they speak, they all knock our heads [criticize us]. I do not pay at-
> tention, but serve and serve. There is no alternative. To serve as cadre is always most

difficult—people curse you coming and going. Thus, I served well, but I am getting old. It needs a rather younger person to do it well.

In the past, people used to talk about unity. Now they do not talk about it. It is just selfishness and self-profit. In the middle of the office headquarters is a flower platform. The party secretary contributed rose bushes. When they flowered, he saw other people go and pick them. Then he said "I'm not going to stand for it" and he chopped down the rose bushes. It is a pity. Now, when I retire, the others are thinking of choosing a man. Why it is that way, I do not know.

Last year I spent ten yuan of my own money, and I called five people to put up a wall at the temple meeting place. But people were saying hateful things. To manage your village does it have to be that way? I thought about it: I alone manage this place, but I, too, will not pay attention anymore whether there is more or less. If you call people to build the wall, they should at least come or else they should pay a fine. As a result, there is still no one who has looked after it.

Mrs. Gao identified some of the circumstances that initially led to her election as team leader when she was a young woman, particularly the small number of families in her hamlet, the lack of qualified people, and the long hours required. She noted that cadres made enemies and faced resentment at times, and that in recent years the spirit of public service is in decline. She also believed the commitment to gender equality was declining in that few new women leaders were being selected. Nonetheless, after Mrs. Gao retired, another woman became a team leader of a different team.

## The Village Women's Director

The women's director of Greater Lu Village also described some of the resistance and difficulties that women cadres faced in exercising leadership. She was also a long-serving cadre who was accustomed to speaking in public when called upon. She provided many years of loyal service to the Communist Party, which had raised her family up from extreme poverty.

Before Liberation, my mother was alone raising three children and depended on weaving straw shoes to earn a living. Life was very bitter, and we often didn't have enough to eat. After Liberation they gave my mother, brother, and I some land and life got a little better.

In 1958 (during the Great Leap Forward), the men in the team were all sent to the city to become workers, to repair the water reservoir (*shuiku*). There were more women in the team than men. Most of the time all the work was done by women. I, too, went to work on the water reservoir for eight months, and it was really tiring. Yet my own thinking was still very optimistic. Every day when I got home from manual labor, I used to sing songs (she is a well-known village story-song singer). From 1958 until 1980, there were always very few men in the village. The majority went to the mines, the railroads, or the steel mill. I also went to the mines in another district for half a month, where I worked as a cook. After they divided the land

and redistributed it back to households, the number of men in the village then started to increase.

Since I was a team leader and Communist Party member, I always had to take the lead in threshing or carrying rice on my back, and when I returned home I also had to do everything else myself. Serving as team leader, I had to carry loads of rice and loads of dirt. I used to carry up to 150 kgs of rice or of earth, when I myself only weighed 47 kgs. I routinely carried 100 kgs. As I was getting older, serving as team leader became too tiring, so I declined and then I served as treasurer. Serving as team leader, I used to earn thirty work points per month. But by 1979, my health was bad, and my back was hurting.

When I was team leader, some men commune members looked down on me. If I wanted the commune members to carry manure to the fields, I had to do it myself. And some men deliberately dug up the manure in the fields and carried it out again. [This was to illustrate that they were not willing to obey her.] Sometimes at night when it was necessary to irrigate the fields, the men also made it necessary for me to go, otherwise they would not do the work. [According to custom, women do not irrigate the fields at night.] So I had to order a few educated young women (*zhi qing*) who had been sent down from the cities to go together with me. The other male team leaders' evaluation (*pingjia*) of me was always very high, and they supported me. They also tried to protect me, not wanting me to carry rice sacks or to plow the fields. But the team leader is responsible for production, and the completion of production targets always depended on me taking the lead myself. Today, serving as team leader is very light and relaxed (*qing song de*). You only have to reach (*shang ji*) the production target, to pass on instructions from above, and bring up the suggestions of the masses. That's about all.

This account implicitly speaks to the danger of sexual harassment or molestation that women experienced if they were required to work at night outside of their homes, unless there were two or three women working together. This woman who had served as a village cadre all her adult life, as team leader and women's director, also had an older brother who was a team leader in central Lu Village for fourteen years (1971–1985). Access to kin who also have political positions is an important factor for both women and men (including the former party secretary) in exercising and retaining political power in Lu Village, as in villages across China[13]

## Cadre Grooming and Dismissal

In 1995, I learned that one of the younger women cadres had been dismissed, even though the older officials had been grooming her to serve as the next women's director. The explanation this woman gave was that, although she was married, she had been unjustly accused of having an affair with a married male cadre with whom she had worked closely. The leaders decided that on moral grounds she was unfit for her job and dismissed her, but they did not dismiss the man with whom she was accused of having this relationship. Not only did she lose her job, but her husband was angry and physically abusive toward her, demanding a divorce. She was distraught and concerned about her children.

The dismissed woman cadre was not in the village during my next visits, and for some years I was not able to learn more about her fate. I subsequently saw the man who was the "other party" to the alleged affair participating in a village wedding as a cadre and member of the community in good standing. Other village women seemed convinced the affair took place and that the woman was guilty. There was no tactful way for me to find out any more about her or her whereabouts on several later visits, but it seemed she had nobody in the village on her side other than her own mother. Although this story was suppressed by people's general concern with shame, it mirrored familiar stories in North America, where women and men have often faced different consequences, including dismissal or demotion, for alleged sexual misconduct.

In 1999, I finally learned that, despite dismissal, this capable woman had resolved some of her difficulties. She was divorced and had obtained half the house, divided down the middle with a wall constructed between her own part and that of her ex-husband. Already one of the better-educated women, during the intervening years she had gone to the county town for paramedical training and was now supporting herself and her children as a medical practitioner at a small village clinic. She also had an allotment of farmland that she managed herself.

## Cadres and Kinship: Sisters and Daughters

In Lu Village, as elsewhere in rural China (Diamond 1975; Ruf 1998), cadre positions seem to stay disproportionately within certain family circles, with siblings and in-laws paving the way for others to achieve government positions. For instance, Dou Changfu served as a team leader for fourteen years, from 1971 to 1985. Although he never attended primary school, he attended half a year of literacy training when he was in the army and can read. This man was the older brother of one of the women who served on the village council. Dou Changfu's younger sister[14] spoke in public with confidence. I watched her run the women representatives' meeting with considerable authority and composure—it was a fairly routine meeting, but speaking in public is not something most village women are accustomed to do. As with men, the presence of influential kin within the community probably gave her confidence. In the case of the women's director, her position within the community was enhanced not only by her brother, a team leader himself, but also by her son, who married the girl next door and thereby allied his family[15] with one of the old families, with numerous kin, some of them cadres, and considerable influence in the village. Similarly, the young woman who served as agricultural technician was the daughter of a woman who formerly served as team leader, women's director, and propagandist.

In 1999, another example of kinship in the cadre ranks arose. The young woman newly selected to take over the family planning position was none other than the married daughter of the village director, which placed two members of one family on the executive committee. With the new family planning officer only twenty-six years old, villagers muttered about the favoritism involved and her obvious lack of experience. While enforcing the family planning regulations probably requires a woman to have powerful backing, it suggests that cadres mainly trust and reward their kin.

## The Party Secretary: Crown Thy Good with Brotherhood

The party secretary of Lu Village, Xia Wending, long held the position of greatest power in the village. Yet surprisingly, Party Secretary Xia, who served from 1964 to 1997, had married into his wife's household. According to Fei's view, this form of marriage, normally a sign of poverty and poor prospects, should have condemned him to a lowly station in the village. Was Xia's success a product of the revolutionary inversion of class status? After former landlords had been deposed, the revolution elevated poor peasants to political positions. This may have been part of the story. But the official emphasis on class analysis and distribution of landed wealth has meant that power relations based on kinship networks were less apparent.

In 1938, clan lands demonstrated clan power within the village. Lu Village had several collective clan holdings belonging to branches tracing descent to an imperial official, but another significant clan landholding, twenty-eight mu, belonged to the Xia clan. The long service of Party Secretary Xia, as well as other cadre families, hints at continuity in the lines of power.[16]

Xia Wending was born to a family of ten children. In a family wedding picture, his eight surviving siblings were all past middle age. Even if his parents had originally had adequate landholdings, equal division of land among five sons and provision of dowries for three daughters would have left the descendants with small shares, a process of downward mobility Fei described in the 1930s. There was little likelihood that the fifth son would inherit a house or land; uxorilocal marriage was an attractive solution for such younger brothers (Wolf 1972). Yet by marrying uxorilocally to a woman resident in the same village, Xia Wending remained in close contact with his natal (patrilineal) kin. Moreover, because his wife's mother was a widow with only one daughter, Wending's position in the household would be unchallenged by a senior male. His bonds to his brothers within the village would have given him support given that he did not compete with them for land.

The revolution brought about a major shift in Xia Wending's prospects as a poor younger brother. The squeeze on family land experienced by younger brothers in families with many sons was resolved by the land reform. Indeed, the classification of villagers into landlord or poor peasant status may have been influenced by differences in the number of male siblings who divided the inheritance rather than by a difference in wealth in the parental generation. Xia Wending benefited, whereas a man without brothers whose father had the same quantity of land may have been classed as a landlord and treated as a class enemy.

Two of Xia Wending's four brothers and one of his three sisters remained and married within Lu Village but belonged to different teams. His youngest brother obtained a nonagricultural job in a factory in Lufeng. In addition, one of his sisters married out and moved to Kunming, a connection that may have provided him with additional resources. However, the one sibling who probably had the greatest influence on his political career was his third older brother. This brother achieved the position of party secretary in another district by 1954. In 1960, he was sent to a position outside the province and then to a party training school. He then served for many years as party secretary in different districts in Lufeng township and other nearby counties. Finally, he held a position in the township forestry department until he retired in 1989. It seems highly likely that the success of the third older brother helped Xia Wending and his younger brother to achieve their successful government positions as village party secretary and as a town worker. Xia Wending described the way his brother's experience affected his own knowledge of the wider world: "Because my brother went to many places, I too went to many places to see him." This broader experience outside his natal village, along with his early military service, probably gave him insights as well as connections to the larger political structure that helped him to hold power for such a long time.

## The Illustrious Ming Family

The interwoven network of cadre positions can perhaps be illustrated by one family—a branch of descendants from the celebrated imperial official—whose daughters have managed to avoid marrying out of their village. Mrs. Ming, for instance, was an official in charge of family planning and later became women's director. Her husband, son of a former party secretary, was head of the local savings and loan society, based in the town. Her son was an official working for the railway, and her younger sister became a team leader. Her older sister's daughter obtained a government teaching position in another town, and another sister married the son and nephew of former cadres. Clearly, particular families (like the Bush and Gore families in U.S. politics) have a fairly high concentration of lineal and affinal relatives who serve as cadres or hold other kinds of government employment.

## POLITICS IN EDUCATION, RELIGION, AND CULTURE

Thus far, I have portrayed village politics in terms of the institutions of leadership and the conduct of village administration, particularly in regard to farming and family planning. But apart from these economic and demographic concerns, the political leaders and local government have played an important role in education, religion, and culture. More specifically, the Communist-led government has instituted mass public education, promoted Communist Party culture, and suppressed religion.

### Public Education

The achievements of village government in providing mass public education and equal education for girls at the primary level have been impressive. In the 1930s, under the Nationalist government, public education in Lu Village was incipient. The village had a primary school with free education covering the first four grades. Beyond that, students had to walk to Lufeng town. Very few girls were even sent to the local school. Fei reported that only two Lu Village students were attending the town school. Students who went on to middle school required family and clan financing that was beyond the capacity of most villagers. Lu Village had one college graduate, Fei's classmate at Yanjing (formerly written Yenching) University, who was funded by clan and church scholarships (Fei and Zhang 1945:130). Fei wrote nothing more about Christian missionary education funding, but it is noteworthy that Christian missionaries were actively promoting education in Lu Village at that time. Nonetheless, before the revolution, the majority of men, and almost all women, were illiterate. By 1990, this had changed dramatically.

In 1990, the average education level for Lu Village adults age twenty and above was 4.4 years. Examining differences by gender showed that men averaged 5.2 years of schooling compared to 3.7 years for women. With about 1.5 years more schooling, men were more likely to reach the threshold, at around four years of schooling, where literacy skills in Chinese are retained. This is because Chinese children cannot achieve literacy by memorizing the sounds of just twenty-six alphabetic characters but, instead, require years to memorize how to read and write several thousand Chinese characters. Even with a simplified system of writing, this is a daunting task. Lu Village school enrollment records by grade show that participation by girls and boys is very close to equal (table 9.4). Township records show that this is not a local anomaly; indeed the aggregate sex ratio is equal at 50:50, although there are small variations from year to year (table 9.5).

The improvement in women's education is also evident in the group ages 15–30 (in 1990), for whom the literacy rate reached 89 percent, with the remainder semiliterate. The average education level for women in this age group had reached 6.8 years, despite the disruptions to education experienced during the Cultural Revolution (1965–1975). Clearly, most girls have attended junior middle school (currently grades six to eight). Beyond this level, the system becomes more selective, with fewer places. This is based on my interview sample (n=272 adults age twenty and over) from 1990. For instance, one of the party secretary's daughters qualified to become a teacher in town. The family planning officer's niece also completed postsecondary training and obtained a government teaching position outside the village. While the majority of Lu Village students now complete junior middle school, those who continue their education beyond that level generally have parents who are successful in business or government positions. These educated children, in turn, often take jobs in town.

The national and local government policy of equal education for boys and girls has clearly born fruit in Lu Village, as in the majority of villages across China, where the rate of primary school enrollment for girls is 95 percent that of boys. This presents a striking contrast to other large agrarian states, such as India and Pakistan, where female primary education lags badly behind that of males at 55 and 74 percent, respectively (United Nations Development Program 1995:52–53). The high rates of female literacy in rural China indicate that the official policy of equal education has been implemented, at least at

**Table 9.4. Lu Village Primary School Enrollment by Grade and Sex, 1991**

| Year | Boys | Girls | Total | Percent Girls |
|------|------|-------|-------|---------------|
| 1 | 28 | 19 | 47 | 40 |
| 2 | 18 | 20 | 38 | 53 |
| 3 | 20 | 20 | 40 | 50 |
| 4 | 38 | 23 | 61 | 38 |
| 5 | 45 | 34 | 79 | 43 |
| 6 | 36 | 46 | 82 | 56 |
| Total | 185 | 162 | 347 | 47 |

*Source:* Lu Village records, 1991.

**Table 9.5.   Lufeng Township Primary School Enrollment by Grade and Sex, 1991**

| Year | Boys | Girls | Total | Percent Girls |
|---|---|---|---|---|
| 1 | 242 | 224 | 466 | 48 |
| 2 | 233 | 255 | 488 | 52 |
| 3 | 256 | 225 | 481 | 47 |
| 4 | 309 | 291 | 600 | 49 |
| 5 | 387 | 247 | 734 | 47 |
| 6 | 377 | 433 | 810 | 53 |
| Total | 1,804 | 1,775 | 3,579 | 50 |

*Source:* Lufeng Township government, 1991.

the primary school level. This has initiated a very important shift over the long run in rural women's access to knowledge, opportunity, and power.

## Religious Retreat

In Lu Village, as elsewhere in China, the Communist Party suppressed religion and took control of culture for many years. The party secretary said that before the revolution there had been a temple in the village, with a big Buddha statue. His mother-in-law had gone to the temple meetings. He recalled that, if there was a drought, people would make a large dragon boat, put a dog in the boat, and sprinkle water: "Sprinkle, sprinkle, then it was supposed to rain." His description recalls villagers' earlier beliefs in the supernatural, seen in chapter 5. After Liberation, however, they turned away from the temple;

*Boys and girls in Lu Village school (1989).*

they went to the big Buddha and struck it down with one blow on the back. Across China, the long-term effects of efforts at religious suppression have been quite variable, with religious ceremonial revivals and temple rebuilding proceeding more rapidly in some regions than others. So far, there seems to be greater apathy toward the revival of religious practice in Lu Village than in some other regions.

In 1938, Fei commented that the Temple of the Lord of the Earth in Lu Village had "all the appurtenances of a place of worship" (Fei and Zhang 1945:54). In the 1990s, the surviving temple and clan buildings housed agricultural equipment, such as threshing machines, or they had been converted into multifamily residences. There was very little evidence of religious practice in Lu Village in the early '90s (although I was not there during Spring Festival). A few people burned incense or had small shrines or altars in their homes, but they had not erected new temples. Moreover, people whose families were known to have been Christian in Fei's study now denied that affiliation and acted as if there never was much Christianity there. Some of the older women sporadically attended the Buddhist temple on the outskirts of the town, which previously served a large number of villages. The temple is being restored, with brand new statues of brightly painted gods (to replace those that were destroyed), but there were generally few people attending the several times that I visited. On a feast day, there were only about thirty women present, and very few from Lu Village. Older women like to go on the first and fifteenth of the month to have a vegetarian meal together. The party secretary used to bring his aged mother-in-law to the temple, riding her on the back of his bicycle, before she died in the early '90s, suggesting that even party members could now afford to be more tolerant of religion. This temple used to have nuns and still has a few very old women. Younger people clearly know less about the rituals but show courtesy and mild interest toward those who go. The youth are more attracted by the new fashions, music, and movies available in the town.

## Culture and Communist Morality

In contrast to the suppression of religion, other realms of cultural performance have been promoted and shaped by the state. Lu Village has gained recognition at the township level for its cultural performances involving theatrical performances, music, and dance. An interest in cultural performance is certainly not new to Lu Village, for Fei recorded a Daoist music society as holding fourteen mu of land to fund its activities (Fei and Zhang 1945:55). In discussing the "leisure class," Fei mentioned that a son of this class had been found one evening "with a number of village notables in a near-by temple, whither we had been led by the strains of music. He was participating as a musician in a big ceremony, organized by his father for the purpose of 'warding off enemy bombing planes.' He had been free to spend all his days and nights in the temple during the two months the ceremony had been in progress because it was not necessary for him to work on the farm" (42).

## The Seventieth Anniversary of the Communist Party and the Cultural Performance Competition

In July 1991, after the rice had been transplanted, about thirty people in Lu Village began to rehearse plays and dances for a township performance competition. The competition was to be held in the town center auditorium, where each of the different villages of the district would stage performances. The Lu Village performances consisted of several minority dances (vigorously danced by Han village youth dressed up in bright clothing) and two plays. These performances involved about ten actors and about twenty dancers. Every day, the performers came to the village headquarters, where they put a great deal of time and energy into rehearsals. There were even some artistic directors who came for a few days from the prefectural capital, Chuxiong, to give them advice. Performers were also given a government subsidy of about four yuan per day for their practice time. The occasion for all this effort was the seventieth anniversary of the founding of the Chinese Communist Party. On the night of the performance in the town auditorium, I observed that most of the skits or short plays were similar to the two presented by people of Lu Village—they were morality plays showing the proper way to deal with social problems such as marriage introductions for older people, corruption, or prejudices against the disabled. Here is a brief description of the content of the two plays put on by Lu Village.

### The Blind Date

The first play involved a middle-aged man and middle-aged woman, both unmarried, who had been sent to a particular corner to meet each other (like a blind date) and are each waiting in the rain for a stranger to come. They have a misunderstanding, each thinking the other is not the one they are expected to meet. Then as they chat, the woman explains that she sells eggs but can't get enough to sell, and the man explains that he raises chickens but can't sell all the eggs they lay. They each realize, eventually, that they have met the unknown person they were told to wait for, and they decide to get married and live happily ever after. There is much humorous double entendre in the play, but it is interesting that complementarity of economic pursuits makes the marriage a good proposition. The theme of the play is that introducing or matching middle-aged men and women who have no partners is very difficult. Yet it portrays them as making their own choice and speaking together as equals and potential partners. It also implicitly treats commercial activities as legitimate purposes (which would not have been the case during the Cultural Revolution).

## The Cadre's Corrupt Wife

The second play portrayed a village team leader's wife who is soliciting bribes for influencing the granting of the contract to the village orchard. She wants to be able to pay for her son to go to university. She is afraid that her husband will not earn enough as a cadre. When he discovers her, her husband furiously confronts her, and in response to his anger, she threatens to drink insecticide, screaming "I'm going to drink DDV! I'm going to drink DDV!"[17] In the end, she does not drink it, and her upstanding cadre husband returns the goods. During the scene when she threatens to drink DDV, the entire audience laughed. This did not really surprise me, but it struck me as rather insensitive, for in my interviews I had encountered several cases in the past few years in which women of Lu Village had committed suicide by drinking insecticide. This threat evidently plays upon a well-known theme, yet I could not help but find it very disturbing that the audience found the woman's threat so familiar and so amusing. Rural China has one of the highest rates of female suicide in the world, predominantly because of the high rate in rural areas. In the conclusion of the play, the wife admits her wrongdoing, the worthy couple get the apple orchard contract, and the party secretary gets a raise so that (his wife's) temptation to take bribes will disappear and his son can go to university.

These two plays were presented to large audiences in town and illustrate the ways in which the party attempts to combine entertainment with moral messages and happy endings. This combination of politics and culture has shaped village culture for a whole generation. When I was invited to evening parties and weddings, many of the folk songs sung by the regular (middle-aged) village singers were standard revolutionary songs they learned as young cadres on propaganda teams. One of the cadres told me she had been a finalist in a provincial competition in 1956 for singing story-plays (*huadeng*). In 1991, Lu Village won the township cultural competition once again and, thus, added another commemorative award banner to the collection in the office.

## Fears of Corruption

During one of my later visits, I learned that the township director was in jail on charges of corruption. He had been under investigation (*shou hui*) for about a month, allegedly over some ¥280,000 that were missing. A local driver was said to be in jail for stealing more than ¥1000. He allegedly stole when transferring money between the central and branch savings societies. No one wanted to say much about the cases, so I did not press for the details. Later, I heard that the director was released and not charged.

In many parts of China, people believe that corruption is endemic and that prosecutions barely address the problem. The problem is recognized by popular opinion and officials alike. Perhaps because I did nothing to suggest I was interested in such rumors, no one presented me particular accounts of corruption among the village leaders, although everyone knows that having connections is vital to economic success. In contrast, bitter memories dating to the land reform, the Great Leap Famine, or Cultural Revolution did surface from time to time. The widespread concern about corruption is part of local culture, even officially sponsored culture, as seen in the cultural performance described above.

## CONCLUSION

The formal politics and political culture of Lu Village have changed considerably since Fei Xiaotong's time. All the same, there are signs of underlying continuity in the ways families gain positions of power and of the emergence of a cluster of families that have disproportionate success in obtaining government positions. This group, holding administrative and teaching positions in the village, bears a certain resemblance to the old gentry that Fei described: the landowners, headman, tax collector, and school master.

One important change is that women of ordinary households participate in team meetings, and women's representatives come together in the village headquarters for meetings to discuss policies that matter to women: farming and family planning. The village leadership, composed of team leaders and the executive committee, still shows a heavy preponderance of males, but Lu Village women have a greater presence than women in other areas of rural China. Moreover, Lu Village women form a sizable minority within the Communist Party.

The current political system has left in place the unbalanced foundations of traditional patrilineal descent and patrilocal residence, which still give village men the advantage of kin support in local politics. The fraction of women who actively participate in politics are, similarly, those who have unusually strong kin networks in the village, much as they were when Norma Diamond (1975) called attention to this situation in rural China more than two decades ago. Lu Village women leaders are those who married a man of the same village; they are women whose parents, brothers, and sisters live nearby. In that sense, the few women who exercise local political power are much like politically active men: they are surrounded and supported by their kin and by people whom they have known since childhood.

If we examine the power of the local officials over the lives of villagers, it is clear that they have considerably less power than they did in the collectivist years; but they still retain power in the management of agricultural resources and revenues. They organize the allocation of land and the provision of irrigation, fertilizer, pesticides, and various other agricultural tasks. They also exercise control over the rate of reproduction by licensing marriage and reproduction at certain ages and intervals and by imposing quotas on the number of children per couple. For all the liberalization of the reform period, the state remains a strong actor in the village and in the household, much stronger than in the time of Fei's research.

In everyday life, village cadres do not posture as authoritarian figures. I have seen them exhorting, persuading, and warning, but I have also seen villagers disregard, ignore, and evade the leaders' instructions. Under normal circumstances, the cadres' power seems to rest on the passive consent of the governed and the villagers' expectation that local leaders will deliver reasonable services as well as implement and buffer commands from above. But clearly, times past—such as the Cultural Revolution and Great Leap Forward—contain painful memories of political rigidity and physical coercion. Greater coercive power and authority resides in the higher levels of township government. While township officials in general exude a sense of confidence rarely found among villagers, the township director with whom I was most familiar preferred a glad-hand style of hearty joking when interacting with villagers. Nonetheless, township officials had access to far more visible trappings of power: vehicles, chauffeurs, telephones, copy machines, and maps. And they had networks that extended to unknown regions and power figures.

Village government rests on the old bedrock of patriarchal institutions, but it has also introduced educational and reproductive institutions that anticipate a very different kind of society, one with more informed citizens and small families. The extent to which the present village government is freely chosen by villagers is doubtful, given the length of service and the general control of the party over appointments. Nonetheless, the local political elite appear to act in good faith to further the interests of the villagers much of the time, for these include their neighbors and kin. Lu Village leaders are themselves highly constrained to achieve the agricultural productivity and the fertility declines that the higher levels of government require. When the gap between these requirements and the expectations or requirements of village households becomes too great, the leaders probably have to maneuver, inveigle, and fudge the results. Yet with every passing year, there is an increasing proportion of the population, male and female, that has become educated and has gained better comprehension of the wider political society. The expectations for accountability and participation are likely to grow.

## NOTES

1. This statement was made in the early 1990s by an individual who did not want to be identified.

2. See Fei's section on "Taxes and Dues" (Fei and Zhang 1945:97–98).

3. I have not found a standard terminology for local government. Judd (1994:77–81) describes village committees (usually groups of five to eight) for villages in Shandong. Others (Brugger and Reglar 1994; Ogden 1995) do not specify other positions, such as team leaders working under the village committee. Bernstein mentions the "disappearance of the lowest tier . . . the production team. . . . although in some areas a version of the team continued to exist under the label *group (zu)*" (1992:143).

4. Judd observes "no indication that the separation between Party and government advocated in China in the early 1980s had become effective" in any of the villages she studied (1994:78).

5. Chance (1991), Seybolt (1996), and Judd (1994) mention gender in village government.

6. On average the women are forty-four years old with five years of education.

7. Seybolt (1996:89) describes a party secretary with similarly long service, thirty years.

8. See note 5 above.

9. Caldwell, Reddy, and Caldwell's study of rural South India (1988) reported that senior women in the past controlled junior women's fertility by controlling where young daughters-in-law slept, with their husband or in another bed. I found no evidence for a similar tradition in Lu Villagers' past.

10. "Doubly Civilized" households were also given awards, but I did not discover what these were based on. Judd also discussed "civilized households" (1994:277) without specifying criteria.

11. The idea that even ripening of the crop was a reason for cooperative labor in transplanting differs from Fei (Fei and Zhang 1945:36), who thought that staggering planting dates facilitated exchange labor because crops would not ripen simultaneously. Both may be true: different plots ripen at different times, but the crop in a single field ripens at a uniform time if the task is completed quickly.

12. The total price for obtaining household registration (*hukou*) for those children was unclear. There were also fines for children spaced too closely. In 1990, the fine of 10 yuan per month under the permissible minimum of 48 months spacing was considered too low and was raised to a higher figure.

13. Seybolt (1993) describes a party secretary whose long tenure seemed closely linked to relatives in high places. Similarly, Qin (1998) illustrates the way the political promotions and demotions of a party leader corresponded with the perceived importance of his brother, an ethnographer, who had studied overseas.

14. Mrs. Dou was the women's director in the early 1990s.

15. Unusually, the women's director and her brother were born outside Lu Village.

16. Fei did not discuss this clan any further, as he devoted most of his attention to two other prominent families with whom he had more contact. The relationship between the current party secretary and the landholding clan was obscured earlier by Fei's English mistranslation of the name, perhaps due to his Suzhou dialect. Only when I compared names with the original Chinese text did I discover that the current party secretary belonged to a family that had been quite wealthy in the 1930s (Fei and Zhang 1945:55).

17. Didiwei is the Chinese way of pronouncing DDV (Dichlorvos), an insecticide that is locally familiar to everyone.

*Chapter Ten*

# Unbinding China's Peasants

Gender in rural China remains an enormous puzzle, despite many years of research addressing the subject. This book has concentrated on one of the big pieces of the puzzle, an ethnographic study of regional variation. At the outset, I outlined the general theories that have been used to explain why rural Chinese women have experienced such restriction and subordination, particularly in the north, and posed questions about the social and economic traditions and conditions that lead to strong or weak patriarchal controls and to greater or lesser gender inequality.

## GENDER AND DEVELOPMENT

Where women were previously ignored by development theorists, we now expect development studies to document the multiplicity of women's economic roles, social adaptations, and family strategies. The ways women are integrated into or excluded from the market economy are important subjects, differentiating them from men, and are too complex for a simple formulaic approach. Gender is slowly being integrated into studies of China's economic development, its labor-intensive economy, its social strata, and its population problems, yet, overall, research on gender and rural development in China is still at a rudimentary stage.

The ethnographic approach used here cannot by itself justify sweeping claims about *all* of rural China. However, it enables us to reexamine prevailing generalizations and stereotypes, showing when they do and do not fit. Ethnographic studies are thus vital to improving the understanding of evolving gender systems in rural China. Fei and Zhang's ambition to provide a series of comparable ethnographic studies of different types of villages responding to the industrial challenge and changing world markets is as relevant for anthropologists today as it was in the 1930s. None of these studies can, by itself, represent all of China, but taken together they can illustrate macrosocial processes in the context of variable local conditions. When Fei studied Lu Village in the 1930s, he presented sufficient detail that his study has been used again and again for insights into the prerevolutionary period. Because of his enormous influence, it has been important to go over much of the same ground and refine our understanding of the Lu Village economy as a *gender* system. Throughout the book, I have used his work as a starting point, verifying and modifying the impressions he left us—as future generations will hopefully do with this work. As a result, Lu Village can continue to provide insights into regional variations in China.

Building on Fei's study, my research has examined local historical processes that can be compared with other Chinese villages. The relationships between farm economy, gender divisions of labor, forms of marriage, and unequal sex ratios thus become more comprehensible. General hypotheses about such relationships, informed by national or ethnographic perspectives, can now be confronted by a body of evidence from Lu Village that stretches across sixty years, a unique resource for comparative research on Chinese women and rural development.

Reviewing the changes that occurred in Lu Village during a large portion of the twentieth century has shown how often they are occasioned by changes in the larger society and in the world economy. The title of Fei and Zhang's early comparison of Yunnan villages, *Earthbound China*, emphasized the way villagers were tied to the soil. Even though Yunnan was a province traversed with long-distance trade routes, the vast majority of the population stayed put much of the time and hoped to live from the soil and to bind the soil to themselves, in the form of landed property. At the same time, they were bound to their village and agrarian pursuits through lack of opportunities and knowledge about the outside world. Nonetheless, world trade and industrial revolution in distant countries significantly affected villages in Yunnan by the late nineteenth century, causing some of them to specialize in opium growing and others to give up cotton spinning and specialize in cotton weaving. These changes, I have argued, had a tremendous impact on rural families, inducing them to reallocate their male and female labor to different combinations of activities.

## Trade and the Textile Revolution

The mass production of industrial textiles proceeded in stages, but the trade in cheaper textiles quickly spread to different parts of the world following old and new trade routes. Global trade meant that it became increasingly uneconomical for most rural regions to produce textiles locally. In the twentieth century, these changes in textile production removed the linchpin from China's footbound gendered economy that kept so many women of all classes at home, their broken feet bound in cloth and their hands free to work at the spinning wheel, loom, or at embroidery, producing the cloth that bound them to local and long-distance markets. In Lu Village and other villages that converted early to an economy based on the purchase of cloth, women had strong incentives to step out of the courtyard economy earlier than those who clung to weaving. Despite interruptions in trade during wartime and revolution, home textile production was on the way out. Both through the coercive mechanisms of revolution and through the reintroduction of open markets in clothing, domestic weaving has finally been abandoned. The needles and threads, spinning wheels and looms that bound Chinese women to the home have been cast aside in most of rural China, just as they were in Europe (Parker 1989). My reflections on the timing of the demise of footbinding in Lu Village in relation to changing patterns of trade in Yunnan will, I hope, stimulate researchers to explore this relationship in other parts of rural China.

## The Market and the State

The nineteenth century had already opened channels for trade in industrial products, which contributed to the collapse of the imperial state in 1911. The twentieth century let loose a flood of global commercial enterprise in new and ever-changing industrial products. Inside China, the transportation revolution of the nineteenth century, with its steamships and railroads, has finally been superseded in the late twentieth century by automobiles, airplanes, and electronic communications. The political revolution of the Communist Party government, seeking to control the disruptive effects of trade and the industrial revolution and to guarantee everyone a livelihood, stopped the clock on most technological change. In so doing, China paid the price of lack of innovation and freedom to pursue improvements through technology and information exchange. The state controls particularly hurt the countryside. Men and women who had been leaving the countryside for the cities in the first part of the twentieth century found themselves forced to stay, and even return, to be bound to the soil once again as peasant farmers in state-run collectives where manual labor was glorified. Throughout the 1980s and 1990s, the reforms have released many rural laborers from the physical drudgery of farmwork, by removing the extreme constraints of the Maoist collective period and allowing rural men and women to travel to cities to buy, sell, and work. But unbinding rural Chinese society is an ongoing, incomplete process.

Open markets in land and housing have only begun to be developed, and village women's access to them cannot be taken for granted.

## Gender and China's Regional Agricultural Contrasts

When Pasternak and Salaff wrote of the Chinese Way (discussed in chapter 1), they referred to an agrarian tradition of intensive family farming. Although the study of Lu Village illustrates the particular workings of larger transformative processes that have affected all of China, it also demonstrates the importance of understanding the relationship of gender to regional agricultural environments and the labor requirements of different cropping systems as well as cottage industries.

In Lu Village, the complex schedule of activities involved in planting winter wheat followed by summer rice means the preparation of irrigated fields and rice transplanting coincides with the winter wheat harvest. This labor bottleneck suggests that, historically, double cropping adaptations were likely to bring *all* family labor into the fields, including that of the women. Moreover, the need to quickly transplant rice to large irrigated fields required dependable nonfamily labor, which women's kin in neighboring villages could often supply.

In north China, where winters froze most crops and wheat was grown as a rain-fed summer crop, the basic template for the gender division of labor differed. There was less need to mobilize all family labor for field work in wheat, except perhaps under the pressure of harvest, when women might contribute. In areas where only a single crop per year could be grown, there would not have been a labor bottleneck to harvest and plant simultaneously. At the same time, northerners must have always outstripped southerners in their need for plenty of warm clothing and bedding. For northerners, textiles were more a matter of survival than of embellishment. Unless reliably connected with areas that specialized in cloth production, they would have had to devote far more resources to cloth production, growing cotton, and producing cotton cloth for their needs. Cotton crops were much more labor-intensive than wheat, often bringing women into the fields. Cotton clothing production was still more labor intensive. Preindustrial cotton cloth production would have needed women in virtually every family working indoors, spinning, weaving, and dying cloth, as well as sewing warm shoes, jackets, and bed quilts for their families. Cloth was also produced for commerce and to pay taxes. In the north, the winter season was a time for women to concentrate on domestic cloth production, while men worked in construction or transport or migrated to find seasonal work. In the north, then, two main concerns of rural production—food grain and cotton cloth—account for the

351 Unbinding China's Peasants

regional tendency to find north China associated with a history of less work in the fields for women and closer domestic control and confinement of women as spinners and weavers.

In the simplistic version of the north-south contrast, rice-producing south China was associated with a history of greater contributions by women to agriculture. This was taken to mean that women were more equal partners in the south and less valued economic dependents in the north. With double cropping more common in the south due to the longer growing seasons and more ample rainfall, rice agriculture would provide a steadier source of year-round employment for both men and women. Many have commented on the greater propensity of women to work alongside men in southern agriculture. H. S. Chen (1936:107, cited in Watson 1994:29) even wrote in the 1930s about the "feminization" of agriculture in Guangdong, a concept that has wide currency in developing countries today.

In single-cropping northern regions, women in the nineteenth and early twentieth centuries were at home trying to outweave the industrial textile mill. The disruptions to trade caused by the banditry of the warlord era, the Anti-Japanese War, and the Communist revolution meant that home weaving in remote villages died out relatively late, because alternate supplies were intermittent. But the many misfortunate women who tried to maintain the traditional division of labor, which had them working indoors, faced low and declining returns from work at the family loom. This would have contributed to the devaluation of women in general and a reluctance to invest in girls.

Lu Village, as an illustration of gendered labor in agriculture, has contributed to the reevaluation of the north-south gradient. It is not a simple divide that can be mapped by latitude and longitude coordinates or by the current distribution of double cropping or by rice and wheat divisions. Examining the histories of changing agricultural practices in a particular region, as well as the characteristics of cloth production, as homemade products or as trade goods, has allowed us to understand gender as a system of allocating household labor to competing economic activities. To this day, there are still too few development economists and anthropologists who take a holistic view of the local household economies that have always mobilized men and women for complex combinations of useful work.

## Technology and Gender

In a relatively closed or locally adjusted economy, when certain traditional gendered occupations suddenly lose their value due to new technology or new transportation of better or cheaper goods, both men and women can experience jolting shocks to their traditional livelihoods. Over the past

century, women have been displaced from household textile production
and, with an extra hard push from the revolution, were integrated into village farm labor, which restored their value to the farm economy. Today, the
agricultural sector is saturated from the requirement that it absorb labor.
Indeed, as agriculture experiences technological change, it becomes soggy,
if not awash, with surplus labor. In the past, traditional morality viewed
women as attached to children and both as needing protection from dangers outside the household. Thus, men were first to seek jobs outside the
family, the village, and the local town. By their mobility, they were better
able to adjust to shifting economic conditions and shifting labor markets
than were women.

Today, it is still true that more men seek and find jobs outside the village,
but women have more education, fewer children, and fewer moral encum-
brances than in the past. To the extent that basic law and order are preserved
in towns and cities, women are increasingly willing to risk migration and seek
opportunities in new sectors of the economy. While many rural women get
caught in dead-end jobs in restaurants or beauty parlors, or in prostitution,
there is also a steadily increasing savvy among rural women about how to survive and make use of the resources in urban settings.

## The Demise of Footbinding

My aim in restudying Lu Village has been to improve our understanding of
contemporary gender relations by reexamining the community before the
revolutionary enterprise took control. By reviewing the insights Fei provided
and deepening them through interviews with elderly women, a sharper image of the economic forces that often motivate cultural change comes into
focus. In particular, the village-based analysis of the early disappearance of
the debilitating fashion of footbinding, so long an emblem of the depressed
status of Chinese women, offers new insights into an old puzzle. Psychological explanations that emphasize the erotic appeal of the bound foot, or the
inculcation of feminine submission through pain, have contributed to the illusion that footbound women's economic activities were unimportant. Psychological approaches, however well they illuminate states of mind, have not
yet produced convincing explanations for why footbinding should be so unevenly distributed across China and why it should decline so rapidly during
the first part of the twentieth century. Through examination of the uneven
demise of footbinding in Lu Village and central Yunnan, and through comparison with the earlier process in northeast China, I have shown how the
demise of footbinding coincided with the rise of new transport technologies
in international trade and with the demise of the domestic textile industry of

spinning and weaving. That is, the custom of footbinding was extinguished by the industrial revolution in textiles.

This is an ambitious claim but does not propose that missionary preaching, Nationalist rhetoric, and police enforcement of Nationalist laws had no impact. Rather, I make a case for closer attention to revolutionary economic and technological changes that often stimulate decisive activity in social, cultural, and political spheres. Without understanding the incredible power of the industrial revolution in textiles and transport, and their destructive impact on domestic textile producers, we miss the dynamic of change and come to expect that simply changing people's ideologies or enforcing laws can change entrenched habits. Families experienced terrible hardship as women's domestic labor lost value, wrenching women from familiar rural surroundings to join the twentieth-century trek to towns and cities and to perform nonagrarian forms of work. At the same time, as part of this process, footbinding declined and eventually disappeared. These results, at first glance disparate and even contradictory, are manifestly part of one historical process.

## LAND AND LABOR IN FARMING

The distribution of land in Lu Village has been an ongoing concern from Fei's time to the present. Fei's interpretation of the land problem in 1938 took into account population growth and partible inheritance among sons, predicting that the way out of poverty would require nonagricultural solutions. His study of Lu Village reflected an emphasis on land and grain, with less attention given to commercial activities and trade in general or to handicrafts such as needlework.

A careful review of land tenure in Lu Village showed that, although generally denied direct land rights, women were sometimes viewed as proprietors, usually when widowed, and could even increase their landholdings. Yet both men and women were constrained by village and clan social relationships so that market transactions in land were restricted. There was little evidence of changes toward more capitalistic forms of farming, whether on a large or small scale, but ties to a woman's natal kin in nearby villages facilitated rental of plots in their villages for diversification.

In reexamining gender in the landholding struggles of the revolutionary period, I proposed that the fixation of class labels by landownership obscured the implications of age and gender. The revolutionary practice of labeling and condemning landlords ignored age and probably favored youth and targeted widows and elderly people who were more likely to hire labor than to work the land themselves. This gender-age dimension has not been explicitly raised in most studies.

Bernard gives a classic example, arising out of Sri Lankan data, of the methodological problems of estimating landlessness that Chinese Communists must have encountered when they classified the population:

> In 1957, N. K. Sarkar and S. J. Tambiah published a study, based on questionnaire data, about economic and social disintegration in a Sri Lankan village. They concluded that about two-thirds of the villagers were landless. The British anthropologist, Edmund Leach, did not accept that finding (Leach, 1967). He had done participant observation fieldwork in the area and knew that the villagers practiced patrilocal residence after marriage. By local custom, a young man might receive *use* of some of his father's land even though legal ownership might not pass to the son until after the father's death. (Bernard 1994:141–42)

Today, land remains the property of the village, which allocates land in long-term contracts to village families. Periodic readjustments in the quantity of land allocated to each household on the basis of household registration have been performed up to 1995, providing the same amount per capita regardless of sex or age. Such egalitarian policies were not implemented in all parts of China, for exceptions favoring men were reported in various villages in east China. The recent policy to eliminate the land readjustments, effectively extending the length of the contracts and making them more like private property, may jeopardize in-marrying women's sense of adding to the amount of land a family contracts. If each family has its portion fixed, the size of future landholdings will depend upon the number of heirs. Under the limitations of the family planning policy there are likely to be, at most, two heirs per family. Families that keep just one son or daughter at home as heir while the other marries into a different family will not experience further subdivision of their land. Problems are most likely to arise if a number of families have two sons or daughters who marry at home and expect equal shares of the land. If patrilineal principals are retained, sons would likely oppose the claims of the daughters.

## Unbinding the Farmers: The Attractions of Jobs and Businesses in Town

The extended life history of an apparently successful woman shaman in the 1930s showed how rare and how hard it was for women to follow unconventional, independent paths and to accumulate wealth once they were successful. The seeress was able to earn considerable income for her services, but officials and bandits found ways to relieve her of it. When her husband and young son died, her hopes for family security were shattered. The seeress was one of the very few women in a prominent position in Lu Village in the 1930s. There is no comparable woman practicing spiritualism in the village today.

Today, single women in rural areas may still face grave difficulties in accumulating wealth independently. While some young women are seeking commercial opportunities, they generally do so as married women. The banking system, according to many villagers I asked, does not distinguish individual from joint accounts. If village women want to set aside separate savings their husbands cannot control, they cannot simply open an account in their own name.

Lu Village women have witnessed some progress toward legal protection of their wealth and individual rights, but family relations are still the most important form of protection for the majority. Young educated women who seek independent incomes have a wider spectrum of opportunities. These opportunities are less likely to be in handicrafts, such as shoemaking, or in "seeing," in the old fashioned form. Women are working as teachers, shopkeepers, and salesclerks and in hospitals and manufacturing in town. Some even make it to the provincial capital, the rapidly modernizing city of Kunming. In these new occupations, their cash incomes earn them respect and influence in their families.

Older married women with young or grown children are most likely to be found managing the field work, gardening, and pig raising activities that make up their occupation as farmers. These women have reasonably secure rights to a share of land, although they cannot sell it. When the need to care for dependents, small children, or aging parents also ties them to the home, women are the most likely candidates to remain in the farming sector. Farmwork has an honorable history, but it is still manual labor bringing relatively low returns. Families continue to value the food and security it provides, but older women, as they age, increasingly find it difficult to persuade the younger generation of women to take their place. To rephrase an old question, "How are you going to keep them down on the farm once they have seen Kunming?" The younger generation, exposed to television, advertising, and various new visions of urban life, is increasingly restless with farmwork, submitting to it during busy seasons but seeking alternatives in cleaner, lighter jobs in commerce, education, transport, and communication. At the close of 1999, judging by the explosion of computer education in the local high schools and urban universities, the computer age is in the offing.

## ECONOMY, FAMILY, AND DEMOGRAPHY

China's strict policies toward family planning have stimulated great interest, receiving both cautious praise and criticism in the West. The Chinese state

has confronted agrarian family traditions favoring many children and instituted a system of universal family planning permitting but two children in rural areas. What has been the effect on women? Various studies have suggested
that the family planning policies are causing China's rural populations to return to the tradition of son preference, killing or abandoning daughters who
fall outside the quota. The government use of incentives and coercive policy
enforcement, faced with peasant resistance and evasion, has sparked considerable disapproval, particularly as China's census data have shown increasingly abnormal sex ratios, with a shortage of girls. Studies that examine these
questions against detailed field research are still rare. This is another area
where the analysis of my local-level data has shed some light.

In Lu Village, the relationship of government policy to birth sex ratios
has not produced the same shortage of girls reported in many other regions.
Even though policy enforcement has been strict, reported sex ratios have
been within the normal range of variation. This suggests that Lu Villagers
are less obsessive about the need to produce sons or male heirs than are Chinese villagers in other areas. In exploring the reasons for Lu Village's more
equal sex ratios, I have proposed that other characteristics of the local economy and society need to be taken into consideration. These include an established tradition of participation by women in farming, gardening, and pig
raising, and a higher degree of flexibility concerning uxorilocal marriage.
Ongoing relationships between parents and daughters' families are generally
strong, and calling in a son-in-law is an accepted alternative in Lu Village.
High rates of village endogamy have also contributed to a community in
which young wives are in close contact with their natal kin and are able to
call upon them for exchange labor (or baby-sitting) during periods of intensive farmwork. Giving birth to two daughters seems to be less often regarded
as a tragedy in this community than in other parts of China. This may well
be because women's important role in rice and bean farming, as well as pig
raising, has been long established, to say nothing of their role in opium
farming in the early part of the century. Even as I make this claim, however,
I am aware that many local conditions can change and Lu Village might
come to resemble more closely the disturbing situation found in many other
parts of China, where the lack of a son spells doom for the family and,
hence, doom for some daughters.

I do not suggest that all of south China's rice farming systems that employ
female family labor in transplanting have evolved similar degrees of flexibility about uxorilocal marriage, and similarly close cooperation with women's
kin in surrounding communities. Rice farming is only *one* of many ingredients in the rural household economy. Other components that must be considered are the combinations of other crops, handicrafts, and livestock rais-

ing undertaken by the household, as well as the traditions of male migration for trade, mining, or construction.

The study of Lu Village has demonstrated the advantages of taking a closer anthropological look at the local traditions of footbinding in relation to household combinations of farmwork and cottage textile production and at the timing of technological changes that push local populations into new configurations of the family labor force. Comparing Lu Village to other villages in Yunnan, I suggest that the later the domestic textile tradition was extinguished, the longer local women were bound to a greatly devalued, unprofitable economic sector. Under conditions of world trade in industrial textiles, their femininity (as defined by footbinding) was under attack and their work became worthless. The transfer of rural women from the skill of weaving to new forms of work was not easy, as new standards of femininity, virtue, and competence in work outside the home take time to develop. With relatively poor preparation for direct participation in the competitive market economy, it probably required more than a generation to evolve new employment and social skills for women outside the home. In rural areas where women still cannot participate and compete in the more dynamic sectors of the economy, stronger son preference is predictable.

Lu Village may be less patriarchal than other Chinese villages, but it still largely follows a patriarchal model. Some of the ways that patriarchal family structures take their toll on women have been examined. Selling of daughters and daughters-in-law was clearly practiced in the past. Although alarming reports of wife selling, abduction, or marriage by deceit are again surfacing in reform China, there is little evidence so far that this has been a problem for the daughters of Lu Village in the reform period. Lu Villagers generally marry someone they know who lives in the vicinity. Some marriages may still be arranged by parents and relatives who negotiate the economic terms, but the sons and daughters of Lu Village marry later, are better educated, and have a legal, and increasingly accepted, right to refuse the candidates introduced to them. The influence of television, which has become pervasive over the past decades, undoubtedly reinforces youthful desires to fall in love and choose their own partner.

The most disturbing aspect of the family system that I encountered was the number of reports of female suicide. These were cases of young mothers who had babies and did heavy field work, middle-aged mothers with a number of teenagers, and older women in conflict with their daughters-in-law. In listening to these stories, I noted that they seemed to involve women in distress through overwork and a lack of cooperation, support, or respect from family members. Even if women have kin nearby, the kin may not always be sympathetic. The burdens of physical labor placed on rural women in extended or large families are often very heavy. Accusations or gossip impugning a woman's sexual conduct were also mentioned as factors. The occurrence of such suicides in Lu Village corresponds to China's national pattern of exceptionally high suicide rates for rural women. Here again, urban employment appears to offer some improvements for women by weakening the power of the patriarchal family to isolate and overload them with unrewarding work.

## WOMEN'S POLITICAL PARTICIPATION

There were no women who had recognizable political roles in Lu Village in Fei's account. The most noteworthy or influential women were an aging family matriarch and the seeress—although we never learned much about the role of outside women, such as Fei's aunt, who was there as a Christian missionary. In the current political system, although women's role is still limited within the village executive committee, women have served as team leaders, women's director, family planning officer, and agricultural technician. For all the shortcomings of the one-party Communist system, it has managed to sustain a political presence for women in Lu Village committees, in the party, and in various kinds of village meetings over a long period of time. Between 1990 and 1998, women's representation on the village council shrunk from 17 to 11 percent as the council itself lost two positions. In contrast, as Communist Party membership increased, women's share increased from 17 to 20 percent.

In these contexts, as well as in the public schools and hospitals, people have become accustomed to seeing local women act and speak publicly. They have also become accustomed to having women gather in public, in mixed groups, although informal gender segregation is common among the elderly. It is possible to exaggerate the significance of this kind of activity, for surely women went to markets and attended weddings, funerals, and other rituals in Lu Village before the revolution. Yet it *is* noteworthy that many village matters, pertaining to agriculture, land distribution, and yes, family planning quotas, call forth women's public participation. However, the women who become politically influential are typically those who grew up in the village rather than incoming wives. A better understanding of Lu Village political power and its glass ceiling for women awaits closer scrutiny of the role of party, military service, and the leaders' links to town officials—subjects that remained beyond my reach. At the cultural level, however, it is clear that women were fully integrated into state-sponsored performances, as actresses, singers, and dancers. The high participation of women in "folk arts" can be traced to the early years of the revolution, when training cultural and propaganda teams was supported by the Communist Party. In the 1990s, jobs as "cultural workers" continue to be funded by the state, much as Western governments hire public relations firms to explain and promote their policies.

## THE EXPANDING RANGE OF OCCUPATIONS AND INCOMES

Careful review of Fei's observations, combined with interviews with older Lu Village women, revealed that women performed varied forms of nonagricultural labor in the 1930s. They worked in family enterprises such as the inns and shops; they worked as porters and as servants. They produced handicrafts, sold goods in the market, and even gained income through moneylending. Many of these activities were suppressed during the revolutionary period, and most women became farmers, working on village production teams. With the breakup of the collective approach to farming, women continued to farm, but those with a strong interest in commerce resumed part-time activities that had been abandoned or confined to the black market. Some women went into food processing, bean-curd making, storekeeping, and marketing. A few supplemented farmwork with other manual labor (such as road building), and a number found informal work in the plastic recycling factory. By the late 1990s, improvements in transportation (more plentiful bicycles, horse-cart taxis, and buses) made it easier for village women to commute to town jobs, ranging from government office jobs, teaching, and factory work to commerce. While less than half as many women as men had full-time nonfarm jobs, women were fairly well-represented in factory, commercial, government, and health care employment. Women remained underrepresented in construction and transportation, two specialties that have had comparable gender segregation in many Western countries. Even here, however, Lu Village women (as well as women I observed in and around Lufeng) defy traditional stereotypes, as some young women have already demonstrated their skills at driving horse carts and minivans. To my surprise, young village women are already getting jobs at computer shops in town, which puts them into close contact with the latest technology. While Lu Village women's cash incomes have generally been considerably below those of men, in 1997 working women in their early twenties were actually earning as much as men in their age cohort. This is the result of the superior education of young women compared to their elders, making them well qualified for town jobs in education, government, health, and commerce.

These initial changes in employment under the reforms resulted in the feminization of farming, leaving married women in charge of much of the farmwork while men migrated to earn more cash in the slow seasons. Most recently, the surge in town employment among young women suggests that the era of women as farmers of small plots may be drawing to a close, much as the sun has set on the era of home weaving. Increasingly, younger women will resist the path of farming unless it is profitable. With smaller families and more employment choices, it may become harder to recruit labor. Eventually, this should raise the cost of farm labor and stimulate mechanization. If labor costs rise enough, the pressure to abandon farming, or mechanize more of it, will grow and technology will be adapted to local conditions. What might delay this process for places like Lu Village, however, could be the supply of poorer villagers in the mountains who are willing to farm their plots for low wages. By the late 1990s, many villagers were hiring migrant farmworkers to harvest their fields, a pattern Fei noted in the 1930s, when educated sons of landowners preferred to avoid work in the fields themselves. In 1999, several villagers experimented with hiring operators of a large mechanical rice harvester that could, if plots were large enough, perform the work at lower cost.

The reappearance of wealth differences in Lu Village is obvious. As in Fei's time, farmers with sufficient land can "get by" but cannot flourish. Outside sources of cash income are eagerly sought, and men have been the first to pursue them. However, many young women seem eager to follow the same path. The opportunity for some to accumulate capital and become wealthy entrepreneurs has thus far centered on men, but this has begun to benefit the women in the families of these men, as families increasingly invest in daughters' educations and in training, leading to prized credentials such as driver's licenses. Gender inequality persists, now complicated by class differences.

## THE SIGNIFICANCE OF LU VILLAGE

As an example of a Han village in southwest China, Lu Village is fairly typical. Certainly there are many other distinctive types of Han villages located in Yunnan, as *Earthbound China* demonstrated when it appeared in 1945, let alone in China. However, Lu Village did not open up early and was not treated as a model village during the periods when the Chinese government was trying to showcase its successes. Lu Village does not seem to have been the beneficiary of any special subsidies or any unusual efforts to instill socialist values. It was not spared the horrors of famine during the Great Leap Forward nor the turmoil of the Cultural Revolution. Today, its standard of living falls toward the average for the province, while Yunnan itself is generally considered one of China's poorer and less-developed provinces.

The undoubted improvements in material well-being that the village has seen over the past twenty years since the reform period began have also been occurring across rural China. In Lu Village, agricultural output, which was essentially stagnant from Fei's time to the late 1970s, has since increased by 20 percent per unit of land and doubled per unit of labor. Village per capita incomes have increased at roughly a 4 percent annual rate in real terms over the same period. All of these numbers, of course, are affected by weather conditions, reporting biases, and many other factors. What is clear is that the people of Lu Village, like most of rural China, have improving access to televisions and modern transport, rice cookers and running shoes. In short, they are rapidly gaining access to a myriad of modern products, technologies, and options to an extent unimagined a generation earlier. Poverty has not vanished, but it has been noticeably reduced.

At the same time, and also in response to these very forces, gender relations have changed in several ways. Greater economic freedom has provided most women with more material comfort, if not wealth, for their labors. Retreat from Communist ideology has, in some ways, however, allowed greater social inequality to reemerge. Communist rhetoric regarding gender equality has subsided, but village society has not quickly reverted to traditional values. Women in Lu Village seem to have gained overall, but this may well be related to what has been, even in the time of Fei Xiaotong, a less rigidly patriarchal society than that in many other Chinese villages. While I am hopeful that increasing nonfarm opportunities for women, and a shrinking need for "earthbound" agricultural labor, will continue to favor greater material well-being, greater gender equality, and the achievement of what Amartya Sen has called "development as freedom," no one can be certain that these trends will continue. What is certain is that the daily substance of most women's lives will, as has been the case in developed countries, revolve less around agriculture in the future.

Amid the uncertainties of economic development and rapid social change, conservative pressures to reinforce family values and limit the rights of women persist, just as in the West. The opening of China's markets and loosening of family controls represent an enormous challenge, full of risk and opportunity, for Chinese rural women. In communities like Lu Village, as well as in villages with more emphatic patrilineal biases, we can observe and compare the tensions between the state and market, the kin group and the individual, men and women, and in so doing better understand what rural development means for Chinese women.

This study has emphasized the links between economy, family, and demography, yet some of the greatest challenges ahead lie in the political sphere. Although village women participate in local government, there are as yet no signs of an autonomous woman's movement to support women against entrenched interests. The ongoing reliance on patrilineal kin groups for security and advancement still puts women at a disadvantage unless their kin are nearby. Women's commitment to development, their incentives to seek education and outside employment, and to rely on smaller numbers of children are linked to the uncertain ability and willingness of the state to promote job opportunities and guarantee property rights, personal liberty, and full citizenship for women.

# Glossary

*bai xiongdi* 拜兄弟  become a sworn brother

*baochan daohu* 包产到户  household responsibility system

*baolai* 抱来  to adopt a child

*caili* 彩礼  bridewealth

*chang bi dui* 长臂队  Long Arm team

*chaosheng haizi* 超生孩子  out-of-quota child

*cubu* 粗布  rough, or handmade cloth

*cunmin* 村民  village citizen

*cunmin xiaozu* 村民小组  villagers' small group

*da jiemei* 搭姐妹  become a sworn sister

*dama* 大妈  aunt, or literally "big mother" (a polite address for elderly woman)

*da guo fan* 大锅饭  big rice bowl

*da guo xi fan* 大锅稀饭  big bowl of thin rice gruel

*dan* 担  1 dan = 10 dou, 350 liters

*dou* 斗  the (nonstandard) Lufeng *dou* is thirty-five liters

*duizhang* 队长  team leader

*fandong* 反动  counterrevolutionary

*fang yin* 放阴  release the underworld

*fei nongmin* 非农民  nonagricultural

*fen* 分  one-tenth of a *mu*

*fengfeng diandian de* 疯疯癫癫的  crazy

*funong* 富农  rich peasant

*ganbu* 干部  a government official or bureaucrat

*ganma* 干妈  dry mother, godmother

*getihu* 个体户  individually owned enterprise

*gong* 工  a measure of land area, 0.4 *mu*

*gonggong* 公公  father-in-law, for a woman

*gongshe* 公社  commune

*guan gui* 关鬼  call spirits

*guma* 姑妈  paternal aunt

*guye* 姑爷  son-in-law

*huanggua jiao* 黄瓜脚  cucumber foot, a shape of bound foot

*hukou* 户口  household registration, official residence status, urban or rural

*jiebai* 结拜  become sworn brothers or sisters

*jiemei* 姐妹  siblings, sisters

*jiapu* 家谱  family tree

*jiazhuang* 嫁妆  dowry

*jiehun* 结婚  to marry

*jiejie* 姐姐  older sister

*jiti* 集体  collective

*jin* 斤  1.1 pounds, or 0.5 kilogram

*jiujiu* 舅舅  maternal uncle, or mother's younger brother

*jiu shehui* 旧社会  the "old society" before 1949

*kuaiji* 会计  accountant, treasurer

*laodong gaizao* 劳动改造, also *laogai* 劳改  "labor reform," a type of prison sentence

*lao zuzu* 老祖祖  the old ancestors

*li di bu li xiang* 离地不离乡  leave the soil, not the village

*luohu fei* 落户费  resettlement fee

*mao* 毛  one tenth of a yuan

*meimei* 妹妹  younger sister

*mixian* 米线  rice noodles

*mixin* 迷信  superstition

*mu* 亩  a unit of land, "mow"

*nainai* 奶奶  paternal grandmother

*niangjia* 娘家 mother's home, usually a married woman's natal kin

*nongmin* 农民 farmer, or peasant; literally agricultural person/people

*nuwu* 女巫 female witch

*peitong* 陪同 a companion, or escort

*pojia* 婆家 mother-in-law's house

*popo* 婆婆 mother-in-law

*po-xi* 婆媳 mother-in-law, daughter-in-law relations

*sancun jin lian* 三寸金莲 "three inch golden lily," a tightly bound foot

*shangmen* 上门 uxorilocal, a man who marries into wife's family

*shao guodi* 烧锅底 "burn the pot bottom," a ritual to establish a separate kitchen

*shao guo jiao* 烧裹脚 burn foot bindings

*sheng* 升 a liter

*shengchan dui* 生产队 production team

*shiniang* 师娘 mistress, skilled woman, a term of respect

*shiniang po de hanzi* 师娘婆的汉子 old lady's husband, an insult

*shumai* 赎买 ransom

*shushu* 叔叔 paternal uncle; or father's younger brother

*shun jiao* 顺脚 smooth feet

*tao lai* 逃来 to escape; to seek refuge

*tang-ki* 童乩 (in Taiwan) a shaman, diviner; (in Mandarin, *tongji*)

*tao xifu* 讨媳妇 to ask for a daughter-in-law

*tongyangxi* 童养媳 adopted daughter-in-law (raised together with future husband)

*tufei* 土匪 bandits

*waiguoren* 外国人 foreigner

*wailaide* 外来的 outsiders

*waipo* 外婆 mother's mother, grandmother

*wupo* 巫婆 female shaman, seeress, or witch

*xifu* 媳妇 daughter-in-law, or the young wife in a family

*xiaogong* 小工 casual labor

*xiaozu* 小组 small group

*yexing* 野性 wild

*yi ku* 忆苦 to recall bitterness, "speak bitterness"

*zhao guye* 招姑爷 seek a son-in-law, find an uxorilocal husband for a daughter

*zisha* 自杀 suicide

*zhong nan qing nu* 重男轻女 male superiority; literally, men are important, women are trivial

*zhongnong* 中农 middle peasant

# Bibliography

## ABBREVIATIONS

*Note: The following abbreviations are used in the bibliography.*

ACWF   All China Women's Federation
LCY     *Lufeng County Yearbook*
LCG    *Lufeng County Gazette*
NPSY   National 1% Population Sample Investigation, Material for Yunnan
SSB     State Statistical Bureau
YPSB   Yunnan Province Statistical Bureau
USCB   United States Census Bureau

## BIBLIOGRAPHY

Agarwal, Bina. 1994. *A Field of One's Own: Gender and Land Rights in South Asia.* Cambridge: Cambridge University Press.

Ahern, Emily. 1973. *The Cult of the Dead in a Chinese Village.* Stanford, Calif.: Stanford University Press.

Aird, John S. 1990. *Slaughter of the Innocents: Coercive Birth Control in China.* Washington, D.C.: American Enterprise Institute.

All China Women's Federation (ACWF). 1991. *Zhongguo xingbie tongji ziliao 1949–1989* (Statistics on Chinese women, 1949–1989). Beijing: China Statistical Publishing House for the Research Institute of All China Women's Federation and Research Office of Shaanxi Provincial Women's Federation.

———. 1998. *Zhongguo xingbie tongji ziliao 1990–1995* (Gender statistics in China, 1990–1995). Beijing: China Statistical Publishing House for the Research Institute of All China Women's Federation, Department of Social, Science and Technology Statistical Bureau.

Arkush, David. 1981. *Fei Xiaotong and Sociology in Revolutionary China*. Cambridge, Mass.: Council of East Asian Studies, Harvard University.

Attwood, Donald W. 1995. *Inequality among Brothers and Sisters*. Centre for Society, Technology and Development (STANDD) Working Paper, Gender and Property Series, McGill University.

Baker, Hugh. 1979. *Chinese Family and Kinship*. London: Macmillan.

Banister, Judith. 1987. *China's Changing Population*. Stanford, Calif.: Stanford University Press.

———. 1992. "China's Changing Mortality." In *The Population of Modern China*, ed. Dudley L. Poston Jr. and David Yaukey, 164–224. New York: Plenum.

Barclay, George W., Ansley J. Coale, Michael A. Stoto, and T. James Trussell. 1976. "A Reassessment of the Demography of Traditional Rural China," *Population Index* 42: 606–35.

Barnett, A. Doak. 1993. *China's Far West: Four Decades of Change*. Boulder, Colo.: Westview.

Becker, Jasper. 1996. *Hungry Ghosts: China's Secret Famine*. London: Murray.

———. 1999. "Home Truths about One-Child Policy." *South China Morning Post, Internet Edition*. <http://www.scmp.com/Special/Template/PrintArticle.asp> (March 31, 1999).

Beijing Foreign Languages Institute. 1993. *The Pinyin Chinese-English Dictionary*. Hong Kong: Commercial Press.

Benedict, Carol. 1996. *Bubonic Plague in Nineteenth Century China*. Stanford, Calif.: Stanford University Press.

Bernard, H. Russell. 1994. *Research Methods in Anthropology*. Thousand Oaks, Calif.: Sage.

Bernstein, Thomas P. 1992. "Ideology and Rural Reform: The Paradox of Contingent Stability." In *State and Society in China: The Consequences of Reform*, ed. Arthur L. Rosenbaum, 143–165. Boulder, Colo.: Westview.

Berreman, Gerald. 1962. *Behind Many Masks*. Lexington: University of Kentucky and the Society for Applied Anthropology.

Blake, C. Fred. 1994. "Footbinding in Neo-Confucian China and the Appropriation of Female Labor," *Signs* 19, no. 3:676–712.

Bloomberg, Ltd. 2001. *China CPI*. Bloomberg Professional Service, www.bloomberg.com.

Boserup, Ester. 1970. *Women's Role in Economic Development*. New York: St. Martin's.

Bossen, Laurel. 1975. "Women in Modernizing Societies," *American Ethnologist* 2, no. 4: 587–601.

———. 1984. *The Redivision of Labor: Women and Economic Choice in Four Guatemalan Communities*. Albany: State University of New York Press.

———. 1988. "Toward a Theory of Marriage: The Economic Anthropology of Marriage Transactions," *Ethnology* 27, no. 2:127–44.

———. 1990. "The Han Gender System in Yunnan." Paper presented at American Anthropological Association Meeting, New Orleans, December 2.

———. 1991. "Changing Land Tenure Systems in China: Common Problem, Uncommon Solution," *Sociological Bulletin: Journal of the Indian Sociological Society* 40, nos. 1–2: 47–67.

———. 1992. "Chinese Rural Women: What Keeps Them Down on the Farm?" Paper presented at the international conference on "Engendering China: Women, Culture and the State," Harvard University and Wellesley College, Cambridge, Mass., February 7–9.

———. 1994a. "Zhongguo nongcun funu: shenma yuanyin shi tamen liu zai nong tian li?" (Chinese rural women: What keeps them down on the farm?). In *Xingbie yu Zhongguo* (Gender and China), ed. Li Xiaojiang, Zhu Hong, and Dong Xiuyu, 128–54. Beijing: Shenghuo-Dushu-Xinhe Sanlian Shudian (SDX Joint Publishing Company).

———. 1994b. "Gender and Economic Reform in Southwest China." In *Femmes, feminisme, et developpement/Women, Feminism and Development*, ed. Huguette Dagenais and Denise Piché, 223–40. Montréal: McGill-Queens University Press.

———. 1994c. "The Household Economy in Rural China: Is the Involution Over?" In *Anthropology and Institutional Economics*, ed. James Acheson, 167–91. Monographs in Economic Anthropology, no. 12. Lanham: University Press of America.

———. 1995a. "All Words and No Deeds." Centre for Society, Technology and Development Working Papers, Gender and Property Series, McGill University.

———. 1995b. "Unmaking the Chinese Peasantry—Releasing Collected Energy?" *Anthropology of Work Review* 16, nos. 3–4:8–14.

———. 1998. "Trade and Beauty: The Demise of Footbinding in Rural Yunnan." Seminar paper, Department of Anthropology, McGill University, November 23.

———. 1999. Women in Development. In *Understanding Modern China*, ed. Robert Gamer, 293–320. Boulder, Colo.: Rienner.

———. 2000. "Women Farmers, Small Plots and Changing Markets in China." In *Women Farmers and Commercial Ventures: Increasing Food Security in Developing Countries*, ed. Anita Spring. Boulder, Colo.: Rienner.

———. n.d. "Deciphering Fei's Rosetta Stone: Calculating Lu Village Output per Mu in 1938." (Author's files.)

Bradley, Neville. 1945. *The Old Burma Road: A Journey of Foot and Muleback*. London: William Heinemann.

Brandt, Loren. 1989. *Commercialization and Agricultural Development: Central and Eastern China, 1870–1937*. Cambridge: Cambridge University Press.

Bray, Francesca. 1997. *Technology and Gender: Fabrics of Power in Late Imperial China*. Berkeley: University of California Press.

Brugger, Bill, and Stephen Reglar. 1994. *Politics, Economy and Society in Contemporary China*. Stanford, Calif.: Stanford University Press.

Bruun, Ole. 1993. *Business and Bureaucracy in a Chinese City: An Ethnography of Private Business Households in Contemporary China*. Berkeley: Institute for East Asian Studies, University of California.

Buck, John Lossing. 1930. *Chinese Farm Economy*. Chicago: University of Chicago Press.

———. 1937a. *Land Utilization in China: A Study of 16,786 Farms in 168 Localities, and 38,256 Farm Families in Twenty-two Provinces in China, 1929–1933*. Shanghai: University of Nanking.

———. 1937b. *Land Utilization in China: Statistics*. Shanghai: University of Nanking.

———. 1957. *Land Utilization in China*. New York: Council on Economic & Cultural Affairs.

———. 1966. *Food and Agriculture in Communist China*. Stanford, Calif.: Hoover Institution.

Butler, Steven B. 1985. "Price Scissors and Commune Administration in Post-Mao China." In *Chinese Rural Development: The Great Transformation*, ed. William Parish, 95–114. Armonk, N.Y.: Sharpe.

Caldwell, John, P. H. Reddy, and Pat Caldwell. 1988. *The Causes of Demographic Change: Experimental Research in South India*. Madison: University of Wisconsin Press.

Carter, Colin, Funing Zhong, and Fang Cai. 1996. *China's Ongoing Agricultural Reform.* South San Francisco, Calif.: The 1990 Institute.

CBC Radio. 1997. <http://www.radio.cbc/programs/quirks/archives/97-98/nov197.thm.> (November 1, 1997).

Chambers, Robert. 1983. *Rural Development: Putting the Last First.* New York: Longman.

Chan, Anita, R. Madsen, and J. Unger. 1992. *Chen Village under Mao and Deng.* Berkeley: University of California Press.

Chance, Norman. 1991. *China's Urban Villagers: Changing Life in a Beijing Suburb.* Fort Worth, Tex.: Holt, Rinehart and Winston.

Chang, Jung. 1991. *Wild Swans: Three Daughters of China.* New York: Anchor Doubleday.

Chang, Pang-Mei Natasha. 1996. *Bound Feet and Western Dress.* New York: Doubleday.

Chen, H. S. 1936. *Landlord and Peasant in China: A Study of the Agrarian Crisis in South China.* New York: International.

Chu Junhong. 2001. "Prenatal Sex Determination and Sex Selective Abortion in Rural Central China," *Population and Development Review* 27 no. 2: 259–281.

Coale, Ansley J., and Judith Banister. 1994. "Five Decades of Missing Females in China," *Demography* 31, no 3:459–79.

Cohen, Myron. 1993. "Cultural and Political Inventions in Modern China: The Case of the Chinese 'Peasant'," *Daedalus: Journal of the American Academy of Arts and Sciences* 122, no. 2:151–70.

———. 1999. "North China Rural Families: Changes During the Communist Era," *Etudes chinoises* 16, nos. 1–2:59–153.

Colquhoun, Archibald R. 1883. *Across Chrysë: From Canton to Mandalay. Being the Narrative of a Journey of Exploration through the South China Border Lands from Canton to Mandalay.* 2 vol. London: Sampson Low, Marston, Searle, and Rivington.

Cooper, Eugene. 2000. *Adventures in a Chinese Bureaucracy: A Meta-Anthropological Saga.* Huntington, N.Y.: Nova Science.

Cooper, T. T. 1871. *Travels of a Pioneer of Commerce in Pigtail and Petticoats: Or An Overland Journey from China towards India.* London: J. Murray.

Croll, Elizabeth. 1981. *The Politics of Marriage in Contemporary China.* Cambridge: Cambridge University Press.

———. 1983. *Chinese Women Since Mao.* London: Zed.

———. 1994. *From Heaven to Earth: Images and Experiences of Development in China.* London: Routledge.

———. 1995. *Changing Identities of Chinese Women: Rhetoric, Experience and Self-Perception in Twentieth Century China.* London: Hong Kong University Press.

Davies, Major H. R. 1909. *Yun-nan: The Link Between India and the Yangtze.* London: Cambridge University Press.

Davin, Delia. 1975. "Women in the Countryside of China." In *Women in Chinese Society,* ed. Margery Wolf and R. Witke, 243–73. Stanford, Calif.: Stanford University Press.

———. 1976. *Woman-work: Women and the Party in Revolutionary China.* Oxford: Clarendon.

———. 1985. "The Single-Child Policy in the Countryside." In *China's One-child Family Policy,* ed. Elizabeth Croll, Delia Davin, and Penny Kane, 37–82. London: Macmillan.

Davison, Jean. 1997. *Gender, Lineage, and Ethnicity in Southern Africa.* Boulder, Colo.: Westview.

Diamond, Jared. 1997. *Guns, Germs, and Steel: The Fates of Human Societies.* New York: Norton.

Diamond, Norma. 1975. "Collectivization, Kinship, and the Status of Women in Rural China." In *Toward an Anthropology of Women*, ed. Rayna Reiter, 372–95. New York: Monthly Review Press.

Dietrich, Craig. 1972. "Cotton Culture and Manufacture in Early Ch'ing China." In *Economic Organization in Chinese Society*, ed. W. E. Willmott, 109–135. Stanford, Calif.: Stanford University Press.

Dikotter, Frank. 1995. *Sex, Culture and Modernity in China: Medical Science and the Construction of Sexual Identities in the Early Republican Period.* Honolulu: University of Hawaii Press.

Drèze, Jean, and Amartya Sen, eds. 1989. *Hunger and Political Action.* Oxford: Clarendon.

———. 1996. *Indian Development: Selected Regional Perspectives.* Delhi: Oxford University Press.

Eades, J. S. 1998. "Eastern and Western Research in Rural China." Paper presented at the International Congress of Anthropological and Ethnological Sciences, Williamsburg, Va., July 28–Aug 2.

Ebrey, Patricia Buckley. 1990. "Women, Marriage, and the Family in Chinese History." In *Heritage of China: Contemporary Perspectives on Chinese Civilization*, ed. Paul Ropp, 197–223. Berkeley: University of California Press.

———. 1991. "Shifts in Marriage Finance from the Sixth to Thirteenth Century." In *Marriage and Inequality in Chinese Society*, eds. Rubie Watson and Patricia Buckley Ebrey, 97–132. Berkeley: University of California Press.

———. 1993. *The Inner Quarters: Marriage and the Lives of Chinese Women in the Sung Period.* Berkeley: University of California Press.

———, ed. 1981. *Chinese Civilization and Society: A Sourcebook.* New York: Free Press.

*Economist.* 2000. "Kidnapping in China." 23 December–5 January, pp. 53–54.

Elliot, Alan. 1955. *Chinese Spirit Medium Cults in Singapore.* Monographs on Social Anthropology, no. 14. London: London School of Economics and Political Science.

Elvin, Mark. 1972. "The High-Level Equilibrium Trap." In *Economic Organization in Chinese Society*, ed. W. E. Wilmott, 137–72. Stanford, Calif.: Stanford University Press.

Endicott, Stephen. 1989. *Red Earth: Revolution in a Sichuan Village.* Toronto: University of Toronto-York University Joint Centre for Asia Pacific Studies.

Fei Xiaotong (Fei Hsiao Tung). 1949. *Peasant Life in China: A Field Study of Country Life in the Yangtze Valley.* London: Routledge and Kegan Paul. (Also published in 1939 as *Peasant Life in China: A Field Study of Country Life in the Yangtze Valley.* New York: Dutton.)

———. 1983. *China Village Close-up.* Beijing: New World Press.

———. 1991. "Chong fangwen Yunnan san cun" (Revisit to Yunnan's three villages), *Zhongguo Shehui Kexue* (Chinese Social Science) 12, no. 1:169–178.

———. 1992. *From the Soil: The Foundations of Chinese Society. A Translation of Fei Xiaotong's Xiangtu Zhongguo with an Introduction and Epilogue by Gary G. Hamilton and Wang Zheng.* Berkeley: University of California Press.

Fei Xiaotong [Fei Hsiao Tung] and Zhang Zhiyi [Chang Chih-I]. 1945. *Earthbound China: A Study of Rural Economy in Yunnan.* Chicago: University of Chicago Press.

———. 1990. *Yunnan San Cun* (Yunnan Three Villages). Tianjin: Tianjin People's Publishing House.

Fitzgerald, C. P. 1941. *The Tower of Five Glories: A Study of the Min Chia of Ta Li, Yunnan.* London: Cresset.

Franck, Harry A. 1925. *Roving through Southern China.* New York: Century.

Friedman, Edward, Paul Pickowicz, and Mark Seldon with Kay A. Johnson. 1991. *Chinese Village, Socialist State.* New Haven, Conn.: Yale University Press.

Gamble, Sidney. 1954. *Ting Hsien: A North China Rural Community.* Stanford, Calif.: Stanford University Press.

Gao Mobo C. F. 1999. *Gao Village: Rural Life in Modern China.* Hong Kong: Hong Kong University Press.

Gates, Hill. 1989. "The Commoditization of Chinese Women," *Signs* 14, no. 4:799–832.

———. 1991. "Narrow Hearts and Petty Capitalism." In *Marxist Approaches in Economic Anthropology*, ed. Alice Littlefield and Hill Gates, 13–36. Lanham, Md.: University Press of America.

———. 1993. "Cultural Support for Birth Limitation among Urban Capital-owning Women." In *Chinese Families in the Post-Mao Era*, ed. Deborah Davis and Stevan Harrell, 251–76. Berkeley: University of California Press.

———. 1995. "Footloose in Fujian: Economic Correlates of Footbinding." Paper presented for "Workshop: Fukien and Taiwan in the Nineteenth and Twentieth Centuries: Contacts and Contrasts," Leiden University, Leiden, The Netherlands, July 5–8.

———. 1996. *China's Motor: A Thousand Years of Petty Capitalism.* Ithaca, N.Y.: Cornell University Press.

———. 1997. "Footbinding and Handspinning in Sichuan: Capitalism's Ambiguous Gifts to Petty Capitalism." In *Constructing China: The Interaction of Culture and Economics*, ed. Kenneth G. Lieberthal, Shuen-fu Lin, and Ernest P. Young, 177–194. Ann Arbor: University of Michigan Press.

Gilmartin, Christina. 1990. "Violence against Women in Contemporary China." In *Violence in China*, ed. J. Lipman and S. Harrell, 203–219. Albany: State University of New York Press.

Gilmartin, Christina, G. Hershatter, L. Rofel, and Tyrene White, eds. 1994. *Engendering China: Women, Culture and the State.* Cambridge: Harvard University Press.

Goody, Jack. 1990. *The Oriental, the Ancient, and the Primitive: Systems of Marriage and the Family in the Pre-industrial Societies of Eurasia.* Cambridge: Cambridge University Press.

Goody, Jack, and S. J. Tambiah. 1973. *Bridewealth and Dowry.* Cambridge: Cambridge University Press.

Gould-Martin, Katherine. 1978. "Ong-Ia-Kong: The Plague God as Modern Physician." In *Culture and Healing in Asian Societies: Anthropological, Psychiatric and Public Health Studies*, ed. A. Kleinman et al., 41–67. Boston: G. K. Hall.

Graham, David Crockett. 1961. *Folk Religion in Southwest China.* Washington: Smithsonian Institution. Miscellaneous Collections, Vol. 142, no. 2.

Greenhalgh, Susan. 1985. "Is Inequality Demographically Induced? The Family Cycle and the Distribution of Income in Taiwan," *American Anthropologist* 87:571–94.

———. 1990. "The Evolution of the One-Child Policy in Shaanxi," *China Quarterly*, no. 122 (June): 191–229.

———. 1992. "Negotiating Birth Control in Village China." Population Council, Research Division, Working Paper #38.

———. 1993. "The Changing Value of Children in the Transition from Socialism: The View from Three Chinese Villages." Population Council, Research Division, Working Paper. Prepared for Elizabeth Brumfiel, ed. *The Economic Anthropology of the State.* Lanham, Md.: University Press of America.

Greenhalgh, Susan, and Jaili Li. 1995. "Engendering Reproductive Policy and Practice in Peasant China: For a Feminist Demography of Reproduction," *Signs* 20, no. 3:601–41.

Hall, Christine, 1997. *Daughters of the Dragon: Women's Lives in Contemporary China*. London: Scarlet.

Harrell, Stevan. 1993. "Geography, Demography, and Family Composition in Three Southwestern Villages." In *Chinese Families in the Post-Mao Era*, ed. Deborah Davis and Stevan Harrell, 77–102. Berkeley: University of California Press.

Hartford, Kathleen. 1985. "Socialist Agriculture Is Dead: Long Live Socialist Agriculture! Organizational Transformations in Rural China." In *The Political Economy of Reform in Post-Mao China*, ed. Elizabeth Perry and Christine Wong, 31–61. Cambridge: Council on East Asian Studies, Harvard University.

He Liyi. 1993. *Mr. China's Son: A Villager's Life*. Boulder, Colo.: Westview.

Hinton, Carma, director. 1984. *Small Happiness* (video). Long Bow Group, Inc. Richard Gorden, Kathy Kline, and Daniel Sipp, producers. New York: New Day Films.

Hinton, William. 1966. *Fanshen: A Documentary of Revolution in a Chinese Village*. New York: Vintage.

Honig, Emily, and Gail Hershatter. 1988. *Personal Voices: Chinese Women in the 1980's*. Stanford, Calif.: Stanford University Press.

Hosie, Alexander. 1890. *Three Years in Western China; A Narrative of Three Journeys in Ssuchuan, Kuei-chow, and Yun-nan*. London: George Philip and Son.

Hsieh, Ping-ying. 1986 [1945]. *Autobiography of a Chinese Girl*. London: Allen and Unwin.

Hsu, Francis. 1952. *Religion, Science, and Human Crises: A Study of China in Transition and Its Implications for the West*. London: Routledge and Kegan Paul.

———. 1967 [1948]. *Under the Ancestor's Shadow: Kinship, Personality and Social Mobility in Village China*. Garden City, N.Y.: Doubleday.

Huang, Philip C. C. 1985. *The Peasant Economy and Social Change in North China*. Stanford, Calif.: Stanford University Press.

———. 1990. *The Peasant Family and Rural Development in the Yangzi Delta, 1350–1988*. Stanford, Calif.: Stanford University Press.

Huang Shu-min. 1989. *The Spiral Road: Change in a Chinese Village Through the Eyes of a Communist Party Leader*. Boulder, Colo.: Westview.

Ikels, Charlotte. 1996. *The Return of the God of Wealth: The Transition to a Market Economy in Urban China*. Stanford, Calif.: Stanford University Press.

Jacka, Tamara. 1997. *Women's Work in Rural China: Change and Continuity in an Era of Reform*. Cambridge: Cambridge University Press.

Jankowiak, William. 1993. *Sex, Death and Hierarchy in a Chinese City*. New York: Columbia University Press.

Jaschok, Maria. 1988. *Concubines and Bondservants: The Social History of a Chinese Custom*. Hong Kong: Oxford University Press.

———. 1994. "Chinese 'Slave' Girls in Yunnan-Fu: Saving (Chinese) Womanhood and (Western) Souls, 1930–1991." In *Women and Chinese Patriarchy: Submission, Servitude and Escape*, ed. Maria Jaschok and Suzanne Miers, 171–97. Hong Kong University Press.

Jaschok, Maria, and Suzanne Miers, eds. 1994. *Women and Chinese Patriarchy*. London: Hong Kong University Press.

Jeffery, Patricia, Roger Jeffery, and Andrew Lyon. 1989. *Labour Pains and Labour Power: Women and Childbearing in India*. London: Zed.

Jeffery, Roger, and Patricia Jeffery. 1997. *Population, Gender and Politics: Demographic Change in Rural North India*. Cambridge: Cambridge University Press.

Jing Jun. 1996. *The Temple of Memories: History, Power, and Morality in a Chinese Village.* Stanford, Calif.: Stanford University Press.

Johnson, Graham. 1993. "Family Strategies and Economic Transformation in Rural China: Some Evidence from the Pearl River Delta." In *Chinese Families in the Post-Mao Era,* ed. Deborah Davis and Stevan Harrell, 103–38. Berkeley: University of California Press.

Johnson, Kay Ann. 1983. *Women, the Family, and Peasant Revolution in China.* Chicago: University of Chicago Press.

———. 1996. "The Politics of Infant Abandonment in China," *Population and Development Review* 22, no. 1: 77–98.

Jordan, David K. 1972. *Gods, Ghosts and Ancestors: The Folk Religions of a Taiwanese Village.* Berkeley: University of California Press.

Judd, Ellen. 1989. "Niangjia: Chinese Women and Their Natal Families," *Journal of Asian Studies* 48, no. 3:525–44.

———. 1994. *Gender and Power in Rural North China.* Stanford, Calif.: Stanford University Press.

King, Haitung, and Frances B. Locke. 1983. "Selected Indicators of Current Health Status and Major Causes of Death in the People's Republic of China. An Historical Perspective." In *China Facts and Figures Annual,* Vol. 6, ed. John L. Scherer, 375–422. Gulf Breeze, Fla.: Academic International Press.

Kleinman, Arthur. 1980. *Patients and Healers in the Context of Culture: An Exploration of the Borderland Between Anthropology, Medicine, and Psychiatry.* Berkeley: University of California Press.

Ko, Dorothy. 1994. *Teachers of the Inner Chambers: Women and Culture in Seventeenth-Century China.* Stanford, Calif.: Stanford University Press.

Lavely, William. 1991. "Marriage and Mobility under Rural Collectivism." In *Marriage and Inequality in Chinese Society,* ed. Rubie S. Watson and Patricia B. Ebrey, 286–312. Berkeley: University of California Press.

Lay, G. Tradescent. 1843. *The Chinese as They Are: Their Moral and Social Character, Manners, Customs, and Language with Remarks on Their Arts and Sciences, Their Medical Skill, the Extent of Missionary Enterprise, etc.* Albany, N.Y.: Geo. Jones.

Leach, Edmund. 1967. "An Anthropologist's Reflection on a Social Survey." In *Anthropologists in the Field,* ed. D. C. Jongman and P. C. Gutkind, 75–88. Assen, Netherlands: Van Gorcum.

Lee, Ching Kwan. 1998. *Gender and the South China Miracle: Two Worlds of Factory Women.* Berkeley: University of California Press.

Lee, James. 1982. "Food Supply and Population Growth in Southwest China, 1250–1850," *Journal of Asian Studies* 41, no. 4:711–801.

Levy, Howard. 1991 [1966]. *The Lotus Lovers: The Complete History of the Curious Erotic Custom of Footbinding in China.* Buffalo, N.Y.: Prometheus.

Li Jiali. 1994. "China's Family Planning Program: How and How Well, Did it Work?" Population Council Working Paper no. 65.

Lin Yueh-Hwa. 1947. *The Golden Wing: A Sociological Study of Chinese Familism.* London: Kegan Paul, Trench, Trubner & Company.

Lufeng County Gazette (LCG) Editorial Committee. 1997. *Lufeng xian zhi* (Lufeng County Gazette). Kunming: Yunnan People's Publishing House.

Lufeng County Yearbook (LCY) Editorial Committee. 1999. *Lufeng xian nianjian* (Lufeng County Yearbook). Mangshi, Dehong, Yunnan: Dehong Nationalities Publishing House.

Maclachlan, Morgan. 1983. *Why They Did Not Starve: Biocultural Adaptation in a South In-dian Village*. Philadelphia: Institute for the Study of Human Issues.

Mann, Susan. 1991. "Grooming a Daughter for Marriage." In *Marriage and Inequality in Chinese Society*, ed. Rubie Watson and Patricia Buckley Ebrey, 204–30. Berkeley: University of California Press.

———. 1997. *Precious Records: Women in China's Long Eighteenth Century*. Stanford, Calif.: Stanford University Press.

Mao Zedong. 1990. *Report from Xunwu*. Translated with an introduction by Roger Thompson. Stanford, Calif.: Stanford University Press.

McGough, James. 1979. *Fei Hsiao-t'ung: The Dilemma of a Chinese Intellectual*. White Plains, N.Y.: Sharpe.

Miller, Barbara. 1981. *The Endangered Sex: Neglect of Female Children in Rural North India*. Ithaca, N.Y.: Cornell University Press.

Mosher, Stephen. 1993. *A Mother's Ordeal: One Woman's Fight Against the One-Child Policy*. New York: HarperPerennial.

Muegglar, Erik. 1998. "The Poetics of Grief and the Price of Hemp in Southwest China," *Journal of Asian Studies* 17, no. 4:979–1008.

Mundlak, Yair, Donald Larson, and Al Crego. 1997. "Agricultural and Development," *World Bank Policy and Research Bulletin* 8, no. 1:1–4.

Naquin, Susan, and Evelyn Rawski. 1987. *Chinese Society in the Eighteenth Century*. New Haven, Conn.: Yale University Press.

National 1% Population Sample Investigation Material for Yunnan (NPSY). 1997. *Quanguo 1% renkou chaoyang diaocha ziliao: Yunnan fence* (1995 National 1% Population Sample Investigation Material for Yunnan). Beijing: China Statistical Publishing House.

Nussbaum, Martha. 1999. *Sex and Social Justice*. Oxford: Oxford University Press.

Ocko, Jonathan K. 1991. "Women, Property and the Law in the People's Republic of China." In *Marriage and Inequality in Chinese Society*, ed. Rubie Watson and Patricia B. Ebrey, 313–46. Berkeley: University of California Press.

Ogden, Suzanne. 1995. *China's Unresolved Issues: Politics, Development, and Culture*. 3d ed. Englewood Cliffs, N.J.: Prentice Hall.

Osborne, Milton. 1996 [1975]. *River Road to China: The Search for the Source of the Mekong*. New York: Atlantic Monthly Press.

Osgood, Cornelius. 1963. *Village Life in Old China*. New York: Ronald Press.

Oxfeld, Ellen. 1993. *Blood, Sweat, and Mahjong: Family and Enterprise in an Overseas Chinese Community*. Ithaca, N.Y.: Cornell University Press.

Papanek, Hanna. 1990. "To Each Less Than She Needs, from Each More Than She Can Do: Allocations, Entitlements and Value." In *Persistent Inequalities: Women and World Development*, ed. Irene Tinker, 162–181. New York: Oxford University Press.

Parker, Rozsika. 1989. *The Subversive Stitch: Embroidery and the Making of the Feminine*. New York: Routledge.

Parrish, William, ed. 1985. *Chinese Rural Development: The Great Transformation*. Armonk, N.Y.: Sharpe.

Pasternak, Burton. 1983. *Guests in the Dragon: Social Demography of a Chinese District, 1895–1946*. New York: Columbia University Press.

———. 1985. *Marriage and Fertility in Tianjin China: 50 Years of Transition*. Honolulu: East-West Population Institute.

Pasternak, Burton, and Janet W. Salaff. 1993. *Cowboys and Cultivators: The Chinese of Inner Mongolia.* Boulder, Colo.: Westview.

Population Census of Yunnan Province (PCYP). 1991. *Yunnan sheng de si ci renkou pucha shouhui zongziliao* (Major figures of manual tabulation on 1990 population census of Yunnan Province). Kunming: Yunnan People's Publishing House.

Population Census Office. 1987. *The Population Atlas of China.* Oxford: Oxford University Press.

Poston, Dudley L., Jr., and David Yaukey, eds. 1992. *The Population of Modern China.* New York: Plenum.

Potter, Jack. 1974. "Cantonese Shamanism." In *Religion and Ritual in Chinese Society,* ed. Arthur Wolf, 207–301. Stanford, Calif.: Stanford University Press.

Potter, Sulamith, and Jack Potter. 1990. *China's Peasants: The Anthropology of a Revolution.* Cambridge: Cambridge University Press.

Pruitt, Ida. 1945. *A Daughter of Han: The Autobiography of a Chinese Working Woman.* Stanford, Calif.: Stanford University Press.

Putterman, Louis. 1985. "The Restoration of the Peasant Household as Farm Production Unit in China: Some Incentive Theoretic Analysis." In *The Political Economy of Reform in Post-Mao China,* ed. Elizabeth Perry and Christine Wong, 63–82. Cambridge: Council on East Asian Studies, Harvard University.

Qian Chengrun, Du Jinhong, and Shi Yueling. 1985. "Yi District's 'Lu Village' Past and Present." In *Yizu wenhua yanjiu wenji* (Collected Essays on Yi Minority Research). Kunming, China: Yunnan People's Publishing House; Yunnan Social Science Academy; Chuxiong Yi Minority Cultural Research Institute.

Qian Chengrun, Shi Yueling, and Du Jinhong. 1995. *Fei Xiaotong Lucun Nongtian Wushi Nian.* Kunming, China: Yunnan People's Publishing House.

Qin Zhaoxiong. 1998. "The Politics of Change in a Chinese Village: A Native Anthropologist's Perspective." Paper presented at the International Congress of Anthropological and Ethnological Sciences (ICAES) meeting, Williamsburg, Va., July 30.

Rofel, Lisa. 1999. *Other Modernities: Gendered Yearnings in China After Socialism.* Berkeley: University of California Press.

Rosen, Stanley. 1995. "Women and Political Participation in China," *Pacific Affairs* 68, no. 3:315–341.

Rosen, Stanley, ed. 1987–1988. "Chinese Women: 1987–88," *Chinese Sociology and Anthropology: A Journal of Translations* 20, no. 1–3.

Ruf, Gregory A. 1998. *Cadres and Kin: Making a Socialist Village in West China, 1921–1991.* Stanford, Calif.: Stanford University Press

Sachs, Carolyn. 1996. *Gendered Fields: Rural Women, Agriculture, and Environment.* Boulder, Colo.: Westview.

Salisbury, Harrison. 1992. *The New Emperors: China in the Era of Mao and Deng.* Boston: Little, Brown.

Schein, Luisa. 2000. *Minority Rules: The Miao and the Feminine in China's Cultural Politics.* Durham, N.C.: Duke University Press.

Sen, Amartya. 1997. "Marriage, Family and Gender Bias in India." In *Indian Development: Selected Regional Perspectives,* ed. Jean Drèze and Amartya Sen. Delhi: Oxford University Press.

———. 1999. *Development as Freedom.* New York: Knopf.

Sen, Gita, and Caren Grown. 1987. *Development, Crises and Alternative Visions: Third World Women's Perspectives.* London: Earthscan.

Seybolt, Peter J. 1996. *Throwing the Emperor from His Horse: Portrait of a Village Leader in China, 1923–1995.* Boulder, Colo.: Westview.

Sheridan, Mary. 1984. "Contemporary Generations. Zhao Xiuyin: Lady of the Sties." In *Lives: Chinese Working Women,* ed. Mary Sheridan and Janet Salaff, 204–235. Bloomington: Indiana University Press.

Simon, Scott. 1994. *The Economics of the Tao: Social and Economic Dimensions of a Taoist Monastery.* M.A. thesis, Department of Anthropology, McGill University.

Sinn, Elizabeth. 1994. "The Protection of Women in 19th-Century Hong Kong." In *Women and Chinese Patriarchy: Submission, Servitude and Escape,* ed. Maria Jaschok and Suzanne Miers. London: Zed.

Siu, Helen. 1989. *Agents and Victims in South China: Accomplices in Rural Revolution.* New Haven, Conn.: Yale University Press.

Skinner, G. William. 1997. "Family Systems and Demographic Processes." In *Anthropological Demography: Toward a New Synthesis,* ed. David I. Kertzer and Tom Fricke, 53–95. Chicago: University of Chicago Press.

Smil, Vaclav. 1993. *China's Environmental Crisis: An Inquiry into the Limits of National Development.* Armonk, N.Y.: Sharpe.

Smith, Christopher. 1990. *China: People and Places in the Land of One Billion.* Boulder, Colo.: Westview.

Smith, Nicol. 1940. *Burma Road.* Indianapolis: Bobbs-Merrill.

So, Alvin. 1986. *The South China Silk District: Local Historical Transformation and World-System Theory.* Albany: State University of New York Press.

Spence, Jonathan. 1990. *The Search for Modern China.* New York: Norton.

Stacey, Judith. 1983. *Patriarchy and Socialist Revolution.* Berkeley: University of California Press.

State Statistical Bureau (SSB). 1992. *Zhongguo tongji nianjian* (China Statistical Yearbook). Beijing: China Statistical Publishing House.

———. 1995. *Zhongguo renkou tongji nianjian* (China Population Statistics Yearbook). Beijing: China Statistical Publishing House for the Department of Population and Employment Statistics.

———. 1996. *Zhongguo laodong tongji nianjian 1995* (China Labor Statistics Yearbook 1995). Beijing: China Statistical Publishing House for the Department of Population and Employment Statistics.

———. 1999. *Zhongguo tongji nianjin* (China Statistical Yearbook). Beijing: China Statistical Publishing House.

Statistics Canada. 2001. CANSIM, Matrix 6367. 8 August 2001, www.statcan.ca/english/Pgdb/People/Population/demo10a.htm.

Stockard, Janice. 1989. *Daughters of the Canton Delta: Marriage Patterns and Economic Strategies in South China, 1860–1930.* Stanford, Calif.: Stanford University Press.

Tian Rukang [T'ien Ju-K'ang]. 1944. "Supplementary Chapter: Female Workers in a Cotton Textile Mill." In *China Enters the Machine Age,* ed. Kuo-heng Shih, 178–98. Cambridge: Harvard University Press.

Topley, Marjorie. 1975. "Marriage Resistance in Rural Kwangtung." In *Women in Chinese Society,* ed. Margery Wolf and Roxanne Witke. Stanford, Calif.: Stanford University Press.

Unger, Jonathan, and Jean Xiong. 1990. "Life in the Chinese Hinterlands under the Rural Economic Reforms," *Bulletin of Concerned Asian Scholars* 22, no. 2:4–17.

United Nations Development Program (UNDP). 1995. *Human Development Report 1995.* New York: Oxford University Press.

U.S. Census Bureau (USCB). 1999. International Data Base. Table 010. <http://www.census.gov/cgi-bin/ipc/idbagg> (February 25, 2000).

Vogel, Ezra F. 1989. *One Step Ahead in China: Guangdong under Reform*. Cambridge: Harvard University Press.

Walker, Kathy Le Mons. 1993. "Marginalization, and the Sexual Division of Labor in Early Twentieth-Century China: Women's Work in Nantong County," *Modern China* 19, no. 3:354–86.

Wang Ping. 2000. *Aching for Beauty: Footbinding in China*. Minneapolis: University of Minnesota Press.

Wang, Shaoxian, and Virginia Li, eds. 1994. *Yunnan Nongcun Funu de Xinsheng* (Women's voice from rural Yunnan: Needs assessment of reproductive health). Beijing: Beijing Medical College, Lianhe Chubanshe (United Publishing House).

Watson, James. 1980. "Transactions in People: The Chinese Market in Slaves, Servants, and Heirs." In *Asian and African Systems of Slavery*, ed. James L. Watson. Oxford: Basil Blackwell.

Watson, Rubie. 1984. "Women's Property in Republican China: Rights and Practice," *Republican China* 10, no. 1a:1–12.

———. 1985. *Inequality among Brothers: Class and Kinship in South China*. Cambridge: Cambridge University Press.

———. 1986. "The Named and the Nameless: Gender and Person in Chinese Society." *American Ethnologist* 13, no. 4:619–31.

———. 1991a. "Wives, Concubines, and Maids: Servitude and Kinship in the Hong Kong Region 1900–1940." In *Marriage and Inequality in Chinese Society*, ed. Rubie Watson and Patricia Ebrey. Berkeley: University of California Press.

———. 1991b. "Marriage and Gender in Chinese Society: An Afterward." In *Marriage and Inequality in Chinese Society*, ed. Rubie Watson and Patricia Ebrey. Berkeley: University of California Press.

———. 1994. "Girls' Houses and Working Women: Expressive Culture in the Pearl River Delta, 1900–41." In *Women and Chinese Patriarchy*, ed. Maria Jaschok and Suzanne Miers, 25–44. London: Hong Kong University Press.

Watson, Rubie, and Patricia B. Ebrey, eds. 1991. *Marriage and Inequality in Chinese Society*. Berkeley: University of California Press.

Wilhelm, Kathy. 1992. "Land Wars: Peasants Fight Back after Businesses Evict Them from Small Plots of Land." Associated Press, in the *Montreal Gazette*, 22 April, A10.

Wilk, Richard. 1989. "Decision Making and Resource Flows within the Household: Beyond the Black Box." In *The Household Economy: Reconsidering the Domestic Mode of Production*, ed. Richard Wilk, 23–52. Boulder, Colo.: Westview.

Wolf, Arthur, and Huang, Chieh-shan. 1980. *Marriage and Adoption in China, 1945–1945*. Stanford, Calif.: Stanford University Press.

Wolf, Margery. 1972. *Women and the Family in Rural Taiwan*. Stanford, Calif.: Stanford University Press.

———. 1975. "Women and Suicide in China." In *Women in Chinese Society*, ed. Margery Wolf and Roxane Witke, 111–42. Stanford, Calif.: Stanford University Press.

———. 1985. *Revolution Postponed: Women in Contemporary China*. Stanford, Calif.: Stanford University Press.

———. 1990. "The Woman Who Didn't Become a Shaman," *American Ethnologist* 17, no. 3.

———. 1992. *A Thrice-Told Tale: Feminism, Postmodernism, and Ethnographic Responsibility.* Stanford, Calif.: Stanford University Press.

Wolf, M., and R. Witke, eds. 1975. *Women in Chinese Society.* Stanford, Calif.: Stanford University Press.

Wong, Jan. 1996. *Red China Blues: My Long March from Mao to Now.* Toronto: Doubleday Anchor.

Woon, Yuen-fong. 1990. "From Mao to Deng: Life Satisfaction among Rural Women in an Emigrant Community in South China," *Australian Journal of Chinese Affairs,* no. 25: 139–169.

World Bank. 1992. *China: Strategies for Reducing Poverty in the 1990s.* Washington, D.C.: World Bank.

———. 1995. *Staff Appraisal Report: China Southwest Poverty Reduction Project.* Report No. 13968-CHA. Washington, D.C.: Agricultural Operations Division, China and Mongolia Department, East Asia and Pacific Regional Office.

Wu Harry Hongda. 1992. *Laogai: The Chinese Gulag.* Boulder, Colo.: Westview.

Xiang Jingyun [Hsiang Ching-yuen Patrick]. 1940. "Tenure of Land in China: A Preface to China's Land Problems and Policies." Ph.D. diss., University of Wisconsin, Department of Agricultural Economics.

Xiang Jingyun [Hsiang Ching-yuen Patrick] and Liu Dewei [Liu Pearl]. 1999. *Staying Power: Patrick Xiang across China's Twentieth Century,* ed. Laurel Bossen. Boulder, Colo.: Gold Hill.

Yan Yunxiang. 1996. *The Flow of Gifts: Reciprocity and Social Networks in a Chinese Village.* Stanford, Calif.: Stanford University Press.

Yang, Mayfair Mei-hui. 1994. *Gifts, Favors and Banquets: The Art of Social Relationships in China.* Ithaca, N.Y.: Cornell University Press.

Yunnan Province. 1991. *Yunnan sheng de si ci renkou pucha shouhui zongziliao* (Major figures of manual tabulation of the 1990 Population Census of Yunnan Province). Kunming: Yunnan People's Publishing House.

Yunnan Province Statistical Bureau (YPSB). 1992. *Yunnan tongji nianjian 1992* (Yunnan Statistical Yearbook 1992). Kunming: China Statistical Publishing House.

———. 1995. *Yunnan tongji nianjin 1995* (Yunnan Statistical Yearbook 1995). Beijing: China Statistical Publishing House.

———. 1999. *Yunnan tongji nianjin 1999* (Yunnan Statistical Yearbook 1999). Beijing: China Statistical Publishing House.

Zappi, Elda Gentili. 1991. *If Eight Hours Seem Too Few: Mobilization of Women Workers in the Italian Rice Fields.* Albany: State University of New York Press.

Zeng Yi et al. 1993. "Causes and Implications of the Increase in China's Reported Sex Ratio at Birth," *Population and Development Review* 19, no. 2:283–302.

Zhao Shiqing, Qu Guang, Peng Zhenglong, and Peng Tiensen. 1994. "The Sex Ratio of Suicide Rates in China," *Crisis* 15, no. 1:44–48.

Zhao Xiong He and David Lester. 1997. "The Gender Difference in Chinese Suicide Rates," *Archives of Suicide Research* 3:81–97.

Zhou, Kate Xiao. 1996. *How the Farmers Changed China: Power of the People.* Boulder, Colo.: Westview.

Zhu Ling. 1991. *Rural Reform and Peasant Income in China: The Impact of Post-Mao Rural Reforms in Selected Regions.* New York: St. Martins.

# Index

*Note:* The following convention has been used: *f* for figure or photograph, *m* for map, and *t* for table.

# About the Author

*The author (left) is guided by a Lu Village farmer out to her fields.*

**Laurel Bossen** is associate professor of anthropology at McGill University.

393